HIGHER EDUCATION:
Handbook of Theory and Research

Volume V

Associate Editors

HIGHER EDUCATION:
Handbook of Theory and Research

Volume V

Edited by

John C. Smart

University of Illinois at Chicago

Published under the sponsorship of
The Association for Institutional Research (AIR)
and
The Association for the Study of Higher Education (ASHE)

AGATHON PRESS
New York

© 1989 Agathon Press
111 Eighth Avenue
New York, NY 10011

ISBN: 0-87586-093-1
ISSN: 0882-4126

Printed in the United States

Contents

The Contributors

JAMES T. AUSTIN is a Visiting Assistant Professor of Psychology in the social-organizational division at the University of Illinois in Champaign-Urbana. His interest lies in industrial and quantitative areas, with an emphasis on the study of goals.

ROBERT BIRNBAUM is Professor of Higher Education at the University of Maryland, College Park, and director of the Institutional Leadership Project at the National Center for Postsecondary Governance and Finance. His research findings appear regularly in higher education journals, and his most recent articles have used organizational and cognitive perspectives to examine phenomena such as faculty senates, the effects of leadership succession, biases in administrative judgments, and presidential searches. His most recent book is *How Colleges Work: The Cybernetics of Academic Organization and Leadership* (1988).

JOHN M. BRAXTON is Assistant Professor of Higher Education at Syracuse University. One of his major research interests is the college student experience including such topics as the college choice process, the student attrition process, and the effects of college on students. His recent publications in such journals as *The Journal of College Student Development, Research in Higher Education,* and *The Review of Higher Education* have focused on these topics. He also serves as a consulting editor for *Research in Higher Education.*

JOHN A. CENTRA is Professor and Chair of the Higher/Postsecondary Education Program at Syracuse University. His research interests over the past 25 years have focused on faculty evaluation and development, the improvement of teaching, college quality and its effect on students, and other issues in the study of higher education.

ELLEN EARLE CHAFFEE is Associate Commissioner for Academic Affairs for the North Dakota State Board of Higher Education. She is also president of the Association for the Study of Higher Education. Previously, she held various positions at the National Center for Higher Education Management Systems, Stanford University, the University of Colorado, and North Dakota State University. She recently co-authored *Collegiate Culture and Leadership Strategies* with William G. Tierney.

GEORGIA A. COOPERSMITH is a Ph.D. candidate in Higher Education at Syracuse University. She holds a B.F.A. in Fine Art from the Rochester Institute of Technology and an M.F.A. in Museum Studies from Syracuse University. Currently she is Museum Director/Coordinator of the Arts at SUNY Potsdam.

DENNIS E. HINKLE is Professor of Educational Research at Virginia Polytechnic Institute and State University. He has published two textbooks on applied statistics and numerous articles on statistical applications. He is currently directing the university's undergraduate student assessment program.

DON HOSSLER is Associate Professor of Educational Leadership and Policy Studies at Indiana University. The author of several books and articles, his writing and research have focused upon the areas of student college choice, enrollment management, and higher education as a field of study.

MARSHA VAN DYKE KROTSENG is Assistant Director of Planning and Institutional Research at the University of Hartford. She previously served as Institutional Research Associate and as Assistant Professor of Higher Education at the University of Mississippi. She is active in the Association for Institutional Research and served on the Board of Directors for the Association for the Study of Higher Education. Her articles and reviews have been published in Jossey-Bass' *New Directions* series on faculty, and in *Educational Studies* and *The Review of Education*.

YVONNA S. LINCOLN is Associate Professor of Educational Leadership and Higher Education at Vanderbilt University. Her research and teaching interests are concerned with organizational theory, alternative research paradigms for the social sciences, program evaluation in higher education, and the effect of changing paradigms on the institution of higher education. She is the co-author of *Effective Evaluation, Naturalistic Inquiry* and the forthcoming *Fourth Generation Evaluation* with Egon Guba.

GERALD W. MCLAUGHLIN is Associate Director for Institutional Research and Planning Analysis at Virginia Polytechnic Institute and State University. His current interests include applied analytical methodology, distributed institutional research support of decision systems, and the data-information-intelligence support of organizational management.

MICHAEL S. MCPHERSON is Professor and Chair of the Economics Department at Williams College. He is interested in the financing of higher education and in the economic behavior of colleges and universities.

JAMES L. MORRISON is Professor of Education, University of North Carolina at Chapel Hill. He is former Vice President, American Educational Research Association (Division J-Postsecondary Education), and former Chair, Special Interest Group in Futures Research. He is author and coauthor of numerous publications focusing on the application of environmental analysis/forecasting techniques in educational planning and policy analysis, including *Applying Methods and Techniques of Futures Research* and *Futures Research and the Strategic Planning Process*.

THOMAS V. MECCA is Vice President for Planning and Development, Piedmont Technical College. He has extensive experience in applying ED QUEST to the strategic management process of that institution. He also serves as President, Institute for Future Systems Research, Inc., a nonprofit consulting firm.

JOHN R. THELIN is Chancellor Professor at The College of William and Mary in Virginia. He is Director of the Higher Education Doctoral Program and a member of the

American Studies and Public Policy Studies program faculties. In 1986 he received the Phi Beta Kappa Award for Faculty Contribution to Scholarship. He serves as Essay Review Editor for *The Review of Higher Education* and in 1989 was awarded a three-year major grant from the Spencer Foundation for an historical study of intercollegiate athletics and academic policy, circa 1930 to 1980.

ALAN P. WAGNER is Principal Administrator, Centre for Educational Research and Innovation at the Organisation for Economic Cooperation and Development (Paris). An economist specializing in the analysis of policies and practices in education and training, he has examined issues in such areas as student financial aid, foreign students and study abroad, adult education and training, education finance, teachers and teacher education, and school organisation.

JOHN C. WEIDMAN is Professor of Education and Sociology at the University of Pittsburgh. He also chairs the Department of Administrative and Policy Studies in the School of Education. His research and teaching interests are in the sociology of higher education with a focus on the socialization of both undergraduate and graduate students, including career development in the years immediately following degree completion.

NANCY A. WILLIE-SCHIFF is a researcher in the New York State Education Department's Office of Postsecondary Education Policy Analysis. She is interested in student aid, prices facing postsecondary students, and the financing of higher education.

TED I. K. YOUN teaches at the School of Education of Boston College. His research focuses on the sociological analysis of academic organizations, academic careers, and academic labor markets. His work has appeared in sociology and higher education journals. He is co-author of a number of books on academic power and academic labor markets, and the author of the forthcoming *Career Mobility in Academic Hierarchies* (1990).

Strategy and Effectiveness in Systems of Higher Education

Ellen Earle Chaffee

Associate Commissioner for Academic Affairs
North Dakota State Board of Higher Education

Systems of higher education have grown in number and importance in recent years, yet the literature has given relatively little attention to them. Except for occasional descriptions of what exists and prescriptive pronouncements arising out of specific experiences, writers have rarely considered what systems are and how they can improve. This chapter takes a different approach, applying to higher-education systems the substantial work that has addressed similar issues with respect to organizations, in the hope of stimulating more theory-based discussion and research on higher education systems.

Although the following discussion is based on academic theory, it asks the same questions as did the intuition of a seasoned participant in higher education, Stephen Bailey (quoted in French and Berdahl, 1980), when he proposed the following questions as fundamental guides to assessing system effectiveness:

1. Is the intellectual/analytical work of the system board of high quality?
2. Is there a sense on the part of the governor and the legislature that the system board's activities are helpful to them in making at least quasi-rational judgments about higher education support and development?
3. Do the affected colleges and universities feel that they are being dealt with by the system board in a fair and understanding manner—granted disagreements about final recommendations?
4. Does the system board operate on the basis of a philosophy of higher education that goes beyond simplistic manpower, occupational, and formula projections, and that endorses a maximum amount of institutional autonomy in making decremental as well as incremental decisions?

I am grateful for the helpful suggestions of Robert Birnbaum, James Mingle, Russell Poulin, Marijo Shide, Barbara Taylor, Pat Terenzini, William Tierney, and Raymond Zammuto. The State Higher Education Executive Officers published an earlier version of this paper.

1

Strategies	Effectivenesss
Linear (analysis)	Goal achievement
Adaptive (external relations)	Resource acquisition
Interpretive (philosophy)	Constituent satisfaction

FIG. 1. Strategy and effectiveness.

Specifically, the chapter uses work on organizational effectiveness and strategic management to discuss system effectiveness and strategy. It suggests that organizational concepts apply at the system level, with some modification. It examines whether systems, like organizations, need to concern themselves with three kinds of effectiveness—goal achievement, resource acquisition, and constituent satisfaction—and three kinds of strategy to become more effective— linear strategy, adaptive strategy, and interpretive strategy (see Figure 1). The chapter will describe these concepts, showing that linear strategy is similar to Bailey's question about the board's analytical work; adaptive strategy relates to Bailey's question about relations with the governor and legislature; and interpretive strategy, the most important system task, addresses Bailey's questions about institutional relations and board philosophy.

The chapter suggests an approach systems can use to deal with their multifaceted, complex tasks. As organizations that are composed of other organizations, systems can benefit from a cybernetic approach to effectiveness and strategy in which the system does not attempt to control everything. Instead, it seeks to recognize the variables that are crucial and to respond to feedback from monitors on those variables that act like thermostats to alert the system when a variable falls below an acceptable threshold.

Three additional concepts, system leadership, policy making, and system strategic management direct attention to the fact that much of a system's most vital activity deals with (a) systemwide issues that transcend the institutions, (b) policy, not management, with regard to the institutions, and (c) strategic management of the system itself. System leadership and system strategic management are fundamental to system success, but they rarely receive conscious attention from system officials. In fact, most system activity occurs in areas that are relatively concrete and management-oriented rather than conceptual and policy-oriented. The major contribution of an organization-theory approach to system effectiveness and strategy is that it highlights fundamental concerns with which systems should be dealing.

SYSTEMS IN HIGHER EDUCATION

Generally, a system is a collection of public institutions of higher education with a governing board and a central staff. In some systems, institutions also have their own boards of trustees, or there is a system of systems in which a coordinating board adjudicates among two or more governing-board systems. The ideas presented here pertain to any system that is, in effect, an organization with formal governance responsibilities regarding other organizations.

Although rarely considered as organizations, systems too have multiple subunits, constituencies, purposes, complex interactions, and other organizational characteristics. However, institutions, which are the operating units of systems, are more self-contained, less interdependent than the operating units of universities, including schools, divisions, and departments. While universities have many people who consider themselves members of the organization, few people (such as university presidents, board members and staff, and government officials) interact directly with a system. For these and other reasons, systems typically seem to be a peculiar aggregate of "real" organizations. Those who do not see a system as an organization in its own right lose sight of many broad issues and tasks that belong to the system as a whole. They miss the opportunities and responsibilities that derive from the fact that the whole is greater than the sum of its parts.

Higher education system officials are tightrope walkers. They exist at the boundary between institutions of higher education and their constituencies. The constituencies of systems include the students, faculties, staffs, and administrators of the institutions they govern, as well as the state's governor, legislature, taxpayers, and potential students. Systems have grown in number and power during the past twenty years, largely in response to increasing consumer and legislative expectations for academic and fiscal accountability and, in many cases, decreasing enrollments and financial resources. Notably absent from the list of system-producing forces is any institutional desire for benefits that might arise from establishing a system. Institutions have tended to fear system developments, not promote them.

The forces that gave rise to systems carried expectations that explain the institutions' lack of enthusiasm for the system concept. Systems were to impose rationality on what appeared to be chaos. They were to enhance efficient delivery of services and impose difficult decisions on institutions that appeared incapable of making those decisions themselves.

However, the forces that tend to protect the interests of institutions within a system are real, not rhetorical. Certain inherent dynamics seek to preserve institutional integrity. First, and perhaps foremost, systems have no students, alumni, or football teams. In the eyes of most constituency groups, systems do not exist. Hence, system officials have difficulty mobilizing support for the system. Then, too, institutions of higher education are professional organizations. Their functioning depends ultimately on how faculty members choose to conduct themselves. Central authorities are limited in their capacity to influence faculty behavior—limited by their traditions, faculty expertise, faculty tenure, faculty expectations for collegial decision making, and faculty mobility, among other factors. Furthermore, system authorities cannot know as much about each institution as its own management knows.

These countervailing forces explain why system officials must walk a tightrope. They are accountable to such diverse constituencies (for example, legislators who want access, students who want low cost, and governors who want economic development) that they have no hope of fully satisfying all simultaneously. In fact, no organization at any level can hope to accomplish all these ends. How, then, can one rate the effectiveness of an organization or a system? And once this is known, how can organizations or systems act so that they become more effective? These questions are the subject of considerable discussion and research as they pertain to individual organizations. The purpose of this paper is to suggest ways in which one might apply that literature to systems of higher education.

TOWARD A CONCEPT OF SYSTEM EFFECTIVENESS

Organizational theorists and researchers have identified three major approaches to organizational effectiveness: goal achievement, resource acquisition, and constituent satisfaction (Cameron, 1981). Each has some bearing on a concept of system effectiveness.

Goal Achievement

Early theorists posited that the effective organization was one that achieved its goals (Etzioni, 1964; Perrow, 1970; Price, 1972). Assessing effectiveness consisted of identifying the goals of the organization, defining how one would know if those goals were achieved, examining the indicators of goal achievement, and determining how well the organization achieved its goals.

However complex an organization may be, it has goals. In fact, organizations may be defined as collections of people who affiliate with one another because they want to pursue a goal that requires more than one person. Higher education institutions have such goals as educating students, preparing students for employment, contributing to knowledge, and serving the public. Measuring the achievement of these goals is difficult because they are multifaceted, intangible, value-laden, and sometimes incompatible with one another. Moreover, they are limitless—how much education is enough? When has an institution accomplished its contribution to knowledge? Nevertheless, it is possible to make valuable efforts toward measuring goal achievement. When such measures are taken repeatedly over time, it is possible to tell whether the institution is doing better now than it once did. This is the thrust of the current interest in assessing the outcomes of higher education.

Systems, too, have goals. For example, they typically seek to ensure that the component institutions provide programs that the state needs and values, to allocate or change missions and guard against overlap, to coordinate boundary functions such as student transfer among system institutions, and to ensure that the institutions are adequately and equitably funded for their tasks. Whether a system achieves such goals can be assessed, albeit imperfectly, if only by assessing the extent to which problems do or do not arise.

The problems in assessing system goal achievement are numerous, however. The first problem is to identify all of the system's goals. The second is to identify methods for assessing the achievement of goals that are intangible and value-laden. In the process of undertaking these tasks, systems are likely to find that some goals conflict—for example, ensuring both high quality and low cost. Goal achievement is one way of assessing system effectiveness, but it is not the only way, and it may not be the best way.

Resource Acquisition

Another approach to effectiveness is to define it in terms of the extent to which an organization obtains the resources it needs to carry out its functions (Keeley, 1978; Connolly, Conlon, and Deutsch, 1980). Clearly, higher education institutions must have competent faculty, able students, adequate equipment and space, and the funds that make these components possible.

Systems, too, require resources. Most of what they need can be defined as the composite needs of the member institutions. However, they also require talented, influential board members and competent staff. A system's capacity to affect institutions is enhanced when it also has funds to allocate for special purposes. The importance of resource acquisition to systems highlights the centrality of legislatures for effective system functioning, since the funds that enable systems to acquire other resources typically depend on legislative action. Therefore, a key question for systems is, what motivates legislatures to provide adequate resources for higher education? Such a question is central to the resource acquisition approach, but not satisfactorily answered. The approach implies that systems should do all they can to please or persuade the legislature. But legislators change, they have limited knowledge of higher education, and they represent only some of the interests that higher education institutions must satisfy.

Like goal achievement, resource acquisition can play only one important part in system effectiveness. Taking both concepts together permits a more comprehensive view of effectiveness, dealing with whether the system is doing what it intends to do and eliciting the resources it needs to do so. However, a third approach takes a different view.

Constituent Satisfaction

The constituent satisfaction approach to effectiveness suggests that organizations continue to exist and prosper to the extent that they satisfy their constituents (Yuchtman and Seashore, 1967; Zammuto, 1982, 1984). If a higher education organization satisfies its students, faculty, financial contributors, board, and relevant portions of the public, it may be said to be effective because it continues to elicit the contributions of energy, expertise, dollars, and other raw materials that enable it to go forward. The constituent satisfaction approach incorporates the other two by assuming that if an organization accomplishes the right goals, it will obtain needed resources because those who contribute the resources will be satisfied and will continue to contribute. The capacity of this approach to incorporate others is one reason why constituent satisfaction is the prevailing approach to effectiveness in current theory and research.

Satisfying constituents requires that the organization define its constituencies, understand what they want from the organization, and provide it. Since organizations typically cannot provide all of what every constituency wants, four methods of helping organizations deal with this dilemma have arisen (Zammuto, 1984). First, the relativist method recommends balance, suggesting that the organization do as much as it can for each constituency without acting to the detriment of any. The second method, dominant coalitionism, points out that every organization tends to have key interest groups with so much power that their satisfaction should be the preeminent goal of the organization.

Third, those who take the social justice approach recommend that the organization provide equality of opportunity for every constituency to benefit from the organization. When discriminatory action cannot be avoided, it should favor the least advantaged constituency. In the case of higher education, one could argue that students typically have the least advantage in influencing the organization, so their needs should come first.

Finally, the evolutionary view of constituent satisfaction points out that constituent preferences and organizational conditions change over time, so effectiveness exists in the organization's capacity to adapt to diverse preferences. In this view, the focus of attention is on becoming effective, not being effective. Organizations need sensitivity to constituent preferences, flexibility, and willingness to respond.

The four theoretical approaches to constituent satisfaction do not provide clear guidance for system response. For example, systems sometimes do well when they seek balanced responses to all constituencies, when they yield to the wishes of a dominant coalition, when they ensure equality of opportunity to all constituencies, or when they adapt over time to changing preferences. Equally often, system behavior in one mode generates strong opposing pressure to behave in another mode.

The literature does not provide definitive guidance about how to define or assess system effectiveness. Perhaps that is one reason for the tendency of most systems not to try. Systems, like organizations, tend to focus on dealing with immediate problems and making things better at the margin. They establish statewide incentive programs to improve undergraduate instruction, or statewide formulas to improve equity in resource distribution, but they rarely take a comprehensive look at how well they are doing. They must provide for monitoring and feedback if they are to improve, for which a cybernetic approach can be useful.

The Cybernetic System

Cybernetic logic has been proposed as an alternative to rational, analytic logic. Rationality requires full knowledge of goals, alternatives, processes, and outcomes, but people acting in complex situations cannot hope to achieve such knowledge. Cybernetic logic suggests that full knowledge is not necessary. Instead, people, organizations, or systems can focus on selected key features of their situation and use that information to make reasonable decisions (Steinbruner, 1974).

A major principle of cybernetics is the law of requisite variety (Ashby, 1956), which states that control devices must have as much variety as the system being controlled so that the devices will register appropriate information and prompt needed responses. In other words, people in organizations need to define a variety of key factors, establish control mechanisms for those factors, and respond when the mechanisms indicate unacceptable changes in those factors. They do not need to oversee all factors at all times if they have set up such devices.

The analogy of the thermostat is useful. Personal comfort is a function of humidity, drafts, and other qualities of the environment in addition to temperature. However, we have generally decided that temperature is the key component, and we have established heating and cooling systems attached to a regulator that activates those systems when the temperature falls outside defined parameters. The thermostat does not recognize directly the effects of other changes in the atmosphere, but people who do can change the parameters accordingly. The resultant change in temperature increases personal comfort under existing conditions. Note, however, that different circumstances may require additional kinds of thermostats, as in the need for humidity controls in rooms housing major computing equipment.

The point is, it is not necessary to control everything in order to achieve a desired result. However, it is necessary to define the key ingredients for a given setting and establish methods to recognize and correct unacceptable changes in those ingredients. In a system of higher education, monitors could include regularly scheduled data analyses, standard operating procedures, or meetings of people with diverse points of view to discuss key issues.

The cybernetic approach suggests that the methods for correcting unacceptable changes arise through trial and error. Those involved in the system have experience that permits them to identify potential solutions. If the first solution they select does not work, the monitor will again register an error. Participants continue to select solutions until the monitor no longer registers problematic conditions. Because of the complexity of organizations and systems, participants will often find that correcting one condition sets off alarms in other areas. Policy makers and administrators recognize that such interdependencies exist and often seek to minimize potentially harmful effects as they choose a course of corrective action. Having effective monitors in place does not prevent unintended consequences, but it does help ensure that they will come to decision makers' attention when they occur.

Extending the analogy to organizations and systems suggests that they need to know what they must be sensitive to, given that they cannot be sensitive to everything that might be considered relevant. Those adopting a cybernetic approach risk overlooking important indicators, but they can minimize that risk in several ways. One important way is to increase the access of existing monitors to the decision-making process or increase the number of participants in the monitoring process, making each participant responsible for a limited set of concerns. Doing so increases the number of concerns they can monitor. Relatedly, the risk is less when they have effective information and communication systems so that monitors provide accurate readings and troublesome readings will elicit appropriate and effective responses. They also need to learn when monitors should be established or abandoned and when new parameters are needed for existing monitors.

What does this mean for systems of higher education? First, systems need to know what they have to monitor. Among the candidates for this list are legislative opinion, gubernatorial positions, and the state's needs for specific kinds of education and training. They also need to monitor institutional performance not only so that they can correct deficiencies but also so that they can communicate the merits of system institutions to key external constituencies.

In order to know what they must monitor, systems must know their purposes. They may define their purposes *a priori*, but they will also discover purposes as they learn by experience. Policy makers' first impulse often is to define system purposes as those of the institutions, writ large. They seek to ensure quality education, research, and public service at individual institutions and collectively.

Appropriate monitors include indicators of faculty quality, teaching effectiveness, adequacy of facilities and equipment, and program quality. This definition of system purpose is legitimate, but it is unfortunate if it leads policy makers too close to management concerns and operational issues. Systems can establish goals with institutions, set broad parameters for them, and define minimum acceptable performance, but those closest to the action are usually in the best position to make managerial and operational decisions.

In any case, these are only a few of the purposes of systems. Systems also enhance the economic development of the state. Some of the monitors for this purpose should assess state needs for skilled employees and system incentives for faculty to work with business and industry. In addition, systems ensure efficient utilization of resources allocated to higher education. They need monitors of costs per student, program costs, program duplication, and program proliferation.

A typical system may have all these purposes and more, including resource acquisition and constituent satisfaction. One way to deal with some system purposes is to delegate them to the campuses, each with its own monitor to keep institutional behavior within an acceptable range. Similar monitors might exist at the system level for a limited number of concerns that individual institutions cannot or will not address. Two obvious areas that may need system monitors are statewide issues (such as the overall ability of the system's institutions to address economic development needs, access to higher education, or the credibility of public higher education among legislators) and selected indicators of institutional failure to address the problems that the system has delegated to local administration.

A hypothetical example illustrates this approach. A system board identified its primary concerns at the state and institution levels. At the state level, these concerns were meeting economic development needs, ensuring a sensible statewide program inventory, distributing resources equitably among institutions, dealing effectively with political forces, and ensuring that students had access to higher education at reasonable cost. As illustrated in Figure 2, the system board established monitors for each of these concerns. For example, system staff prepared an annual report to the board (a) showing current state needs for economic development as they related to higher education functions such as skilled employees, new knowledge, and incentive structures and (b) analyzing the ways in which higher education might be more responsive.

For institution-level issues, Figure 2 shows that this system takes a dual approach. The system delegates responsibility for such issues as faculty quality, efficiency, program quality, and adequacy of support functions to the institutions (smaller thermostats), but it maintains two forms of oversight (larger thermostats). First, the system requires the institution to create and use local procedures for monitoring selected issues. For example, system policy requires each

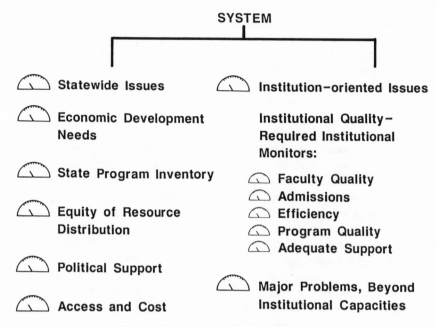

FIG. 2. Monitors in a hypothetical system.

institution to evaluate every instructional program every five years. Other issues, such as faculty quality, are subject only to an occasional request from the system for information about such gross indicators as the proportion of faculty holding the doctorate. These requests more often produce public relations statements than policy directives.

The second form of oversight the system uses for institution-oriented issues can be likened to the "tilt" indicator on a pinball machine. The system wants to know when the institution experiences fundamental problems with which it is unable to deal alone. For many institutions in recent years, the rapid development pace and high cost of equipment for graduate study and research has created such a problem. The system's monitors in this area consist of structured opportunities for the institutions to raise such issues (the annual budget process is a prime example) and a few pulse-taking exercises to satisfy the system that the institution is functioning well. In this system, the exercises consist of a presidential evaluation procedure and an annual look at cost per student.

This system is hypothetical. Other systems will have other monitors, depending on various factors. Monitors may reflect mandates contained in the state constitution, statutes, or by-laws of the system board. Major issues or crises may give rise to new monitors that become part of a system's standard operating procedures. In the ideal situation, monitors reflect conscious attempts to anticipate problems before they arise, and they reflect that the system knows what it needs to do in order to be effective. Defining and implementing what the system needs to do constitute system strategy. The next section explains strategy in a system context and ties strategy back to the concept of effectiveness.

STRATEGY IN HIGHER EDUCATION SYSTEMS

Strategy in organizations is the actions taken by top-level administrators and policy makers to position the organization to be effective (Hambrick, 1980; for a broad review of literature on strategy in business and higher education, see Chaffee, 1985). A higher education system is supraorganizational in that it is an organization of organizations. This fact complicates the application of strategy to a system but does not invalidate it. The chief danger of applying strategy to systems is the risk that doing so will take a system too deeply into the management of the constituent institutions.

To minimize that risk, one must distinguish between the common term *strategic management* and three other concepts, *system leadership, policy making*, and *system strategic management*. These are the responsibility of the system, as shown in areas 1, 2, and 3 of Figure 3. In this terminology, systems should confine themselves to the three system-based areas and leave the institutions to conduct their own strategic management, the fourth area in Figure 3.

Area 1 in Figure 3 depicts system leadership. In this area, the system has overall responsibility for central system welfare and institutional welfare, and it exercises this responsibility with reference not only to internal concerns but also in response to the constituencies that support the system and institutions. Encircling area 1 with a dotted line indicates the importance of relationships between internal and external constituencies. Government officials, the public, and those inside the institutions need to have mutual understandings about why the system exists, how it discharges its responsibilities, and where it is going. Establishing and maintaining these understandings are vitally important system functions.

Area 2 in the figure is where system strategic management occurs. System officials often think of themselves as agents of other organizations, especially the constituent institutions, but they must also recognize that the system is itself an organization. On behalf of the system organization, officials need to consider strategies that will enhance system functioning. Such strategies could include maintaining the credibility of central leadership through selection of board members and board staff or building trust with legislative leaders.

Area 3 is where the system and the institutions interact as the system engages in policy making. The major system activities in this area are establishing parameters within which the institutions are to function and monitoring key institutional functions. Institution strategic management, area 4 in the figure, is

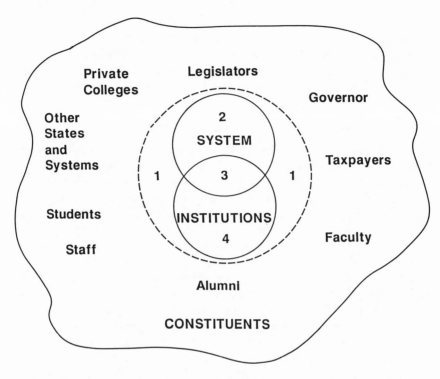

FIG. 3. Four types of strategy. (1) System leadership; (2) system strategic management; (3) policy making; (4) institution strategic management.

the responsibility of the institution's chief executive officer and will not be discussed here.

A higher education system engages in system leadership, system strategic management, and policy making. Before examining these three activities separately, however, this section provides a discussion of the concept of strategy in general and relates it to the three approaches to effectiveness.

The Concept of Strategy
A basic premise of strategy is that the organization and its environment are inseparable (Biggadike, 1981; Lenz, 1980). The organization uses strategy to deal with changing environments. Strategic decisions are never routine, structured, or predictable because constant, often unpredictable changes occur in both the organization and its environment. Strategic decisions, by definition, are important enough to affect the overall welfare and effectiveness of an organization.

The strategy that an organization implements is composed typically of actions that may or may not have been planned in advance. Therefore, all organizations or systems make strategy, even if they do not do so consciously. They make strategic decisions, whether they call them that or not. According to the literature on strategy, summarized in Chaffee (1985), their strategies may fall into one of three categories, each of which corresponds to one of the approaches to effectiveness described above. The three categories are best illustrated by analogy to three kinds of systems found in individual people. Extended discussion of each category follows a brief analogy for each.

Individual people have machinelike systems, adaptive systems, and cultural systems. The skeleton is an example of a machinelike system, in which characteristics and relationships are highly predictable. Skilled observers can easily identify the location and nature of a break in the skeletal system, and they can predict the behavioral consequences of a given skeletal type or abnormality. These properties make the skeletal system analogous to a predictable, rational, goal-oriented approach to effectiveness, which is comparable to what is called the linear approach to strategy.

People also adapt to circumstances and changes, both physically and psychologically. If they hunger for attention and get it by screaming, they learn to scream more. If they lose one sense, they become able to learn more from their remaining senses.These capacities parallel a resource-acquisition approach to effectiveness and what we will call the adaptive approach to strategy.

Finally, people are cultural systems. They receive, process,and send communications; they develop beliefs about fundamental philosophical issues and specific situations; they express emotions and affiliations in complex relationships with other people. These systems correspond to the constituent-satisfaction approach to effectiveness and the interpretive approach to strategy. They are the least predictable, the least susceptible to analysis, and the most complex human systems. They are also the most fundamental in terms of their capacity to distinguish humans from other animals and one human from another.

Interpretive-satisfaction issues are the most complex, and they are the source from which all other actions should derive for maximum effectiveness. They are the most difficult issues to understand and address, but also the most important ones. Once they are understood, the identification of adaptive-resource actions and linear-goal actions is a straightforward exercise in drawing implications and making extrapolations. Before dealing with these interrelationships, it is useful to examine each approach to strategy separately.

Linear Strategy.
Linear strategy is highly rational and oriented toward planning (Chandler, 1962). The term *strategic planning* represents linear strategy well. According to this view, strategy consists of integrated decisions, actions, or plans that will set and

achieve viable organizational goals. Linear strategy is therefore related to the goal approach to effectiveness, discussed earlier. The direct route to achieving organizational goals is to use linear strategy. As the word *linear* suggests, in this mode strategy is methodical, direct, sequential, and plan-based.

Successfully engaging in linear strategy carries several requirements. Top administrators must have considerable capacity to change the organization to comply with their plans, which they make by identifying their goals, generating alternative methods of achieving them, weighing the likelihood that alternative methods will succeed, and deciding which ones to implement. They aim to capitalize on those future trends and events that are favorable while avoiding or counteracting those that are not. The utility of the linear approach depends either on having a relatively predictable environment or on insulating the organization from its environment. To the extent that the environment is unpredictable and directly affects the organization, unforeseen events can ruin linear-strategy plans.

Despite the increasing volatility and vulnerability of the world of higher education, linear strategy has a place in institutions and systems. Some key features of management and policy making will yield to this approach. For example, enrollment levels are certainly strategic variables for higher education. Although they cannot be predicted perfectly, enough is known about the demographics of the traditional college age group and the participation patterns of the older population groups to permit useful forecasting and planning to deal with projected changes in enrollment. Many financial functions, too, can be planned. At the policy level, systems working with institutions can assess current costs for programs, identify areas where major capital investments may become necessary to keep a program or institution viable, and predict changes in financial needs well enough to know whether major efforts will be required to handle them.

The usefulness of linear strategy for higher education is limited by the multiple, conflicting goals of higher education, its inability to predict many key environmental circumstances, and its inability to buffer institutions from the environment. Furthermore, managers and policy makers have difficulty in creating change expeditiously because of norms that require high participation in decision making and organizational inflexibilities such as faculty tenure, faculty specialization, and inability to "move the plant to a better location."

Adaptive Strategy.
Adaptive strategy recognizes volatile environments and the need for organizations to adapt if they are to continue to exist (Hofer, 1973). The purpose of adaptive strategy is to develop a viable match between the demands of the environment and the activities of the organization. The idea of a viable match is

as close as this approach gets to suggesting that organizations should have goals—the goal is the viable match. But the goal is never achieved because environments continue to change. Adaptive strategy is a constant process of change in search of a viable match. The implicit aim of the match is to enable the organization to attract resources from the environment, so adaptive strategy is a potential route to effectiveness as defined in the resource acquisition approach.

Adaptive strategy supports the idea of looking into the future, both to identify predictable changes such as those appropriate for linear strategy and, perhaps more important, to guess what the major unpredictable changes might be. Adaptive strategy also suggests that the organization constantly examine its present circumstances to identify mismatches between what it does and what is needed. Compared with linear strategy, adaptive strategy is less centralized in top management, more multifaceted,and generally less integrated into an overall view of the organization's identity and future.

Probably the single most significant change in the higher education industry since 1970 has been its conscious shift toward adaptive strategy. The ivory tower has become an anachronism as colleges and universities shifted from admissions viewed as a selection function to admissions as recruitment, and from intellectual discussions about new program ideas to market-based discussions regarding whether the new program would attract enough students and provide them with jobs upon graduation. Higher education institutions began offering courses in the evenings, taking courses to convenient locations, and serving adult students in other special ways. Only the most elite or well-situated institutions have been exempt from the need to adapt to declining public support for higher education, increasing demand for employment-preparation as a goal of undergraduate education, and declining numbers of traditional-age students.

As valuable as adaptive strategy has been for many colleges and universities, it has limits. These institutions express certain purposes and traditions that cannot be abrogated without betraying their charters and fundamental reasons for existence. A business can change its products radically; a college cannot. Furthermore, even desirable changes may take considerable time to implement because of the institutions' dependence on personnel rather than capital, the specialized nature of faculty expertise, and the relatively low rate of faculty turnover. Higher education can adapt, but usually slowly and always within fairly narrow limits.

Interpretive Strategy.
The third form of strategy suggests that organizations consist of implicit contracts among people, making an organization a collection of cooperative agreements entered into by individuals with free will (Chaffee, 1984; Pettigrew, 1977; Van Cauwenbergh and Cool, 1982; Weick and Daft, 1983). The organization's ex-

istence depends on its ability to attract enough individuals to cooperate in a mutually beneficial exchange. Interpretive strategy aims to attract and hold the individuals in an organization by ensuring that they perceive the benefits of participation.

For example, among the potential benefits of higher education to a student are opportunities to learn about interesting ideas, prepare for a job, participate in a congenial community, and attend cultural and athletic events. But sometimes students get bored, wonder if they'll be employable, feel like outsiders, or in other ways fail to perceive the benefits of participation, whether those benefits are really there or not. Interpretive strategy focuses attention on the importance of perception: just because a college is known for its high placement ratio for graduates doesn't mean that students never drop out because they see no vocational future for themselves there. Are people wrong about the college, or are these students simply unable to connect? For these students, it doesn't matter—they see the college as unlikely to provide what they want and they leave. Interpretive strategy points out the importance of discovering how various constituencies perceive an organization and taking appropriate action to reinforce positive perceptions and repair negative ones.

Satisfaction is an attitude that bears only a moderate relationship to truth—that is, some people may be satisfied by inefficient or ineffective organizations or dissatisfied with organizations that accomplish their goals remarkably well. Stanford and Harvard have their disillusioned dropouts; Bootstrap University has its fervently loyal alumni.

Therefore, interpretive strategy deals with two worlds. One is the world of decisions, actions, and events, such as those that comprise linear and adaptive strategy. The other is the world of communication, norms, language, attitudes, symbols, perception, and relationships. The organization needs to act in ways that satisfy its constituents, but it also needs to interpret what it is doing so that constituents will see the organization as it wishes to be seen. The current emphasis on the importance of leadership with vision is a call for interpretation. Vision brings a sense of direction that enables everyone to contribute and feel significant.

What an organization does and what it says may differ from one another, but logic suggests that the greater the difference and the longer it persists uncorrected, the more likely constituents are to see the difference. This dynamic helps prevent interpretive strategy from being an amoral manipulation of gullible constituents. Organizational leaders cannot long convey an erroneous interpretation of the organization because constituents have many sources of information that the leaders cannot control. Ultimately, the best interests of the organization are more likely to be served by truthfulness than by deceit. A central message of interpretive strategy is the importance of communicating about the organization, even when it may be painful to do so.

TABLE 1. Parallel Views of Strategy and Effectiveness

Effectiveness can be	Strategy can be	Managerial Motto
Goal achievement	Linear	Plan ahead
Resource acquisition	Adaptive	Serve the public
Constituent satisfaction	Interpretive	For the good of the cause

Interpretive strategy is one direct route to effectiveness, as described in the constituent satisfaction model. In fact, although the effectiveness and strategy literatures are fairly independent of one another, Table 1 shows similarities in the approaches discussed here. Goal achievement corresponds to linear strategy, where "plan ahead" might be the managerial motto. Resource acquisition is closely related to adaptive strategy, and organizations seek most of all to serve the public. Constituent satisfaction is linked with interpretive strategy, where the goal is to develop a feeling that we're in this together, for the good of the cause.

Integrating Three Views of Strategy and Effectiveness
Current theory holds what common knowledge would verify: organizations need to use all three approaches to strategy and seek all three forms of effectiveness. Doing so is not as complicated as it might seem, for two reasons. Table 1 illustrates the first reason. Each approach to strategy bears a natural relationship to one of the forms of effectiveness. Therefore, organizations have a tool (an approach to strategy) with which to address each of their desired outcomes (forms of effectiveness). Interpretive strategy has special significance because by articulating institutional values, it provides a framework within which to incorporate and orient adaptive and linear strategy.

Second, the three forms of strategy and effectiveness represent an implicit hierarchy of complexity that guides decisions about how the three should relate to one another. At the top of the hierarchy is the interpretive model, followed by the adaptive, and then the linear. Hierarchical does not mean sequential. It is not necessary to go through the adaptive level in order to move between the linear and the interpretive. Hierarchical means that the interpretive model, complex enough in itself, embraces also the complexities of the adaptive and linear models. The adaptive model incorporates the linear elements of the person or organization, but it does not include the interpretive elements. The linear model excludes both the adaptive and the interpretive.

Starting at the most complex level, organizations and systems need to develop interpretive strategies to enhance constituent satisfaction, and to let those interpretive strategies guide their decisions about adaptation (for resource acquisition) and linear planning (for goal achievement). Interpretive strategy makes adaptation sensible and coherent, rather than random, and it defines the organization's goals, some of which may be achieved through planning.

The next section takes these admittedly abstract concepts and applies them to systems of higher education, using the distinctions established in Figure 3 among system leadership, system strategic management, and policy making.

SYSTEM LEADERSHIP, MANAGEMENT, AND POLICY MAKING

System leadership is a system function, oriented toward statewide issues and the system as an organization that is greater than the sum of its parts. System strategic management is also a system function, in which the system ensures that its central functions are headed in the right direction. In policy making, where system and institutions overlap, the system and the institution share responsibility. The major system activities in this area are to set policies about such matters as budget and personnel procedures or academic program development and to monitor key institutional functions such as the president's performance. Institution strategic management relates to many local decisions within parameters set by the system and is the responsibility of the institution's chief executive officer. The three kinds of activity (system leadership, system strategic management, and policy making) that apply to the system level can be distinguished in the abstract, but in practice considerable overlap occurs. A system need not be actively engaged in all three at all times, but it is useful to pause occasionally to assess whether any of the three is being neglected.

Systems arose because of a perceived need for a statewide perspective on institutional management. That is, systems were created to engage in policy making. However, system leadership and system strategic management are necessary preconditions for effective policy making. Systems are beginning to recognize this fact, but in too many cases system leadership remains the most important and most overlooked function of systems.

System Leadership
System leadership requires all three levels of strategy (interpretive, adaptive, and linear) as shown in Figure 4. The interpretive level dominates and focuses system leadership. This is where systems create aspirations and establish direction. They do so with regard to the higher education industry in the state, the institutions collectively, and the mix of institutional roles in the system. System leadership requires conscious, continual, energetic attention if it is to succeed, but it is often forgotten except in times of crisis.

The three fundamental tasks of system leadership at the interpretive level are articulating key elements of the system's identity, purposes, and beliefs; setting

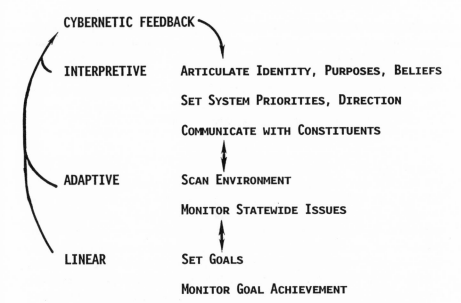

FIG. 4. System Leadership. *Key issues*: Define system identity; define key constituencies.

direction and priorities for the system; and communicating with constituencies. Certain adaptive and linear strategies supplement and inform these tasks.

The two major adaptive tasks are to scan the environment and monitor statewide issues. Scanning the environment means that the system actively seeks information about current and future conditions that may affect the system. Systems need to know about impending changes in the economic climate; political, educational, and social circumstances; demographic parameters; and other broad-scale shifts.

Where feasible, the system needs to set specific goals and monitor progress toward achieving the goals. At the interpretive level, a system may see a need to improve its relationships with the legislature. To do so, it may decide to contact legislators, encourage others to contact legislators, publish documents for legislators, and so on. These activities lend themselves to goal setting (how many legislators must be contacted, what changes are expected, and how will we know when the changes have occurred).

In the process of implementing system leadership initiatives, the system should establish monitors to provide feedback about the system as it is experienced by key constituencies. Such feedback allows the system to take corrective action when necessary.

In the system leadership process, two key issues are central to success. First, the system must have a clear definition of its identity—what is it, why does it exist, what are its values? Second, the system should try to define its key constituencies and recognize when it is responding to some constituencies in preference, and perhaps to the detriment, of others. Systems may respond differentially to constituencies from one specific issue or time to another, but the reasons for such preferences should be clear and consistent and the system should recognize that it may incur important costs as well as benefits when it acts preferentially.

System Strategic Management

The need for system strategic management arises from the fact that the system must organize itself so that it is capable of implementing both system leadership for higher education and policy making for the institutions. System leadership pertains to higher education in general, system strategic management to the system board and staff, and policy making to the system-institution interface. One way to think of the differences among the three is that institutional presidents might willingly help accomplish the goals of system leadership (unless, for example, system leadership involves cutting back resources); they would not be involved in system strategic management; and they may sometimes resist policy making as a perceived intrusion on their prerogatives.

At the system strategic management level, systems can be more oriented toward their own operational issues than broad-brush conceptual issues. The focus here is on the board members and board staff and how they conduct business for the system as a whole.

The system needs to recognize and deal with those elements of system leadership that have little to do with the institutions. For example, if the board itself has low credibility because it is seen as highly politicized, that problem can become an input to system strategic management at the interpretive level. Possible solutions could include changes in who communicates what about the system (interpretive), the issues that capture board attention (adaptive), or how the board organizes its meetings (linear).

At the interpretive level, Figure 5 suggests that system strategic management also includes how the central part of the system represents itself to both internal and external constituencies, as well as how authority is distributed among the board, staff, and other actors (what is reserved for the legislative or executive branches, the coordinating board, or the institutions). The system needs to adapt as issues rise or fall in salience and as legislation is proposed by the board or by others. The system uses linear strategies such as written plans, formal analysis, staffing patterns, and meeting agenda structure. In fact, some of the most fundamental concerns of system strategic management are linear. They include personnel decisions (board members and staff) and rules or legislation authorizing the system board and delimiting its activities.

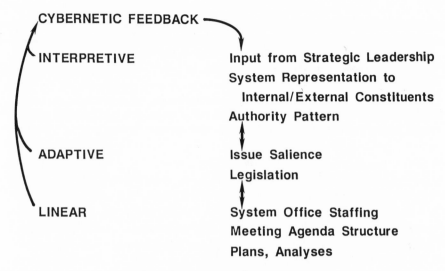

FIG. 5. System strategic management.

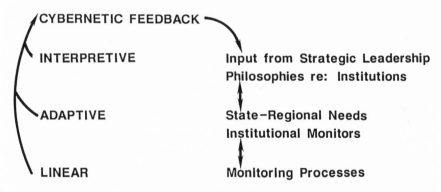

FIG.6. Policy making.

Policy Making

Policy making deals with the interface between the system and the institutions, and it, too, requires all three levels of strategy, with the interpretive level dominating the other two (see Figure 6). The interpretive level should reflect the results of the process of system leadership, for example, by including the system's philosophy regarding institutional diversity in policies that deal with academic program development. The roles of the system board and its staff with respect to the institutions should be articulated, and the individuals selected to fill those roles should reflect and act consistently with system leadership decisions.

At the adaptive level, the system needs to establish monitors that give information about both the needs of the state or region and the performance of the institutions. Key issues that such monitors are likely to address include academic programs, access to higher education, research and development, academic quality, and public service.

The linear level provides a vehicle for accomplishing many of the changes that the adaptive monitors or interpretive values may suggest. The system needs to establish policies and monitors regarding institutional performance in various areas. The literature on system activities suggests that the following areas are some of the most central to system functioning: goals, plans, and analyses; system-institutional relations; missions (including program review, state needs, and access issues); and financial issues (including resource acquisition, budgeting, student charges and aid, and physical plant). Policies and monitors in these areas can communicate the expectations the system holds for the institutions, express the system's priorities and values, and provide feedback to the system when something goes wrong.

A study of how systems typically allocate their time and attention would probably show the majority at the linear level of policy making. Systems produce a great many rules and decisions regarding institutional management, a process that accounts for much of their effort. The second greatest activity level is probably adaptive policy making, with systems encouraging and approving institutional changes that are designed to respond to environmental changes.

This focus on relatively operational, institution-oriented activities is understandable. These are the areas in which system boards have leverage on their focal constituency and can achieve results. Furthermore, the system as a whole is an abstract entity. It does not make presentations at board meetings. The few people who are most likely to make pleas on its behalf—the board's staff—are thereby more likely to be charged with self-interest or power mongering than with caring for some greater good.

If systems operate mainly at the level of linear and adaptive policy making, all levels of system leadership, system strategic management, and the interpretive level of policy making occur implicitly rather than explicitly. When these fundamental tasks are overlooked, the results are likely to be inconsistent and incomplete. Systems run the risk of violating their beliefs, failing to notice important priorities, and missing valuable opportunities. They may inadvertently set up conflicting expectations of their institutions. Thus, if a system is to be effective, it must address issues of system leadership, interpretive system strategic management, and interpretive policy making.

TOWARD AN EFFECTIVE SYSTEM OF HIGHER EDUCATION

Systems, like less complex organizations, are effective to the extent that they satisfy key constituencies, attract needed resources, and achieve goals. To satisfy key constituencies, interpretive strategy contributes an emphasis on the importance of the system being aware of its identity and dealing with the perceptions of its constituencies. To attract needed resources, adaptive strategy suggests the importance of recognizing constituencies' needs and responding to them. To achieve goals, linear strategy suggests the value of structuring situations, obtaining and using data, and assigning responsibility for action.

Achieving system effectiveness is exceptionally complex. In general, a system's external constituency groups are more diverse and more far-flung than those of individual institutions. Systems tend to have less detailed knowledge of and less control over their internal components (institutions) than institutions have of theirs (schools, divisions, and departments). Therefore, the cybernetic approach is especially useful to systems, suggesting that systems be decentralized to the maximum feasible extent with regard to institutional activities, but they should also use monitors to ensure that vital processes are working and effective.

In the ideal system, all levels of system leadership, system strategic management, and policy making occur simultaneously and interactively. It is therefore difficult to prescribe steps that a system should take to implement these ideas. Generally speaking, a system should:

1. Develop the interpretive levels of all three strategies, ensuring consistency among them;

2. Identify the implications and needed actions to implement the results of its interpretive deliberations;

3. Review existing statements, procedures, and monitors to ensure that they correspond to the desired results of the interpretive strategies;

4. Develop new and drop old statements, procedures, and monitors, as may be necessary to enact its interpretive strategies;

5. Establish diverse monitors of system and institutional functioning;

6. Receive and act on the results of its monitoring processes;

7. Go through these steps regularly as personnel and conditions change over time.

A checklist for some important elements of an effective system arises from these ideas. An effective system:

Has a conscious, explicit identity, purposes, beliefs, priorities, and expectations
   of its institutions
Knows what the state needs and wants with respect to higher education
Recognizes and corrects when the system does not meet appropriate state needs
Acts to acquire or reallocate resources necessary to meet state needs
Communicates effectively with key internal and external constituencies
Ensures that institutions know what is expected of them

Decentralizes authority to the institutions except with regard to systemwide concerns

Draws conflicting interests together in a way that ensures credibility and support for the system

Promotes interinstitutional cooperation, rather than competition

Corrects deficiencies in a manner that is consistent with its own authority and the norms of the academic community.

Systems may spend far too much time on the last item in this list and far too little on the others. An effective system must search constantly for an appropriate balance among them.

Among the practical implications of these recommendations, one of the most important relates to the system board's selection of a system chief executive officer. Systems need CEOs who have developed a clear personal philosophy about the roles and value of higher education generally and the type(s) of institutions that comprise the system in question. The philosophy must be consistent with the existing or desired philosophy of the state setting. CEOs need to be able to lead the system board to discuss and deal with abstract ideas, building toward consensus and appropriate action. CEOs need exceptionally strong communication skills to articulate and generate enthusiasm for the system view among many diverse constituencies.

CEOs also need the capacity to discern mismatches and inadequacies in the board, system staff, and institutions. They need strong skills in synthesis and extrapolation so that they can juxtapose seemingly unrelated circumstances (such as the need for a shift in the state's economic base and the nature of higher education offerings in the system) and foresee their implications for the system.

Finally, CEOs need to be persuasive and to ensure compliance with high standards, but they should not be controlling when it comes to institutional operations. Rather, they need to know what kinds of monitors are important and how to use them as cybernetic processes.

In other words, the stronger the interpretive skills of system CEOs, the more likely they will be able to lead in areas systems most often overlook. When CEOs lead systems to attend to state-higher education issues (system leadership) and the system as an organization (system strategic management), they can enhance the credibility of higher education in the state for the benefit of all.

These recommendations imply that boards will spend more time on system issues than institutional issues, and that institutions will be involved not only in their own concerns but also in system issues. McGuinness (1987) suggests that systems should spend 75% of their time on system issues and 25% on the institutions, reversing the figures for how institutions should spend their time. The suggestion is consistent with the point of view developed here. Yet many board agendas do not reflect this allocation. One way to move toward the ideas expressed here is simply to reallocate board agenda time to ensure that more is devoted to system issues. Another way is to set aside a special time, perhaps annually, to discuss system leadership or interpretive strategy issues. This is not to say that a system should distance itself from its component institutions. The institutions provide critical intelligence on important issues and feasible solutions. The point is that many boards can profitably spend more time on system issues with institutional advice and less on institution-specific issues.

System boards will find it difficult to make this kind of shift in what they attend to, if only because institutional matters are often numerous and pressing. Furthermore, system board members probably obtain greater satisfaction from dealing with people—notably institutional leaders—than with abstractions. People offer the possibility of immediate results, philosophy rarely does. A crucial issue facing those who seek to act on the recommendations proposed here is that of identifying incentives for board members to expend greater effort on behalf of the higher education system as a whole. The long-term benefits can be great, but the short-term benefits are not usually apparent. However large the collective benefits of taking this approach may be, it will not be adopted unless it also carries personal benefits for board members.

The system that acts according to these recommendations can become what Ewell (1984) has called "self-regarding." It can see and adjust to broad evolutionary changes as well as short-term crises. It can recognize major points of imbalance and get them on the agenda. It can anticipate potential problems and resolve them before they become debilitating. The system itself can learn. It will have the foundation on which to engage in constant betterment of higher education for the good of the state.

RESEARCH NEEDED ON SYSTEM STRATEGY AND EFFECTIVENESS

Most of the material listed in the reference section that follows is descriptive or prescriptive. It explains governance arrangements at the state level, which is tantamount to the system level in some states, but not the majority. It outlines actions that are recommended on the basis of experience and common sense. If there is a difference between those documents and this one, it is only that this one makes an explicit attempt to define potentially promising theories for understanding system dynamics.

Theory-based research on systems is scarce. The National Center for Postsecondary Governance and Finance (NCPGF), headquartered at the University of Maryland, is currently conducting a set of theory-based studies on the institutional impact of state initiatives to improve quality. While this focus is not directly related to systems as such, since initiatives to improve quality may come from other state-level agents, the project may be the first major empirical effort to explain suprainstitutional dynamics in ways that move beyond the descriptive toward the predictive.

The preceding discussion raises a very large number of researchable questions. The applicability of existing models of effectiveness and strategy to system operations is untested. Does system functioning, however defined, improve when systems accomplish goals, acquire resources, and/or satisfy constituents? Must systems be effective in other ways? Are some goals, resources, and constituents more important to systems than others? Do systems face unique linear-strategy issues as they set and work toward goals that may require institutional collaboration? What are the adaptive pressures on systems and how do they respond—at the system level, institutional level, or both? Can system leaders successfully interpret the system and higher education itself to external constituencies? To their own institutions? Is it important that they do so?

Is it useful for systems to act in ways described here as system leadership, system strategic management, and policy making? What kinds of monitors do they use to obtain feedback in these areas? What monitors work best? What array of responses do systems use when monitors indicate action is needed?

At the level of system leadership, no one has yet studied whether system mission statements exist, how they vary, and whether they relate to policy statements and system board decisions. What kinds of tools do systems use to relate to external constituencies through vehicles such as publications, hearings, or blue-ribbon commissions, and with what effects? Does it matter if systems have no mission statements or external-relations programs?

With regard to system strategic management, the State Higher Education Executive Officers organization has classified the states according to the state-level authority structures for higher education, and it reports state staffing numbers, but no one has analyzed the functions performed by system staff members, how they relate to board members, or whether variations in such behaviors affect system effectiveness.

The NCPGF studies described above will establish a potentially important beginning in the area of system policy making by examining the effects on institutions of state incentive programs. The field would benefit also from studies of system policies of many kinds, including how they vary and their effects on institutions. The process for establishing institutional budget requests is also likely to vary substantially among systems, from strong institutional initiative to strong system parameter-setting. Such variations may affect not only how much state funding institutions receive, but also their ability to use resources efficiently and effectively.

In addition to research questions that arise directly from the preceding discussion, system leaders would benefit from studies based in other kinds of theories. For example, sociologists have developed theories about interorganizational relations that could prove useful in examining institution-system dynamics and the effects of competition versus cooperation among institutions within a system. Systems may have diverse cultures regarding which anthropological methods may yield valuable insights. System dynamics may correspond to interest-group theories from political science.

To expand on one set of possibilities, Pfeffer (1982) applies a variety of social science theories to organizations. Selecting from his list, one might examine individual leaders in systems, such as board members, board staff members, and campus presidents, from the perspective of expectancy theory, need theory, exchange theory, socialization theory, role theory, or power theory. Such theories are candidate explanations for what motivates these individuals as they relate to each other or the system and how they influence one another.

With regard to relations among institutions, the board, and the legislature, resource dependence theory is potentially powerful. Resource dependence theory posits that "organizational behavior becomes externally influenced because the focal organization must attend to the demands of those in its environment that provide resources necessary and important for its continued survival" (Pfeffer, 1982, p. 193). Hence, a resource-dependence view could elaborate the structure of such interdependencies and trace their implications for action by the various participating groups.

On the other hand, organizations have been described in social construction theory as elaborate systems of shared meaning created by the participants. The theory may be especially apt for higher education systems, which lack the physical presence and committed members that are typical of many organizations. A social constructionist approach could elucidate the methods participants use to create the identity and nature of the system, thereby enhancing understanding of why participants do what they do within it.

System-level research may require special research methods. Fourteen states have statewide governing boards for all public institutions. Another eight have such boards for all except the two-year colleges. In these eight and the remaining twenty-eight states, multicampus governing boards with varying scopes (statewide community colleges, universities in a region, community colleges in a region, and so on) exist. The total national number of system governing boards of a given type is unlikely to exceed fifty. Few important research questions will be simple enough to yield to statistical methods—the number of variables may often approach or exceed the number of cases.

Hence, system-level research will probably depend heavily on case studies with sample sizes of one to a dozen or so, in many studies probably including the entire population of a given type of system. Researchers will need to take exceptional care in selecting cases for study to ensure that the cases are comparable on some variables and diverse on others, as the research question suggests. Current knowledge of systems is so sparse that single case studies, especially longitudinal ones, could be unusually effective.

Inquiry into many important questions will necessarily begin with purely descriptive work, since little is yet known about systems on many key points such as budget-setting processes, meeting and agenda patterns, staffing patterns, and the nature of system policies. Research to generate hypotheses that may apply to systems outside the study is also needed. In short, the field would benefit from studies with limited ambition regarding size, scope, and generalizability, but maximum ambition regarding depth,duration, and careful design. Ideally, individual studies will be part of larger research programs, each study intended to fill in a piece of the mosaic.

The need for system-level studies is due partly to the larger number of institutions now incorporated in systems than once was true, but also because systems and states have greatly expanded their roles. No longer do they focus on institutional efficiency; they also seek to improve academic quality. It appears that higher education itself can no longer assume public support; it must actively cultivate such support. Systems have considerable potential power to affect higher education, yet systems as such do not enroll a single student, do not teach a single class. System leaders desperately need research to help them understand how their potential power can best be used for the advancement and transmission of knowledge.

REFERENCES

Ashby, W. R. (1956). *An Introduction to Cybernetics*. London: University Paperbacks.
Biggadike, E. R. (1981). The contributions of marketing to strategic management. *Academy of Management Review* 6: 621–632.
Birnbaum, R. (1988). *How Colleges Work*. San Francisco: Jossey-Bass.
Cameron, K. S. (1981). The enigma of organizational effectiveness. In *New Directions for Program Evaluation: Measuring Effectiveness*, No. 11, pp. 1–13. San Francisco: Jossey-Bass.
Chaffee, E. E. (1984). Successful strategic management in small private colleges. *Journal of Higher Education* 55: 212–241.
Chaffee, E. E. (1985). The concept of strategy: From business to higher education. In J. C. Smart (ed.), *Higher Education: Handbook of Theory and Research*, Vol. I, pp. 133–171. New York: Agathon Press.
Chandler, A. D., Jr. (1962). *Strategy and Structure*. Cambridge, Mass.: MIT Press.
Connolly, T., Conlon, E. J., and Deutsch, S. J. (1980). Organizational effectiveness: A multiple-constituency approach. *Academy of Management Review* 5: 211–217.
Etzioni, A. (1964). *Modern Organizations*. Englewood Cliffs, NJ: Prentice-Hall.
Ewell, P. (1984). *The Self-Regarding Institution: Information for Excellence*. Boulder, CO: National Center for Higher Education Management Systems.
French, E., and Berdahl, R. (1980). Who guards the guardians? The evaluation of statewide boards of higher education. Occasional Paper No. 7. Department of Higher Education, State University of New York at Buffalo, August.
Hambrick, D. C. (1980). Operationalizing the concept of business-level strategy in research. *Academy of Management Review* 5: 567–575.
Hofer, C. W. (1973). Some preliminary research on patterns of strategic behavior. *Academy of Management Proceedings*, pp. 46–59.

Keeley, M. (1978). A social justice approach to organizational evaluation. *Administrative Science Quarterly* 22: 272–292.

Lenz, R. T. (1980). Environment, strategy, organization structure and performance: Patterns in one industry. *Strategic Management Journal* 1: 209–226.

McGuinness, A. (1987). Acting in concert: Suggestions for system board members. Denver: SHEEO Task Force on Role and Mission.

Perrow, C. (1970). *Organizational Analysis: A Sociological View*. Belmont, CA: Wadsworth.

Pettigrew, A. M. (1977). Strategy formulation as a political process. *International Studies of Management and Organization* 7: 78–87.

Pfeffer, J. (1977). Usefulness of the Concept. In P. S. Goodman, J. M. Pennings, and Associates. *New Perspectives on Organizational Effectiveness*, pp. 132–145. San Francisco: Jossey-Bass.

Pfeffer, J. (1982). *Organizations and Organization Theory*. Marshfield, Mass.: Pitman.

Price, J. (1972). The study of organizational effectiveness. *Sociological Quarterly* 13: 3–15.

Steinbruner, J. D. (1974). *The Cybernetic Theory of Decision*. Priceton, NJ: Princeton University Press.

Van Cauwenbergh, A., and Cool, K. (1982). Strategic management in a new framework. *Strategic Management Journal* 3: 245–265.

Weick, K. E., and Daft, R. L. (1983). The effectiveness of interpretation systems. In K. S. Cameron and D. A. Whetten (eds.), *Organizational Effectiveness: A Comparison of Multiple Models*. New York: Academic Press.

Yuchtman, E., and Seashore, S. (1967). A system resource approach to organizational effectiveness. *American Sociological Review* 32: 891–903.

Zammuto, R. F. (1982). *Assessing Organizational Effectiveness*. Albany: State University of New York Press.

Zammuto, R. F. (1984). A comparison of multiple constituency models of organizational effectiveness. *Academy of Management Review* 9: 606–616.

Selected References on Systems

Association of Governing Boards (1983). *Self-Study Guidelines and Criteria for Governing Boards of Public Multicampus Higher Education Systems*. Washington, D.C.

Berdahl, R. O. (1971). *Statewide Coordination of Higher Education*. Washington, D.C.: American Council on Education.

Berdahl, R. O. (1975). *Evaluating Statewide Boards*. New Directions for Institutional Research, No. 5. San Francisco: Jossey-Bass.

Dressel, P. L. ed. (1980). *The Autonomy of Public Colleges*. New Directions for Institutional Research, No. 26. San Francisco: Jossey-Bass.

Education Commission of the States (1973). *Coordination or Chaos? Report of the Task Force on Coordination, Governance and Structure of Postsecondary Education*. Denver.

Education Commission of the States (1979). *Accountability and Academe: A Report of the National Task Force on the Accountability of Higher Education to the State*. Denver.

Education Commission of the States (1980). *Challenge: Coordination and Governance in the '80s*. Denver.

Floyd, C. E. (1982). *State Planning, Budgeting, and Accountability: Approaches for Higher Education*. AAHE-ERIC/Higher Education Research Report No. 6. Washington, D.C.: American Association for Higher Education.

Glenny, L. (1985). *State Coordination of Higher Education: The Modern Concept.* Denver. State Higher Education Executive Officers.

Halstead, D. K. (1974). *Statewide Planning in Higher Education.* Washington, D.C.: U.S. Department of Health, Education, and Welfare.

Kauffman, J. F. (1980). *At the Pleasure of the Board: The Service of the College and University President.* Washington, D.C.: American Council on Education.

Lee, E. C., and Bowen, F. M. (1975). *Managing Multicampus Systems: Effective Administration in an Unsteady State.* San Franciso: Jossey-Bass.

Leslie, L. L., and Hyatt, J., eds. (1981). *Higher Education Financing Policies: States/Institutions and Their Interaction.* Tucson: Center for the Study of Higher Education, University of Arizona.

Millard, R. M. (1976). *State Boards of Higher Education.* ERIC/Higher Education Research Report No. 4, 1976. Washington, D.C.: American Association for Higher Education.

National Center for Higher Education Management Systems (1979). *Postsecondary-Education Information Planning at the State Level.* Five-volume series. Boulder, CO.

Perkins, J. A., and Israel, B. B., eds. (1972). *Higher Education: From Autonomy to Systems.* New York: International Council for Economic Development.

Wing, P., McLaughlin, J. N., and Allman, K. A. (1975). *An Overview and Guide to the Use of the Statewide Measures Inventory.* Boulder, CO: National Center for Higher Education Management Systems at Western Interstate Commission for Higher Education.

Wing, P., McLaughlin, J. N., and Allman, K. A. (1975). *Statewide Measures Inventory: An Inventory of Items of Information Relevant to Statewide Postsecondary Education Planning and Management.* Boulder, CO: National Center for Higher Education Management Systems at Western Interstate Commission for Higher Education.

Responsibility Without Authority: the Impossible Job of the College President

Robert Birnbaum
Project Director, National Center for Postsecondary Governance and Finance, University of Maryland, College Park

If any man wishes to be humbled and mortified, let him become president of Harvard College (plaintive cry of Harvard President Edward Holyoke on his deathbed in 1769, cited in Horn, 1969, p. 389).

What kind of a place is this? I give an order and nothing happens. People pay no attention to what I say or reply that they will take it under advisement. I ask for an opinion on how to proceed and I get fifty different opinions. I propose what I think is a capital idea and it produces a faculty wrangle. How does a man get things done in a place like this? (poignant question asked by a military man after taking over a university presidency, cited in Jones, Stanford, and White, 1964, p. 30).

Presidents never feel in charge because universities are too diffuse. You are less in charge in universities than in other organizations (realistic appraisal of college president in the Institutional Leadership Project (ILP), 1987).

Every decade, about 5,000 persons serve as college or university presidents. Over a term of office averaging less than seven years the president is expected to serve simultaneously as the chief administrator of a large and complex bureaucracy, as the convening colleague of a professional community, as a symbolic elder in a campus culture of shared values and symbols, and (in some institutions) as a public official accountable to a public board and responsive to the demands of other governmental agencies. Balancing the conflicting expectations of these roles has always been difficult; changing demographic trends, fiscal constraints, and unrealistic public expectations now make it virtually

This document was prepared pursuant to a grant from the Office of Educational Research and Improvement/Department of Education (OERI/ED). However, the opinions expressed herein do not necessarily reflect the position or policy of the OERI/ED, and no official endorsement by the OERI/ED, should be inferred.

impossible for presidents to provide the leadership that is expected from the position.

The college presidency may not be the second oldest profession in America, but the role has existed in this country from the time of the founding of Harvard in 1636, a century and half before there was a nation. From the colonial period until the Civil War, institutions were for the most part small, simply structured, and controlled by their lay boards of trustees, leading to a "weak presidency." The president's role even in those days was a demanding one that included teaching, preaching, fund raising, record keeping, and (most especially) student discipline, but in a simpler world of certain knowledge and accepted authority, most presidents were able to perform effectively the tasks expected of them.

The period between the Civil War and World War I was one of expansion and transformation in higher education. New and more complex institutions were created as research and public service were added to the traditional teaching mission. The late nineteenth and early twentieth centuries were times of the "great men" presidents who often wielded unchecked authority to create great institutions. Trustee boards were increasingly composed of businessmen who embraced the developing concepts of scientific management. Viewing the college as comparable to a business firm, faculty were considered to be employees hired to do as they were told, and the president, in Veblen's (1918/1957) caustic terms, was the "Captain of Erudition" responsible for increasing enrollment, capital, and reputation, while controlling costs.

The job was clearly becoming more difficult, and observers of that day could note that "the duties imposed upon the modern university president are so multifarious that it is becoming exceedingly difficult to find a man capable of filling the position in the larger institutions" (Slosson, 1913). But although the role had become more complex, it was still one possible to fulfill; presidents had the power, and if they wished (and many did), they could administer following the precept attributed to Jowett, the head of Balliol College, Oxford: "Never retract. Never explain. Get the thing done and let them howl!"

As institutions became more comprehensive and involved in scholarship, the faculty became more specialized, more professionalized, and less tolerant of administrative controls. Increasingly until World War II, and then with accelerating force during the 1950s and 1960s, faculty claimed for themselves not only the right to make decisions concerning the major educational activities of the institution, but also to participate fully in setting institutional policy and to have a voice in its management. The growing power of the faculty, a change significant enough to justify referring to it as the "academic revolution" (Jencks and Riesman, 1968), was one of the forces that led postwar presidents to claim that "the fundamental difficulty with the office of university president arises out of the current system of controlling modern universities. . . . He has vast responsibilities for all phases of the life and welfare of the university, but he has no power'' (Rainey, 1960, p. 00).

Presidential discretion was being increasingly limited not only by forces within the academy but by those outside as well. In particular, federal and state agencies were exerting influence over matters that had previously been considered internal institutional prerogatives. The loss of effective presidential authority, related internally to changes in organizational complexity and patterns of influence, and externally to increased environmental constraints, helped to transform the role from a difficult job to an impossible one.

This claim must be accompanied by a caveat. There are over 3,300 colleges and universities today, most (but not all) headed by a chief executive officer with the title of president (or, less frequently, chancellor). The composite public image of a small number of the more visible institutions tends to obscure their great diversity in size, wealth, program level, complexity, student selectivity, faculty preparation, and public or private sponsorship—all factors that affect presidential authority and therefore the extent to which presidents can be effective. The historical generalizations that have already been made, and the analyses that follow, must therefore be applied with caution. In discussing the presidential role, this chapter will focus primarily upon institutions with at least moderate enrollments, multiple missions, and comprehensive programs. Such institutions enroll most of the students in higher education, but they probably represent less than half of the total number of the nation's colleges and universities.

THE PRESIDENTIAL ROLE

There is no standard definition of the presidency, or description of the expectations placed on the performance of its incumbents. Presidents traditionally have no stated term of office but serve ''at the pleasure'' of a public or private board of lay trustees. Institutional statutes or bylaws commonly identify the president as the chief executive and administrative officer of the board as well as the chief academic officer of the faculty, and delegate to the president all powers necessary to perform these functions. Statements of such sweeping authority may appear to the uninitiated to offer almost unlimited control over administrative and programmatic initiatives, but the reality of presidential influence is quite different. As one president has commented, ''regardless of what may appear in the charter and bylaws, the authority of the president, his real leadership, depends on the willingness of the campus to accept him as a leader. If it will not, well there are other ways for him to earn a living'' (Ness, 1971, p. 49).

There are many ways of looking at the components of the presidential role. One typical listing identifies and describes responsibilities inside and outside the institution. Inside, the president is responsible for managing the finances of the institution and its budget, long-range institutional planning, coordination of the academic program and the maintenance of appropriate standards of quality, personnel policies, and student affairs. Outside, the president solicits support from donors, represents the institution to legislative and other external audiences, deals with alumni and athletics, protects academic freedom, and makes public pronouncements on educational issues (Demerath, Stephens, and Taylor, 1967).

From a more analytical perspective, presidential tasks can be seen as comprising administrative, political, and entrepreneurial components (Cohen and March, 1974). As administrator, the president carries out the policies of the trustees, supervises subordinates, allocates resources, establishes systems of accountability, and performs functions similar to those found in any complex organization. As politician, the president must be responsive to the needs of various constituencies whose support is critical to the maintenance of his or her position. The interests of groups and subgroups of faculty, students, alumni, and others whose actions may constrain presidential discretion must be considered and courted, and the president must often form coalitions and propose compromises that will permit peace with progress. A president may go from table to table in the faculty club dining room or the Rotary luncheon much as a politician "works" a cocktail party, building relationships that can later be used to construct acceptable programs. As entrepreneur, the president is expected to develop and exploit markets that offer necessary resources for the institution. Fund raising is perhaps the most visible component of this role, but communicating with legislators in the State House or in Washington, securing grants, developing marketing plans, and managing institutional relations programs are important and time-consuming activities as well.

There may be agreement on the components of the role, but there is no model of the presidency that identifies priorities between them. Presidential activities are to a great extent contingent on the characteristics of their institutions, the inexorable ebb and flow of the academic calendar, the emerging exigencies of the environment, and their own personal interests. Over a span of only several hours, presidents may find themselves meeting with a potential donor, responding to a faculty complaint about parking, presiding over a solemn ceremony, smoothing the ruffled feathers of an irate athletic booster, preparing testimony for a legislative hearing, convening a meeting of vice-presidents, and reviewing the elements of a budget that can run into the hundreds of millions of dollars. Some presidents spend a majority of their time in fund raising, public representation, and related resource-acquisition activities. The typical presidential spends little time on academic matters.

The pace, intensity, and comprehensiveness of the presidency are in many ways comparable to those of managers and executives in other settings (Mintzberg, 1973). But there is a fundamental difference. On a college campus the exercise of authority in governance is not solely an administrative preroga-tive, but rather a shared responsibility and joint effort that properly involves all important campus constituencies, with particular emphasis given to the partici-pation of the faculty. The influential 1966 "Joint Statement on Government of Colleges and Universities" (American Association of University Professors, 1984), for example, gives to the faculty the "primary responsibility" for "curriculum, subject matter and methods of instruction, research, faculty status, and those aspects of student life which relate to the educational process" (p. 109). In such matters the president is expected to "concur with the faculty judgment except in rare instances and for compelling reasons which should be stated in detail" (p. 109). If, as it is generally agreed, the central questions that define the essential nature of a college or university are Who should teach? What should be taught? and Who shall be taught?, such normative statements reserve these matters for the direct control of the faculty, and not for either the president or the trustees.

The Joint Statement codified what had been true for many years at academi-cally strong campuses and what was evolving as good practice at many others. In doing so, it highlighted the basic managerial dilemma of the president: Essential questions of institutional "production" or service, which would be considered matters of managerial prerogative in other settings, were in colleges and universities to be decided by the faculty, who were "employees."

In a business firm, the president or CEO is solely accountable to a board of directors. In higher education, the president functions between two layers of organizational operations—the trustees and the faculty—and is accountable to both. Conflict between constituent groups is common in many organizations, but its importance and consequences for the college president may be unique. In a business firm, presidential tenure is the sole prerogative of the board of directors. Within many colleges or universities, however, faculty (and often other groups as well) assert the right to participate in presidential selection and evaluation. And as many presidents have discovered, a faculty vote of no confidence often has the same power to end a presidential career as does a formal vote by the trustees. Sometimes such a vote is implicit in the president's inability to gain faculty support for presidential initiatives, or in a growing campuswide sense of faculty distrust or institutional disengagement. Occasionally it is explicit, with motions presented in faculty senates, debated, and voted.

WHY THE JOB IS IMPOSSIBLE

There is no educational, social, or political consensus on exactly what it is higher education should be doing, what constituencies it should serve, and how it should serve them. At different times and on different campuses emphasis has been given to transmitting values, to discovering knowledge, or to improving society. Some of the manifest purposes of higher education—the education and development of individual students, transmitting the culture and advancing society in general, providing for educational justice and social mobility, supporting intellectual and artistic creativity, and evaluating society so that it can become self-renewing (Carnegie Commission, 1973)—enjoy general support as principles, but they become contentious as people attempt to describe how such vague ideals should best be implemented.

In addition to these obvious aims, colleges and universities have latent purposes as well. Among other things, they serve a custodial function by removing from parents the burden of controlling the behavior of young adults, they serve as a means of certifying to employers that graduates possess diligence and at least a modicum of intelligence, they socialize students and help them develop networks that will prove useful later in life, and they perpetuate the existing social order. These latter functions often conflict with the avowed purposes of colleges and universities, and although less often discussed, they are nonetheless important. To illustrate in terms of the custodial function, consider which would be the more effective faculty strike: one at which faculty came to class but didn't teach, or one in which classes were canceled and students came home.

Goals of access, quality, and diversity, which are in conflict and which call for quite different institutional structures and responses, appear and then wane on the public policy agenda in cycles; the essential educational missions of teaching, research, and service compete with each other for resources; and there is no rational way to assess the legitimacy of the competing and incompatible demands of many internal and external groups. Internally, faculty and administrators may disagree on appropriate levels of work load or salary, students and faculty may be in conflict about degree requirements or the academic calendar, alumni and trustees may debate the virtues of tradition and change, and students may disagree with administrative perspectives on investments or on campus recruitment by intelligence agencies. Externally, institutions may find themselves arguing with local governments over the cost and availability of civic services, with environmental groups about waste disposal, with neighboring institutions offering competing programs, or with industries asking that curriculums be developed to meet their needs.

Virtually all of these demands have some merit, and few can be dismissed out of hand. Yet there is no accepted criterion presidents can employ to judge the benefits of one course of action over another, as well as little assurance that they could implement their preferences even if they could specify them. Presidential authority is limited, complete understanding of the scope and complexity of the enterprise exceeds human cognitive capability, and unforeseen changes in demographic, political, and economic conditions often overwhelm campus plans. Presidents fortunate enough to preside during good times may reap the benefits of a munificent environment over which they have had no control, and even the incompetent may appear heroic; presidents during times of depression or social ferment may reap a whirlwind they did not sow.

This section will consider four factors that make presidential leadership impossible: the constraints on presidential discretion, the unique characteristics of academic organizations, the problems of assessing effectiveness, and the limitations of the presidential role itself. In this and following sections, generalizations have in some cases been illustrated with direct quotes from presidents. Some of these have been taken from unpublished interviews of presidents participating in the Institutional Leadership Project (ILP, 1987), an ongoing longitudinal study of 32 campuses being conducted at the University of Maryland, College Park, and Teachers College, Columbia University as part of the National Center for Postsecondary Governance and Finance.

Constraints on Presidential Discretion

Many factors have increasingly limited presidential leadership (Commission on Strengthening . . . , 1984). Some of these result from interactions with other organizations in their environments, while others arise within the institutions themselves. Environmental constraints include more federal and state controls; greater involvement by the courts in academic decision-making; more layers of governance, particularly in institutions that are part of statewide systems; fewer opportunities for growth, and consequently for changes accompanying growth; questions of the importance of the missions of higher education; less acceptance of authority in general; and fewer potential applicants and therefore greater responsiveness to the student market. Within institutions themselves, constraints on leadership arise due to greater involvement by faculties in academic and personnel decisions; faculty collective bargaining; greater goal ambiguity; greater fractionation of the campus into interest groups, leading to a loss of consensus and of community; greater involvement by trustees in campus operations; and increased bureaucracy and specialization among campus administrators. Presidents are very conscious of these constraints. One said,

> leadership in higher education is becoming more difficult. . . . There was a time when the president was really in charge. There are so many constituents now that have an impact. Too often you find yourself rolling with the punches. It's like treading in a mine field—trying to be sure you alienate as few people among these constituencies as possible. It is a subject of concern—how [the president can] be in charge and know he can run the place. (ILP, 1987).

Statewide coordinating or governing boards in almost all states exercise increasing influence over matters reserved in the past to the campus, including such critical issues as faculty personnel policies, or the review of academic programs. For example, public institutions may be required to follow mandated procedures for personnel searches, to employ stipulated criteria for appointment, and to restrict the number of promotions they are able to make. State boards may also review both existing and proposed academic programs in order to assess their quality and cost; in some instances, programs have been closed or merged in the face of institutional objections. Other state executive or legislative agencies have become involved in facilities reviews (what buildings are needed, how big should they be, what they should look like), administrative operations (what computers can be purchased, what travel is permitted, how nonacademic employees can be hired), budgeting (how many personnel positions are available, how much money can be allocated to research, who has to approve mid-year changes), and planning (what future enrollments should be, what new programs will be permitted, what changes in institutional mission are acceptable). Although these intrusions focus primarily upon public institutions, which include approximately 80% of all enrollments, they may directly or indirectly affect private institutions in some states as well. As the locus of influence moves from the campus to the state, public sector presidents may find themselves becoming more like middle managers in public agencies than campus leaders. Faculty may respond to increased centralization of control by centralizing their own participation through processes of collective bargaining that often ritualize disruptive conflict. The loss of ability to exert local influence leads to faculty-administration scapegoating, end runs to state offices that further reduce presidential authority, and a diminished sense of both campus responsibility and accountability.

As patterns of authority become confused, particularly in larger and more complex institutions, schools or departments become the locus of educational decision-making. The institution may become an academic holding company for a federation of quasi-autonomous subunits. Unable to influence the larger institution, faculty may retreat into the small subunit for which they feel affinity and from which they can defend their influence and status, and presidential influence over their activities decreases still further. As a consequence, it appears that "fewer decisions can be made because of more veto power; that those decisions that can be made are made more slowly due to extensive consultation and confrontation; that there is less of a central vision for the institution and more of a congeries of competing visions; that 'nobody is in charge'" (Kerr and Gade, 1986, p. 143).

In addition to these political and structural constraints, presidential influence is severely limited by both the paucity of resources available and the short-term difficulties in internally reallocating those resources that exist. Some important intangible campus resources, such as institutional prestige or attractiveness to students or to potential donors, are tied into a network of external relationships that are virtually impossible to change in the short run, and that are difficult to alter even over long periods of time. Internally, on most campuses the personnel complement is largely fixed through tenure and contractual provisions, program change is constrained by faculty interests and structures as well as facilities limitations, and yearly planning begins with the largest share of the budget pre-committed.

Organizational Factors

The administration of colleges and universities presents "a unique dualism in organizational structure" (Corson, 1960, p. 43), with two structures existing in parallel. One is the conventional bureaucratic hierarchy responsive to the will of the trustees; the other is the structure through which faculty make decisions regarding those aspects of the institution over which they have professional jurisdiction. Members of boards of trustees differ markedly from faculty in terms of their ideology and their attitudes about higher education (Hartnett, 1969), and presidents often find themselves caught between the incompatible demands of the two groups. Trustees, who hold all legal authority, are primarily business executives who are more likely than the faculty to see the organization as comparable to business firms in their structure and authority patterns and to support the idea of "top-down" management. The president, viewed as their CEO, is expected to carry out their wishes and to be accountably for faculty performance. The faculty, on the other hand, expect to exercise primary authority over educational processes, and trustee or presidential intrusion into academic affairs is likely to be viewed as illegitimate.

The problems caused by dualism of control are exacerbated by the conflicting nature of administrative and professional authority. In most organizations, the major goals activities are subject to the bureaucratic authority of administrators which arises from their position within the hierarchy, and from their legal right to give directives. The professional authority of faculty members, on the other hand, comes from their expertise and training (Blau, 1973). Administrative and professional authority are not only different, but mutually inconsistent. It is not only the existence in colleges and universities of two different structures—one administrative and one faculty—that creates the problems of governance related to "dualism of controls," but also the fact that the two structures are primarily driven by incompatible systems of authority. The president is imbedded in both authority systems and therefore is continually subject to incompatible demands and behavioral expectations (Baldridge et al., 1978; Birnbaum, 1989). As the leader of a bureaucracy, the president is expected to establish goals, decide how they are to be achieved, scientifically organize the work of subordinates, plan, and monitor organizational functioning. As the head of a professional and collegial body, the president is expected to be "first among equals," and to move the group toward consensus by listening, proposing, mediating, persuading, and influencing through information sharing and appeals to reason. The use of legal authority or status differentials, which is an important means of gaining influence in one system, is illegitimate and unacceptable in the other.

Assessing Effectiveness

The particular organizational complexities of colleges and universities, exacerbated by the conflicting demands of their environments and the difficulty of understanding exactly how they function, have led to their identification as "organized anarchies." An organized anarchy exhibits three characteristics; problematic goals, an unclear technology, and fluid participation. Cohen and March (1974) state that

> these properties are not limited to educational institutions, but they are particularly conspicuous there. The American college or university is a prototypical organized anarchy. It does not know what it is doing. Its goals are either vague or in dispute. Its technology is familiar but not understood. Its major participants wander in and out of the organization. These factors do not make the university a bad organization, or a disorganized one. But they do make it a problem to describe, understand, and lead. (p. 3)

The concept of the organized anarchy suggests that colleges and universities often make choices through a process of "garbage-can decision making" (Cohen, March, and Olsen, 1972). Problems, solutions, and participants form steady streams that flow through the organization as if they were poured into a large can. When one tries to make a decision, other people or issues in the can may become attached to it because they are contemporaneous, even though they may not appear to be logically connected. For example, a presidential decision to build a faculty parking lot on some unused campus land would appear to be easily made if there were enough data on parking needs and available resources to perform a cost-benefit analysis. But such apparently simple decisions become incredibly complex as elements seen by the decision maker as extraneous (that is, "garbage") become attached to it. The biology department may argue that the lot will destroy adjacent trees and may use the incident to press its continuing proposal for an institutional environmental master plan; a candidate for student government office may use the lot as a symbol of administration indifference to student needs, and may ask for student membership on the board of trustees; and a faculty member may link the cost to recent cuts in library budgets and use the incident as a forum for discussing educational priorities. Since "garbage" is in the eyes of the beholder, it is possible for almost any two issues to be seen by someone on campus as connected and for any problem to become coupled to any decision. Making a decision on the parking lot may be impossible unless some way can be found of severing its connection to environmental plans, student trustees, and educational priorities.

Institutional outcomes may be a result of only modestly interdependent activities and are often neither planned nor predictable. For example, a campus may receive a federal research grant because a president gave additional resources to a department, because a grant proposal was assigned by chance to one reviewer rather than another, or because the granting agency was obliged to seek a geographic distribution in its awards. People in different parts of the organization may have access to information making any of these or other explanations plausible. Such ambiguity inhibits the making of valid inferences about cause and effect, and presidential learning becomes exceptionally difficult. Presidents may spend more time in sense making (Weick, 1979), and in engaging in activities that verify or enhance their status, than in decision making. The decoupling of choices and outcomes makes symbolic behavior particularly important.

The ambiguities of institutional life are intensified by the absence in colleges and universities of accepted and valid indicators of effectiveness. There are different definitions of effectiveness, all of which are difficult to measure (Cameron, 1984); different audiences use different criteria to make the assessment (Cameron and Whetten, 1983); and achievement of effectiveness in one area of institutional functioning may inhibit or prevent it in another (Cameron, 1978). Without measures of organizational effectiveness, it becomes difficult for presidents—or others—to objectively assess presidential effectiveness. Presidents feel this frustration very keenly. As one said,

> I am discouraged, the faculty are on me, the press too. I don't know how you know you are being effective. History will tell. The experience of the presidency itself is a marvelous one. Whether or not I have been successful will be determined much down the line (ILP, 1987)

Institutional outcomes in general, and perceptions of presidential success or failure in particular, may be "largely a matter of luck. . . . The president is always in a war, and whether he wins or loses bears only a marginal relation to his foresight, his wisdom, his charm, his blood pressure." (Ness, 1971, p. 8).

The Role

Much of the extensive literature on presidential roles comes from presidents themselves. There is a tendency by some to celebrate their own accomplishments, but there is often a strong undercurrent of despair or anger, and of resignation that in the long run their success or failure may be due more to the vagaries of luck and history than to their own dedication and skill. Presidents are subject both to role overload and to role ambiguity as they respond both to their own personal interpretations of their roles and to the legitimate demands of many groups. Claims for their attention are long; time and energy are short. Kerr's (1963) famous depiction captures the nature of the problem:

> The university president in the United States is expected to be a friend of the students, a colleague with the faculty, a good fellow with the alumni, a sound administrator with the trustees, a good speaker with the public, an astute bargainer with the foundations and the federal agencies, a politician with the state legislature, a friend of industry, labor, and agriculture, a persuasive diplomat with donors, a champion of education generally, a supporter of the professions (particularly law and medicine), a spokesman to the press, a scholar in his own right, a public servant at the state and national levels, a devotee of opera and football equally, a decent human being, a good husband and father, an active member of the church. Above all, he must enjoy travelling in airplanes, eating his meals in public, and attending public ceremonies. No one can be all of these things. Some succeed at being none. (pp. 29–30)

One consequence of multiple and conflicting roles is that any actions of the president, while applauded by some, are likely to result in criticism from others. A well-known president (Hesburgh, 1970) commented that "criticism is a far greater part of presidential life than plaudits or gratitude" (p. 44). Criticism may be related to specific issues or just generally to the tensions of academic life.

Many of their responsibilities lead presidents to find themselves always "on stage": "the spotlight of publicity plays upon him so continuously that it leaves him not even intermittent shadows within which he and his family may make an unmarked move" (Stoke, 1959, p. 10). The pace, the unrelenting pressures, and the marginal membership of presidents in many conflicting groups affect the physical as well as the mental health of presidents. Presidents know that every decision will have its personal costs, and that it will be difficult to find private time for family or recreation. As one said,

> Most presidents work too hard and discover along the way that being president of a university is a way of life. It means being on call seven days, 24 hours a day—demonstrating a presence on the schedule of other people. Any time you make changes there are people who will feel you will make the wrong decisions. Many decisions are lose/lose decisions. (ILP, 1987)

The popular view of the role may identify the president as a larger-than-life heroic leader whose wise decisions and forceful administration solve problems and advance the institution's fortunes. But in fact, presidential decisions may have little effect on disparate organizational subsystems, changes in the environment may often overpower any changes that are attempted internally, administrative structures and processes of organization and control are relatively weak when compared to the autonomous action of professional participants, and a president can attend to only a small number of potentially important matters—and there is no way of knowing beforehand (or often even afterward, for that matter) whether or not these are the most important. These problems led Cohen and March (1974) to say that the presidency is an illusion:

Important aspects of the role seem to disappear on close examination. Compared to the heroic expectations he and others might have, the president has modest control over the events of college life. The contributions he makes can easily be swamped by outside events or the diffuse quality of university decision making. (p. 2)

Many presidents reject this perspective; some recognize and accept it, such as the president who said,

I have very little influence. My faculty has lifetime tenure; they are like the Supreme Court. There is a great assumption that the president has great influence. That is not true. I can coddle and berate [the faculty] in a teasing way, but that is all. For the most part we just leave each other alone. (ILP, 1987)

Other presidents may have a greater sense of their influence, but they also recognize that random events may come to play an important—occasionally a decisive—role in their lives. One said,

you can't ever be off your guard. You can never feel on top of things because some things are out of your control. It is part of the job. And you need to live with this. . . . Any day you can be knocked out of office by something unexpected. (ILP, 1987)

These limits on influence and the ambiguities of purpose, power, experience, and success (Cohen and March, 1974) make it difficult for presidents to learn from their experience. If the institution has ambiguous and multiple purposes, and if it lacks a sense of shared direction, how can presidents justify their actions or know if they have been successful? If influence is dispersed throughout the institution and decentralized, how can presidents know how much power they have, or what they can or cannot do? If what happens on a campus depends as much on the actions of others and on environment pressures as it does on presidential behavior, what can presidents accurately learn from their experiences? And if presidents have confirmed their success earlier in their careers because they have been promoted, how can they assess their present success when promotion is no longer possible?

A college or university president is the executive, administrative, academic, and symbolic head of an organization whose performance cannot be measured and that resists leadership. The president "confronts problems which may have no solutions or, at best, only proximate solutions. He confronts innumerable, diverse, and warring constituencies, whose separate goals and drives may be irreconcilable" (Bennis, 1976, p. 148).

Presidents realize that these conflicting expectations often place them in no-win situations. For example,

The right thinks I'm too feminist. The left thinks I'm not feminist enough. Some would like for me to take a harder line on things, but they would be murderous if I did. (ILP, 1987)

Every decision that supports the interests of one group at the same time opposes the interests of another. There are probably no presidential actions that can enjoy universal support, and presidents come to realize that

> friends come and go, but enemies accumulate. There are lots of toes you can walk on. It's hard to think of an important action that doesn't step on some people's toes. (ILP, 1987)

BEHAVIORAL AND COGNITIVE STRATEGIES

Survival requires the development of coping mechanisms that help the organization and the people within it make sense of the ambiguities of their daily lives. Colleges and universities have evolved ways of responding to the difficulties caused by their complex environmental relationships, inchoate influence patterns, and inability to rationalize their technology. For example, institutions meet the conflicting demands of interest groups by decentralizing and permitting subunits to operate in a quasi-autonomous fashion. Subunits can then meet different needs, but at high cost: presidential authority is diminished, it becomes almost impossible to coordinate activities, and maintaining a sense of coherence and common purpose is extremely difficult.

Institutions may attempt to cope with the difficulty of assessing effectiveness by publicly focusing attention on inputs (such as the percentage of faculty with the doctorate) rather than outputs (how much a student has learned), and by actively discouraging inspection and relying instead upon established reputation, tradition, and goodwill to justify continued political and fiscal support.

Presidents find themselves expected to provide leadership, direction, coherence, and progress in an organization with conflicting authority structures, multiple social systems, and contested goals. There is a general acknowledgment that presidents are not able to effectively meet these expectations. Individual presidents view their confreres and say,

> I guess I am concerned about the quality of leadership in higher education. I see so many of my colleagues being blown by the winds of concern. Many of them are so unable to do what they can. I think the agenda of higher education is not really being addressed sufficiently, and largely for political reasons. (ILP, 1987)

A recent national commission on the presidency (Commission on Strengthening . . . , 1984) agreed. It endorsed the finding that "our colleges and universities are in desperate need of leadership" (p. xii) and noted that the presidency is weaker and less attractive to persons of talent now than in the past. The commission found that a quarter of all presidents were dissatisfied, some despairingly so, and that the turnover rate among presidents was about 30% every two years. Presidents are acutely aware of limitations in performing their roles and of the difficulties a president faces in getting things done.

External observers who criticize higher education leadership and the conduct of the presidency have offered suggestions meant to make the job more "possible." Many of their approaches would presumably increase presidential authority by one of several means: strengthening the presidency, increasing rationality and management controls, or reducing constraints on presidential discretion.

One common proposal suggests strengthening the presidency through the selecting of better presidents. It assumes (although without supporting data) that today's presidents do not have the same characteristics of courage and decisiveness as presidents of the past. The obvious solution is for presidential search committees to seek stronger and more decisive candidates. Alternatively, the presidency could be strengthened by increasing the legal authority of the position and curtailing the influence of other groups. A former president (Fisher, 1984) proposed that trustees consider suspending all existing college policies regarding shared authority and grant exclusive authority to the president for the conduct of all campus affairs. The president could then give other campus groups, as a privilege, the opportunity to participate in governance at the president's discretion. A less radical proposal is that presidents be given greater internal discretion to act without engaging in the full panoply of consultation and consensus building, while ensuring accountability through periodic reviews of their performance (Mortimer and McConnell, 1978).

If one of the causes of impossibility is the anarchical nature of the organization, then one possible solution is to increase the extent to which decisions are made using rational rather than political or symbolic processes. The many attempts to do so, through the imposition of management systems, personnel policies increasing administrative discretion to reduce staff size, or formulas for budget allocations, have by and large not had the desired and expected effects. In many cases, processes set up to respond to problems have themselves exacerbated them.

Many factors limiting presidential authority (and probably the most critical ones) are outside the control of the academy itself. However, it has been suggested that presidential effectiveness might be improved if trustee boards provided more support to their presidents, gave the president a leadership position on the board, encouraged faculty support for the president, resisted attempts to involve themselves in administration, used the president as the sole conduit into the administrative structure, and provided presidents a sense of security (Commission on Strengthening . . . , 1984). The frantic pace of presidential life has also been identified as a major constraint upon presidential effectiveness. It has often been suggested that providing presidents with more personal assistance would free their time for contemplation and long-term planning. This suggestion almost always overlooks the possibility that presidents don't become busy people; busy people become presidents. Presidents constantly complain about the lack of time for contemplation, but there is no reason to believe that if presidents had more "free" time they would use it in that way.

There is no dearth of advice for presidents. Various authorities have suggested that they can be successful by remaining distant or by being intimately involvement with constituents; by emphasizing resource acquisition or by focusing on academic matters; by stressing accountability or by fostering creativity; by setting goals or by helping others to achieve their own goals. The proposals are inconsistent, and their behavioral implications are unclear. Nevertheless, this section will suggest some presidential administrative strategies that appear more likely to increase presidents' effectiveness and improve their institutions, and it will identify others that are frequently unsuccessful. It will also examine some of the cognitive and symbolic strategies that permit presidents and institutions to cope with the discrepancies between their authority and their responsibility, and between their expectations and their achievement. Finally, it will consider the possibility that, because of certain characteristics of colleges and universities, a weak presidency may have important, but latent, organizational functions.

Successful Administrative Strategies

Successful presidents are likely to be realists rather than idealists. They accept a decentralized structure, conflicting authority systems, and loose coupling as inherent organizational characteristics and try to work within these constraints. They know that essential institutional functions are likely to continue to operate, even in the absence of presidential direction, because of ongoing administrative systems and the largely autonomous activities of professional faculties. In many ways, the organization works as a cybernetic system (Birnbaum, 1989) in which negative feedback serves to activate processes that maintain the institution's current level of functioning. Presidents appreciate that some of their energy will be occupied with the day-to-day activities of monitoring these processes, and of identifying and attending to institutional weaknesses and problems.

However, they also recognize that they can have an impact on the institution if they focus on a small number of limited objectives or programs and devote extraordinary energy to them. Presidents can be effective even in areas such as curriculum, in which administrative influence is traditionally weak, if they are willing to accept the inevitable cost of other opportunities foregone. Presidents who try to do too many things, either at their own initiative or in response to perceived environmental demands, often end up accomplishing none of them.

Effective presidents understand the culture of their institution and the symbolic aspects of their positions. Recognizing that their effectiveness as leaders depends upon the willingness of highly trained professionals to be followers, they avoid actions that would violate cultural and academic norms and thereby diminish their own status. Effective presidents spend a great deal of time in understanding their institutional culture. They go out of their way to walk around their campuses to see and be seen, to confer with other formal and informal campus leaders and solicit opinions and advice, to learn institutional histories, and to understand the expectations others have of presidential behavior. They also recognize that as a symbolic leader they must consistently articulate the core values of the institution and relate them to all aspects of institutional life in order to sustain and reinvigorate the myths that create a common reality. Management skills may be a necessary, but usually not a sufficient, concomitant of presidential success. For example. studies (Chaffee, 1984), suggest that presidents who focus on resource acquisition strategies alone to resolve fiscal crises are not as successful as those who also combine them with interpretative strategies that change campus perceptions and attitudes.

Since centralized control cannot be achieved, effective presidents realize that prevention of error is not possible in complex, nonlinear, social systems. They therefore emphasize the design of systems to detect error and make institutional processes self-correcting. They support the regular collection, analysis, and public dissemination of data reflecting key aspects of institutional functioning that permit various interest groups to continually monitor the institution. Organizational stability is increased as institutional components pay attention to different aspects of the environment, and serve as controls and checks on each other's activities. The effectiveness of a free flow of information is increased when presidents support and publicly articulate throughout the institution the value of open communication and a willingness to tolerate and encourage, rather than to punish, disagreement. One president has codified these ideas in the motto "no surprises, no reprisals."

Effective presidents recognize that the inherent specialization and fractionation essential to the maintenance of quality and responsiveness must be coordinated unobtrusively in order to avoid alienation. They do this in part by establishing formal opportunities for interaction, and they emphasize particularly forums such as senates, cabinets, retreats, and task forces, that bring together persons representing different constituencies and different institutional levels. Senate presidents who sit on administrative councils, deans who attend senate meetings, and students, faculty, and administrators who serve on joint committees, interact in ways that make their perceptions and interests more consistent.

Presidential effectiveness is based as much upon influence as upon authority, and influence in an academic institution depends upon mutual and reciprocal processes of social exchange. Effective presidents influence others by allowing themselves to be influenced. This requires presidents to listen carefully, a behavior that is difficult for many presidents who have come to believe that the proper role of leaders is to tell others what to do.

Unsuccessful Administrative Strategies

To some extent, the strategies of unsuccessful presidents are likely to be the reverse images of successful ones. They do not accept the institution's characteristics but consider them as indications of institutional pathology. They attempt comprehensive rather than incremental change, violate norms and procedural expectations, try to prevent error through complex management systems, control and filter communication, and emphasize one-way rather than two-way influence.

These strategies reflect simplicity, and it can be suggested that less effective presidents have simpler understandings of their institutions and their roles than do successful presidents. There is evidence that presidents become more cognitively complex as they become more experienced, either as a result of learning or because the less complex do not remain long in office (Bensimon, 1989; Neumann, 1987). Presidents are called upon in many situations to function simultaneously as chief administrative officer, as colleague, as symbol, and as public official. Each of these roles may require different—and mutually inconsistent—behaviors, so that actions that are effective in one context may cause difficulty in another. Because of knowledge, skill, or luck, successful presidents have developed complex behavioral repertoires enabling them to balance these roles. Unsuccessful presidents are more likely to emphasize only one —to act as a manager without sensitivity to academic values, or to stress institutional culture without attending to the interests of external political audiences, for example.

Probably the most common problem of unsuccessful presidents is the management of the disruption caused by the adoption of management control systems. Both critics and supporters of higher education have accused colleges and universities of being poorly managed. Presidents interact with a world that expects accountability and may make institutional survival dependent upon conforming to "rationalized myths" (Meyer and Rowan, 1983) of management, even at the cost of institutional effectiveness. Presidents can cope with these conflicting pressures in several ways. At some institutions, presidents who believe that the implementation of rationalized management systems is inconsistent with organizational performance may appear to comply with external demands for accountability and control, but do so in a way that buffers operational units from their impact. They may develop a five year plan with the tacit understanding that it will not be implemented, or accept a system for evaluating faculty as long as it is never used when making personnel decisions.

Other presidents may accept new management techniques in the belief that they will improve organizational performance, or because their endorsement serves as a symbol of their own managerial competence. Over the last several decades many processes for increasing university effectiveness have been touted. The consequences for each have largely been the same, as master planning has been succeeded in turn by program budgeting, zero based budgeting, management information systems, management by objectives, strategic planning, and entrepreneurship; initial administration enthusiasm is followed by faculty resistance, disappointment, and ultimate failure. Each adoption has tended to produce disruption which has justified further efforts to bring order out of apparent disorder.

Another form of adoption that may result in disruption is the presidential penchant for reorganization, particularly shortly after their initial appointment. Organizational structure is not irrelevant, and indeed some presidents use structural revisions to exert an important influence over organizational communication, management, or decision systems. But structural revisions of others may have other purposes; a symbol that the institution is now "under new management," an apparent response to an insoluble problem that has in the past been attributed to structural defects (and which everyone knows will not be resolved by the new organization), or the comfort of installing familiar systems used in previous experiences. For one or another reason, many ILP presidents made reorganization a major priority when they took office, some to decrease the number of officers reporting directly to them, and others to increase it. Sometimes restructuring can ameliorate a problem, but even if it does not, the appearance of response that restructuring provides may assist in deflecting criticism.

Presidents have little control over the basic processes of the academic program that is the *raison d'être* of their institution, so it is not surprising that almost every study of the presidency suggests that they spend little time dealing with academic matters. When they do turn to academics, effective presidents identify high-leverage issues (for example, development of a core curriculum) from which success ripples through other programs. Less effective presidents become involved in specific programs which are based on personal interest rather than strategic importance, and which have little effect on institutional operations even if they are successful. Many of the presidents in the ILP had specific programs in which they saw themselves as playing a leading role. Like the proverbial 900-pound gorillas who can sleep wherever they want to, presidents can involve themselves in almost any individual program they wish. Programs that are the recipients of presidential interest (and the deans who must pick up the pieces or find resources to continue the support when the president loses interest or finds other projects) are as likely to consider it to be a meddlesome albatross as a welcome support. But it does permit presidents to believe—some with more justification than others—that they are providing academic leadership and improving their institutions.

Unsuccessful presidents may remove themselves from academic activities altogether and in a classic demonstration of means-ends reversal, may become totally consumed with involvement in management, public relations, and other essential yet peripheral procedural and support activities. Others give emphasis only to short-term goals that can be precisely defined and assessed through short-run evaluations.

Unsuccessful presidents may find themselves engaged in negative behavior characterized by "isolation, platitudes and prevarication, inertia and excessive busyness" (Demerath et al., 1967, p. 221) or comparable manifestations of behavioral or organizational pathology. Inertia and busyness can arise because there are so many things to which a president may attend that it is easy to justify doing almost anything and, in the process, to end up doing nothing of any consequence. Robert Hutchins said it best: "The temptation to bury oneself in routine is tremendous. There are so many reports, so many meetings, so many signatures, so many people to see—all that have some value to the institution, that you can conscientiously draw your salary and never administer at all" (cited in Demerath, et al., 1967, p. 87).

Presidents are likely to be unsuccessful when they pay too much attention either to too many things or to too few.

Cognitive and Symbolic Strategies

Individuals typically become presidents after successful performance in a series of related positions of increasing responsibility. One reason for defining the presidency as an impossible job is the extensive criticism by reputable sources directed at the presumably failing efforts of so many previously accomplished people. Presidents rely upon unconscious cognitive strategies to reconcile this discrepancy between past achievement and present criticism. They see themselves as successful even as others may see them as failing.

Academic presidents occupy a prestigious position in American life. They are major figures in their communities, sought after as speakers for local functions, and interviewed by the media. They are at the core of impressive academic ceremonies, they have the highest salaries and most significant perquisites a campus has to offer, and they are surrounded by respectful aides and by associates with vested interests in maintaining a successful presidency.

Presidents talk easily about the deficiencies of their confreres, but when asked about their own performance, their self-assessments are almost uniformly positive. In one study (Birnbaum, 1986) a sample of 252 presidents rated the quality of their own "institutional leadership" as 77, while they rated that of the "average president" as 66 and that of their predecessor as only 52 on a 100-point scale. They also indicated that the quality of their own campus had improved on each of seven dimensions since they had become president, a finding of individual success that collectively is contradicted by a host of recent reports critical of American higher education. Successes were also emphasized in the ILP study; all presidents interviewed pointed to significant campus improvements under their leadership, and none stated that the campus was worse now than when they took office. Presidents appear to cope with impossible situations through psychological processes that affect their perceptions and judgments. They focus attention on institutional successes and attribute at least some of that success to their own performance.

Presidents build schemas of effectiveness based upon previous career success. When they encounter new and ambiguous situations, they are likely to anticipate, and therefore to observe, successful outcomes, and to attribute these to their own efforts. When presidents were asked to identify a recent event that had had positive outcomes on their campus, for example, 74% indicated that they had initiated it. But when asked to identify an event with a negative outcome, only 14% accepted responsibility (Birnbaum, 1986). There seems to be evidence of a success bias (March, 1982) that leads these successful people to believe that they have been responsible for successful outcomes, and that permits them to disassociate themselves from failure.

The Latent Organizational Functions of Impossibility

It may be so vital, for symbolic reasons, for organizational members to believe that their leaders are important that both leaders and followers may cope with the reality of weak presidents' influence by constructing an illusion of their power. We have developed highly romanticized, heroic views of leadership—what leaders do, what they are able to accomplish, and the general effects they have upon our lives. It amounts to what might be considered a faith in the potential, if not in the actual, efficacy of those individuals (Meindl, Ehrlich, and Dukerich, 1985).

In many situations presidential leadership may not be real but is, rather, a social attribution—a result of the tendency of campus constituents to assign to a president the responsibility for unusual institutional outcomes because the leader fills a role identified as a leader, because presidents are very visible and prominent, because presidents spend a great deal of time doing leaderlike things (such as engaging in ceremonial and symbolic activities), and because we all have the need to believe in the effectiveness of individual control. Leaders are people believed by followers to have caused events. "Successful leaders," says Pfeffer (1977), "are those who can separate themselves from organizational failures and associate themselves with organizational successes." (p. 110) As one president put it,

> things have happened during my presidency, and I'll take credit for them. If you have to get blamed for the rain, you might as well take credit for the sunshine. (ILP, 1987)

In organizations with clear goals, understood technologies, and hierarchical power structures, illusionary leadership may be dysfunctional. Increasing the authority of competent leaders would reduce the extent to which their job might be thought of as impossible and, in the process of doing so, would increase organizational effectiveness. But when these organizational characteristics are not present, it is highly questionable whether increasing presidential power would yield positive outcomes. It may even be that the very factors responsible for the impossibility of the presidential role are also important components of organizational effectiveness, and that action taken to strengthen the one would weaken the other. Higher education may be effective not *despite* its arational characteristics, but *because* of them.

While presidents may rail against the frustrations of their job, they assumed their positions aware of the constraints they would face. Some may have been enticed primarily by egocentric motives, but for most, a natural interest in power, money, and prestige is strongly tempered by a sense of dedication to the enduring values of education and a commitment to serve the interests of their institution. If the presidency had greater authority than it does, it might attract to it a different kind of person—one perhaps less committed to the concept of the leader as institutional servant and more likely to see the leader as institutional master.

It might be that if presidents had greater authority, they might enjoy it more, but in Stoke's (1959) thoughtful aphorism, "those who enjoy it are not very successful, and those who are successful are not very happy. . . . Those who enjoy exercising power shouldn't have it, and those who should exercise it are not likely to enjoy it" (p. 20).

The collegial traditions of higher education suggest that presidential vacancies are filled by faculty who are selected by their colleagues, who serve them in leadership roles for limited terms, and who then return to their first love of teaching and research. While this may be more a fondly remembered fantasy than an established fact, it accurately reflects the normative sense among many academics that while college teaching may be a profession, high administrative office is only one of several temporary roles within it. The difference between seeing the presidency as a profession and as a role is a critical one. Incumbents who view the presidency as a profession are apt to see the maintenance of their position as a major objective. Such presidents "simplify their task by making only one calculation—calculating what is contributory to the welfare of the president, given the incentives to do so in the presence of job insecurity on the one hand and the impossibility of a precise definition of the institution's general welfare on the other" (Kerr and Gade, 1986, p. 53). In contrast, incumbents who see the presidency as a role can give primary attention to the needs of the institution, rather than of themselves. This makes it possible for them to accept that the greatest service a president can sometimes perform is to leave office, because "the survival of the president is not the goal. The leader is temporary and, if necessary, expendable in service to the potential value of the institution" (Kauffman, 1980, p. 14). Presidents who view their obligations as part of a role are able to enjoy the roller coaster of the presidency during its initial phases and then are able to leave without regret. Said one,

I am now excited about the job, but four or five years from now I may get tired, when I have shot my wad and need a new venue to re-charge. (ILP, 1987)

They are able to see themselves as an important—but replaceable—component in a large, cybernetic organization, and they are able to "cope by perceiving exit as a symbolic, political act of a pluralistic democratic organization, not as a threat to managerial competence" (Walker, 1977, p. 57). They are also able to separate their role from their personal identity:

I don't take what I do all that seriously. I watch myself at work with some amusement and distance. My real gut is not engaged in this job. I can get excited [for the institution] but not for myself. People play their roles to the president of [the institution], not to me [as a person]. There is a perceived and palpable difference between what I am and what I do. To get emotionally involved is damaging to your health. (ILP, 1987)

Some presidents never come to terms with the impossible nature of their jobs. Frustrated in their attempts to have the influence they desire, they may eventually find solace in cognitive distortions that lead them to see what they wish to believe. Others may follow the route of the zealot and may redouble their efforts as they lose sight of their goals. One consequence of these behaviors is to create self-fulfilling prophesies in which aggressive administrative action leads to resistance, which in turn becomes the justification for still more assertive presidential behavior.

But other presidents make peace with their positions by bringing to them a more complex understanding of the peculiar nature of the organizations and of the presidential role within it. Their goal is a peaceful balance of institutional interests within which they can make marginal improvements in a limited number of areas. They reconcile themselves to the possibility of future failure by acknowledging the role played by uncontrollable external sources, and by recognizing that some of what happens to them—both good and bad—may be a product of luck. One president said,

I've been lucky, and by and large I've gotten away with [the risks I've taken]. If my luck runs out . . . I can work up to a point, but then it's in the lap of the gods. (ILP, 1987)

Another, after making an unpopular decision, survived an extended period of personal attacks not only by the press but also by his own board and later commented,

It changed the way I looked at life, like having a heart attack changes your view of life. It changed the way I looked at leadership. I'm more relaxed and philosophical about things now. No matter how good and virtuous you may be, you may not survive to the end. (ILP, 1987)

The presidential role may be as much a product of social attributions as it is a set of desirable behaviors. By creating roles that we declare will provide leadership to an organization, we construct the attribution that organizational effects are due to leaders' behavior (Pfeffer, 1977). This allows us to simplify and make sense of complex organizational processes that would otherwise be impossible to comprehend (Meindl et al., 1985). It is perhaps as sensible to say that successful organizational events cause effective presidents as it is to say that effective presidents cause successful events.

Recognizing the significant limits to presidential leadership may be personally and organizationally useful. It may reduce somewhat the unrealistic aspirations of presidents and their constituencies. When presidents have had the experience of trying, their views moderate. They no longer need to feel in control of everything and will settle for influence over some things. They may also come to see their role less as that of an activist change-agent with comprehensive responsibility for institutional performance and more as that of a coordinator who is in a position to provide unusual leverage leading to incremental improvements in limited areas. They can come to see that

> the university existed before you came, and it will continue after you leave. [The president] has a cheerleader role—making an institution feel good about itself by the symbolic things you can do. . . . You tell people how good they are . . . you honor their accomplishments. (ILP, 1987)

One of the reasons that colleges and universities have been so successful is that as their environments have become more complex, they have responded through the creation of decentralized, flexible, and only moderately interdependent structures that collectively have been more effective in responding to environmental change than any centralized mechanism could be. This may make coordination by the president exceptionally difficult, but the same forces that limit presidential authority are also those that make these organizations exceptionally adaptable and stable. The paradox of an institution that gives precedence to professional rather than administrative authority is that management weakness may be a significant source of organizational strength.

REFERENCES

American Association of University Professors (1984). Joint statement on government of colleges and universities. In *Policy Documents and Reports, 1984 Edition*. Washington, DC: American Association of University Professors.

Baldridge, J. V., Curtis, D. V., Ecker, G., and Riley, G. L. (1978). *Policy Making and Effective Leadership: A National Study of Academic Management*. San Francisco: Jossey-Bass.

Bennis, W. G. (1976). *The Unconscious Conspiracy*. New York: AMACOM.

Bensimon, E. M. (1989). The meaning of "good presidential leadership": a frame analysis. *Review of Higher Education* 12:107–123.

Birnbaum, R. (1986). Leadership and learning: the college president as intuitive scientist. *Review of Higher Education* 9: 381–395.

Birnbaum, R. (1989). *How Colleges Work: The Cybernetics of Academic Organization and Leadership*. San Francisco: Jossey-Bass.

Blau, P. M. (1973). *The Organization of Academic Work*. New York: Wiley.

Cameron, K. S. (1978). Measuring organizational effectiveness in institutions of higher education. *Administrative Science Quarterly* 23: 604–632.

Cameron, K. S. (1984). The effectiveness of ineffectiveness. In B. M. Staw and L. L. Cummings (eds.), *Research in Organizational Behavior* Vol. 6. Greenwich, CT: JAI.

Cameron, K. S., and Whetten, D. A. (1983). *Organizational Effectiveness*. New York: Academic Press.

Carnegie Commission (1973). *The Purposes and Performance of Higher Education in the United States*. New York: McGraw-Hill.

Chaffee, E. E. (1984). Successful strategic management in small private colleges. *Journal of Higher Education*. 55: 212–241.

Cohen, M. D., and March, J. G. (1974). *Leadership and Ambiguity: The American College President*. New York: McGraw-Hill.

Cohen, M. D., March, J. G., and Olsen, J. P. (1972). Garbage can model of organizational choice. *Administrative Science Quarterly* 17: 1–25.

Commission on Strengthening Presidential Leadership (1984). *Presidents Make a Difference: Strengthening Leadership in Colleges and Universities*. Washington, DC: Association of Governing Boards of Colleges and Universities.

Corson, J. J. (1960) *Governance of Colleges and Universities*. New York: McGraw-Hill.

Demerath, N. J., Stephens, R. W., and Taylor, R. R. (1967). *Power, Presidents, and Professors*. New York: Basic Books.

Fisher, J. L. (1984). Presidents will lead—if we let them. *AGB Reports* (July/August): 11–14.

Hartnett, R. T. (1969). *College and University Trustees: Their Backgrounds, Roles, and Educational Attitudes*. Princeton, NJ: Educational Testing Service.

Hesburgh, T. (1970). The college presidency: life between a rock and hard place. *Change* (May–June) 43–47.

Horn, F. S. (1969). The job of the presidency. *Liberal Education* (October): 387–392.

Institutional Leadership Project (1987). Unpublished data from the Institutional Leadership Project, National Center for Postsecondary Governance and Finance, Teachers College, Columbia University.

Jencks, C., and Riesman, D. (1968). *The Academic Revolution*. New York: Doubleday.

Jones, T. E., Stanford, E. V., and White, G. C. (1964). *Letters to College Presidents*. Englewood Cliffs, NJ: Prentice-Hall.

Kauffman, J. F. (1980). *At the Pleasure of the Board*. Washington, DC: American Council on Education.

Kerr, C. (1963). *The Uses of the University*. New York: Harper & Row.

Kerr, C., and Gade, M. (1986). *The Many Lives of the Academic President*. Washington, DC: Association of Governing Boards of Colleges and Universities.

March, J. G. (1982). Emerging developments in the study of organizations. *Review of Higher Education* 6: 1–18.

Meindl, J. R., Ehrlich, S. B., and Dukerich, J. M. (1985). The romance of leadership. *Administrative Science Quarterly* 30: 78–102.

Meyer, J. W., and Rowan, B. (1983). Institutionalized organizations: formal structure as myth and ceremony. In J. W. Meyer and W. R. Scott (eds.), *Organizational Environments* Beverly Hills, CA: Sage.

Mintzberg, H. (1973). *The Nature of Managerial Work*. New York: Harper & Row.

Mortimer, K. P., and McConnell, T. R. (1978). *Sharing Authority Effectively*. San Francisco: Jossey-Bass.

Ness, F. F. (1971). *An Uncertain Glory*. San Francisco: Jossey-Bass.

Neumann, A. (1989). Strategic leadership: the changing orientation of college presidents. *Review of Higher Education*, 12:137–151.

Pfeffer, J. (1977). The ambiguity of leadership. *Academy of Management Review* 2: 104–119.

Rainey, H. P. (1960). How shall we control our universities? Why college presidents leave their jobs. *Journal of Higher Education* 31: 376–383.

Slosson, E. E. (1913). Universities, American endowed. In P. Monroe, *Cyclopedia of Education*, Vol. 5 (pp. 663–673. New York: Macmillan.

Stoke, H. W. (1959). *The American College President*. New York: Harper & Row.

Veblen, T. (1957). *The Higher Learning in America*. New York: Sagamore Press. (Originally Published in 1918.)

Walker, D. E. (1977). Goodbye, Mr. President, and good luck! *Educational Record*. (Winter): 53–58.

Weick, K. E. (1979). *The Social Psychology of Organizing*. Reading, MA: Addison-Wesley.

Trouble in the Land:
The Paradigm Revolution in
the Academic Disciplines

Yvonna S. Lincoln
Vanderbilt University
Department of Educational Leadership

I know that most men, including those at ease with problems of the greatest complexity, can seldom accept even the simplest and most obvious truth if it be such as would oblige them to admit the falsity of conclusions which they have delighted in explaining to their colleagues, which they have proudly taught to others, and which they have woven, thread by thread, into the fabric of their lives (Tolstoy, quoted by Joseph Ford, in Gleich, *Chaos*, 1987, pp. 37–38).

Tolstoy never had access to Thomas Kuhn, but he understood a fundamental truth about scientific revolutions (and probably other kinds as well): when persons have made careers on some idea, they are loathe to give it up, whatever the evidence that the idea is not longer very serviceable. But the person who contends that there is no fire in his basement will soon either admit to the truth, or perish.

There are several ways in which one might approach the topic of a paradigm revolution in the academic disciplines. The first is to deny that the debate is important, or that it has any meaning. This posture has been taken by some (Miles and Huberman, 1984) who argue that debates about epistemological matters are best left to those who have a compelling interest in them, or who have nothing better to do with their scholarly time. The second is to recognize that there is a debate raging, but to reaffirm that the "scientific method" model of research is still our single best weapon in the war on coming-to-know, leading to social and technological advances. The third posture is to deny that there is a debate, and to continue to do as one has always done. The fourth stance is to exhibit intense curiosity, and attempt to inform oneself what the parameters of the debate might be. The purpose of this paper is to address the fourth stance, by setting some of the boundaries of the debate, and by specifying exactly what the arguments address. Although the formal definition will be taken up shortly, by *paradigm revolution*, I mean to denote the call for abandoning scientific method which is occurring in many academic disciplines.

The exercise here departs slightly from the formats of other pieces contained in past volumes. The purpose of many chapters to date has been to take an area of research, review the literature extensively, and provide a summary of what we know about the topic. The editor's advice to the author was that she "think of what you might expect in a paper in *Review of Educational Research* or *Review of Research in Education*. The expectation is that the existing literature, either theoretical or empirical, will be reviewed" (personal communication, Pascarella, 1987). There is no way, however, that the "existing literature" on the (problematic) paradigm revolution in the academic disciplines can be reviewed in its totality. To accomplish such a purpose would require fleets of graduate assistants, trained in the hard and social sciences, and rather more than a decade of time simply to read and digest such a body of work—assuming a moratorium on writing about the topic. A more practical and managable task is simply to demonstrate, by reviewing many articles across a dozen disciplines, that the social sciences (as well as the hard sciences) are in an uproar. Readers will immediately recognize that I have limited my comments to the social sciences, in the main. That is because the revolution has already occurred (and become orthodoxy) in the hard sciences, particularly chemistry, quantum mechanics and physics, mathematics, microbiology, and biology. Those arenas will be discussed, but mainly to demonstrate that traditional logical positivism (i.e., conventional or "scientific" inquiry) has been abandoned by theoreticians in those fields, one by one, since the turn of the century.

I will not argue for a particular standpoint, although I have argued the appropriateness, or "fittingness," point elsewhere (Guba and Lincoln, 1981; Lincoln and Guba, 1985; Lincoln, 1988). My interest is to demonstrate Cole's (1985) assertion that "science is less a statement of truth than a running argument" (p. 99), and to show that the argument is rapidly becoming pandemic in the academic disciplines.

WHY WOULD WE BE INTERESTED IN KNOWING ABOUT THE ARGUMENT?

There are several reasons. First, scholars in higher education are themselves affected by the spreading unease characterizing the paradigm revolution (Keller, 1985; Lincoln, 1987), including the call to abjure trivial, but quantifiable, questions in favor of grappling with inquiries which aim at larger understandings, even if at the expense of some rigor, and the call to reemphasize context and the criticality of diversity when explaining findings, or attempting to generalize about higher education experiences. Second, administrators in higher education need to understand that scholars on their campuses are engaged in battles which go far beyond scientific findings. They are fighting over the problems of primacy and legitimacy, and they are fighting over access: access to outlets for publication, and fair review of their nonconventional theorizing and research. To the extent that administrators in higher education realize this internecine struggle over who will control the journals and other avenues of publication, they can provide internal supports to their maverick faculty members who are not currently recognized as mainstream (but who may well be on the farthest edges in their respective disciplines). Finally, those among the higher education scholars who are historians of this unique institution will someday chronicle the revolution. A major part of the revolution still lies underground, but historians of contemporary culture—historians who attempt to "do history" as it is being written—will recognize that the paradigm revolution may well rank, in terms of its power to change the face of modern institutions forever, alongside the student "free speech" movement, the universalization of higher education in the U.S., and civil rights movements on campus. Thus, the revolution has aspects of the "watershed" phenomenon.

WHAT IS THIS PARADIGM REVOLUTION, AND WHERE DOES IT COME FROM?

Gregory Bateson postulated over thirty years ago that we were entering a period he called "deutero-learning." Deutero-learning involves learning about how we go about learning. Bateson (1972) contended that paradigm revolutions have occurred in other times and places, but that those who were part of the revolutions were unaware that their conception of the universe was changing forever. Some common "paradigm revolutions," known to any undergraduate student in Western civilization courses, would include the shift from the bicameral to the unicameral mind (Jaynes, 1976); the transition from the polytheocracy of the Greek and Roman worlds to the monotheocracy of medieval and feudal societies (Bark, 1960; Sullivan, 1960; Pirenne, 1937; Knowles, 1962; Heer, 1962; Lot, 1961; Southern, 1953; Dawson, 1956); the rise of the Renaissance (Haskins, 1965; Huizinga, 1954); the Industrial Revolution in Europe (Weber, 1958; Tawney, 1926; Landes, 1966; Schumpeter, 1950; Mantoux, 1961; Deane, 1967); and the civil rights movement in the United States. The point of deutero-learning is that most historical shifts in consciousness are traced only *after* the revolution has occurred. Bateson believed, however, that we are now sophisticated enough as a culture to *watch ourselves changing while we are in the process of changing*.

Indeed, that is part of the point of being, for some, a contemporary historian, that is, writing history as it happens (Salisbury, 1967, Manchester, 1974, and Halberstam, 1972, are good examples of this genre), or quite soon thereafter. A part of the fun of being a contemporary historian (or watching one) is that writers about contemporary phenomena have the pleasure not only of watching the actual events in progress but, more importantly, of *creating labels, metaphors, and names for the events* which capture something of their meaning and import.

In that sense, we behave as constructivists alongside historians, deciding whether their metaphors are apt and believable, deciding whether we will keep them, or discard them as fads. *Paradigm revolution* is one label which appears to have great staying power.

Thomas Kuhn can be credited with inventing the term *paradigm revolution*, and virtually no one in academic circles today is unfamiliar with at least the term, if not the ongoing debate. But what is meant by it? Thomas Kuhn is a historian of science, best known for a small book titled *The Structure of Scientific Revolutions* (1970). Although it is sometimes asserted that the book has had far more impact than it had any right to, and although Kuhn himself has expressed some surprise that the work has exhibited the staying power that it has, the work has nevertheless caught the imagination of all manner of scholars. The simple reason for this is that the book offers a way of viewing how new conventions about doing science come into being.

Briefly, the model postulates this: There is a period of "normal science," when the scientific community (particularly in the hard sciences) enjoys some wide or universal agreement concerning how "science" will be done, some common language for talking about what is known or should be known (called the *discourse of science*), and a mutuality of philosophical worldview (or paradigm). The philosophical paradigm, or model, is nothing more than a set of agreements about what we think the nature of reality is (the ontological agreement), what we think is possible to know (the epistemological agreement), how we ought best to come to know it (the methodological agreement, which in this case has been "scientific method"), and what we believe the role of values in inquiry ought to be (the axiological agreement). When an entire scientific community operates on a set of tacit or taken-for-granted agreements about the four axioms above, we have a period of relative quiet within the community, which Kuhn terms "normal science." Scientists proceed with their individual and group research projects with the same underlying assumptions, and with a common language of discourse, typically called *scientific terminology*.

As scientists proceed with their work, anomalies occasionally occur. These anomalies represent phenomena which cannot be either understood or explained by current and existing theories. For some period of time, the anomalies are simply understood as anomalies, until the sheer number and weight of them begins to stretch a given theory's credibility to the point of collapse (or indeed until the anomalies are numerous enough and bizarre enough to challenge the entire discipline's theoretical base). This takes a long time, of course, since one purpose of a theory is to "wall off" contrary evidence, to treat anomalous data and observations as though they were "outliers," interesting but statistically insignificant.

Sooner or later, however, the anomalies begin to take on the appearance of regularities, and a crisis is precipitated, according to Kuhn. In simplest terms, the crisis revolves about whether the scientific community will reject traditional theory and begin anew to construct theory which accounts for the anomalies, or whether it will remain tied to classical theory. A battle ensues between the classicists and the emergent theoreticians, a battle which is, according to Darwin, rarely ever fully won until the last of the classicists dies off or retires from scholarly circles, and a completely new generation of scholars is hired. The battle's lines are almost never drawn around the question of *scientific proofs*. Kuhn (1974) himself says, "The competition between paradigms is not the sort of battle that can be resolved by proofs. . . . The transfer of allegiance from paradigm to paradigm is a conversion experience that cannot be forced" (p. 43). After a generation or so of the battle, the "new paradigm" (or set of new theoretical or philosophical models) emerges victorious. It then goes on to become the "new orthodoxy," establishing its theories in the place of primacy, establishing its language as the new, and more appropriate, language of discourse.

Sometimes, the paradigm revolution occurs *within* disciplines as, for example, when physics shifted from classical physics to quantum mechanics; at other times, the shift occurs at a more abstract level and reaches *across* disciplines. It is that latter shift to which this work refers.

What is the Shape and Form of the Paradigm Debate?
The paradigm revolution debate has many shapes and forms, particularly as it cuts across disciplines. Different disciplines have found different reasons to call for abandonment of the conventional, logical positivist framework for doing science. Some understanding of how different groups, different disciplines, and different individuals have *framed* the debate is critical for understanding how each discipline frames its response, or what a given group or discipline believes will remediate the problems it sees with the old paradigm. There are at least four ways to "frame" the debate:

The "Impoverished" Debate
To some critics, the debate is little more than a debate regarding enlarging the armamentarium of methodological tools at the disposal of conventional scientists, largely by incorporation of qualitative methods in addition to quantitative methods, thereby adding richness, texture, depth, and increased understanding to research studies. Miles and Huberman (1984), Miles (1984), Cook and Reichardt (1979), Goetz and Lecompte (1984), and Patton (1980, 1981, 1982) would be examples of this posture in educational research, or research methods used widely in education. Williamson, et al. (1981), Glaser (1978), Jick (1979), and Glaser and Strauss (1967) would be examples in the larger social science community. The approach is what I call (although many of the authors above would not) the *impoverished argument*. The debate is simply that quantitative

methods alone tell us less than we need to know about the situations and contexts in which we do research. Qualitative methods, in this form of the debate, are useful and necessary, albeit an "attractive nuisance" (Miles, 1979), for increasing our understanding of the phenomena under investigation. "Mixing qualitative and quantitative methods" (Jick, 1979, p. 602), particularly with an eye toward providing power and robustness in the form of triangulation, is viewed as a path to additional rigor in data analysis.

The impoverished argument, or the argument for inadequacy, simply says that we have too long ignored a source of richness in our data collection and analyses. We could, as researchers, profit from its inclusion or, in some cases (where we do not know enough), from its exclusive use. The latter posture suggests that qualitative methods are fine when not much is known about the phenomenon, implying, of course, that once more is known, one can move to the more rigorous scientific and quantitative methods.

Adherents for the impoverished or inadequate debate can and do strongly suggest that the same criteria for rigor nevertheless apply to qualitative methods as apply to quantitative methods, although extraordinary care must be taken to meet such criteria, and occasionally, or perhaps most of the time, qualitative data will fail on the strictest reading of the criteria. The press for adoption of qualitative methods by this particular group, however, is grounded in the determination that such data are absolutely needed; that they may provide additional evidence of the rigor of quantitative data; and that researchers must content themselves with less-than-perfect data in return for enhanced understanding.

The reader should notice that in the impoverished or inadequate debate, the presumption is that any criticisms of the scientific or conventional paradigm can and should be resolved at a *methods* level. The answer to criticisms of scientific method has been the expansion of methods, as well as the cessation of reliance on strictly quantitative and experimental modes for doing science. Supporters of this strategy to address the shortcomings of science are adamant that ontological, epistemological, and axiological arguments do not need to be addressed, and that expansion of the repertoire of *methods* available to the conventional scientist is quite enough to solve any problems arising from the limitations of traditional and conventional science.

Other social scientists, however, have found the inadequacy argument, focusing as it does strictly on methods, to be itself impoverished. Equally skilled scientists have argued that other problems inhere in the conventional scientific paradigm, and that those problems must also be addressed.

The "Exclusion" Debate
Another stern set of criticisms of the conventional paradigm for science has come from an unexpected quarter: women scientists, and feminist theorists. Strange as

it may appear, female scientists and feminist theorists—a group originating, in part, from comparative literature, literary criticism, and history—have made common cause on the issue of whether or not science is a male-dominated activity. While scholars can and have separated the criticisms of female scientists from female theorists, there is little conceptual reason to do so here, since their arguments are strikingly similar, and since they finally arrive at the same conclusions regarding the *social structure of science*—and therefore, its onto-logical, epistemological, methodological and axiological *biases*. The paradigm debate here has taken the form of a scientific criticism of science as a "gendered" (i.e., traditionally male-dominated) social enterprise. As a "gen-dered enterprise," it has been labeled sexist and, therefore, biased in its appearance of neutrality in portraying women's natures. Namenwirth (1986) has captured this particular debate well:

> The predominance of white, middle-class men in science has resulted in excessive reliance on conceptual paradigms related to the social preoccupations of this group. . . . The effect of male bias on scientific research is most dramatic in fields closely related to sex and gender. In the study of primate social behavior, for example, scientists have exaggerated the extent and importance of male dominance hierarchies and male aggression, initiative, and competition in controlling troop behavior. . . . This astigmatism has seriously compromised data collection and theory construction in animal behavior and evolution. Another example of distortion can be found in the near-obsessive focus on discovering a biological basis for small average differences between the sexes in behavior, or in the scores achieved on some kind of cognitive test. *Thus, in areas of biological research related (sometimes unconsciously) to human sexuality or gender, male bias in the scientific establishment has frequently resulted in misleading, unreliable research.* (p. 25, emphases added)

Fee (1986) echoes the criticism, when she develops the arguments that support the assertion, "We have been used to a virtual male monopoly of the production of scientific knowledge and discourses about science, its history and meaning" (p. 42). The response of the scientific community to criticisms from feminists (and from scientists who are themselves women and feminists) has been "a conservative ideological movement within science . . . mobilized to defend inequality, protect the status quo, and create barriers to change; sociobiological theories are among the weapons of the ideological warfare" (p. 43).

The criticisms from the gender debate focus on two issues. First, science as traditionally done has portrayed women in ways which continue to support inequality and discriminatory treatment. Second, the undergirding propositions of science force this supposed value-neutrality and objectification of the subjects of scientific research. Each of the arguments, however, focuses on the male-oriented conception of "science" as the offending characteristic, and the suggested response is a "feminization" of science (Reinharz, 1979; Harding, 1986; Bleier, 1984, 1986; Keller, 1974, 1978, 1982, 1983a), including a return to more qualitatively oriented studies which attempt to honor the perspectives of women, to focus on the holism of women's experiences, and to retreat from researcher-directed frames of response. The "if this, then that" quality of the debate mounted by feminists is explained by the brief history of the arguments proffered by Fee (1986):

> This new body of work has encompassed several different and sometimes contradictory strands, but as a collective body of theory it seeks to defend women from ideological attacks conducted in the name of "science"—and also it goes much further in challenging the entire tradition of Western science by exposing how the foundations of our knowledge have been built on the assumptions of male domination and patriarchal power. . . .
>
> This round of confrontation with scientific knowledge began as critiques of specific theories, historical and contemporary, and showed how those theories represented (often outrageously) biased accounts of women and of sex differences. . . . *Critiques of specific theories were often initiated with the intent of improving science by removing some of its worst abuses, but they also tended to raise questions about science in general—particularly, the authoritarian epistemological claims made on behalf of scientific knowledge and method.* (p. 43, emphases added)

The debate about paradigms began, thus, with an argument that much of what science had to say about women was wrong, and it proceeded from a model the political overtones of which were sexism, discrimination, and second-class citizenship. The political overtones were argued to extend to others besides women: homosexuals, persons of color, and even primates (Haraway, 1986; Rose, 1986). Following hard on the heels of straightforward feminist criticism, however, were growing critiques of science as a socially constructed activity (Reinharz, 1979; Keller, 1985; Bleier, 1984). Feminists and female scientists began with a concern for the "role of science in the creation of an elaborate mythology of women's biological inferiority as an explanation for their subordinate position in the cultures of Western civilizations" (Bleier, 1984, p. vii) but moved much farther to describe science as a gendered—and therefore, paradigmatically limited—knowledge production function (Epstein, 1981).

Much more will be said about the call for a new paradigm in women's studies, feminist studies, and feminist criticism later in this chapter, when the issue of discipline-bound criticisms is taken up. For now, it is sufficient to say that alongside those who debate the paradigm revolution as a move to employ more qualitative methods, there are the feminists who believe that method is only the tip of the iceberg. But joining those two groups is yet another group, those who have specific axiomatic complaints.

The "Exception" Debate

Still another set of scholars has undertaken criticism of science by calling for a mediation on one or another of the specific axioms of scientific inquiry.[1] So, for example, we can see educational psychologists (Cronbach, 1975) calling for an abandonment of the traditional concept of generalization, in favor of the "working hypothesis." The working hypothesis has, Cronbach argues, the strength that it recognizes that all science is "mostly history" (shortly after it is science), and that all knowledge is, or should be, treated as though it were tentative, requiring testing in each new context. Policy analysts and political scientists argue publicly that science is not, and cannot be, value-free (Bahm, 1971). Psychologists and sociologists call for a constructivist view of reality (Berger and Luckman, 1973; Bakan, 1972); that is, they deny the possibility of a single "reality" onto which science must converge. Physicists back them up with the newest theories in quantum mechanics, which postulate (in simplest terms) that reality is quite possibly a created phenomenon (cf. "Schrödinger's cat," in Zukav, 1979).

Historians, likewise, have criticized the assumption that it is possible to write a "scientific, value-free history," although that has been a disciplinary aspiration for generations of scholars until recently (Winkler, 1986). The call by Professor Hexter noted in this *Chronicle of Higher Education* article is far more widespread than it would appear to be, and it revolves about what he calls a need for "moral judgment in research." This moral judgment denies the necessity of ridding "scholarship of value judgments," a relic of the "Cartesian transformation" which "obliterated that pervasive value-bearing element which permeated the pre-Copernican universe" (p. 10). Hexter argues that there are three ways of knowing: one has "to do with ways of coming to conclusions about the validity of sources and about the veracity of witnesses who are rarely directly accessible"; a second is the Cartesian method, a "precise mathematical measuring of the universe" which he describes as "a mistake not just about method, but about knowing itself"; and a third way, which he describes as the Marksian method (not Marx, but Marks, after his grandmother), a method of knowing which is informed by moral judgment, by interpretation, and by the understanding that "moral judgments can be [and are] different" between historians (or, by extension, other social scientists; p. 11).

Likewise, other social scientists have taken up the call for a return to research which is characterized by clear sets of values, more limited claims regarding causal chains, and an increased attention to "interpretation" (Winkler, 1985). That these calls have been issued at national professional meetings, and have met with favorable response, signals that whole professions are listening and contemplating the same message.

The "Whole Paradigm" Debate

Howe (1985) has pointed out that the repudiation of logical positivism occurred more than 30 years ago, with Quine's demolition of two buttressing beliefs of the philosophical system, the "quantitative-qualitative distinction and the fact-value distinction." But educational research has long held on to these two beliefs, and to the central axioms of logical positivism, although it will be clear shortly that the rest of the academic world, and particularly the hard sciences, has long since abandoned such propositions in favor of either what it is now called *post-positivism*,[2] or for a constructivist or phenomenological philosophical system.

The root distinction between adherents for and against in this debate has been their willingness to mount a criticism of the entire (apparent) supporting system of logical positivism. The most vocal of these critics have been Lincoln and Guba (Guba, 1978, 1982; Guba and Lincoln, 1981, 1982; Lincoln and Guba, 1985a, 1985b, 1986). Some review of my (and our) work is not inappropriate here, since it follows a style which has been undertaken at the same time—but unknown to us then—at the Stanford Research Institute by Schwartz and Ogilvy (1979, 1980), whose work will also be reviewed shortly.

In the course of teaching a course, we[3] became aware that belief systems in which we had both been trained were inadequate to explain the rampant non-use of evaluation results (Guba, 1972), the resistance to even highly positive evaluation efforts which rarely jeopardized anyone's position, and the national waste of resources involved in funding evaluation projects whose results never saw the light of the day (Guba and Lincoln, 1981). Three central beliefs occurred to us immediately as a source of the problem, and we set about explicating how those beliefs "interfered" with performing evaluation studies which were actually utilized.

The central beliefs were the belief in a single reality, on which it was believed that any study's findings should converge; an adherence to the proposition that the researcher and researched can and ought to remain "objectively" distanced from one another, with proper safeguards taken either to avoid or to account for reactivity or interactivity; and the belief that each inquiry ought to lead to a set of generalizations, time- and context-free statements which embodied some law of nature (Guba and Lincoln, 1981).

A content analysis of major works in educational research led us to believe that these were pervasive and inescapable axioms of conventional, or logical positivist, inquiry. Those three axioms, in their reversed form, were declared to be the system for "naturalistic" inquiry,[4] and we set about repudiating conventional, scientific, or positivistic inquiry as not fitting the human behavioral sciences (for a much longer explanation of why, see Guba, 1978).

In the process, we also derived a set of "postures" (now called *implications*), choices which were more or less mandated, but at least preferred, when carrying out naturalistic inquiry. They represented both methods and methodological choices which a naturalist would find more congenial than those typically utilized in conventional inquiry. For instance, we argued that a naturalist would rarely, and probably never, take an inquiry to a laboratory but would rather take it to a natural setting, since contextual factors were thought to be important to the inquiry, and since the purpose of a laboratory was to screen out contextual (contaminating) factors, under circumstances of great control. We also argued that qualitative methods were the methods of most frequent choice, since qualitative methods were those which enabled inquirers to tap into the multiple reality constructions of respondents, since those were the methods which enabled holistic, rich, textural and context-bound data to emerge, and since those were the methods most congenial to the human-as-instrument.

There were a number of these postures, or implications, but increasing encounters with readers of the 1981 volume began to press on other issues. Not long after the appearance of that work, we realized, either from the penetrating questions of scholars and practitioners, or from our own reanalysis of the original research design literature we had reviewed, that two of the "postures," or implications, were in fact of the stature of axioms themselves. In brief, they were the assumption about causality and the assumption regarding whether or not inquiry can be value-free. The literature was quite clear, either directly or indirectly, that one aim of science was to arrive at some certain knowledge of the causal chains which linked events. Discussion of how an inquirer might go about this led us to believe that causal chains (in conventional inquiry) could be expressed as "if-then" statements (such as occurred in many, if not most, texts on research design and methods) and were conceived of as linear in nature.

The other assumption, first treated as a posture, was that inquiry should be—in conventional inquiry—conceived of as value-free. Already the hard scientists and psychologists were beginning to reject this assumption (Bahm, 1971) and others appeared to be fast behind, as noted earlier. Upon completion of a reanalysis of the literature on this point, we came to realize that a given inquiry is bounded by value choices on five sides: in the choice of a problem to research; in the choice of a paradigm to guide the inquiry; in the choice of methods used to collect and analyze data; with respect to the values which inhere in all natural contexts; and with respect to whether all of those choices exhibit congruence, or *resonance*, with each other. If there were internal mismatches, the inquiry could be termed *dissonant*. An early article (Guba and Lincoln, 1982) outlined the complete paradigm from the perspective of whole-system critique and was followed in three years with the first whole-paradigm book-length critique (Lincoln and Guba, 1985).

At the same time as Lincoln and Guba began their own explication of the new paradigm, an interesting and near-parallel project was under way at SRI in Menlo Park, California. Under the direction of two senior researchers, Peter Schwartz and James Ogilvy, the Values and Lifestyles Program Project was preparing to write the seventh of a number of critical monographs. The Values and Lifestyle Program was a piece of proprietary research (and thus is not generally available in the public domain) undertaken to aid manufacturers, industrial concerns, and a variety of service providers in understanding what products and services would be needed by the American public (and indeed, the developed world) into the 21st century. As one way of assessing "who" the American public might be past the year 2000, Schwartz and Ogilvy conducted a content-analysis-like survey of academic disciplines since the turn of the century. They were searching for emergent concepts likely to have an impact—sooner or later—on the way in which not only academicians and scientists and product design personnel saw the world, but on the way in which John Q. Public saw it also. The results were startling.

In a variety of disciplines and subspecialties of disciplines (and subjects which are treated as disciplines in academic institutions)—including chemistry, mathematics, physics, brain theory, ecology and biology, evolutionary theory, philosophy, politics and political theory, philosophy, linguistics, religion, studies of types of consciousness (as in biofeedback and the like), and the arts—they have abstracted "seven major characteristics of the 'new paradigm' that are virtually opposed to those of the dominant paradigm" (logical positivism; Lincoln and Guba, 1985, p. 51). While it is not possible in a limited space to treat their findings with the justice they deserve, a review of them is essential to understanding how two sets of scholars unknown to each other could arrive at essentially the same conclusions regarding the major philosophy guiding science in the Western world (logical positivism) and concepts (or axioms) regarding the ultimate nature of the universe.

Schwartz and Ogilvy (1979) precede their analysis with the concept from Bateson (1972) used earlier in this chapter, that of deutero-learning. They comment that

> Among the greatest of the changes [occurring over the centuries] is the capacity to make just this kind of leap: from a series of thoughts about phenomena on one level to an entirely different level of thought about *those* thoughts on the first level. Not just more and different thoughts on the first level, but meta-leap to meta-laws covering the laws on the first order of generality: *thinking about thinking and knowing.*
>
> So, for example, organic change—growth—was the paradigm or pattern for change for an entire epoch of science. . . . Now the pattern is changing once again. Neither the teleological interpretation of organic growth nor the causal account of physical mechanism is adequate any longer. And we know it.
>
> Further, *we know that we know it.* We know that we have accomplished a break from our previous paradigms. We know that there are such things as paradigms. Before our era, most people didn't think of themselves as caught within a paradigm. Having never consciously experienced a shift of paradigms, the very existence of paradigms could not be perceived. Now, however, not only do we appear to be on the edge of the new paradigm, but in addition, we know that there are paradigms. Precisely that awareness is part of the new paradigm, and how meta-leap to a self-reflective stance on all of one's thoughts, and how it is, finally that thought thinks about itself. (pp. 4–5; first and last emphases in the original, others added)

TABLE 1. Changes in Basic Beliefs—Dominant Versus Emergent Paradigm

Dominant paradigm from	Emergent paradigm toward
Simple	Complex
Hierarchy	Heterarchy
Mechanical	Holographic
Determinate	Indeterminate
Linearly causal	Mutually causal
Assembly	Morphogenesis
Objective	Perspective

Source: Lincoln and Guba, 1985 (p. 52), based on Schwartz and Ogilvy, 1979 (p. 13).

Schwartz and Ogilvy summarize succinctly the characterizations of positions described earlier in this chapter as forms and shapes of the debate. They noted that

> In our culture, there are different sequential patterns: old, current and emergent. The old pattern is the Newtonian paradigm that succeeded the Aristotelian world view. At the common level, that old pattern is still dominant. And, for many purposes, even in the formal disciplines the old paradigm is still valid but in a more limited way. *In the formal disciplines, the current pattern is a fractured one*, hardly a pattern at all—more appropriately, the fragments of a pattern. The emergent pattern is for the future. It is the underpinnings of future values and beliefs. Its *outline is becoming visible.* (pp. 5–6, emphasis added)

They have charted the "emergent pattern" on seven different dimensions of change, displayed in Table 1. Some discussion of what those dimensions mean will lend a flavor to the revolutionary nature of their description.

1. *The shift from simple to complex realities.* Schwartz and Ogilvy (1979) point out that in the past, the universe was thought to be characterized by a lack of diversity, by phenomena which were not interactive, and which stood as separate systems. Now, they say, it is becoming apparent to scientists that it is more often the case that diversity and interactivity are *inherent characteristics* of most phenomena and systems. One cannot simply "abstract out for intense study one or a few elements (variables?) while holding 'everything else constant.' Variation is the order of all contexts . . . , it is, 'in principle impossible to separate a thing from its environment'" (p. 13). One can no longer assume that a phenomenon is the sum of its parts, since the movement to increasingly complex systems means that each system develops properties which are unique to the system and which account for more variation than that which is indicated in the individual parts themselves.

2. *Movement from hierarchic to heterarchic concepts of order.* In the Newtonian universe, the appropriate model for science required that systems— whether ecological, mechanical, biological, or chemical—be viewed as hierarchic, that is, possessing an inherent order from the simplest to the most complex. This was reflected in social systems which cast certain members of society as second-class citizens (such as women and persons of color), in the monarchical systems which supported the "divine right of kings," in the periodic table of chemical elements, and in the common assumptions regarding how the natural world was taxonomically ordered into increasingly complex organisms. The idea of a "pecking order, a chain of command, higher- and lower-order principles" has *given way* to systems which are not pyramidal, but rather characterized by heterarchies with "mutual constraints and influence [and] movement that is unpredictable and different from those of the particular component interests" (p. 13).

3. *Movement from mechanical toward holographic.* The older paradigm viewed the universe as a vast mechanical object (the clock is the most widely used metaphor), which, when put into motion, simply moves until it winds down or runs out of energy. But the image of the universe as a vast piece of machinery which can be understood by taking apart its components no longer appears very serviceable, in view of the fact that we now see aspects of complexity and heterarchy which were not apparent to us in an earlier paradigm. A more apt model is posited to be the holograph, the image of which "is created by a dynamic process of interaction and differentiation" (p. 14). Unlike a mechanical model, a holographic image has information that is "distributed throughout . . . at each point [in the holographic image] information about the whole is contained in the part . . . everything is *interconnected* like a vast network of interference patterns" (p. 14, emphasis in the original). The implication here, of course, is that information about, for instance, organizations, can be found in each of their parts—and indeed, in all of their parts—and that it would not be possible to wall off information within specific suborganizations about the operations of the larger organizations. The image of the universe as a vast clockwork or other machine is replaced by the image of the universe as a holographic image composed by a dynamic process of interconnection, steady differentiation, and interaction.

4. *Movement from determinacy toward indeterminacy.* The image of a vast clockwork or a massive machine as a description of the universe lent credence to deterministic arguments in a variety of fields. Mechanistic models of the universe supported religious, social, and scientific theses for determinism. As Schwartz and Ogilvy put it, "If the world consists wholly of particles and fields of force whose behavior is mathematically describable, then, given sufficiently sophisticated computational abilities [or sufficiently 'intelligent' computers], the behavior of whole aggregations should be predictable. Even if calculation is not

possible in practice, the system is still strictly determined" (p. 14). But the presumed determinacy of the universe was put to rest forever with the advancement of the Heisenberg uncertainty principle, which states that we cannot know the future state of a subatomic particle (it is in theory not predictable), and that the very action which we take to determine what or where it is, or how much it weighs, will determine what we see. In research terms, the implication of this realization is that the very act of asking questions about a phenomenon—that is, what questions are asked, and in which way, and the order in which they are asked—determines what we will come to know regarding the phenomenon. More than that, Schwartz and Ogilvy (1979) argue that

> Qualitatively, the implication of this is not that there are no causal linkages between past, present, and future; rather, in complex systems *possibilities* can be known, but precise outcomes cannot be predicted. It means that *ambiguity* about the future *is a condition of nature*. (p. 14, first and last emphases added, second emphasis in original text)

The shift from determinism to indeterminism echoes other shifts which preceded it, particularly in the social and political sciences.

5. *Movement from linear to mutual causality.* Causal models in the old paradigm reflected strongly the hierarchy, mechanism, and determinacy concepts inherent in the Newtonian universe. In the Newtonian-Cartesian universe, the best causal model is always that one which is simplest, and therefore linear. It is best expressed in the usual "if-then" statements which undergird the formation of hypotheses in conventional scientific inquiry. But newer conceptualizations from both physics and chemistry suggest that some complex systems may be operating in ways which make causality, as we currently understand it, implausible. There is the possibility that A and B do not interact in such a way that A causes (or brings about) B, but rather that A and B interact in such a way that they "evolve and change together, each affecting the other in such a way as to make the distinction between cause and effect meaningless. . . . [they exhibit, in other words, a] symbiosis" (p. 14).

6. *Movement from assembly to morphogenesis.* Schwartz and Ogilvy observed that as conceptions of the universe have changed, so have traditional conceptions of the change process. From chemistry and astronomy had come the concept of *morphogenesis* to describe what was thought to be the evolution of planets and other galactic material from chaos, or from primordial matter. The concept involves the "sense of order emerging from disorder" and posits systems which are significant for their "diversity, openness, complexity, mutual causality and indeterminacy" (p. 14), which hold the possibility not of quantitative, but of qualitative, change. The mathematics of René Thom describes the phenomenon, under the rubric "catastrophe theory." In short, morphogenesis is consonant with other characteristics of the emerging system, most particularly in the sense

that it is impossible to have a morphogenetic change without the other emerging constructs demonstrated in the phenomenon.

7. *Movement from objective toward perspective.* The final conventional scientific assumption to be denied by the emerging paradigm of thought and belief is that of objectivity. Historians credit Descartes with this particular transformation of Western civilization, noting that ways of knowing in the Cartesian universe included the "disinterested observer," the use of reasoning as a way of coming to understanding, and the distancing of the observer from the thing to be observed (Winkler, 1986). But objectivity, and the distancing of researchers from the researched, thought to be achievable with instrumentation which reduced interactivity or reactivity, turns out to be an illusion. Scientists, however, who feel they are left with the alternative of subjectivity only, and who find subjectivity is a poor substitute for the (nevertheless impossible) objectivity, have increasingly turned to "perspective" as a way of coping with the value-bound nature of their inquiries. Perspective, suggests the SRI group, "connotes a view at a distance from a particular focus. Where we look from affects what we see. This means that any one focus of observation gives only a *partial result; no single discipline ever gives a complete picture. A whole picture is an image generated morphogenetically from multiple perspectives*" (Schwartz and Ogilvy, 1979, p. 15, emphasis added).

Schwartz and Ogilvy (1979) do not attempt to deal here with whether or not there is a "real" reality out there (the ontological argument); rather they argue that, if there is a real reality "out there," it will nevertheless resist our attempts to know it, since "every time we try to discover what it is, our efforts will be [no more than] partial" (p. 16). The "new metaphor," they contend, is

somewhat like a change in metaphor from reality as a machine toward reality as a conscious organism. Machines are mechanical and relatively simple. . . . A conscious being—say, a human being—is very complex and unpredictable. . . . Because of this complexity of interaction, people don't always see the same things; they have unique perspectives. In the same way, the emergent paradigm of the actual world is complex, holographic, heterarchial, indeterminate, mutually causal, morphogenetic and perspectival. The shift in metaphor is from the machine to the human being. We are like the world we see. (p. 16)

Schwartz and Ogilvy do not represent a true case of the paradigm debate in the sense that they set about to *criticize* the axioms of the old paradigm. Quite the opposite. Their charge was simply to project dominant, undergirding social beliefs for the next century. They were themselves amazed at their findings. They simply analyzed what scientists and those in the academic disciplines are saying about the nature of the world, and they have found that the scientific world looks very different to those on the cutting edge of their disciplines. Since these changes in perspectives on the nature of the cosmos will take some time to filter down to nonacademic circles, these two researchers have termed the paradigm of the future "emergent."

But others would argue that it is not emergent, that it is here. Thus, Lincoln and Guba (1985) argue that the philosophical base for the new pattern of research is upon us, in place, and reflects the political, ethical, and social realities found in the world of educational, social, and behavioral research. Support for that position has been amply documented by the SRI International research work, however unintentionally. As a result, a reading of one set of literature—that, for instance, which the SRI group reviewed from the academic disciplines— buttresses the critics of the conventional paradigm, although the groups may not have been aware of each other's work prior to publication, now were they attending to the same conceptual task. The implications are clear. Schwartz and Ogilvy (1979), who care little about "fittingness" arguments advanced by others, nevertheless see a total reconceptualization of the universe in Western thought, which they call "a shift in paradigm, the evolution of new conceptual maps, a change in world view . . . akin in kind, diversity, and magnitude to the emergence of the Enlightenment in the seventeenth and eighteenth centuries" (p. 16).

Schwartz and Ogilvy observed that as conceptions of the universe changed so must traditional conceptions of the change process—that is, how change occurs, or how it may be brought about—be altered. From a model of the universe as mechanistic, as a complicated "Rube Goldberg" machine, the shift is made to a model of the universe, and the systems within it, as a complex living cell, with systems and subsystems within it, interacting, and differentiating in order to accomplish multiple functions at which we can only begin to guess. Change within a living-cell model must be seen in the same interactive, delicate, differentiating way. Push-pull conceptions of how change is brought about in (mechanical) systems must be abandoned.

Stances on the Paradigm Revolution

Although there are four broad stances on the paradigm revolution and its importance, significance, and potential solutions, it should be noted that there are variations on each theme within the four stances or postures. The "impoverished" or "method-inadequate" group argue variously among themselves as to whether the problem may be solved by applying the same standards of rigor to qualitative methods, or whether different standards of rigor may be appropriate for different methods (Marshall, 1985; M. L. Smith, 1987). Within the "exclusion" debate, feminists occasionally argue that what is needed are new voices, voices which are given respect and legitimacy, while women scientists argue now for a totally altered conception of science as a socially produced knowledge production function, criticizable not only for its findings, but also for the gender and class interests *reflected* in those findings. The "exception" debate is split on which of the specific axioms of conventional inquiry may need to be "fixed." And the "whole paradigm" congeries of arguments revolves about whether we need to discard all of conventional inquiry in favor of more phenomenological and/or constructivist paradigms or worldviews, or whether we ought to replace logical positivism with postpositivism or, as Donald T. Campbell has suggested, post-postpositivism.

Nevertheless, the four major stances on the paradigm revolution are fairly well represented by the summary arguments presented here. These summaries are balanced and comprehensive enough to capture both the flavor and some of the critical literature entering the debate.

A fair question which might be raised here is why anyone would bother becoming a part of the debate. Besides Cole's reminder that science is less a statement of truth than a running argument, there are more forceful reasons to become informed about the revolution and its surrounding debates. The first important reason is *the question of legitimacy and primacy*. The second reason is that *the revolution is pandemic*, spreading throughout the disciplines (an assertion I shall demonstrate shortly). Scientists, particularly higher education specialists, need to be aware that they are not confronting an anomaly. Rather, they are confronting a challenge which seeks to overthrow the existing theoretical bases of many, or most, academic disciplines.

Legitimacy and Primacy
The legitimacy and primacy problem, referred to earlier by some feminists, is one which permeates all of the academic disciplines. It has transfused the disciplines for the simple reason that primacy and legitimacy influence hiring decisions ("Are you primarily a quantitative or a qualitative researcher?"); promotion and tenure decisions ("Does this candidate's research record reflect *mainstream* research interests, or is this candidate out in left field?"); access to scholarly outlets ("Do we want to publish this 40-page case study, or could we more profitably fit in two 20-page conventional scholarly studies?"); and funding and entrepreneurial opportunities ("Will the Department of Education fund a study which includes an 'emergent design' and interview protocols which are incomplete because the principal investigator is not certain what the salient questions or issues might be?"). Reinharz and Rowles (1988) characterize the primary and legitimacy questions clearly when they aver

> It is certainly not our intention to polarize and exacerbate mistrust between the [quantitative and qualitative] research styles. However, in our view, these myths [that qualitative and quantitative research are mutually exclusive; that qualitative methods are always subjective, whereas quantitative methods are always "uncontaminated" by context and are objective; that qualitative researchers are unconcerned about the issues

of generalizability, validity, and reliability, whereas quantitative researchers are satisfied with superficial insights] are fed by *differences in power*. Since quantification is associated with a reified view of science, which is dominant in the ethos of Western culture, and description is associated with literature, journalism, and the world of everyday interaction, quantifiers have the upper hand in a kind of power struggle in universities and research centers. Some have argued that this epistemological struggle ultimately rests on the fact that science has become gendered; i.e., numbers are defined as hard data, which are equated with reason and masculinity; language is defined as soft data, which are equated with emotion and femininity. . . .

When, as is frequently the case, power resides in the hands of those engaged in quantitative research, people wishing to engage in qualitative scholarship may be denied publication opportunities, research funding, or jobs. By excluding qualitative research, quantitative researchers limit competing viewpoints. As a result, the quantitative paradigm is reinforced, reproduced in succeeding generations of researchers, and further institutionalized. Researchers who use qualitative methods become obliged to present extraordinary justification for their choice. . . . They may also be forced to work within a milieu in which their research is viewed as inferior or peropheral to the core scientific enterprise. (p. 14, emphases added)

It would, of course, end the debate conclusively if one were able to show that power interests operated in such a way as to provide maximum opportunity for qualitative (phenomenological, constructivist, case study) research and researchers, but of course, that is not the case, whence the debate. Primacy of paradigm provides the power base from which exclusion of qualitative researchers and research operates, and legitimation of this power base provides the means for preventing qualitative research from gaining a foothold in the journals and funding channels, and qualitative researchers from having their findings seriously considered in the policy circles which consider and consume research findings. The arguments which Reinharz and Rowles mount are serious, have their basis in realities faced by qualitative researchers, and pose heavy policy and moral dilemmas for institutions of higher education. The debate reflects the hidden question of who will comprise the faculties of the next generation. Many serious scholars—those who are engaged in the debate and those who merely watch it—understand it as a debate about who will be heard in the marketplace of ideas in the future. That is one reason the paradigm revolution will be of interest to historians of education (and historians of science) and to faculties and administrators in higher education in the coming years.

The Spreading Crisis

Another reason to note the crisis in paradigms is its pervasiveness. And its pervasiveness is the real substance of this chapter.

Those who rarely read out of their own academic disciplines will be largely unaware of the extensiveness, fervor, or urgent quality of the paradigm crisis and its surrounding debate. But systematic search of the literature in different disciplines leads one to a sense of unquiet, to an unease regarding proper, appropriate, and accepted methods, methodologies,[5] and paradigms (world-views). The debates take radically different tacks, many of which can be described by the four "stances" described earlier. Some are rather soft calls for incorporating qualitative methods more extensively in research designs, while others are arguments for paradigm replacement that are strident, argumentative, and aggressive. The tone depends on the journal or outlet, the established reputation of the author, and the perspective on where the various disciplines might align themselves on the question of a paradigm shift. But every source reflects the sense that science is somehow fraught with inadequacy as it is currently configured, and that the presumed inadequacy must somehow be addressed.

The remainder of this chapter will address a number of academic disciplines in an effort to help researchers and students alike understand the variety, extent, and complexity of the paradigm debate as well as the pervasiveness of the paradigm revolution.

TROUBLE IN THE LAND

It should be remembered here that the debate takes vastly different forms, depending on what the discipline is and what the problem with conventional, logical positivist inquiry is construed to be. For some researchers, redressing the imbalance between quantitative and qualitative inquiry effectively "mends" what is wrong with conventional science; for others, nothing short of replacing the dominant paradigm with one which has equal legitimacy (or, for some, primacy) will do. But no effort will be made to distinguish between what position various authors adopt. The literature will be used in a primarily monolithic way, underscoring the scope, magnitude, range, and intensity of the debate. Thus, I shall be using different authors as buttresses in the larger argument, while regrettably passing over many of the subtleties and nuances of their individual arguments. Space limitations prevent a full exploration of those individual interests.

The Start of It All: The Hard Sciences in a Nutshell

Strange as it may seem, the paradigm revolution began shortly after the turn of the century in the academic disciplines thought of as most conservative: the hard sciences. Physics, the queen of theoretical sciences, provided the opening salvo. While the keynote speaker for the 1893 international conference of physicists had declared that it was unprofitable for young men to enter the field since there was little left for them to do, within twelve years Einstein's theory of relatively had set physics on an entirely new course. Erwin Schrödinger's "cat," a metaphor for a reality which is "created" rather than "discovered" by the investigator, overturned classical Cartesian formulations of a single "real" reality, ultimately discoverable (able to be converged upon) by scientists. Werner Heisenberg's announcement of what has come to be called the uncertainty or indeterminacy principle made it clear as early as 1927 that deterministic physics was dead. It was impossible to determine both the position and the momentum of a particle at the same time; focusing on one made the other forever indeterminate. Furthermore, the outcome was the result of a conscious choice made by the investigator; it made clear that the results of an inquiry into the motion of a particle was influenced at least as much by the nature of the question asked as by the status of nature. The results of inquiries were created by the interaction of the inquirer and the inquired-into; so much for objectivity. The elimination of reality, determinism, and objectivity as possible aspects of the inquiry process (i.e., of methodology) radically changed the face of physics and moved it into an utterly new realm of discourse and theoretical underpinning.

Physics has moved on, but the argument is made (informally) that the social sciences, seeking the kind of respectability granted the hard sciences (and their exquisite stepchildren, technologies) adopted—rather uncritically—"scientific method" and its attendant focus on logical positivist formulations of the universe. In an effort to appear "scientific," and therefore as rigorous, "hard," and ultimately fundable as physics, chemistry, and genetics, the social sciences took unto themselves a set of methods, criteria for judging rigor, and a closed system of inquiry more suitable to gases, solid particles, and visible matter. Whatever the reasons, the hard sciences were in the process of abandoning many of the axiomatic beliefs which characterized conventional science at a time when the social sciences were busily embracing them.

The "running argument" today in the social sciences, and in education as an applied social science, has to do with whether researchers will acknowledge and give equal time to a worldview which has emerged in the physical sciences, and which is well ahead of the positivism of the 19th century. Should we entertain a worldview of human systems which reflects what we have come to know about the physical world? Or should we remain lodged in a worldview which reflects neither the physical nor the social systems in which we currently move? The question begs to be answered. The social sciences, described by Schwartz and Ogilvy (1979) as "fractured," are nevertheless seeking to make themselves whole and unified again. The next sections will try to show how the arguments are being mounted in a variety of disciplines.

Business Administration and Organizational Theory
A bellwether discipline for understanding the paradigm revolution is business administration and organizational theory. A scant thirty years ago, organizational

theory was scarcely a part of business administration programs. The focus of such courses of study was the creation of a cadre of skilled managers to direct the processes of industry, capital formation, profit, and national and international markets. Slowly and subtly, schools and colleges of business began to change their particular worldviews, moving from theoretical models of administration which focused initially on time and motion studies toward others stressing the interpersonal dynamics of the workplace. The emphasis on the man-machine-task interface eventually gave way to a focus on the motivations, desires, personal and group needs, and interpersonal structures which comprise the "organization"—the human relations focus (Graham, 1980). Attendant on this new concern for the worker and her or his frameworks within the organization came a concern for what kinds of data would prove convincing in studies of human factors in organizational settings. The question was answered with a call for an increase in the use of case studies—of organizational settings, of particularly productive companies and corporations (e.g., Peters and Waterman's work, 1982), or of successful individuals within organizational settings, including women of the corporation (see, for instance, Hennig and Jardim's *The Managerial Woman*, 1978).

One of several journals in the area of administrative theory, the *Administrative Science Quarterly*, has already sponsored two focused issues on qualitative methodology (Van Maanen, 1979a) and ethnography in organizational studies (Jelinek, Smircich, and Hersh, 1983). In the first of those edited and focused issues, such diverse topics as "The Ethnographic Paradigm," "Mixing Qualitative and Quantitative Methods," "Qualitative Research Techniques in Economics," and "On Studying Organizational Cultures" were included. The second volume was equally diverse, suggesting that many actors in schools and colleges of business, in organizational studies, and in administrative science felt they had something urgent and important to say.

An equally powerful article in the *Academy of Management Review* urged upon researchers a serious consideration of qualitative research in organizational theory (Morgan and Smircich, 1980). The authors argue that calls for qualitative rather than quantitative methods in organizational theory reflect "a somewhat crude and oversimplified dichotomization" and fail to reflect careful consideration of concomitant concerns when methods questions are raised. Those concomitant concerns include ontology, assumptions regarding human nature, and epistemology (p. 491).

New terminology, a new discourse of management and administrative science, is making itself heard. "Organizational culture" (implying that organizations have properties which are culturelike, that is, like the units which anthropologists describe as cultures; Frost, et al., 1985), "garbage can" models of organizational decision-making (Cohen, March, and Olsen, 1972), uncertainty and ambiguity (Cohen and March, 1974), "loose coupling" (Weick, 1976, 1985), bounded rationality, superstitious learning (Hedberg, 1981), cognitive mapping (Goodman, 1968), thick description (Geertz, 1973)—all are terms which would have been virtually unheard of, let alone commonly used in the organizational theory literature, a quarter century ago. The new terminology suggests that researchers are "seeing" aspects of organizations and organizational functioning which previously escaped them, or which, because of the strictures dictated by any given worldview, they were prevented from seeing. The words, terms, and phrases of the new organizational discourse reflect the inadequacy of earlier language and metaphors to capture the realities of contemporary organizations. Language such as *chain of command, subordinates, unity of command, authority, line officers, staff officer, tight ship, troops, span of control*, and *standard operating procedures* reflect a worldview steeped in the traditions of bureaucracy (particularly military bureaucracy), ill-suited to today's flexible, flattened, nonhierarchical, highly responsive, egalitarian organizations (Clark, 1985, pp. 48–50). Organizational theorists and administrative scientists are inventing a language and terminology to talk about the organizational characteristics which they are seeing, whether those characteristics have been there all along, or whether they are characteristics of emergent organizational forms which have arisen to compete in today's global economies.

But the current revolution in organizational theory goes far beyond merely calling for the inclusion of qualitative methods. In fact, authors are talking in terminology which would not be at all foreign to Schwartz and Ogilvy. David Hurst (1986) is a good example, although there are clearly others (Mitroff, 1981, 1983; Perrow, 1981, 1986). Hurst (1986) has taken on "strategic management," a model for management and the management process which he says has "dominated . . . North American management thinking" for "the past 35 years" (p. 5). The problem with such a management strategy is that it tends to be sequential, linear, "based heavily upon an objective, rational, systematic assessment of the business and its environment" (p. 5). Its underlying assumptions presume little, if any, environmental change and presume that retrospective knowledge of the state of the organization accurately predicts future knowledge of those states. This, Hurst says, is unlikely. We cannot presume environmental stability (at least not the extent that we need to in order for strategic management to work), and past knowledge of organizational states tells us nothing regarding future organizational states.

Compare that criticism of the dominant management model of the past 35 years with descriptions of the new worldview provided by Schwartz and Ogilvy earlier in this chapter. Past or current states of systems tell us nothing about possible future states. Linear and sequentially ordered interventions reflect linear causal principles but fail to reflect mutual causality. Retrospective knowledge of systems provides us only with possibilities, but never with certainties regarding the shape of the future.

Organizational theorists are talking and writing increasingly as would astronomers, mathematical catastrophe theorists, physicists, chemists, and biologists. Indeterminacy, the inability to predict with precision future states of either organizations or the environment, the inadequacy of linear and sequential decision-making, scanning and planning techniques, complexity, interactivity—all characterize the most contemporary conversations between administrative and organizational theorists.

The material cited here, of course, is only a beginning to the conversation, the running argument, in organizational theory, administrative science, and business administration. But it does represent some of the most widely read literature and should give a sense of the kind of debate which is now abroad. The organizational theorists are not alone, however.

Social Welfare
This applied arena has not been immune to exactly the same kinds of arguments which have characterized the larger debate, particularly in sociology and in education. On the one hand, respected writers in the field have called for a turn away from the "insight" and "feels right" research approach to social work inquiry, and toward the careful use of scientific method (Sheldon, 1978a,b, 1982, 1983, 1984, 1986) in the best positivist tradition. On the other hand, that call has been answered by careful criticism of the limits of positivism in social work research by others (Raynor, 1984, 1985; Paley, 1986; David Smith, 1987; Pieper, 1985, 1987; Heineman (Pieper), 1981). The origination of the debate has apparently been Sheldon's early "advocacy of a strictly 'scientific' approach, using Popperian criteria of falsifiability, riskiness of prediction and so on, to define what is to count as scientific, and therefore which theories should be preferred" (David Smith, 1987, p. 402). The "narrow empiricism and unquestioned positivist assumptions" which have characterized much of earlier social work research, and which have been lately demanded of current inquiry, are rejected on two grounds. First, historians and philosophers of science themselves have "found the assumptions of positivism highly questionable," and second, the experiential base of social work researchers and practitioners leads them to quite valuable insights regarding the structure of their research which are at variance with the strictly Popperian requirements for science (D. Smith, 1987, pp. 403 ff.).

The debate extends far beyond this particular set of journal conversations (Geismar and Wood, 1982; Ruckdeschel and Farris, 1982; Fischer, 1981; Gordon, 1983; Gyarfas, 1983; England, 1986; Karger, 1983). Heineman (1981) and Haworth (1984) both take on the "obsolete scientific imperative" in social work research, but Haworth extends the argument by including the debates regarding single-case-study research design and the question of whether there is any "distinct social work paradigm at all" (p. 343). Heineman, in particular, is critical of the movement in the past thirty years to "declare [social work's] traditional model of research to be insufficiently scientific and [to replace] it with discrete canons of scientific acceptability," especially since "the assumptions underlying these . . . criteria for service models and research *have been abandoned by most philosophers of science*" (Heineman (Pieper), 1981, p. 371, emphasis added). As a part of her criticism, she proffers another, more contemporary model for research in applied social work. That model specifically denies the possibility that "the truthfulness of scientific results can be guaranteed" (p. 287), and instead "concentrate[s] on the practicing scientist as decision maker and problem solver," the purpose of which is to focus science on the "functional and the dynamic rather than [the] normative" (Heineman (Pieper), 1981, p. 387). The end product of such research foci is a reliance on *multiple perspectives*, achieved by

> studying as many aspects of a problem from as many vantage points as possible (by comparing the work of different individuals, focusing on different levels of abstraction of different environment-system boundaries, or employing different theoretical models). (p. 390)

This posture on criteria for science will obviate one persistent problem, she argues: that of having methodology dictate the questions which can be explored, rather than having the interesting questions guide the search for appropriate methodologies. Questions of importance to the social work field could be undertaken for their intrinsic interest rather than for their conformity to elegant research designs which fulfil positivist criteria (pp. 371, 385–391).

Haworth echoes the criticism of unthoughtful adoption of positivist criteria for research. Far from eschewing the intuition and insight which Sheldon (1984) abhors, Haworth (1984) notes that the trend in all of the social sciences has been toward "making the intuitive and implicit more explicit" (p. 351), although the call for more *rigorous* traditional and conventional research would deny that trend. A consequence of heeding the call for a return to more conventional inquiry would be ignoring a central aspect of that process: the problem generated by "the subjective experience of the mind solving problems with some degree of comfort within a set of 'givens,' as if the rules [for science] were external and eternal, rather than *the result of various historical human processes*" (Haworth, 1984, p. 354, emphases added). No, says Haworth, we must look toward a new paradigm, since the social sciences have already committed a grievous error. The social sciences are "where [early positivist] assumptions [were] generally borrowed naively, learned authoritatively, and held tenaciously" (p. 351); it is for these sciences to see the error of such borrowing, and to make the break within themselves. Haworth (1984) repeats Kuhn's assertion that "people doing 'normal science' within an established set of procedures do not take kindly to having their contextual assumptions challenged, and new paradigm thinking must wait for the established opponents to die'' (p. 351).

In ensuing discussions of what must replace the ''obsolete'' scientific paradigm in social work research, Heineman (Pieper) is not alone. Rodwell (1987) also proposes a model for social work assessment: naturalistic inquiry. In criticizing the dominant paradigm of social work assessment, Rodwell contends that many of the problems can be addressed by switching to the more phenomenological and resonant naturalistic inquiry, since

> Including naturalism legitimates other ways of knowing and provides a mechanism for documenting that knowledge. It also provides a different construction of expecta- tions for the profession. . . . It is no longer necessary to determine ''the'' problem and select ''the'' appropriate intervention strategy because problems are multiple just as the appropriate intervention can be one of many. . . . Naturalism allows the acceptance of multiple rationales, conflicting value systems, and separate realities. (p. 243)

Social work and social welfare provide an excellent example of the fourth stance mentioned earlier. The debate in the field and the profession is rarely about methods per se. Rather, the argument has gone directly to the heart of the paradigm revolution and may be viewed as a contest over legitimacy— legitimacy for which model, positivist or phenomenologist, and a critique of the assumptions which guide the former.

Business Communications
It can hardly be fairly said that business communications as a field is undergoing a paradigm revolution. One article was found—but it does point the way to a rethinking of that teaching field in terms of its research capabilities and the interest of faculty in doing research. Essentially, the authors of the single article found (Cochran and Dolan, 1984) call for the inclusion of qualitative methods in the research repertoire of business communications faculty. They note that few faculty actually do research and may have animadversions to the simplistic number- crunching and statistics which appear to characterize ''legitimate'' research, that is, the research which typically appears in the journals. Cochran and Dolan postulate other reasons why business communication teachers do little, if any, research of the sort typically reported in journals. They note that in the social sciences more broadly, scholars ''have become increasingly concerned with the fact that much of the research being done . . . appears to be dominated by a concern for methodology rather than a concern for the means and consequences of research'' (p. 25). This has led to a certain ''restrictiveness of discipline-based research,'' to ''a tendency to support specific and focused research paradigms,'' to the ''fostering of intense but narrow studies of particular and well-defined research topics,'' and to ''a leaning toward methodologies which are far too limited and conventional'' (p. 25). Not unsurprisingly, Cochran and Dolan have

sought guidance in the larger social sciences arena, and they cite the increasingly well-known *Beyond Method: Strategies for Special Research* by Gareth Morgan (1983); their plea is for introducing qualitative methods to the study of business communication. Such a strategy will, they aver, be responsive to at least three concerns: the aversion to statistics held by most instructors of business communications; the rejection of a single, monistic reality, objective and "out there," which is claimed for science; and the indifference to making the subdiscipline of business communication a science, as, say, marketing is rapidly becoming a science (Cochran and Dolan, 1984, p. 26).

The call here is for the incorporation of methods previously ignored, not for a paradigm shift. By implication, one may assume that this is because business communication is thought to be in a preparadigmatic, or aparadigmatic, state as a discipline.

History

As one of the disciplines characterized by many subspecialties, history is more difficult to treat monolithically. What American historians might see as relevant and appropriate to their own specialty, Russian historians who focus on contemporary Stalinism, economic development, or the Christian church in the USSR might find utterly useless or unsuitable. Nevertheless, history is characterized (as a discipline) by a willingness to be reflective about itself, to engage in criticism of the *process* of creating history and of what it means to *write history* (Bloch, 1953; White, 1965; Higham, 1970; Fischer, 1970; Landes and Tilly, 1971; Hexter, 1971). Fischer (1970) spoke of the role of the historian as "someone (anyone) who asks an open-ended question about past events and answers it with *selected facts which are arranged in the form of an explanatory paradigm*" (p. xv, emphases added). The selection process leads one not to "ultimate truth," but rather to one of many possible explanations of things which we know or can use about the past. But we can never know everything. Fischer goes on to say that

> The impossible object is a question for the whole truth—a question which characteristically takes one of three forms. Occasionally, it consists of an attempt to know everything about everything. Sometimes it seeks to learn something about everything. Most often it is a search for everything about something. *None of these purposes is remotely realizable. A historian can only hope to know something about something.* (Ibid., p. 5, emphases added)

If Fischer is to be believed, and if most historians do indeed understand that they can only "know something about something," then that history can be moved toward rejecting pure scientific method in favor of a more interpretive bent should hardly be surprising.

Some signs already indicate that historians intend to talk about the value-centeredness of their discipline. The speech by J. H. Hexter, reported in the *Chronicle* (Winkler, 1986) is but one signal. An early article by Isaiah Berlin (1960) commented on the concept of "scientific history," undergirded by theory generated by social science regarding human behavior. John Higham (1970) spoke of "rival methodologies" and the "schism in American [historical] scholarship," noting the differences between the scientific method in the social sciences and the "humanistic strategy," which he distinguished from the scientific strategy because of its attention to "preserv[ing] amd appreciat[ing] the complexity of experience." Such efforts

> include the use of expressive rather than technically precise language, a greater interest in individual events than in general laws, *a reliance on qualitative rather than quantitative judgment, and a subjective grasp of a totality in preference to a dissection of its parts.* (p. 4, emphases added)

This description of the "humanistic strategy" is a close and careful, if informal, description of naturalistic inquiry, or the phenonmenological paradigm, and its major contrasts with the scientific strategy for knowing. It is utterly appropriate, since Higham notes, too, that there has been a return to the historian as a "moral critic," exactly the same call cited here and earlier in this chapter by Hexter.

Still others have commented on the need for careful consideration of how a "fact" is defined and what use is made of information (Carr, 1962). Others have also taken up the work of T. S. Kuhn on paradigm revolutions, looking for its implications in the doing of history (Hollinger, 1973). Thus, it is not clear whether history is undergoing a paradigm revolution or merely moving to readjust the balance between what some historians would call *scientific history* and *humanistic history.* Clearly, Hexter's call to the American Historical Association this past year is for a redress in returning history to the moral judgments which were once thought to characterize the historical process. Whether the call to historians signals a call to return to more phenomenological approaches, or whether it means that historians needed merely to be reminded, is not clear. But the debate regarding the value-freedom of science has been entered, and historians are concerned about the kind of history they and others have written. Wherever the discipline of history might be, it is clear that some would have the discipline remember its roots, moving away from the scientism which has been the hallmark of 20th-century social science back to a profoundly judgmental posture. The "humanistic strategy" in history has not been abandoned but merely allowed to go dormant under the sway of an emphasis on science in the social sciences.

Theater and Drama

Even scholars of Renaissance drama are quoting Kuhn on the structure of paradigmatic revolutions. There is as yet no call for a paradigm shift; aesthetic fields tend to shift themselves when the dominant paradigm has been explored to its artistic limits. But the fact that aesthetic analysis now proceeds from a Kuhnian perspective (although Kuhn himself believed that aesthetics and science proceeded along different avenues of change, and that his paradigm revolution applied to "the perceptions of scientists but not to those of artists"—Boni, 1982, p. 48) indicates that theater and drama have entered an age of self-conscious thought about aesthetic and structural analysis. Historically situating dramatic analysis by locating criticism within a larger social structure (e.g., the Renaissance and perceptions of man as a free agent in the determination of his own destiny) is a relatively modern phenomenon. If what theater and drama lack is a call for a new paradigm, they are nevertheless conducting dramatic criticism, particularly of historical material, in such a way as to take account of the mind shifts in Western thought. Boni (1982) notes that

> We may, with some confidence, assert a dialectical relationship between artist and paradigm [as we would between scientist and paradigm] in the matter of form and of content. Those whom we do not label "derivative," though they may be painting another *Odalisque* or writing another play exploring human evil, are those who take a form, an idea, to more revealing levels of expression.
>
> Consequently, we begin to see the problems involved with paradigm shifts, the problems artists encounter when they "plunge recklessly into unexplored realms," in Frederick Hartt's terms. . . . [Thus] Renaissance playwrights in England reflected such an attempted shift as they became more concerned with the interior processes of their characters—what we today label as psychological motivation. (pp. 49–51)

So dramatists and playwrights are seen as interacting in a dialectical way with form and content, the product being one of a larger set of aesthetic products which reflect a social, psychological, and moral terrain which characterizes an age. When the terrain is unexplored, as when a playwright breaks new ground in form, content, or human characterization, the field is willing to call that a paradigm shift—although typically in retrospect only (Boni, 1982, pp. 60–63).

It is neither fair nor legitimate to place this field in the midst of a paradigm shift—although critics would no doubt point to the controversy surrounding deconstructionism and would argue that this postmodernist movement represents the best of the paradigm transformation examples. Nevertheless, the intentional usage of Kuhn's work to frame dramatic criticism has to be taken as an indication of the level of awareness of worldview and of the impact of social models on dramatic, artistic, and aesthetic products, of whatever age.

Psychology

Gordon Allport (1955), Willems and Raush (1969), and Lee Cronbach (1975) stand as prophets to the quarrel in psychology. Each has fueled the controversy in some fashion, either by disputing psychology's adamant adherence to the positivist paradigm, by repudiating the strict behaviorism which had taken hold in the post-Freudian era, or by simply reminding the field that there were two, not a single, disciplines of scientific psychology, one of which grew from the positivist tradition, one of which grew from phenomenology. The two disciplines (Cronbach, 1975) or two cultures (Kimble, 1984) are currently competing for legitimacy, although it is strongly argued that they could quite profitably coexist.

Psychology is critical as a discipline since many see the basis for a pedagogy of learning—and therefore for a discipline of education—as originating in psychology, particularly in studies of human cognition, learning, and motivation. Therefore, psychology may hold a key to understanding the position educational researchers finally take on the paradigm issue; whence goes psychology probably goes educational research.

The arguments in this discipline range from those of simply incorporating more qualitative methods, or moving the sites of research out of the laboratory to more natural contexts (Willems and Raush, 1969; Tunnell, 1977; Georgourdi and Rosnow, 1985; Gibbs, 1979), to explanations of what is needed by way of a revolution (Faulconer and Williams, 1985; Bavelas, 1984; Friedlander, 1982; Gergen, 1985; Sampson, 1978). Other courses pursued have included criticism of various aspects of positivism (Faulconer and Williams, 1985), criticism of the field in general (Greenwald, 1980; Paull, 1980; Scarr, 1985), and notes on what a radically expanded image of psychology might include (Packer, 1985; Bakan, 1972; Cronbach, 1975).

At the center of the debate has been the *American Psychologist*, journal of the American Psychological Association and tuning fork for mainstream arguments.[6] Much of the debate has gone on in that channel.[7] But psychologists are not the only persons in the debate. Rom Harré (1987), a philosopher at Oxford, strongly urges that psychology consider its purposes in light of its metaphysical postures and belief systems. Gergen (1985), a psychologist, essentially agrees with Harré in his postulation of new paradigm inquiry but takes issue on the subject of how and in what manner any new paradigm may be warranted as "better" or "preferred" (p. 20) to the old, and on the question of whether or not it is necessary and/or desirable to "retain the empirical warrant for theories of human action" (p. 21). Gergen argues (and I would agree) that "understanding is essentially a hermeneutic or interpretive enterprise [where] objective warrants do not apply" (p. 22). But if the case for a new paradigm in psychology cannot "be secured on empirical grounds, how is new paradigm inquiry to be justified?" (p. 22). Gergen's solution is similar and parallel to Harré's: to treat "theories of human action [as] primarily bodies of socially negotiated discourse" (p. 21), wherein accounts of phenomena which are theoretical are examined by discursive analysis, honoring the rules and conventions of the particular realm of discourse into which one has entered (pp. 21–22). In simple language, a theory becomes a form of discourse which is determined (and located) historically, and discussion of a given theory must take account of the particular rules, conventions, and situation of the theory itself. In obeying the conventions, one can evaluate a given theory (of human action) alongside other bodies of discourse in which one has a vested interest; alongside cultural, social, ethical, and ideological heritages; or alongside our notions of what facilitates action, empowerment, or problem solution (pp. 22–23). Thus, psychology has the rationale for a shift in paradigm from a criticism of the failures of positivism (including "the assumptions of induction, verification-falsification, decontextu-alized theory, meaning, operationism, work-object isomorphism, the criterion of coherence, [and] the cumulative character of science"), and from warrants for how one might achieve validity by subsuming science into a deliberation of social discourse (pp. 21–23).

Psychology is, in some respects, far ahead of other disciplines, in that philosophers have been drawn into the fray and have provided the necessary rationales and criticism from which new paradigm inquiry might be mounted. For this reason, it is possible to consider psychology a bellwether discipline, shifting no faster than any other social science, but with the necessary arguments marshaled and available to support any scholar who wishes to make the shift. Readers should note carefully that psychology, unlike some disciplines, is distinguished by the fourth stance, the call for a complete paradigm shift, rather than simply a call for extension of the repertoire of methods in research.

Economics
Economics was a discipline which remained unassessed by Schwartz and Ogilvy; they found the discipline in "disarray" and declared it incomprehensible for the purposes of charting any kind of shift. But since their work (1979), economics has undergone a subtle change, signaling some larger deliberations for the future. An early piece (Piore, 1979) called for the wider use of qualitative methods in economics research, noting that many questions of interest to economists were routinely un- or underresearched because of the preference for quantitative measures which did not always lend themselves to the questions of interest. The editors' introduction to *Economics and Philosophy* (Vol. 1, Harshman and McPherson, 1985) noted that economics could no longer afford to divorce itself epistemologically from philosophy, simply because theories of economics were reflective of human theories of action. But Kanth (1985) provides perhaps the strongest evidence that economics may be persuaded as the other social sciences are being persuaded. He argues that Ricardian economics, putatively value- and ideology-free, in fact has been finally declared for what it is: an ideological system. Kanth suggests that "both the ship of science and the shallop of ideology were grounded securely in the shoals of the Ricardian sea" (p. 158), leaving the claims of Ricardian science to be "relatively unfiltered and objective" (p. 185)

essentially false. One consequence of such an exploration is to suggest that economics, grounded as it is in the social knowledge production function, operates along premises which are now discredited. This leaves economics ripe for the paradigm picking, and scholars are suggesting that classical economics, rooted in political assumptions which no longer hold, may be ready for renewed thinking about its models (Reich, 1980; Blaug, 1958; Rowthorn, 1974).

Sociology

This discipline does not present a monolithic posture. Sociology, having borrowed its traditions from anthropology, has utilized qualitative methods from its disciplinary infancy. Thus, the call to utilize more quantitative methods may be seen primarily as an argument for redressing the balance between quantitative and qualitative, or, as Bronfenbrenner (1977) has put it, between rigor and relevance. The increasing press for utilizing qualitative methods can be seen in the establishment of new journals (e.g., *Qualitative Sociology*) and in the serious consideration of adapting computer software to the unique problems of analyzing qualitative data bases (Conrad and Reinharz, 1984; Gerson, 1984; Brent, 1984; Weber, 1984). The plethora of new computer programs for qualitative analysis should be evidence enough that qualitative methods are here to stay in the field of sociology. But larger evidence also exists that philosophical considerations of the foundations of science are under attack and serious reflection in this discipline. Two types of evidence may be found.

The first piece of evidence is the rise in power and influence of the neo-Marxists in American sociology. While the neo-Marxists have long had a voice in Europe and particularly in Great Britain, they have had great difficulty in establishing a foothold in academic circles in the U.S. The historical reasons are open for debate (and, for my purposes, are irrelevant), but the situation has changed dramatically in the past 15 years. Faculties are no longer loathe to hire young sociologists of neo-Marxist persuasions, and the situation will, as the neo-Marxists would say, bring about some social reproduction of other young neo-Marxists. These faculty have brought with them a self-consciousness and an awareness of the historical locations of Western science and, concomitantly, social science. While neo-Marxists themselves typically own a realist ontology, nevertheless their criticisms of knowledge as a socially constructed entity have brought increasing awareness to other sociologists who are not themselves neo-Marxists. Along with conventional realist ontologies, however, they have brought with them another "theoretical current," the focus on a theory of collective action (Lash and Urry, 1984). The emphasis on *agency*—collective agency and the power and resources of social classes—has moved some sub-streams of sociology beyond considerations of structure and social class which had been held for nearly 40 years.

The second piece of evidence of a paradigm shift in sociology has been the systematic philosophic deliberation on the conventions of discourse about the science sociologists do (Radnitzky, 1972; Kekes, 1974; Neilsen, 1973; Rosetti, 1976). Heavy reliance on "hard" data (Neilson, 1973), on method (Kekes, 1974), and on value-freedom in social science has led to an impoverishment in which the questions of human values in human sciences have been ignored, twisted, or forgotten. But Radnitzky (1972) warns that all research enterprises ". . . are *embedded in an intellectual milieu*: an 'intellectual climate' and an 'intellectual market.' The *intellectual climate* contains above all world picture hypotheses in the wide sense: philosophical cosmologies (world views) and philosophical anthropologies (images of man . . .). The *Intellectual market* consists of other research enterprises and traditions." (p. 203, emphases in original)

Taking account of such embeddings forces the researcher to make more conscious choices regarding tradition, conventions, paradigm, and intellectual milieus for his or her own research. The presumed ahistoricity of conventional science has been declared nonexistent; social scientists, having tasted of the apple of ideology-tainted social science, cannot go back.

Other authors have referred to the multiparadigmatic nature of sociology, or to the problem of creating a "sociology of sociology" (Friedrichs, 1970); the paradigm revolution is hardly new news in this discipline. Assessing the extent to which the discipline has determined to take the revolution seriously, however, is difficult. Two currents flow against each other: the first from the qualitative methodologists who see understanding *meaning* as the key to understanding human groups, and the second which enjoys the broad grasp of movement by means of demographic, cliometric, and/or quantitative studies. It is quite likely that both groups will continue to exist amicably side by side while philosophically oriented members of the community will disagree regarding whether or not conventional science is sufficiently flawed to be rejected wholesale (Imershein, 1976; Neuhring and Imershein, 1975; Phillips, 1975; Ritzer, 1975).

Other more playful (though no less serious) evidences exist for the disciplinary awareness of the paradigm revolution. As in the case with theater and drama, sociologists are utilizing Kuhn's work to demonstrate metaphorically other arguments they may wish to make. So, for instance, Imershein (1977) uses Kuhn's work to talk about organizational change as paradigm shift, and about organizational activities as analogous to scientific activities (that is, existing within a community which enjoys some common form of discourse). The use and usefulness of Kuhn's work for understanding a wide variety of phenomena has no doubt brought even the most philosophically distant sociologist under its sway, whether or not she or he realizes it.

Sociology is not in theoretic or paradigmatic disarray (a situation which I believe characterizes, for instance, educational research). Since a portion of its tradition has always resided in phenomenology, sociology has never been assaulted by the uniform and strident demand for a shift from strictly conventional positivist science. But the discipline will never again do what it has traditionally done in an unselfconscious manner; the Marxists and critics of positivist science have seen to that.

Occupational Therapy

A cluster of the medical professions are undergoing self-scrutiny regarding what methods and methodologies are consonant with their professional philosophies. Occupational therapy is one; nursing is another. Each of these professional programs grew out of, and adopted, the medical model of research, which has typically utilized scientific method (not without some success) to the exclusion of other models of research. Having been associated with medicine and allied health fields for decades, occupational therapists find it difficult to dissociate themselves from the medical model. The medical model has characteristics which bring it into sharp contrast with the emergent paradigm model for research. The table of contrasts (Table 2) should give the reader some sense of the kinds of contrasts which are faced both by occupational therapists and by nurses in the professional discharge of their duties. The result of the discrepancy between what the medical model demands and what the profession believes is high-quality professional service has brought about several calls for reformulation of the research role (Christiansen, 1981, 1986, 1987; Yerxa, 1981, 1984; Schwartzberg, 1978).

Rogers (1982), on whose work the table is based, has described the conflict between models for research and practice as bringing disorder to the field of occupational therapy. The response has been both additional qualitative and ethnographic studies in the field (Kielhofner, 1981) and calls for redressing the problem perceived (Gilfoyle and Christiansen 1987; Hasselkus, 1987; Kielhofner, 1981; Ottenbacher, 1981, 1985; Schmik, 1981). In addition, at least two national conferences have been held at which the topical theme has been qualitative or naturalistic research. Invitations to guest speakers and conference participants have included researchers noted for their qualitative expertise.

Occupational therapy as a discipline and profession has recognized that it needs to bring its world-as-experienced into line with the world-as-researched and is making moves to accomplish that end. It is a discipline which should undergo its final paradigm revolution soon; the generation in the field now appears to understand the limitations and failures of the medical model, especially with respect to holism, and will move to change research paradigms yet within this generation.

TABLE 2. Contrasts Between the Medical Model and the Occupational Therapy Model

Comparison item	Medical model	OT model
Mind-body concept	Dualistic.	Monistic (unity).
Health	Passive; absence of disease.	Active; *meaningful* participation and productivity.
Standards	Minimal (no disease).	Optimal (competence).
Disorder	Disease; structural or functional abnormalities—a discrete entity.	Disruptions/dysfunctions in performance; a multifaceted entity.
Causes	Unitary; exposure to pathogens; genetic abnormalities.	Multiple mutually interacting factors, including medical but adding cultural deprivation, aging, inappropriate socialization, absence of purpose.
Diagnosis	Objective, esp. laboratory procedures; labeling that targets "right" treatment.	Combined objective and subjective procedures at holistic level; no singular labeling.
Professional posture	Focus on disease and needed treatment; patient freed of accountability.	Take responsibility for whole person; patient shares accountability.
Treatment	Drugs or surgery aimed at restoration.	Learning aimed at promoting optimal performance.
Eligibility for services	Sick.	Sick and attenuated.
Implications for the doing of research	Use of conventional and highly resonant paradigm.	Move to new or emergent-paradigm inquiry resonant with the above.

Source: Constructed by Egon G. Guba, April 1987, but stimulated by Rogers (1982).

Nursing

Like occupational therapy, nursing as both a profession and an academic discipline is in crisis. A part of that crisis has to do with the larger issues of whether nurses are handmaidens to the healing process or full-fledged members of the medical team. That battle is not likely to be won decisively at any time soon and, in any event, is not the proper domain of this chapter.

What is an appropriate domain, however, is the extent to which nursing should continue to do research with a model which is now believed to be antithetical to whole-person therapies. To return to Table 2, the medical model has embodied some of the same assumptions which have forced the call for rejection from other disciplines. The mind-body problem, for instance, is viewed dualistically, as necessitated by the Cartesian formulation. Health is considered to be the absence of disease, while in the new occupational therapy model (a model which could equally well be said to apply to new conceptions of nursing) health is not a passive state, but rather an active one, marked by meaningful participation and productivity. Health is defined as wellness, not as the absence of disease. Disorders in the medical model are either disease or structural or functional abnormalities in the body. In the occupational therapy model, disorder is rather more broad, encompassing not only disease, but also disruptions or dysfunctions in performance. Disorder is not a unitary entity; it is a multifaceted one. The medical model prescribes a mode of diagnosis which is "objective," even in psychiatry. The right procedure is typically determined by a complex battery of laboratory and X-ray tests; psychosomatic relationships are rarely explored, even by persons trained to take careful medical histories. The OT model combines both objective and subjective procedures at a holistic level and generally refuses singular labeling of cause and effect. The professional posture of the medical model has, in the past, focused on diagnosis and needed treatment, largely with the physician assuming responsibility for both, and the patient being freed of accountability so long as she or he "did as the doctor ordered." The emerging occupational-therapy (nursing, physical-therapy, family-practice, and allied-health) model demands a responsiblity for the whole person, while the patient shares accountability with the professional for the healing process. Treatment modalities in allopathic medicine usually are combinations of drugs, surgery, and other physical interventions (such as X rays, traction, and the like) or prescribed changes in lifestyle (smoking cessation, diet, exercise, or rehabilitative programs). The treatment of choice with occupational therapy is learning aimed at promoting optimal performance, whether physical or psychological. The implications for research within the medical model are the use of the conventional and highly resonant scientific model, but under the emerging occupational therapy (and other health-sciences) model, the implications for research are much more consonant with new-paradigm research and the paradigm revolution. Holism prevails, the connection between mind and body is honored, and singular or linear causality for dysfunction is eschewed in favor of multiple considerations of the dysfunction problem.

The importance of Table 2 is that it points out in stark contrast where medical science has been and where the allied health sciences have begun to take exception. With respect to exceptions, nursing may be farther along than even occupational therapy. Nurses have already labeled the growing controversy the "qualitative-quantitative debate" (Duffy, 1985) and are suggesting a move toward more phenomenological approaches (Oiler, 1982). Nursing researchers know that the medical model they have inherited goes against the grain of what nurses believe they are about (Munhall, 1982), and they have entered the philosophical fray, asking whether how one comes to know might not be affected by how one asks the question (Carper, 1978). Without intervention from other fields, nurses have begun to explore ethnographic and qualitative methods (Burns and Greene, 1987; Germain, 1986; Sandelowski, 1986; Robertson and Boyle, 1984; Frank, 1986; Stevens, 1984) and have begun to question why nursing research has persisted for so long in a model which flies in the face of professional experience (Diekelmann, 1986; Downs, 1983; Swanson and Chenitz, 1982; Windsor, 1987).

But a call in the journals is not enough. And indeed, the nurse researchers now have an excellent text (Leininger, 1985), should program directors and/or faculty decide they wish to teach qualitative research methods in nursing research programs. There are rumored to be other texts either in press or in progress, and the field should shortly have its own methodological literature, targeted by a careful choice of research examples to the nursing population (although undoubtedly other health fields would find them equally useful). Nursing is, as a result, slightly ahead of other fields in the health cluster because of the direction and sophistication of the debate. When its members can ask whether nursing philosophy and nursing research are in apposition or in opposition (Munhall, 1982), the field has entered into self-examination worthy of the best philosophy department.

Occupational therapy and nursing, however, are not the only fields in this arena to examine naturalistic or phenomenological inquiry and to wonder about the question of fit.

Medicine and Family Practice
A single voice has been heard in medicine thus far, from family practice. Anton Kuzel, M.D., found *Naturalistic Inquiry* (Lincoln and Guba, 1985) somewhere in the course of his master's work in family practice and wrote a short but exceptionally well-argued master's thesis on the appropriateness of such inquiry to family practice in medicine (1985). Rather more readily available is Kuzel's journal article (1986) based on his thesis research, which attempts to show family practice doctors how and why the emergent paradigm exhibits greater "fit" with family practice than does the traditional medical model. Kuzel's voice may seem small at the moment, but when melded with the voices from occupational therapy, nursing, and other allied health fields, and when considered alongside

the contemporary press for greater holism in patient treatment, for examination of psychological motivations for physical well-being, and for understanding where the motivations come for active lifestyles versus inactive ones, Kuzel's voice may gain stature and resonance. To put it more simply, Kuzel may be part of a larger trend within medicine and health. The person who doubts that this is the case ought simply to visit a comprehensive newsstand and look over the vast number of periodicals and magazines devoted to increasing and maintaining health, fitness, and wellness. The psychological landscape of medicine has changed dramatically, and what was a mere 20 years ago considered ''counter-culture,'' especially with respect to diet and exercise, is now considered mainstream.

Women's Studies

Women's studies and feminist criticism have together provided the strongest and fiercest, and perhaps the most powerfully argued, critique of positivism and its social and political (not to mention scientific) ramifications. As mentioned earlier, the criticism of scientists who looked at the sex, gender, and biological research sought first to correct the most glaring errors about women (Bleier, 1986). But ongoing scrutiny of the research on women uncovered a larger problem: the ''gendered'' nature of research and the social location of science as a knowledge production activity which had a hidden impact on the way in which findings were structured. Women scientists and philosophers of science, at first moved to correct the more obnoxious and obviously prejudicial findings, were at last moved to comment on the nature of the scientific enterprise itself. Calling it bound with the preoccupations of the gender and class which produced the research (white, middle-class, male), women scientists and feminists were appalled at the realization that science's impact on women was not socially neutral but operated, they asserted, to reinforce class and status barriers which maintained second-class status for women. The implication of this assertion for the scientific world has not yet been felt fully, but it is likely that it will be shortly.

Only a scholar who reads in this literature as a professional commitment could possibly keep track of the major themes and voices. Unlike other fields, where occasionally only a faint voice may be heard, there is a virtual cacophony in women's studies, feminist scholarship, and feminist criticism of science (DuBois, et al., 1987; Farnham, 1987; Ferguson, 1984; Gilbert and Mulkay, 1984; Gilligan, 1982; Harding, 1986; Harding and Hintikka, 1983; Harding and O'Barr, 1987; Keller, 1985; Knorr-Cetina, 1981; Knorr-Cetina and Mulkay, 1983; Langland and Gove, 1981; Mahoney, 1976; Rossiter, 1982).

Feminists have taken on science not only as a social activity, but also on issues of ecology and the environment (Cheney, 1987; Merchant, 1982); race (Ladner,

1987; Thomas and Alderfer, 1989); ethics (Gilligan, 1982; Belenky et al., 1986; Freeman, 1989; Deetz, 1985); and organizational and administrative studies (Alvesson, 1984; Calas and Smircich, 1987; Cooper and Barrett, 1984; Denhardt, 1981; Donelson, Van Sell, and Goehle, 1985; Ferguson, 1984; Garland and Dwyer, 1988; Gross and Averill, 1983; Martin, 1987; Scott and Hart, 1979; Smircich and Calas, 1987). And it would be grossly unfair to fail to mention that there is also an extensive literature on women and culture (see, for instance, the journal *Signs*) and significant feminist scholarship on women and literature (Weedon, 1987; Showalter, 1977; Diamond and Edwards, 1977), women and psychology, women and history (that is, women *in* history, as well as women and the *writing* of history; see, for instance, Kolodny, 1984), and women writing about women and postmodernism (Flax, 1987), poststructuralism (Weedon, 1987), and postsecondary education (Rossiter, 1982; Andersen, 1987; Bernstein, 1988; DuBois et al., 1987; Langland and Gove, 1981; Noe, 1988; Abramson, 1975).

But the real issue for the purposes of this work is the criticism by women of science, of the scientific paradigm, and of the political, structural, and equity ramifications that paradigm has on women, society, and the structure of knowledge. And however women scientists, philosophers, and feminist scholars have got there, whether directly or circuitously, and although their research is occasionally contradictory and sometimes internally cantankerous, nevertheless, the combined voices speak with greater and greater clarity: the scientific paradigm cannot be "fixed." There is too much wrong with it, the worst of which is that it supports second-class citizenship for women and probably for racial and ethnic minorities as well. Easlea (1986) noted the bias of science toward the masculine when he wrote that

of long standing is the belief that successful practicioners of scientific method must ruthlessly suppress all extraneous factors, particularly intrusions of an emotional kind, and so allow themselves to be guided by logic and facts alone in order to arrive at their (assumed) goal of genuine knowledge and truth about nature. . . . Such "hard, ruthless analysis of reality" exemplified by suppression of all emotion, speculation and wishful thinking undoubtedly constitutes for many people the hallmark of scientific inquiry and thus greatly contributes to science's overall masculine image. (p. 136)

But the presumed masculinity of science is not the only factor contributing to the pervasiveness of the masculine domination of science as a social enterprise.

There is also the problem of language, which shapes thinking about the realm of the scientist: nature. And the language and imagery have been, typically, feminine. So, for instance, we have scientists trying to grapple with *Mother Nature*, in an attempt to wrest *her* secrets from her; nature "has hidden her secrets in an almost impregnable stronghold" (Easlea, 1986, p. 140); and "science need never encounter an absolute check in its attempt to penetrate more deeply into the secrets of nature'' (Rescher, cited in Easlea, 1986, p. 141). The imagery of force, of penetration, of aggressive sexual motivation is not lost on women. Women have sensed, and probably correctly, a profound misogyny in the conquest and force metaphors and images of male-dominated science. Easlea is not certain the problem will go away:

> it is conceivable that a widespread use of (non-loving) sexual imagery, *particularly aggressive sexual imagery*, is symptomatic of underlying and possibly serious problems that will not conveniently disappear together with a determination among scientists to eliminate the use of sexual imagery from their rhetoric, lectures, popular articles and books. For not only have the feminists compellingly demonstrated that Western culture has consistently been misogynist and sometimes virulently so but they continue to make clear that it also *remains* profoundly misogynist. (p. 141, emphasis in original)

So it is that women have much to fear from science on some level, not simply for the sake of findings which may support prejudicial public policies, but also for the more subtle reason that the very language and imagery of science support rigid masculine stereotypes alongside potent images of nature as a woman on whom nothing short of brute force and mastery will work.

Put into close proximity the axioms of conventional inquiry, with their demand for a focus on reality (truth) to the exclusion of human concern, the demand for the objectification of the research object (Keller, 1983a), and the permitted posture of value-freedom, and you have a system which cannot but be rejected. Women scientists have led the running argument to date, but men are joining in an unanticipated self-criticism. A prophet in the revolution might hazard a guess that the revolution in paradigms will ultimately occur at the confluence of criticism of science and feminist scholarship.

A further word about women's studies, feminist scholarship, and women's critiques of science is in order here. I make no claim to be completely conversant with this literature. I remain certain that many fine pieces—and therefore, many careful arguments—have been missed. But the work which has been reviewed remains substantial enough to be compelling in its accuracy, its quality, its documentation and scholarship, and its extraordinary clarity. It is to be hoped that the women who have provided such criticism will remain to see the change it can make, for it is powerful, reflective, and caring.

TROUBLE IN THE LAND: EDUCATION

Education is a particular problem in the review process, since it is comprised of many subdisciplines and specialties. For those who wish to see what exists in their particular field to which they might refer, I have broken this portion of the review into some of the subspecialties which characterize, typically, professional schools of education. It is clear that other disciplines also see themselves as composed of specialties, but those are academic disciplines where only other specialists should be so bold as to subdivide the literature. Since, however, my early training was in higher education, and since I reside in a professional school of education, I have chosen to treat this field in a more specialized way.

Education as a Broad Field

There is a substantial body of literature which is not subdiscipline-specific. It cuts across education to address that more general group, the community of educational researchers. Within this body of literature, the form and scope of the questions addressed depend more on the particular interests of the writer and the outlet she or he has chosen. The vast majority of the work at this level concerns itself with the topic of the qualitative-quantitative distinction and thus may be said to address the *methods* issue. Methods is certainly a large part of the debate, but as I noted earlier, addressing the question of methods misses the mark, since methods may be used in the service of any paradigm for disciplined inquiry. Within the methods debate, however, the work is not insubstantial (Eisner, 1981, 1988; Evertson and Greene, 1986; Hosie, 1986; Smith and Heshusius, 1986; Weingartner, 1982; Miles and Huberman, 1984; Miles, 1984).

Others have addressed questions of practice and the applied nature of education with respect to whether educational research can be termed scientific (Carr, 1983). Still others have tackled the paradigm revolution directly, with respect either to various axioms (Phillips, 1985) or to some other avenue (Tuthill and Ashton, 1983; Walberg, Schiller, and Haertel, 1979) such as the whole-paradigm argument, including a call for postpositivism (Garrison, 1986). And these citations do not begin to exhaust the literature. They merely suggest the scope and the outlets in which additional indications of a debate might be found. Certainly one of the most frequent publishers of such articles (whatever their cast, for or against, as one might say) has been the *Educational Researcher*, which, as the journal of the American Educational Research Association, has the potential of reaching as many in the research community as any of the more specialized journals. More specialized subdisciplines, however, have created a virtual compendium of remarks on the paradigm revolution.

Counseling and Guidance

This field has begun to experience some of the problems cited previously with allied health disciplines: the experience of its practice is contrary to the demands of the scientific paradigm for research. As a result, researchers in this field want to talk about their models for research. Following Tranel's early article (1981), M. L. Smith (1981) commented on the utility of naturalistic research for the *Personnel and Guidance Journal*. In 1985, a special issue of the *Journal of*

Counseling and Development focused on paradigm shifts as a way of opening discussion within the discipline.

Curriculum

Padgam's (1983) analysis of the "holographic paradigm" and postcritical reconceptualist curriculum theory marks one of the earliest links to the world of emergent paradigms in the hard sciences. The use of the holograph as a paradigm or model reflects contemporary formulations of phenomena in physics, and its deliberate usage with postcritical reconceptualist theory in curriculum probably signals a major attempt at synthesis and appropriation. A second article (Dillon, 1985) takes up the question of appropriate methods and solutions in curriculum inquiry; one suggestion is that an increasing use of qualitative methods would be appropriate.

Adult Education

Only one piece (Rockhill, 1982) could be found in adult education. Its focus was on the potential of qualitative methods for exploring participation in adult education. It is difficult to know what impact a single article might make, but the article is another piece of evidence in the substantiating process.

Art Education

Like adult education, the evidence here is slim, although it might be argued that the substantial work done by Elliot Eisner, himself an art educationist, is testimony enough (although I have not reviewed it here). Nevertheless, Ettinger (1987) creates a taxonomy of styles of on-site descriptive research, a support for the method's adherents, while Brooks (1982) argues for the use of interpretation theory in art education. And Pearse (1983) has taken on the question of paradigms appropriate for art education, arguing that the literature in education more broadly suggests we ought to look at analyzing art education in terms of paradigm building, seeking new ways of viewing the substance of the discipline, and exploring alternatives for considering the aesthetic dimensions of art education. The framework which Pearse suggests is borrowed from Jürgen Habermas (who in turn borrowed from the history of philosophy). The three "orientations" are called the "empirical-analytic" orientation (technical knowing), the "interpretive-hermeneutic orientation" (situational knowing) and the "critical-theoretic" orientation (critical knowing) (Pearse, 1983, p. 159). The point of this argument is that art education has been dominated by a single paradigm (science, or technical knowing) for too long and must incorporate other ways of knowing if it is to comprehend the processes embedded in education about art. Pearse asks, "Who then are the art educational architects of critical theorists in the classroom? They are the teachers who see learning as under-standing and understanding as self-reflection leading to critical 'action, leading to action''' (p. 162). His conclusion is that for art education to become increasingly sophisticated, the world has to be viewed in multiple-perspective frames, each of which contributes something to the set of larger understandings with which we confront the world as aesthetic beings (Aoki, 1978a,b; Beittel, 1973, 1978; Lanier, 1977; Marantz, 1982; Zurmuehlen, 1980).

English Education

A central focus in English education has not been on paradigm, but rather on methods, specifically ethnography as one of the qualitative methods/processes available for studying contexts. Each of four separate sources (Chorney, 1984; Judy, 1984; Kantor, Kirby, and Goetz, 1981; O'Donnel, 1983) referred to the value and utility of ethnographic methods, either in English education broadly, or in research on the teaching of writing and writing skills. Ethnographic studies, particularly as they focus on the context of English education, are seen to be particularly useful; they allow researchers to situate understanding about the acquisition of writing skills (and other English language tools) in contexts, rather than divorcing that understanding from the place in which the skill is acquired and sharpened.

Some of the most interesting work has appeared in *College English*, a journal for teachers and professors of English writing and literature at the college level. That body of work, small as yet but certain to grow voluminous before the end of 1989, has commenced to inspect the new theories of literature criticism. In the early course of that writing, authors attempted to introduce new concepts, particularly those of Barthes, Derrida, and others, to English teachers (Leitch, 1977; Fischer, 1979). Later work has clearly gone on to explore the deconstruc-tionists' and critical theorists' impact on English teaching and literary criticism, some of it quite humorously (Bell, 1981). There is an extensive literature in this highly focused field, although it is ancillary to this piece, since it deals quite specifically with literature. It is important simply to note that literary criticism and the teaching of college English are being affected profoundly by critical traditions such as hermeneutics, critical theory, and deconstructionism. It is too soon to make a judgment regarding what the specific revolution in English education will look like, but since it is drawing from the anthropological field a focus on qualitative methods, from the French concerns about deconstruction-ism, and from the Marxists and critical theorists and concern for that impact upon English, it seems reasonably safe to say that some form of revolution is afoot.

No doubt there are other studies, as yet unfound, which support these references, and which report studies undertaken ethnographically in English education. That this author did not find them does not mean that others, whose substantive interests are in the area of English education, would not find them readily, either to inquire into what has been done, or to examine as models for their own case studies.

Reading

The status of reading research is unclear from a search in the literature. Jerome Harste, who himself has been interested in naturalistic inquiry and new-paradigm research, has provided the reading research community with a "portrait of a new paradigm" which he commends to their attention (1985). In this piece, he explores ways in which moving to a new paradigm can strengthen what is already known about reading and reading processes, and he discusses what questions and domains of knowledge might still be profitably explored by switching to another paradigm for reading research. It remains to be seen whether the research community will heed his call.

Instructional Systems Technology

The revolution is here apparent in all its guises and forms. Some researchers call for the increased use of qualitative methods in performance technology (Jacobs, 1985). Others argue that alternative paradigms (from the scientific, or conventional) might be profitable for the discipline (Driscoll, 1984), and some deplore the tenor of the debate which has cast some researchers as "good guys" and others as "bad guys" (Cunningham, 1986). But others have discussed the paradigm shift in exactly those terms and have attempted to understand the issues of paradigm, method, methodology, culture, and context as they interact to shape research (Bhola, 1987), and to propose the naturalistic paradigm as the paradigm of choice when attempting to understand reality construction and individual interpretation (Koetting, 1984).

Some of the earliest work of Guba (1982) and Guba and Lincoln (1982) appeared in the *Educational Communications and Technology Journal*. Contrary to one wag's witty assessment that Lincoln and Guba could find no other outlets, this occurred because the then-editor of the *ECTJ* became deeply interested in the perplexing problem of how to assess the qualitative (or naturalistic) case studies which were coming to him for publication. He organized a small conference of journal editors to discuss issues of trustworthiness (the naturalistic equivalent of scientific rigor) in naturalistic case studies, and he published the first paper on trustworthiness criteria in his own journal. After that, upon hearing that Lincoln and Guba were revising their system of naturalistic inquiry, he asked for first publication rights on that article also. The intense interest of this field in new-paradigm inquiry bespeaks a part in the revolution, even though the citations here do not look as "dense" as they do in other fields. A prognosis for instructional systems technology is a major rethinking of the disciplinary and theoretical bases which drive the field currently.

Science Education

Science education is also borrowing heavily from the social sciences, weighing the evidence from both sociologists and evaluators to decide whether what those two groups see as profitable might well be adapted to science teaching and research on science teaching. Welch (1983) explored the uses of both the conventional (scientific) and the naturalistic (emergent) paradigms, concluding that there were questions which might be profitably explored under each. Spector (1984) concluded that there exists a "crisis" in science education. That crisis, she contends, might usefully be addressed by generating grounded theory from data-analytic frameworks developed utilizing qualitative methods (pp. 462–464). M. L. Smith (1982) argues convincingly that naturalistic methods lend benefits to research in science education. It is not clear from the latter, however, whether what is meant is a switch in paradigm (worldview) or merely a switch in methods (data collection and analytic techniques) which are more qualitative. Nevertheless, the field is beginning to talk about methods and about paradigms, and the major journal in the discipline has been publishing such articles and their questions for several years.

Special Education

This field may be temperately described as in turmoil. Stainback and Stainback (1984a,b, 1985) have provided some of the more thoughtful discussions available in special education on the qualitative-quantitative debate, although others have been a part of the dialogue.

When doubters of whether there is a revolution in the offing ask whether or not there is any evidence, perhaps the most useful and exemplary case is that of *Special Education in Rural America* (Skrtic, Guba, and Knowlton, 1985), an NIE-funded, multiyear study of interorganizational special education programming in rural areas (final technical report and five case studies). In this-two-and-a-half-year study, five sites were extensively studied (representing five separate geographic regions of the U.S.), and policy recommendations were formulated which attempted to take into account the context and special problems of rural areas in delivering special education services to widely dispersed students with many different handicaps. The real strength of this three-volume set is its ability to make clear to the reader why and under what circumstances policy recommendations have been derived. In short, the contexts have been explored for their particular implications for service delivery. Policy is derived from the *interaction* of federal regulation, local (rural) districts, intermediate education agencies responsible for coordinating the services, and individual parents and teachers. The special problems faced by rural districts in complying with the letter of the law are explored, along with suggestions for revisions of requirements grounded in the extraordinary circumstances of rural life.

There are no doubt other equally compelling case studies in the literature, either available through the ERIC system or available from individual researchers, but this particular set of journal articles and technical report from a funded study should serve as an introduction to subtle changes in the field of special education.

Vocational Education

Vocational education, like adult education, is a small subdiscipline, and the resources located for this specialty were only two in number. Jax (1984) probed the use of interpretive science in vocational education research, and Larkin and Cobb (1984) proposed the usefulness of qualitative methods for doing the same. If these two articles represent the universe of new-paradigm literature (and they likely do not), then it would be fair to characterize this field as focusing initially on the methods stance in the paradigm debate. It is more likely the case that other pieces confront the paradigm issue more directly, although such evidence was not located.

Teaching and Learning: Teacher Education

Research on teachers, teaching and learning, and teacher education is simply too voluminous for anyone but a teacher educator to comment upon. And where would one put the larger issues of "schooling" currently being debated? Under teaching and learning, or under philosophy of education? In a separate section called *schooling*? I have chosen to deal with teacher education in a very narrow sense, that is, by defining it as that body of work which concerns itself most directly with pedagogical issues in teaching teachers; with problems in teacher training; with teaching and learning as practice and theory; and with teaching as the central concept in a professional school of education. It will be apparent, however, to virtually anyone reading this piece that significant portions of research, new and emerging traditions, and transformative thinkers and writers have been omitted from the ongoing discussion. And this is an arbitrary decision. That the works of Dilthy, Freire, Habermas, the critical theorists, and the neo-Marxists should be disregarded is probably heresy. But those writers and thinkers deserve other treatment, as extended at this chapter has been, that deals with the significance and extensiveness of the reaction to their work. The original intent and purpose of this work has been to demonstrate that many disciplines are talking about their theoretical and methodological models, not to explore every instance of it. So omissions which deserve their own compendium have been excluded. Thus, my initial entries here will be limited, numerically and intellectually, to works which are significant, but somewhat more precisely bound than larger questions (such as the processes of schooling). With these caveats in mind, elisions can be ignored temporarily, if not forgotten.

Easley (1982) has contended that social-cognitive mechanisms in teachers are critical in helping researchers understand what the problems of teachers might be. One way to extend our knowledge of such mechanisms is the use of naturalistic case studies, which serve to illuminate meanings, especially those connected to social-cognitive processes. Green (1983) and Evertson and Green (1986) have examined linguistic perspectives on teaching-learning processes and qualitative methods in classroom observation and research. Erickson (1986) has provided some of the clearest and most compelling rationales for using qualitative methods in research on teaching in the entire discipline.

But the debate does not stop there. Others have joined the "running argument." Some have joined the discussion on methods, more precisely explaining what can be problems with ethnography, including Overholt (1980). More than one has suggested that ethnographic research might be useful in the educational policy process (Rist, 1981; Lincoln and Guba, 1986b), and one has suggested that ethnography ought to be "an adventure in interpretive research" (Duignan, 1981). At least one other set of researchers has moved to a global level and has attempted to take on the implications of a shift in the dominant social paradigm for education and teacher education (Bright, Simula, and Smaby, 1984). The latter reference suggests that the "dominant social paradigm of the United States . . . is changing from one that requires social institutions to seek and develop human resources to maintain a position of competitive dominance to an emerging view of world interdependence" (Bright et al., 1984, abstract). The implications for teacher education are that educational processes need to be restructured so that students are taught what it means to live in such a world. Hegemony would give way to interdependence, but not without having citizens prepared to live in such a world (p. 14); the only way to prepare for such a world is to prepare teachers to prepare students to think about the possibility of its existence. That this last work should have been an address at the 1984 annual meeting of the American Association of Colleges of Teacher Education is not surprising; it suggests that already individuals are thinking about the impact of new modes of thinking on the training of teachers and on teaching and learning.

Educational Evaluation

It is with trepidation that this particular summary is undertaken, since much of the encouragement for a paradigm shift in this field has come from the author and her colleague-husband, Egon Guba (Guba, 1978, 1987; Guba and Lincoln, 1986, 1989). But while we have called for a paradigm shift and have attempted to devise a coherent and integrated set of axioms which might guide this form of inquiry, others have engaged the battle in other ways.

So, for instance, some have called for the addition of qualitative methods in educational evaluation activities (see, for instance, the work of Michael Q. Patton, 1980, 1981, 1982, of Cook and Reichardt 1979, of Goetz and LeCompte, 1984, and Miles and Huberman, 1984, and Miles, 1984, among others cited in this chapter). Others have taken up the problem of ensuring that case studies (the usual products of ethnographic, naturalistic, or phenomenological inquiries) met certain minimal requirements for rigor, trustworthiness and authenticity (Stake, 1978; Smircich, 1986; Lincoln, 1986a; Smith and Kleine, 1986; Guba, 1982; Lincoln and Guba, 1986a).

In general, the evaluation community falls into two camps within the paradigm debate. Of the two "central themes," there is evaluation of the first sort, which "treats naturalistic evaluation as a collection of usually qualitative techniques" and evaluation as a "new way of constructing the world, a wholly different paradigm" (Guba, 1987, p. 40). Two inferences may be drawn from knowing about the evaluation literature and its approach. First, among the stances which might be taken, there are virtually no adherents to the stance which declares that various axioms of scientific inquiry might need adjustment. The stance of positivist paradigm adherents is that it does not need adjustment on axiomatic bases; rather it could profit from the inclusion of some qualitative methods in order to provide rich and thick descriptions of natural settings. Others simply call for a radical paradigm shift.

Whatever the position various practitioners and theorists in educational evaluation take, it is quite clear that this subdiscipline of education (and of the social sciences more broadly, for that matter) is in a state of foment and open revolt. That there is a revolution in progress in evaluation cannot be denied.

Educational Administration

This particular arena is an important one, if for not other reason than the staggering numbers of master's and doctoral degrees awarded in any given year. That this field is in disarray is somewhat harder to demonstrate, simply because the methodological literature has not kept pace with the case studies! Fewer researchers write about the fundamental philosophy of their work than actually produce anthropological, phenomenological, naturalistic, or qualitatively oriented research studies in this area. The work of many educational anthropologists bespeaks a long, if quiet, tradition in educational administration. The work of Donald Willower (1981) in trying to sort out philosophical, epistemological, and ethical questions for the field was pivotal. Less well-known, British neo-Marxist David Reynolds (1980–1981) has been extremely articulate in criticizing the naturalistic paradigm from the perspective of Marxist theory. Helen Sungaila's

(1979) plea for paradigmatic ecumenism asks that we preserve all the paradigms for knowledge production, simply because they contribute in their contradictions to a critical dialectic regarding what knowledge is and what kinds of knowledge we might value. Her claim is that "phenomenological inquiry, while being systematic, rigorous and empirical, is not a scientific but rather *a philosophical activity*, which is basically concerned with the *pre-theoretical* understanding we have of our own world" (pp. 87–88, first emphasis added, second emphasis in original).

Thus, the discussion about paradigm does go on, although some have entered the fray mainly in the form of providing qualitative studies in education (some of which are phenomenological and some of which are positivist in orientation). But those who have chosen to engage in discussion regarding paradigms have done so at an extremely sophisticated level (Marshall, 1985), and the level of the discussion reflects some of the most articulate work in education.

Health, Physical Education, and Recreation

Two articles here point to the paradigm problem in this field. Harris (1981, 1983) calls for a "broadening of horizons" in physical education research, incorporating interpretive culture research and hermeneutic method and process in order to broaden understandings of the field, and in order to comprehend the culture in which physical education takes place: the sites, the individuals and the culture(s) of physical educators and their learners.

Higher Education

Little has been said on the paradigm revolution in theh subdiscipline of higher education, although one might argue that construing the field broadly, much has been said, especially on the previous pages. If we look, for instance, at history, the dialogues in that discipline can inform the dialogues in the history of higher education. If we look at the running debate in sociology or the social sciences broadly, directions which the social sciences are taking may guide higher education's research tomorrow. Conversations in the arts will impinge on art and music education, while developments not only in knowledge, but also in method and the worldviews of science and medicine, will affect the manner in which health, physical education, and recreation are taught. Philosophy will inform educational psychology and alter notions of appropriate pedagogical process, just as liberation theologists will reorganize what we now think we know about political science and teaching and learning in Third World countries as well as our own nation. It is not hard to see multiple ways in which what is happening in the academic disciplines, including other specialties in education, will influence scholars who study higher education.

The evidence, likewise, is as readily available to the reader as it is to the author. The increasingly number of case studies, both as books and monographs and as journal articles, and the qualitative empirical studies demonstrate that individual scholars and journal editors alike have found merit and utility in such approaches. It is likely that the revolution in paradigms has already found its way into the study of higher education. Most assuredly, scholars have heard the calls for its usefulness, for its appropriateness (Lincoln, 1986a), and for its power to address questions for which we may not be able to provide precise answers, but for which we need at least some good ideas (G. Keller, 1985, 1986). Weiner (1986) believes that such research is impossible because of the discipline's lack of "a larger and more diverse cadre of provocative scholars to study higher education" (p. 163). The "new market for ideas" in higher education, he says, does not exist and must await new "management of colleges and universities." When new management appears, with a vision of what a scholarly community can be about, there will be a "freshened sense of new possiblities . . . interested in nourishing for dissent and debate, and the easy entrance and exit of individuals with fresh perspectives" (p. 163). Weiner does not see that occurring anytime soon.

Others are more optimistic, both about the fresh ideas that could be turned to good use and about the possibility of useful work's being done without major funding (Thelin, 1986). It would assuredly mean that the potential paradigm revolution would fall on barren ground if higher education scholars were to ignore the profound changes in the academic disciplines.

But the possibility of a paradigm revolution has much larger implications for faculty and administration in higher education, ramifications which should not be missed. If it is the intent of faculties and administrations to be open to respectful dissent, then dissenters must be supported, nourished, encouraged, and re-warded. It is not enough to recognize that they exist; they must be sought out, and their work acknowledged, especially since they are likely to be treated as peripheral and, therefore, extraneous to "mainstream" university activities. Nothing could be farther from the truth. The significance of such work from scholars is that it may provide the impetus for tommorrow's scholarship; it cannot be wasted.

But wasted it will be if those who work in the emergent paradigm are penalized, their ideas shut out of the academic marketplace, and their careers jeopardized for having led where another truth might take them. Since the vast number of persons trained in programs of higher education are, in fact, training to be administrators in postsecondary institutions (rather than scholars of higher education), they have to be introduced early to the philosophy of supporting divergence and dissent. Without such an egalitarian posture, the scholars who work at the cutting edge of their disciplines will be driven into retreat or may leave academia altogether. Training administrators to seek out such persons, to support them in hiring, in tenure and promotion, and with institutional funds for travel and scholarly activity, is critical. It is quite possibly the only way to "nourish" the market for ideas which Weiner (1986) believes higher education so desperately needs.

A Note on Educational Research—The Broader Look

It would be a serious mistake to believe that the foregoing review comprises the whole of the revolution in education, for it does not. There is another body of literature in the journals and textbooks which deals with research more broadly, that is, without reference to any subdiscipline within education. Much of it focuses on the new paradigm (Wolcott, 1985; Wilson, 1977; Rubin, 1982; Everhart, 1976; Spindler and Spindler, 1985; Erickson, 1984; Goetz and LeCompte, 1984; LeCompte and Goetz, 1982), how it can be made rigorous (trustworthy and authentic), and how it may be utilized in the various forms of inquiry (research, evaluation, and policy analysis; Lincoln and Guba, 1986b).

Still other major bodies of work address methods and ideologies which are different again from new-paradigm inquiry, but which will need to be taken into account by scholars pursuing their own work. Such literature includes the revisitation of Marxian analysis (Nash, 1984; Stafford, 1981; Apple, 1981; Liston, 1985; Giroux, 1984), conflict theory (Wood, 1983), emancipatory political action (Giroux, 1983, and see also the works of Paolo Freiere), and other liberationist pedagogies (which share some of their ideological stance with liberation theologies; see, for instance, Grumet, 1978). Although scholars will no doubt pick and choose both ontologies and ideologies consonant with their personal conviction and their personal belief system, nevertheless dissenting voices will make themselves heard. It behooves all manner of scholars to be able to listen comprehendingly to new forms of discourse. Scholars in nondominant ideologies and paradigms have found the dominant language and system of discourse unreflective of their ideas and refuse to use the old terminology. This is no less the case with emergent-paradigm or naturalistic inquiry than it is with Marxism, critical theory, ethnography, liberationist pedagogy, or any of the other competing forms of inquiry and/or discourse. At least a working knowledge of the language and definitions is now *de rigueur*, and I suspect most of us, the author included, fail on that count alone.

The point of this short tangent is to say that emergent-paradigm inquiry is only one of many contested forms of discourse for science or pedagogy. There are others, some of which broadly address the research arena, some of which address the value stances of education, schooling, and pedagogy. Until we have a working knowledge of the language of some, if not all, of them, we are lost in our own field.

WHAT DOES THE INTEGRATED SYSTEM LOOK LIKE?

In part, some indication of the way scholars are thinking about the concepts of new-paradigm inquiry—and the paradigm revolution—has already been presented. Terms like *morphogenesis, mutual causality, holography*, and the like indicate, however, *patterns of thought* more than they reveal what the *philosophical dimensions* of such a paradigm might be like. It will be the purpose of this section to propose what such a philosophical system might be like, and to contrast that with the dominant (conventional, scientific) paradigm.

All philosophical belief systems are comprised of three arenas: the system's ontology, its epistemology, and its methodology. In brief, those three aspects tell one how the belief system configures reality—that is, what is the nature of reality; what it has to say about the nature of causal relationships within that reality and how those may be expressed; what the relationship between the knower and the to-be-known is or ought to be, and what the role of values is within that relationship; and what the dynamic is that governs how it is we can come to know.

In conventional, logical positivist inquiry, the answers to the ontological questions have been widely accepted. Reality, in this paradigm, is a singular entity, "out there." The role of scientists is to converge upon this reality, typically by taking it apart into smaller subsystems and fragments which are called variables, and studying those intensively to understand the relationships between them. These relationships to each other are ordinarily expressed in the form of generalizations, which, when thoroughly studied and aggregated, are capable of being distilled into nomothetic, lawlike causal statements. Scientists may disagree as to the ability to approximate reality—that is, some believe it is ultimately knowable, some believe it is only approximatable, and some believe that we can only model it—but essentially, each knows his or her role in attempting to discover something about the nature of reality.

Conventional-paradigm epistemology, seeing "Nature" as something "out there" and, therefore, as separate from the self, generally supports a dualistic model for the relationship of knower to known. This distancing of the self from the object to be understood is intended to achieve a certain neutrality and objectivity, a dispassionate and disinterested posture believed to lend the clearest view of the phenomenon under investigation. Conventional scientists attempt to minimize or eliminate bias, and therefore contamination, since when those factors enter into an inquiry, they "prevent" us from seeing "true" elements of nature or "real" aspects of causal relationships, and thus they keep us from understanding what the laws are that govern physical or social phenomena and destroy the possibility of generalization. Only when something is seen in as unbiased and objective a manner as possible can we be certain that the laws we write to govern the instance have applicability beyond this situation. Values, either those of the scientist or those that relate to any aspect of the inquiry, are one source of contamination, and therefore a putatively value-free science is demanded.

Methodology in the conventional paradigm is noninteractive, distanced, interventionist (controlling). It is distinguished by a reliance on description and a verificationist stance toward data. Often, in order to comply with the mandate to be objective, data are collected with as little interaction as possible between scientist and subject, generally by means of paper-and-pencil instrumentation in the case of the social sciences.

Reduction, generally numeric, allows for the treatment of large groups so that the probability of being able to make statements about an entire population is enhanced. The reductionist stance moves science toward quintessential "truth," since one function it serves is to sift out extraneous variables of no interest to the study under investigation. The other function of (particularly quantifiable) reduction is, of course, to put the inquirer at least one remove from her or his data.

The naturalistic (or emergent-paradigm, phenomenological, hermeneutic, or case-study, as it has been called) paradigm begins with radically different premises. These premises are not new, but the treatment of them as an integrated system has rarely been undertaken (the exception, for the use of social scientists, has been Lincoln and Guba, 1985). A description of that ontological, epistemological, and methodological system will demonstrate the profound differences between naturalism and logical positivism.

Ontologically, naturalistic inquiry believes that there is no reality "out there" on which science may, ultimately, converge. The ontological position of naturalism (or constructivism, as we prefer to call it now, from its roots in constructivist psychology) is that reality is a social construction—or better yet, multiple social constructions, theoretically infinite, since a social construction may be held by many individuals (or a group, in which case we would call the shared constructions *cultural myths*). Reality is a created social phenomenon, *enacted* by individuals and groups, and bearing no intimations of universality or eternal verity (that is, social constructions can and may be changed, with the changing awareness, education, or sophistication of the constructor). As holistic entities, they are not fragmentable, since to fragment them—say, for the purpose of studying a single portion of the construction—does violence to the seamlessness and embeddedness of the whole in a singular belief system. Ontologically, the whole is indeed greater than the sum of its parts.

Science cannot converge on these multiple constructions; it can only diverge, since to expand an inquiry does not enable the inquirer to distill further, but rather to enlarge, both the scope of her or his understandings and the scope of the constructions under consideration. Since reality is a set of entities which are socially enacted by individuals, causal statements of the linear variety make little sense. A more sensible view of "the way things happen" in naturalistic inquiry is the pattern theory of Kaplan (1964), which posits that human affairs tend to take place in weblike systems of *mutual influence* and *plausible inference*; things, situations, events, are interrelated in such a way as to make traditional causal statements meaningless. Unique local interrelations remove the possibility and utility of generalizations. Instead of lawlike statements which relate the interaction between variables, the inquirer must content herself or himself with what has been called *working hypotheses*, understanding and knowledge of a more tentative sort, demanding testing in each new context to which such hypotheses are transported (an empirical matter).

The vision of reality is thus relativist—since there is no single reality on which we may converge—and determining which reality is "better" than some other is a matter not only for scientists but also for axiologists, ethicists, and politicians. Truth is arrived at consensually, not by extraction, but by the negotiation and the egalitarian participation of the various holders of social constructions. Critics of relativist ontologies point out that such positions on reality leave inquiries and inquirers open to charges that "anything goes." But respondents to this charge point out that relativism does not mean, necessarily, any such thing. All ideas may be weighed against some standard; the most important question here is whether the standards are foundational and absolutist (that is, rooted in a realist ontology) or relative (that is, weighed against other ideas in the history of human ideas). So, for instance, we can weigh *liberty* against the criterion of *equal educational opportunity*. Or we can weigh either, or both, against the criterion of *social and economic cost*. That is done, simplistically, by asking such questions as: How much freedom are we willing to give up in the (social) interests of equal educational opportunity? How much equal educational opportunity are we willing to pay for, either in desegregation efforts, in busing, or in other social or economic ways? Of liberty, equal opportunity, and economic cost, which is the most important social end? The second most important? The least important? And those are questions for ethicists, and for the body politic to determine—in relativist fashion.

The epistemology of naturalistic inquiry requires a recognition of the Heisenbergian universe: it is impossible to separate completely the knower from that which is to be known. This is especially true when that which is to be known is another human being. But the interaction between knower and known is not treated as a threat to objectivity, reliability, or neutrality in this paradigm. Rather it is treated as an opportunity, since it provides the arena in which the inquirer may collect the multiple constructions as faithfully as possible. It is also a chance for inquirer and inquired-into to exchange roles as teacher and learner, moving between each other's worlds and increasing understanding between them of both worlds.

Subjectivity is not, in this paradigm, viewed as compromising the inquiry hopelessly. Rather, subjectivity is seen as one level of understanding which should lead to critical subjectivity, the ability to see other constructions, to empathize, to understand, to comprehend, while still entertaining other levels of awareness, criticality, and the sense of self and other as unique persons. Values are a part of this subjectivity (at each level of it), since human existence cannot be a thing apart from human value. But the inquirer avoids hopelessly prejudicing the study by critical self-awareness, by the comprehension and presentation of her or his own values within the study itself, and by displaying them alongside the values which are embedded in the various contructions found on site and inhering in the site. Increasing awareness of self and the values which the self holds allows both inquirer and outsider (say, a reader of a case study) to locate the inquiry within a historical time, context, and belief system, open to dialogue, criticism, and ideological situation. Subjectivity here is not the confounder of inquiry; it is the first step in coming to know the self as instrument.

The methodology of naturalistic, constructivist inquiry is likewise altered. From the verificationist stance of the logical positivist, inquiry is moved to the hermeneutic, dialectic, and reconstructive forms which are consonant with phenomenological systems. A heavy reliance is placed on human-to-human data collection and analytic modes (such as qualitative methods), since those are the forms of method which allow inquirers to garner the multiple constructions of which realities are made.

"Truth," if such a thing exists, is arrived at in the process of negotiating how and under what circumstances persons are willing to enlarge, expand, or alter their constructions to take account of new information or other, more sophisticated, constructions of which they may become aware. Truth is a temporal (not eternal) entity, tentative, which awaits new information, additional constructions, or a changed context. It is arrived at consensually, with awareness (which the inquirer aids in bringing to the context) of human contradiction, the role of values, and conflict. In any given constructivist inquiry, it is quite likely that there will be no "truth," since there will be no final consensus; there will be multiple truths, each weighed by the individuals involved to determine which values undergirding which truths they will decide have primacy and legitimacy. The process of deciding is one of respectful collaboration and of fair and power-balanced negotiation and arbitration.

Issues and Implications of the Paradigm Contest

There are multiple issues of the contest between paradigms now gathering steam in the disciplines. Many of those have already been covered (Lincoln and Guba, 1985), but two are worth mentioning here, since they have no small impact on the discipline of higher education. They are *fittingness* and *the role of theory*.

By fittingness is meant the match between the phenomenon to be investigated and the paradigm chosen to guide the inquiry. It has long been the contention of phenomenologists and constructivists (among which we count ourselves) that human, social, and behavioral phenomena are not served in the inquiry process by the use of a model which is based on rationalistic, hypotheticodeductive principles. Since much of human behavior is a-rational (that is, not rational, but emotive, poetic, or something else besides logical) and cannot be "tracked" using hypothetic-deductive principles save as a reconstructed logic, it makes little sense to impose such a system on our inquiries of humans. At the very least, this obviates the need to declare much of human behavior, especially in organizations, as irrational, nonrational, or "boundedly" rational. We are freed from that confining language. The conventional system of inquiry was developed and refined for phenomena which behaved in lawlike and logical ways (for instance, gases under pressure) and has ill served social science (although it has not ill served the physical sciences, of course). So the argument is made that the constructivist paradigm is better suited (exhibits more fittingness) to human phenomena, simply because it demonstrates congruence with human experience of reality and coming-to-know.

The other implication has to do with the part theory plays in inquiry. In conventional inquiry, theory is the mechanism by which the lawlike relationships between pieces of reality (variables) are tested and displayed. The larger the theory (*grande théorie*), the larger the "chunk" of reality it supposedly describes. The process of taking several small relationships, building a larger theory, and then testing it is thought to be the pinnacle of conventional science (which explains, in part, the rewards associated with the heavy reliance on *de novo* research and on theory building as opposed to reanalysis, or repetition of research studies).

Quite the opposite posture is ordinarily found in constructivist inquiry. Theory is only built *after* extensive (thick) description and interpretation have been acquired and is considered, like the working hypotheses of which it is made, tentative and subject to immediate disconfirmation upon a change in context or time. Theory is referred to as *grounded*, since it is derived from the data in context themselves. The emphasis is on achieving local understanding, not on building grand, or overarching, theory. Constructivist inquirers would be dismayed at trying to construct theory in their offices, then proceeding to the field to test it. Theory is that pattern explanation which grows from prolonged engagement and persistent observation in the natural context, not that which is derived from attempts to link unrelated data.

This does not mean that the constructivist either begins with an empty head or must reinvent the wheel each time the field is entered. When other resonant (i.e., naturalistic, constructivist) studies have been done, they ought surely to inform the current research. And when such studies have engaged in grounded theory construction, those theories may be tested in the next context (indeed, one hopes that they are and will be); it is an excellent way to test understandings and allows increasing sophistication to emerge. It may even be a way of having knowledge accrue, although that terminology itself bespeaks a model of knowing which may be tied to the old paradigm. Not every study must begin from ground zero. But the knowledge from Study #1 must always be treated as though it were tentative and open to test in Study #2, thus precluding the possibility of generalization.

WHY IN HIGHER EDUCATION?

Why would higher education scholars, administrators, and researchers be interested in this revolution? I have tried to suggest two reasons already. First, higher education scholars should be aware of what is happening in other disciplines. Often, work in higher education is derivative, that is, takes its lead from methods, approaches, and strategies developed in other academic disciplines (and appropriately so). To know and understand what is happening in the academic disciplines can mean more informed and more sophisticated research and practice in our own. Marvin Peterson warned us in 1986 against "our growing *insulation* which cuts us off from the disciplines [inhibiting] the influx of conceptual ideas and methodological debates" (p. 149, emphasis in original). This prevents, too, our "*isomorphism*—freezing our research categories or discussions along conceptual or theory-practice issues," as he called it (p. 149, emphasis in original). It helps, too, in the improvement of "research methods and paradigms" by "*initiat[ing]* more professional discussions and publication activity aimed at examining the applicability of new methods and strategies and understanding new or different paradigms" (ibid., emphasis in original). Awareness brings about discussion and the possibility of change or at least informed decision-making.

Second, I have underscored the importance of having administrators comprehend the necessity of supporting alternative-paradigm faculty members, if for no other reason than ensuring the constant flow of new ideas to higher education. Since many of the persons we train in higher education programs wish ultimately to be administrators, they must be exposed to the debates and to the terminology. Administrators themselves need not make the paradigm shift in their own minds; but they do need to understand its ramifications for their faculty, and to be open to providing support and encouragement for those who hear a different drummer. At the very least, newly minted administrators ought to have some skills in discourse in the new paradigm, especially since scholars are busy writing "dictionaries for languages not yet spoken" (Lincoln, 1985b). The capability of engaging in substantive conversation with new-paradigm inquirers is foreclosed if administrators cannot understand new terminology or what such scholars believe it means.

There is a third reason, however, why knowing about the paradigm debates, or the paradigm revolution, is important. That reason has to do with the nature of a paradigm. It is both the major strength and the major weakness of a model for inquiry that it enables the inquirer to pose some questions extraordinarily well and makes other questions odd, awkward, or incomprehensible. Keller (1985) has already suggested that some questions we *have* asked have produced trivial results, while others *could not* be asked because they could not be framed well or sensibly using the conventional inquiry model. In paradigmatic terms, this makes perfectly good sense. Some questions are answered competently by one model, but others are nonsensical or do not admit of easy resolution. Change models, and questions which have previously made no sense now make strong sense (while others are trivial or useless). An alteration of paradigmatic stance would allow us to address questions which have remained unaddressed. Keller (1985) commented that one British scholar noted that there was no dearth of research, but very little scholarship in higher education, a comment which Keller interpreted to mean that some of what has been done is trivial, unthoughtful, or insignificant. A plethora of trivial or insignificant research does not mean, however, that no questions remain except trivial or insignificant ones. Rather it suggests that the lenses which frame our questions are clouded by our insulation and isomorphism (Peterson, 1986).

Simply said, a switch in paradigms may enable a switch in the questions which we can fruitfully pursue (Lincoln, 1986a). This is not a new idea, simply one which has come of age. I have suggested earlier that institutions of higher education are metamorphosing before our very eyes; they are not the same institutions of even 30 years ago. We need strategies to understand the changes, as well as scholarly thought which enables us to decide whether this is what we want or what we need. And if these changes are not what we want or need, we need to understand how we got here and how we could be somewhere else. Linear, assembly-motif planning and causal models can no longer ensure that the future we plan will be the one which arrives. We need models of thinking and planning built on probability functions, on helical, circular, arational, weblike, or other metaphors which help us to synthesize or comprehend, rather than continuing to aggregate (in the hope that more data will lead us to better decisions and therefore less complicated futures). The terminology of the new organizational theorists—and their lexicons of fresh language—could enable such thinking. But such an effort has to be built on new language, new metaphors, and new images of organizations and people in organizations.

George Orwell's *1984* made clear that the excision of words from a language could bring about the disappearance of the concept from the vocabularies and minds of a people. I would argue that the converse is also true: create a new language, and soon the images will follow. *Loose coupling*—a descriptive rather than prescriptive term, according to its inventor—is one such example. Loose coupling flies in the face of our orderly, systemslike view of bureaucracy and describes handily the way in which many academic departments function with respect to other academic departments. More such terms—a dictionaryful—and we should be able to describe what it is we're seeing, rather than have our terminology dictate what we must see.

Language is critical: the language of a new paradigm, the language of the running argument in science, and the language of description of the world we construct. At the very least, scholars and administrators must have a working vocabulary of some of the debate. There is a revolution at the gates of the ivory tower. Until we have talked to those at the barricades, learned their language, and understood their particular way of seeing both our world and their own, we are like tourists, seeing sights, but not understanding what we see. We are aliens on our own soil, we are "strangers in a strange land."

NOTES

1. A review of the axioms of scientific inquiry (logical positivism) and phenomenological (or naturalistic, or constructivist) inquiry will be undertaken later in this chapter.
2. Postpositivism is here defined as the succeeding generation of positivism, with sharply curtailed or discarded axioms from positivism. Postpositivism, however, in its many shapes and forms, is not to be confused with phenomenology or constructivism. Most postpositivist systems have as their chief defining characteristic the insistence on a realist ontology, or on the necessity for objectivity in research, or both.
3. *We* refers to the author and her colleague, Egon G. Guba, Indiana University.
4. *Naturalistic* is the term we originally used to describe the set of axioms which formed the paradigmatic opposite of conventional inquiry.
5. *Methods* and *methodologies* are here distinguished for the sake of conceptual clarity. The term *Methods* is used to refer to specific data collection and analytic techniques, while *methodology* is used to refer to the overall design strategy utilized to pursue the research question. Methodology includes problem definition, choice of research location, the entire set of data collection and analytic techniques, and consideration of the form and shape of the final report.
6. The reader should here note that none of the major work done in the late 1940s and throughout the 1950s, including the work of the constructivist psychologists, has been reviewed. The focus here has been on debates beginning the last 15–20 years, rather than the historical foundations of the debates. But knowledgeable psychologists will no doubt be astonished to find the works of Schutz and others omitted from this discussion.
7. Clearly, it is not fair to assume that all of the debate has centered on the *American Psychologist*. But as the foremost journal of the largest organization of psychologists in the U.S. (or anywhere), it commands an audience which can be fairly said to be representative of the field.

REFERENCES

Aanstoos, Christopher M. J. (1984). Foundations of phenomenological psychology. Paper presented at the Annual Meeting of the Southeastern Psychological Association, New Orleans, March.

Abramson, Joan (1975). *The Invisible Woman: Discrimination in the Academic Profession*. San Francisco: Jossey-Bass.

Agar, Michael, and Hobbs, Jerry R. (1982). Interpreting discourse: coherence and the analysis of ethnographic interviews. *Discourse Processes* 5(1): 1–32.

Allport, Gordon (1955). *Becoming*. New Haven: Yale University Press.

Alvesson, M. (1984). Questioning rationality and ideology: on critical organization theory. *International Studies of Man and Organization* 14(1): 61–79.

Andersen, M. L. (1987). Changing the curriculum in higher education. *Signs* 12(2): 222–254.

Aoki, T. ed. (1978a). *Curriculum Evaluation in a New Key*. Vancouver: University of British Columbia.

Aoki, T. (1978b). Toward curriculum inquiry in a new key. In J. Victoria and E. Sacca (eds.), *Presentations on Art Education Research*, Number 2: *Phenomenological Description: Potential for Research in Art Education*. Montreal: Concordia University.

Apple, Michael W. (1981). Reproduction, contestation and curriculum: an essay in self-criticism. *Interchange on Educational Policy* 12(2–3): 37–47.

Argyris, Chris, and Schön, Donald A. (1978). *Organizational Learning: A Theory of Action Perspective*. Reading, MA: Addison-Wesley.

Astley, Graham W. (1984). Subjectivity, sophistry, and symbolism in management science. *Journal of Management Studies* 21(3): 259–272.

Bahm, A. J. (1971). Science is not value-free. *Policy Sciences* 2: 391–396.

Bakan, David (1972). Psychology can *now* kick the science habit. *Psychology Today* 11(March): 26–28, 87–88.

Bark, William Carroll (1960). *Origins of the Medieval World*. Garden City, NY: Doubleday.

Barrett, Michele (1984). *Women's Oppression Today: Problems in Marxist Feminist Analysis*. Thetford, England: Thetford Press.

Bartlett, L., et al. (1983). A guide to evaluation design. *Case Study Method*, Vol. 6, pp.1–32. Geolong, Australia: Deakin University Press.

Bateson, Gregory (1972). *Steps Toward an Ecology of Mind*. New York: Ballantine.

Bavelas, Janet Beavin (1984). On naturalistic family research. *Family Process* 23: 337–341.

Beatley, Ralph (1985). The new activist anthropologists. *Newsweek* (January 28), pp. 66–67.

Beittel, K. (1978). Qualitative description of the qualitative. In J. Victoria, and E. Sacca (eds.), *Presentations on Art Education Research* Number 2: *Phenomenological Description: Potential for Research in Art Education*. Montreal: Concordia University.

Beittel, K. (1973). *Alternatives for Art Education Research*. Dubuque, IA: Wm. C. Brown.

Belenky, M. F., Clinchy, B. M., Goldberger, N. R., and Tarule, J. M. (1986). *Women's Ways of Knowing*. New York: Basic Books.

Bell, Robert H. (1981). Erotic hermeneutics. *College English* 43(3): 253–256.

Berger, P. L. and Luckman, T. (1973). *The Social Construction of Reality*. London: Penguin.

Berlin, Isaiah (1960). The concept of scientific history. *History and Theory* 1: 1–31.

Bernstein, R. (1988). History convention reflects change from traditional "gender" studies. *New York Times*. (January 9).

Bhola, H. S. (1987). Evaluation in cross-cultural settings: confounding of methodology by culture and context. Prepared for American Evaluation Association Annual Meeting, Boston, October 15–17.

Blaug, M. (1958). The classical economists and the Factory Acts: a re-examination. *Quarterly Journal of Economics* 72: 211–226.

Bleier, Ruth (1984). *Science and Gender: A Critique of Biology and Its Theories on Women*. Oxford: Pergamon.

Bleier, Ruth, ed. (1986). *Feminist Approaches to Science*. New York: Pergamon.

Bloch, Marc (1953). *The Historian's Craft*. New York: Random House.

Boni, John (1982). From medieval to Renaissance: paradigm shifts and artistic problems in English and Renaissance drama. *Journal of the Rocky Mountain Medieval and Renaissance Association* 3: 45–63.

Bowers, C. A. (1982). The reproduction of technological consciousness: locating the ideological foundations of a radical pedagogy. *Teachers College Record* 85(4): 529–557.

Bramson, Leon (1961). *The Political Context of Sociology*. Princeton, NJ: Princeton University Press.

Brekke, John (1986). Scientific imperatives in social work research: Pluralism is not skepticism. *Social Service Review* 60(December): 539–544.

Brent, Edward (1984). Qualitative computing: approaches and issues. *Qualitative Sociology* 7(1&2): 34–60.

Bright, L. K., Simula, Vern, and Smaby, Marlow H. (1984). The global imperatives for an education paradigm shift. Paper presented at the American Association of Colleges for Teacher Education Annual Meeting, San Antonio, TX.

Bronfenbrenner, Urie (1977). Toward an experimental ecology of human development. *American Psychologist* 32: 513–531.

Brooks, Cathy A. (1982). Using interpretation theory in art education research. *Studies in Art Education* 14: 43–47.

Burns, N., and Greene, S. K. (1987). Introduction to qualitative research. In *The Practice of Nursing Research*. Philadelphia, PA.: W.B. Saunders Company. 75–106.

Burrell, G., and Morgan, G. (1979). *Sociological Paradigms and Organizational Analysis*. London: Heineman.

Calas, M. B., and Smircich, L. (1987). Post-culture: is the organizational culture literature dominant but dead? Paper presented at the 3rd International Conference on Organizational Symbolism and Corporate Culture, Milan, Italy, June 24–26.

Caro, Robert A. (1982). The Path to Power: The Years of Lyndon Johnson. New York: Knopf.

Carper, Barbara A. (1978). Fundamental patterns of knowing in nursing. *ANS/Practice Oriented Theory* 1: 13–23.

Carr, Edward H. (1962). The historian and his facts. In *What Is History?*, pp. 3–35. New York: Knopf.

Carr, Winfred (1983). Can educational research be scientific? *Journal of Philosophy of Education* 77: 35–43.

Caulley, Darrel N., and Dowdy, Irene (1987). Evaluation case histories as parallel to legal case histories: accumulating knowledge and experience in the evaluation and profession. *Evaluation and Program Planning*, 10(4): 359–72.

Caulley, Darrel N. (1986). The evaluation of short-term education programs. Paper presented at the annual conference of the American Evaluation Association, Kansas City, MO.

Cheney, J. (1987). Eco-feminism and deep ecology. *Environmental Ethics* 9(Summer): 115–145.

Chorney, Merron (1984). Endless quest. *English Education*. 16: 22–33.

Christiansen, Charles H. (1987). Research: its relationship to higher education. *The American Journal of Occupational Therapy*. 41: 77–80.

Christiansen, Charles H. (1986). Research as reclamations. *The Occupational Therapy Journal of Research* 6: 323–327.

Christiansen, Charles H. (1981). Toward resolution of crisis: research requisites in occupational therapy. *The Occupational Therapy Journal of Research*. 1(2): 115–123.

Clark, David L. (1985), Emerging paradigms in organizational theory and research. In Y. S. Lincoln, (ed.), *Organizational Theory and Inquiry: The Paradigm Revolution*. Newbury Park, CA: Sage.

Cochran, David S., and Dolan, J. A. (1984). Qualitative research: an alternative to quantitative research in communciation. *The Journal of Business Communication* 21(4): 25–33.

Cohen, Michael D., and March, James G. (1974). *Leadership and Ambiguity* (2nd ed.). Boston: Harvard Business School Press.

Cohen, Michael D., March, J. D., and Olsen, J. P. (1972). A garbage can model of organizational choice. *Administrative Science Quarterly* 17: 1–25.

Cole, Stephen (1985). Is there such a thing as scientific objectivity? *Discover* 6(9): 98–99.

Conrad, Peter, and Reinharz, Shulamit (1984). Computers and qualitative data. Special issue of *Qualitative Sociology* 7(12, Spring/Summer).

Cook, Thomas, and Reichardt, Charles A. eds., (1979). *Qualitative and Quantitative Methods in Education Evaluation*. Beverly Hills, CA: Sage.

Cooper, E. A., and Barrett, G. V. (1984). Equal pay and gender: implications of court cases for personnel practices. *Academy of Management Review* 9(1): 84–94.

Cronbach, Lee J. (1975). Beyond the two disciplines of scientific psychology. *American Psychologist* 30: 116–127.

Cunningham, Donald J. (1986). Good guys and bad guys. *Educational Communication and Technology Journal* 34: 3–7.

Davis, Liane V. (1985). Female and male voices in social work. *Social Work* 30: 106–112.

Dawson, Christopher (1956). *The Making of Europe*. Cleveland: World.

Deane, Phyllis (1967). *The First Industrial Revolution*. Cambridge, England: Cambridge University Press.

Deetz, S. (1985). Ethical considerations in cultural research in organizations. In P. J. Frost, L. F. Moore, M. R. Louis, C. C. Lundberg, and J. Martin (eds.), *Organizational Culture*, pp. 253–269. Beverly Hills, CA: Sage.

Denhardt, R. B. (1981). *In the Shadow of Organization*. Lawrence: The Regents Press of Kansas.

Denzin, Norman K. (1971). The logic of naturalistic inquiry. *Social Forces* 50(December): 166–182.

Diamond, A., and Edwards, L. R., eds. (1977). *The Authority of Experience: Essays in Feminist Criticism*. Amherst: University of Massachusetts Press.

Diekelmann, Nancy (1986). Why research in nursing education? *Nursing Educator*. 11(1): 4–5.

Dillon, J. T. (1985). The problems/methods/solutions of curriculum inquiry. *Journal of Curriculum and Supervision* 1: 18–26.

Dokecki, Paul R. (1986). Methodological futures of the caring professions. *Urban and Social Change Review* 19(1): 3–7.

Donelson, E., Van Sell, M., and Goehl, D. (1985). Gender biases in management research: implications for theory and practice. Presented at Fourth Annual International Conference on Women and Organizations, San Diego, August.

Donovan, Josephine (1985). *Feminist Theory: The Intellectual Traditions of American Feminism*. New York: Frederick Ungar.

Downing, David B. The rigors and scruples of deconstruction: the politics of enlightened critique. Paper presented at Eastern Illinois University, (no date).

Downs, Florence S. (1983). One dark and stormy night. *Nursing Researcher* 32(5): 259.

Driscoll, Marcy P. (1984). Alternative paradigms for research in instructional systems. *Journal of Instructional Development* 7(4): 2–5.

DuBois, E. C., Kelly, G. P., Kennedy, E. L., Korsmeyer, C. W., and Robinson, L. S. (1987). *Feminist Scholarship: Kindling in the Groves of Academe*. Urbana: University of Illinois Press.

Duffy, Mary E. (1985). Designing nursing research: the qualitative-quantitative debate. *Journal of Advanced Nursing* 10: 225–232.

Duignan, Patrick A. (1981). Ethnography: an adventure in intepretive research. *Alberta Journal of Educational Research* 27(September): 285–297.

Eash, M. J., Hood, R., Stake, R., and Shapiro, D. (1985). Evaluation research and program evaluation: retrospect and prospect. *Educational and Policy Analysis* 7(3): 237–252.

Easlea, Brian (1986). The masculine image of science: how much does gender really matter? In Jan Harding (ed.), *Perspectives on Gender and Science*. Philadelphia: Falmer Press.

Easley, J. A. (1982). Naturalistic case studies: exploring social-cognitive mechanisms, and some methodological issues in research on problems of teachers. *Journal of Research in Science Teaching* 19(3): 191–203.

Egler, Frank (1979). Physics envy in ecology. In *The Nature of Vegetation: Its Management and Mismanagement*. Alton, IL: Forest.

Eisner, Elliot W. (1981). On differences between scientific and artistic approaches to qualitative research. *Educational Researcher* 10: 5–9.

Eisner, Elliot W. (1988). The primacy of experience and the politics of method. *Educational Researcher* 17(5): 15–20.

England, Hugh (1986). *Social Work as Art*. London: Allen & Unwin.

Epstein, Cynthia Fuchs (1981). Women in sociological analysis: new scholarship versus old paradigms. In Elizabeth Langland and Walter Gove, (eds). *A Feminist Perspective in the Academy: The Difference It Makes, pp. 149–162*. Chicago: University of Chicago Press.

Erickson, Frederick (1986). Qualitative research on teaching. In Merlin C. Wittrock (ed.), *Handbook of Research on Teaching* (3rd ed.). New York: Macmillan.

Erickson, Frederick (1984). What makes school ethnography "ethnographic"? *Anthropology and Education Quarterly* 15(Spring): 51–66.

Erickson, Frederick (1979). Mere ethnography: some problems in its use in educational practice. *Anthropology and Education Quarterly* 10(Fall): 182–188.

Ettinger, Linda F. (1987). Styles of on-site descriptive research: A taxonomy for art education. *Studies in Art Education* 28(2): 79–95.

Evans, Mary, ed. (1982). *The Woman Question: Readings on the Subordination of Women*. Oxford: Fontana Press.

Everhart, Robert B. (1976). Ethnography and educational policy: love and marriage or strange bedfellows? *Anthropology and Education Quarterly* 7(3): 17–25.

Evertson, Carolyn M., and Green, Judith L. (1986). Observations as inquiry and method.

In Merlin C. Wittrock (ed.), *Handbook of Research on Teaching* (3rd ed.), pp. 162–213. New York: Macmillan.

Farnham, C., ed. (1987). *The Impact of Feminist Research in the Academy*. Bloomington: Indiana Press University.

Faulconer, James E., and Williams, Richard N. (1985). Temporality in human action: an alternative to positivism and historicism. *American Psychologist* 40: 1179–1188.

Fee, Elizabeth (1986). Critiques of modern science: the relationship of feminism to other radical epistemologies. In Ruth Bleier (ed.), *Feminist Approaches to Science. pp. 42–56. New York: Pergamon*.

Ferguson, K. (1984). *The Feminist Case Against Bureaucracy*. Philadelphia: Temple University Press.

Feyerabend, P. K. (1981). *Realism, Rationalism and Scientific Method. Philosophical Papers*, Vol. 1. Cambridge: Cambridge University Press.

Fischer, David Hackett (1970). *Historians' Fallacies: Toward a Logic of Historical Thought*. New York: Harper & Row.

Fischer, Joel (1981). The social work revolution. *Social Work* 26(May): 199–207.

Fischer, Michael (1979). Why realism seems so naive: romanticism, professionalism and contemporary critical theory. *College English* 40(7): 740–750.

Flax, J. (1987). Postmodernism and gender relations in feminist theory. *Signs* 12(4): 621–643.

Frank, Betsy (1986). Choosing a methodology. *Nurse Educator* 11(6): 6–7.

Freeman, R. E. (1988). *Corporate Strategy and the Search for Ethics*. Englewood Cliffs, NJ: Prentice-Hall.

Freire, Paulo (1970). *Pedagogy of the Oppressed* (trans. by Myra Berman Ramos). New York: Harper & Harper.

Friedlander, Frank (1982). Alternative modes of inquiry. *Small Group Behavior* 13: 428–440.

Friedrichs, Robert W. (1970). *A Sociology of Sociology*. New York: Free Press.

Frost, Peter J., Moore, Larry F., Louis, Meryl Reis, Lundberg, Craig C., and Martin, Joanne, eds. (1985). *Organizational Culture*. Newbury Park, CA: Sage.

Gable, Robert, and Roger, Vincent (1987). Taking the terror out of research. *Phi Delta Kappa* 69(8): 690–695.

Garland, S. B., and Dwyer, P. (1988). A return to compassion? *Business Week* (February 1), pp. 63–65.

Garrison, James W. (1986). Some principles of postpositivistic philosophy of science. *Educational Researcher* 15(November): 12–18.

Gasdella, Ibrahim, E., and Cooper, Robert (1978). Towards an epistemology of management. *Social Science Information* 17(3): 249–383.

Geertz, Clifford (1973). *The Interpretation of Cultures*. New York: Basic Books.

Geismar, Ludwig G. (1982) Comments on "The Obsolete Scientific Imperative in Social Work Research." *Social Service Review* 56: 311–312.

Geismar, Ludwig, and Wood, Katherine (1982). Evaluating practice: science as faith. *Social Casework: The Journal of Contemporary Social Work* 63: 272–275.

Georgourdi, Marianthi, and Rosnow, Ralph I. (1985). Notes toward a contextual understanding of social psychology. *Personality and Social Psychology Bulletin 11:* 5–22.

Gergen, Kenneth J. (1985). The social constructionist movement in modern psychology. *American Psychologist* 40(3): 266–275.

Germain, Carol P. (1986). From practice to grounded theory. *Journal of Nursing Scholarship* 18(4): 185–187.

Gerson, Elihu M. (1984). Qualitative research and computers. *Qualitative Sociology* 7(1,2, Spring/Summer): 61–74.

Gibbs, John C. (1979). The meaning of ecological oriented inquiry in contemporary psychology. *American Psychologist* 34: 127–140.

Gilbert, G. N., and Mulkay, M. (1984). *Opening Pandora's Box: A Sociological Analysis of Scientist's Discourse.* Cambridge, England: Cambridge University Press.

Gilfoyle, Elnora M., and Christensen, Charles H. (1987). Research: the quest for truth and the key to excellence. *The American Journal of Occupational Therapy* 41(1): 7–8.

Gilligan, C. (1982). *In a Different Voice: Psychological Theory and Women's Development.* Cambridge: Harvard University Press.

Giroux, Henry A. (1985). Toward a critical theory of education: beyond Marxism with guarantees—a response to Daniel Liston. *Educational Theory* 35(3, Summer): 313–319.

Giroux, Henry A. (1984). Marxism and schooling: the limits of radical discourse. *Educational Theory* 34(2, Spring): 113–135.

Giroux, Henry A. (1983). Ideology and agency in the process of schooling. *Journal of Education* 165(1, Winter): 12–34.

Glaser, Barney G. (1978). *Theoretical Sensitivity: Advances in the Methodology of Grounded Theory.* Mill Valley, CA: Sociology Press.

Glaser, Barney G., and Strauss, Anselm (1967). *The Discovery of Grounded Theory.* Chicago: Aldine.

Gleich, James (1987). *Chaos.* New York: Viking Press.

Goetz, Judith P., and Lecompte, Margaret (1984). *Ethnography and Qualitative Design in Educational Research.* Orlando, FL: Academic Press.

Goodman, P. S. (1968). The measurement of an individual's organization map. *Administrative Science Quarterly* 13: 83–98.

Goodyear, Rodney K., ed. (1987). Special issue on paradigm shifts. *Journal of Counseling and Development* 64.

Gordon, William E. (1983). Social work: revolution or evolution? *Social Work* 29: 181–205.

Graham, Linda Lee (1980). Expectancy theory as a predictor of college student grade-point average, satisfaction and participation. Unpublished dissertation; University of Kansas, Lawrence.

Gray, Elizabeth Dodson (1979). *Green Paradise Lost.* Wellesley, MA: Roundtable Press.

Green, Judith L. (1983). Exploring classroom discourse: linguistic perspective on teaching-learning processes. *Educational Psychologist* 18(3): 180–199.

Greenwald, Anthony G. (1980). The totalitarian ego: fabrications and revision of personal history. *American Psychologist* 35: 603–618.

Gross, M., and Averill, M. B. (1983). Evolution and patriarchal myths of scarcity and competition. In S. Harding and M. B. Hintikka, (eds.), *Discovering Reality*, pp. 71–95. Boston: D. Reidel.

Grover, Robert, and Glazier, Jack (1985). Implications for application of qualitative methods to library and information science research. *Library and Information Science Research* 7: 247–260.

Grumet, Madeleine R. (1978). Curriculum as theater: merely players. *Curriculum Inquiry* 8(1): 37–64.

Guba, Egon G. (1987). Naturalistic evaluation. In D. C. Corday, H. S. Bloom, and R. J. Light (eds), *Evaluation Practice in Review. New Directions for Program Evaluation* No. 34 San Francisco: Jossey-Bass.

Guba, Egon G. (1982). Criteria for assessing the trustworthiness of naturalistic inquiries. *Educational Communications and Technology Journal* 29: 75–92.

Guba, Egon G. (1978). *Toward A Methodology of Naturalistic Inquiry in Educational Evaluation*. CSE Monograph Series in Evaluation, No. 8. Los Angeles: Center for the Study of Evaluation, University of California.

Guba, Egon G. (1972). The failure of educational evaluation. In Weiss Carol (ed.), *Evaluating Action Programs*. Boston: Allyn & Bacon.

Guba, Egon G., and Lincoln, Yvonna S. (1989). *Fourth-Generation Evaluation*. Newbury Park, CA: Sage.

Guba, Egon G., and Lincoln, Yvonna S. (1986). The countenances of fourth-generation evaluation: description, judgment, and negotiation. In David S. Cordray and Mark W. Lipsey (eds.), *Evaluation Studies Review Annual*, Vol. 11. Newbury Park, CA: Sage. (A longer version appears in Dennis J. Palumbo, *The Politics of Evaluation*, pp. 202–234. Newbury Park, CA: Sage, 1987.)

Guba, Egon G., and Lincoln, Y. S. (1982). Epistemological and methodological bases of naturalistic inquiries. *Educational Communication and Technology Journal* 30: 233–252.

Guba, Egon G., and Lincoln, Y. S. (1981). *Effective Evaluation*. San Francisco: Jossey-Bass.

Guettel, Charnie (1974). *Marxism and Feminism*. Toronto: Hunter Rose.

Gyarfas, Mary Govman (1983). The scientific imperative again. *Social Service Review* 57(March): 149–50.

Halberstam, David (1972). *The Best and the Brightest*. New York: Random House.

Hampton, D. R., Summer, C. E., and Webber, R. A. (1987). *Organizational Behavior and the Practice of Management*. Glenview, IL: Scott, Foresman.

Haraway, Donna (1986). Primatology is politics by other means. In Ruth Bleier (ed.), *Feminist Approaches to Science*, pp. 77–118. New York: Pergamon.

Harding, S. (1986). *The Science Question in Feminism*. Ithaca, NY: Cornell University Press.

Harding, S., and Hintikka M. B., ed. (1983). *Discovering Reality: Feminist Perspectives on Epistemology, Metaphysics, Methodology, and Philosophy of Science*. Boston: D. Reidel.

Harding, S., and O'Barr, J. F. (1987). *Sex and Scientific Inquiry*. Chicago: University of Chicago Press.

Harré, Rom (1987). Enlarging the paradigm. *New Ideas in Psychology* 5(1): 3–12.

Harris, Michael H. (1986). The dialectic of defeat: antimonies in research in library and information science. *Library Trends* 34(3): 515–531.

Harris, Janet C. (1983). Broadening horizons: interpretive cultural research, hermeneutics, and scholarly inquiry in physical education. *Quest* 35: 82–97.

Harris, Janet C. (1981). Hermeneutics, interpretive culture research, and the study of sports. *Quest* 35: 72–86.

Harshman, L. F., and McPherson, A. (1985). Editor's introduction to *Economics and Philosophy* 1: 1–7.

Harste, Jerome C. (1985). Reading research: portrait of a new paradigm. In R. J. Spino (ed.), *Reading Research in the 90's*. Hillsdale, NJ: Erlbaum.

Harste, Jerome C. (1982). Research in context: where theory and practice meet. *Australian Journal of Reading* 5(3August): 110–119.

Haskins, Charles Homer (1965). *The Renaissance of the 12th Century*. Cleveland: Meridian Books.

Hasselkus, Betty R. (1987). Letter to the editor. *The American Journal of Occupational Therapy* 41: 471.

Hatch, Amos J. (1983). Applications of qualitative methods to program evaluation in education. *Viewpoints in Teaching and Learning* 59: 1–11.

Haworth, Glenn O. (1984). Social work research, practice and paradigms. *Social Service Review* 58(September): 343–357.

Hedberg, B. (1981). How organizations learn and unlearn. In P. C. Nystrom, and W. H. Starbuck, (eds.), *Handbook of Organizational Design* Vol. 1. New York: Oxford University Press.

Heer, Friedrich (1962). *The Medieval World*. New York: Mentor Books.

Heineman, Martha Brunswick (Pieper) (1981). The obsolete scientific imperative in social work research. *Social Service Review* 55: 371–397.

Hennig, Margaret, and Jardim, Anne (1978). *The Managerial Woman*. Garden City, NY: Anchor Doubleday Books.

Hexter, J. H. (1971). *Doing History*. Bloomington: Indiana University Press.

Higham, John (1970). *Writing American History: Essays on Modern Scholarship*. Bloomington: Indiana University Press.

Hollinger, David A. (1973). T. S. Kuhns's theory of science and its implications for history. *American Historical Review* 78: 370–393.

Hosie, Peter (1986). Some theoretical and methodological issues to consider when using interviews for naturalistic research. *Australian Journal of Education* 30: 200–211.

Howard, George S. (1985). The role of values in the science of psychology. *American Psychologist* 40(3): 255–265.

Howe, Kenneth R. (1985). Two dogmas of educational research. *Educational Researcher* 14(October): 10–18.

Hubbard, R. (1983). Have only men evolved? In S. Harding, and M. B. Hintikka (eds.), *Discovering Reality*, pp. 45–69. Boston: D. Riedel.

Huizinga, J. (1954). *The Waning of the Middle Ages*. Garden City, NY: Doubleday Anchor Books.

Hurst, David K. (1986). Why strategic management is bankrupt. *Organizational Dynamics* 15(Autumn): 5–27.

Imershein, Allen W. (1977). Organizational change as a paradigm shift. *The Sociological Quarterly* 18: 33–43.

Imershein, Allen W. (1976). The epistemological bases of social order: toward ethno-paradigm analysis. In David Heise (ed.), *Sociological Methodology*, pp. 1–51. San Francisco: Jossey-Bass, Inc.

Imre, Roberta Wells (1984). The nature of knowledge in social work. *Social Work* 29: 41–45.

Jacobs, Ronald L. (1985). A rationale for using qualitative methods in performance technology. *Performance and Instructional Journal* 24(5), (June): 20–23.

Jax, Judy (1984). Ethnography: an approach to using interpretive science in vocational education research. *Journal of Vocational Educational Research* 9(4): 8–19.

Jaynes, Julian (1976). *The Origin of Consciousness in the Breakdown of the Bicameral mind*. Boston: Houghton Mifflin.

Jelinek, Mariann, Smircich, Linda, and Hersh, Paul, eds. (1983). Special issue on ethnography. *Administrative Science Quarterly* 28(3).

Jennings, Jerry L. (1986). Husserl revisited: the forgotten distinction between psychology and phenomenology. *American Psychologist*. 41(11): 1231–1240.

Jick, Todd D. (1979). Mixing qualitative and quantitative methods: triangulation in action. *Administrative Science Quarterly* 24: 602–611.

Journal of Counseling and Development (1985). Special issue on paradigm shifts, Vol. 64(May).

Judy, Stephen N. (1984). Recent research and new directions in the teaching of writing. In F. Parkay, F. O'Brien, and M. Hennessy (eds.), *Quest for Quality, Improving Basic Skills Instruction in the 1980's*, pp. 18–22. New York: University Press.

Kanth, K. Rajani (1985). The decline of Ricardian politics: some notes on the paradigm-shift in economics from the classical to the neo-classical persuasion. *European Journal of Political Economy* 1/2: 157–187.

Kantor, K. J., Kirby, D. R., and Goetz, J. P. (1981). Research in context: ethographic studies in English education. *Research in the Teaching of English* 15: 291–309.

Kaplan, Abraham (1964). *The Conduct of Inquiry*. San Francisco: Chandler.

Karger, H. Jacob (1983). Science, research and social work: Who controls the profession? *Social Work* 28(2): 200–205.

Kekes, John (1974). Logical dualism: human values and method in the social sciences. *Cultural Hermeneutics* 2: 61–73.

Keller, Evelyn F. (1985). *Reflections on Gender and Science*. New Haven: Yale University Press.

Keller, Evelyn F. (1983a). Gender and science. In Sandra Harding and Merill B. Hintikka (eds.), *Discovering Reality*, pp. 198–206. Dordrecht, Holland: D. Reidel.

Keller, Evelyn Fox (1983b). *A Feeling for the Organism: The Life and Work of Barbara McClintock*. New York: Freeman.

Keller, Evelyn Fox (1982). Feminism and science. *Signs: Journal of Women in Culture and Society* 7(3): 589–602.

Keller, Evelyn Fox (1980a). Baconian science: a hermaphroditic birth. *Philosophical Forum* 11: 400–411.

Keller, Evelyn Fox (1980b). Feminist critique of science: A forward or backward move? *Fundamenta Scientiae* 1(Summer): 341.

Keller, Evelyn Fox (1979a). Nature as "her." *Proceedings of the Second Sex Conference*. New York University.

Keller, Evelyn Fox (1979b). Cognitive repression in contemporary physics. *American Journal of Physics* 47: 718–721.

Keller, Evelyn Fox (1978). Gender and science. *Psychoanalysis and Contemporary Thought* 1: 409–33.

Keller, Evelyn Fox (1974). Women in science: a social analysis. *Harvard Magazine* (October): 14–19.

Keller, George (1985). Trees without fruit. *Change Magazine* 17(Jan./Feb.): 7–10.

Keller, George (1986). Free at last? Breaking the chains that bind educational research. *The Review of Higher Education* 10(2): 129–134.

Kielhofner, Gary (1987). Qualitative research. *The Occupational Journal of Research* 2: 150–169.

Kielhofner, Gary (1981). An ethnographic study of deinstitutionalized adults: their community settings and daily life experiences. *The Occupational Therapy Journal of Research* 1(2): 125–142.

Kimble, Gregory A. (1984). Psychology's two cultures. *American Psychologist* 39(8): 833–839.

Knorr-Cetina, K. D. (1981). *The Manufacture of Knowledge*. New York: Pergamon.

Knorr-Cetina, K. D., and Mulkay, M. (1983). *Science Observed*. Beverly Hills, CA: Sage.

Knowles, David (1962). *The Evolution of Medieval Thought*. New York: Random House.

Koetting, Randall J. (1984). Foundations for naturalistic inquiry: developing a theory base for understanding individual interpretations of reality. Paper prepared for Association for Educational Communications and Technology, Dallas, January 20–24.

Kolodny, A. (1984). *The Land Before Her: Fantasy and Experience of the American Frontiers*, 1630–1860. Chapel Hill: University of North Carolina Press.

Kuh, George D., Whitt, Elisabeth, J., and Shedd, Jill D. (1987). *Student Affairs Work 2001: A Paradigmatic Odyssey*. Washington, DC: American College Personnel Association.

Kuhn, Thomas S. (1974). Second thoughts on paradigms. In P. Suppes (ed.), *The Structure of Scientific Theories*. pp. 459–515. Urbana: University of Illinois Press.

Kuhn, Thomas S. (1970). *The Structure of Scientific Revolutions* (2nd ed., enlarged). Chicago: University of Chicago Press.

Kuzel, Anton J. (1986). Naturalistic inquiry: an appropriate model for family medicine. *Family Medicine*: 18: 369–374.

Kuzel, Anton J. (1985). Naturalistic inquiry and its place in family medicine research. Unpublished master's thesis, University of Illinois, Chicago.

Ladner, J. (1987). Introduction to *Tomorrow's Tomorrow: The Black Woman*. In S. Harding, (ed.), *Feminism and Methodology*, pp. 74–83. Bloomington: Indiana University Press.

Landes, David S., and Tilly, Charles, eds. (1971). *History as Social Science*. Englewood Cliffs, NJ: Prentice-Hall.

Landes, David S. (1966). *The Rise of Capitalism*. New York: Macmillan.

Langland, E., and Gove, W., eds. (1981). *A Feminist Perspective in the Academy: The Difference It Makes*. Chicago: University of Chicago Press.

Lanier, V. (1977). The five faces of art education. *Studies in Art Education* 18: 7–12.

Larkin, Dave, and Cobb, Brian (1984). A perspective on the usefulness of qualitative research in vocational education. *Journal of Vocational Education Research* 9(2): 36–48.

Lash, Scott, and Urry, John (1984). The new Marxism of collective action: a critical analysis. *Sociology* 18(1): 33–50.

LeCompte, Margaret D., and Goetz, Judith Preissle (1982). Problems of reliability and validity in ethnographic research. *Review of Educational Research* 52(1): 31–60.

Leitch, Vincent B. (1977). A primer of recent critical theories. *College English* 39(2): 138–151.

Leininger, Madeleine (1985). *Qualitative Research Methods in Nursing*. Orlando, FL: Grune & Stratton.

Lincoln, Yvonna S. (1988). The role of ideology in naturalistic inquiry. Paper presented at the annual meeting of the American Educational Research Association, New Orleans.

Lincoln, Yvonna S. (1987). A future-oriented comment on the state of the profession. *The Review of Higher Education*. 10(2): 135–142.

Lincoln, Yvonna S. (1986). Criteria for assessing the authenticity of naturalistic inquiries. Paper presented at the annual meeting of the American Educational Research Association, San Francisco, April.

Lincoln, Yvonna S. (1985a). Naturalistic inquiry in the psychology of music. Keynote address, Research Symposium on the Psychology and Acoustics of Music, University of Kansas, Lawrence.

Lincoln, Yvonna S., ed. (1985b). *Organizational Theory and Inquiry: The Paradigm Revolution*. Newbury Park, CA: Sage.

Lincoln, Yvonna S. (1984). Bridging the gap: new constructs for organizations and appropriate methodologies. Presented at the annual meeting of the Association for the Study of Higher Education, Chicago.

Lincoln, Yvonna S., and Guba, Egon G. (1988). Criteria for assessing the products of naturalistic inquiries. Paper presented at the annual meeting of the American Educational Research Association, New Orleans.

Lincoln, Yvonna S., and Guba, Egon G. (1987). Ethics: the failure of positivist science. Paper presented at the annual meeting of the American Educational Research Association, Washington, DC.

Lincoln, Yvonna S., and Guba, Egon G. (1986a). But is it rigorous? Trustworthiness and authenticity in naturalistic evaluation. In D. D. Williams, (ed.), *Naturalistic Evaluation. New Directions in Program Evaluation* Vol. 30. San Francisco: Jossey-Bass.

Lincoln, Yvonna S., and Guba, Egon G. (1986b). Research, evaluation and policy analysis: Heuristics for disciplined inquiry. *Policy Studies Review* 5: 546–565.

Lincoln, Yvonna S., and Guba, Egon G. (1985). *Naturalistic Inquiry*. Beverly Hills, CA: Sage.

Liston, Daniel P. (1985). Marxism and schooling: a failed or limited tradition? A response to Henry Giroux. *Educational Theory* 35(3, Summer): 307–319.

Lot, Ferdinand (1961). *The End of the Ancient World and the Beginning of the Middle Ages*. New York: Harper & Row.

Lucas, Christopher (1985). Out at the edge: notes on a paradigm shift. *Journal of Counseling and Development* 64(November): 165–172.

Luke, Helen M. (1984). *Woman: Earth and Spirit: The Feminine in Symbol and Myth*. New York: Crossroad Publishing.

Mahoney, M. J. (1976). *Scientist as Subject*. Cambridge, MA: Ballinger.

Manchester, William (1974). *The Glory and the Dream*, Vols. 1 and 2. Boston: Little, Brown.

Mantoux, Paul (1961). *The Industrial Revolution in the Eighteenth Century: An Outline of the Beginnings of the Modern Factory System in England*. New York: Harper & Row.

Marantz, K. (1982). Heresies and other devilish advocacies: a cynical view of art education today. *Annual Journal, Canadian Society for Education Through Art* 13: 4–7.

Marshall, Catherine (1985). Appropriate criteria of trustworthiness and goodness for qualitative research on education organizations. *Quality and Quantity* 19: 353–373.

Martin, J. (1987). The suppression of gender conflict in organizations: deconstructing the fissure between public and private. Unpublished manuscript.

McCann, H. Gilman (1978). *Chemistry Transformed: The Paradigmatic Shift from Phlogiston to Oxygen*. Norwood, NJ: Ablex Publication.

Merchant, Carolyn (1982). *The Death of Nature: Women, Ecology and the Scientific Revolution*. London: Wildwood House.

Metz, Mary Haywood (1985). What can be learned from educational ethnography? *Urban Education* 17(4): 391–418.

Mick, David Glen (1986). Consumer research and semiotics: exploring the morphology of signs, symbols, and significance. *Journal of Consumer Research* 13: 1–18.

Miles, Matthew B. (1979). Qualitative data as an attractive nuisance: the problem of analysis. *Administrative Science Quarterly* 24(4): 590–601.

Miles, M. B., and Huberman, A. M. (1984) Drawing valid meaning from qualitative data: toward a shared craft. *Educational Researcher* 13: 20–30.

Miles, Matthew B. (1984). *Qualitative Data Analysis: A Sourcebook of New Methods*. Beverly Hills, CA: Sage.

Miller, Jean Baker (1976). *Toward a New Psychology of Women*. Boston: Beacon.

Milner, Richard B. (1972). The trickster, the bad nigga, and the urban ethnography: an initial report and editorial code. *Urban Life and Culture* 1(1): 109–117.

Mintzberg, Henry (1979). An emerging strategy of direct research. *Administrative Science Quarterly* 24: 582–589.

Mitroff, Ian I. (1983). *Stakeholders of the Organizational Mind*. San Francisco: Jossey-Bass.

Mitroff, Ian I. (1981). Is a periodic table of the elements for organizational behavior possible? Integrating Jung and TA for organizational analysis. *Human Systems Management* 2: 168–176.

Mitroff, Ian I. (1974a). Norms and counter-norms in a select group of the Apollo moon scientists: a case study of the ambivalence of scientists. *American Sociological Review* 39(August): 579–595.

Mitroff, Ian I. (1974b). *The Subjective Side of Science*. Amsterdam: Elsevier.

Mitroff, Ian I. (1972). The myth of objectivity or why science needs a new psychology of science. *Management Science* 18: B-613–B-618.

Morgan, Gareth (1986). *Images of Organization*. Newbury Park, CA: Sage.

Morgan, Gareth, ed. (1983). *Beyond Method: Strategies for Social Research*. Beverly Hills, CA: Sage.

Morgan, Gareth, and Smircich, Linda (1980). The case for qualitative research. *Academy of Management Review* 5(4): 491–500.

Munhall, Patricia L. (1982). Nursing philosophy and nursing research: in apposition or opposition? *Nursing Research* 31(13): 178–181.

NamenWirth, Marion (1986). Science seen through a feminist prism. In Ruth Bleier (ed.), *Feminist Approaches to Science*, pp. 18–41. New York: Pergamon.

Nash, Roy (1984). On two critiques of the Marxist sociology of education. *British Journal of Sociology of Education* 5(1): 19–31.

Natoli, Joseph P. (1982). Librarianship as a human science: theory, method, and application. *Library Researcher* 4: 163–174.

Neilsen, Kai (1973). Social science and hard data. *Cultural Hermeneutics* 1: 115–143.

Neuhring, Elane, and Imershein, Allen W. (1975). Open systems, organizational research, and the sociology of knowledge. Paper presented at the annual meeting of the Southern Sociological Society.

Noe, R. A. (1988). Women and mentoring: a review and research agenda. *Academy of Management Review* 13(1): 65–78.

Odi, Amusi (1982). Creative research and theory building in library and information sciences. *College and Research Libraries* 43(4): 312–319.

O'Donnel, Holly (1983). Eric/RCS report: agreeing on ethnography. *English Education* 15: 239–245.

Oiler, Carolyn (1982). The phenomelogical approach to nursing research. *Nursing Research* 31: 181–184.

Ortner, S. B. (1974). Is female to male as nature is to culture? In M. Z. Rosaldo, and L. Lamphere, (eds.), *Women, Culture, and Society*, pp. 67–87. Stanford, CA: Stanford University Press.

Ottenbacher, Kenneth J. (1981). Publication trends in occupational therapy. *The Occupational Therapy Journal of Research* 2(2): 80–88.

Ottenbacher, Kenneth J. (1985). Ritual, rigor, and relevance: the design of clinical research. *American Journal of Occupational Therapy* 39(March): 202–203.

Overholt, George (1980). Ethnography and education: limitations and sources of error. *Journal of Thought* 15(Fall): 11–20.

Packer, Martin J. (1985). Hermeneutic inquiry in the study of human conduct. *American Psychologist* 40: 1081–1093.

Padgam, Ronald E. (1983). The holographic paradigm and post critical reconceptualistic curriculum theory. *Journal of Curriculum Theorizing* 5(3): 132–143.

Paley, J. (1986). Review of *Social Work as Art*. *British Journal of Social Work* 16: 693–695.

Panikakar, Raimundo (1979). The myth of pluralism: the tower of Babel—a meditation on non-violence. *Cross-Currents* 29: 197–231.

Pascarella, Ernest (1987). Personal communication, November.

Patton, Michael Quinn (1980). *Qualitative Evaluation Methods*. Beverly Hills, CA: Sage.

Patton, Michael Quinn (1981). *Creative Evaluation*. Beverly Hills, CA: Sage.

Patton, Michael Quinn (1982). *Practical Evaluation*. Beverly Hills, CA: Sage.

Paull, John (1980). Laws of behavior, fact or artifact? *American Psychologist* 35(12): 1081–1083.

Pearse, Harold (1983). Brother, can you paradigm? The theory beneath the practice. *Studies in Art Education* 24(3, Spring): 158–163.

Perloff, Robert, and Perloff, Evelyn, eds. (1980). Values, ethics and standards in evaluation. *New Directions for Program Evaluation*, Vol. 7. San Francisco: Jossey-Bass.

Perrow, Charles (1986). *Complex Organizations: A Critical Essay*. (3rd ed.). New York: Random House.

Perrow, Charles (1981). Deconstructing social science. *New York University Educational Quarterly* 12(Winter): 2–9.

Peshkin, Alan. (1988). Understanding complexity: a gift of qualitative inquiry. *Anthropology and Education Quarterly*, 19(4): 416–424.

Peters, Thomas J., and Robert H. Waterman, Jr. (1982). *In Search of Excellence*. New York: Harper & Row.

Peterson, Marvin W. (1986). Critical choices: from adolescence to maturity in higher-education research. *The Review of Higher Education* 10(2, Winter): 143–150.

Phillips, D. C. (1985). On what scientists know, and how they know it. In Elliot Eisner, ed. *Learning and Teaching the Ways of Knowing*, pp. 37–59. Chicago: University of Chicago Press.

Phillips, Derek L. (1975). Paradigms and incommensurability. *Theory and Society* 2: 37–61.

Pieper, Martha Heineman (1987). Comments on "Scientific imperatives in social work research: pluralism is not skepticism." *Social Services Review* 61(2): 368–370.

Pieper, Martha (1985). The future of social work research. *Social Work Research and Abstracts* 21: 3–11.

Piore, Michael J. (1979). Qualitative research techniques in economics. *Research Techniques in Economics* 24: 560–568.

Pirenne, Henri (1937). *Economic and Social History of Medieval Europe*. New York: Harcourt, Brace & World.

Porter-Gehrie, Cynthia (1980). The ethnographer as insider. *Educational Studies* 11: 123–124.

Radnitzky, Gerard (1972). Toward a theory of research which is neither logical reconstruction nor psychology or sociology of science. *Quality and Quantity* 6(2): 192–238.

Ramirez, Rafael (1979). Action learning: a strategic approach for organizations facing turbulent conditions. *Human Relations* 36: 725–742.

Raynor, Peter (1984). Evaluation with one eye closed: the empiricist agenda in social work research. *British Journal of Social Work* 14: 1–10.

Raynor, Peter (1985). *Social Work, Justice and Control*. Oxford: Blackwell.

Reason, Peter, ed. (1988). *Human Inquiry in Action: Developments in the Practice of New Paradigm Research*. London: Sage.

Reason, Peter, and Rowan, John, eds., (1981). *Human Inquiry: A Sourcebook of New Paradigm Research*. New York: Wiley.

Reich, M. (1980). Empirical and ideological elements in the decline of Ricardian economics. *Review of Radical Political Economics* 12: 1–14.

Reinharz, Shulamit (1986). Experimential analysis: a contribution to feminist research. In G. Bowle and R. Duelli, eds., *Theories of Women's Studies*, pp. 162–191. London: Routledge & Kegan Paul.

Reinharz, Shulamit (1979). *On Becoming a Social Scientist*. San Francisco: Jossey-Bass.

Reinharz, Shulamit, and Rowles, Graham D., eds., (1988). The "gendering" of science: science and power. Chapter in *Qualitative Gerontology*. New York: Springer.

Reynolds, David (1980–1981). The naturalistic method of educational and social research:—a Marxist critique. *Interchange* 11(4): 77–89.

Rist, Ray C. (1981). On the utility of ethnographic research for the policy process. *Urban Education* 15(4, January): 485–494.

Ritzer, George (1975). *Sociology: A Multiple Paradigm Science*. Boston: Allyn & Bacon.

Robertson, Mildred, and Boyle, Joyceen S. (1984). Ethnography: contributions to nursing research. *Journal of Advanced Nursing*. 9: 43–49.

Rockhill, Kathleen (1982). Research participation in adult education: the potential of the qualitative perspective. *Adult Education* 33: 3–19.

Rodwell, Mary K. (1987). Naturalistic inquiry: an alternative model for social work assessment. *Social Service Review* 61: 231–245.

Rogers, Joan C. (1982). Order and disorder in medicine and occupational therapy. *American Journal of Occupational Therapy* 36: 29–35.

Rosaldo, M. Z. (1980). The use and abuse of anthropology: reflections on feminism and cross-cultural understanding. *Signs* 5: 389–417.

Rose, Hilary (1986). Beyond masculinist realities: a feminist epistemology for the sciences. In Ruth Bleier (ed.), *Feminist Approaches to Science*, pp. 57–76. New York: Pergamon.

Rosetti, Carlo (1976). Theory, structure and action in contemporary English social science. *Rassenga Italiana di sociologia* 17: 71–117.

Rossiter, M. (1982). *Women Scientists in America: Struggles and Strategies to 1940*. Baltimore: Johns Hopkins University Press.

Rowthorn, R. (1974). Neo-classicism, neo-Ricardianism, and Marxism. *New Left Review* 86: 63–87.

Rubin, Blanche Mallins (1982). Naturalistic evaluation: its tenets and application. *Studies in Art Education* 24: 57–62.

Ruckdeschel, Roy A., and Farris, Buford E. (1982). Science: critical faith or dogmatic ritual: a rebuttal. *Social Work Research and Abstracts* 63: 272–275.

Ruckdeschel, Roy and Farris, Buford E. (1981). Assessing the practice: a critical look at the single-case design. *Social Casework: The Journal of Contemporary Social Work.* 62(7) 413–419.

Salisbury, Harrison, E. (1967). *Behind the Lines—Hanoi*. New York: Harper & Row.

Sampson, Edward E. (1978). Scientific paradigms and social values: wanted—a scientific revolution. *Journal of Personality and Social Psychology* 36: 1332–1343.

Sanday, Peggy Reeves (1979). The ethnographic paradigm(s). *Administrative Science Quarterly* 24: 527–538.

Sandelowski, Margarette (1986). The problem of rigor in qualitative research. *ANS* 8(3): 27–37.

Scarr, Sandra (1985). Constructing psychology: making facts and fables for our times. *American Psychologist* 40: 499–512.

Schein, Edgar H. (1978). *Organizational Culture and Leadership. San Francisco: Jossey-Bass.*

Schmik, Harriet (1981). Qualitative research and occupational therapy. *American Journal of Occupational Therapy* 35(2): 105–106.

Schön, Donald A. (1984). *The crisis of professional knowledge and the pursuit of an epistemology of practice. Paper presented at Harvard Business Schools' 75th Anniversary Colloquium.*

Schumpeter, Joseph A. (1950). *Capitalism, Socialism and Democracy* (3rd ed.). New York: Harper & Row.

Schwartz, Peter, and Ogilvy, James (1980). *The emergent paradigm: towards an aesthetic of life. Paper presented at the ESOMAR conference, Barcelona, Spain.*

Schwartz, Peter, and Ogilvy, James, (1979). *The emergent paradigm: changing patterns of thought and belief.* Analytical Report #7: Values and Lifestyles Program. SRI International, Menlo Park, CA.

Schwartzberg, Sharan (1978). Letter to the editor. *American Journal of Occupational Therapy. 32(5): 329.*

Scott, W. G., and Hart, D. K. (1979). *Organizational America.* Boston: Houghton Mifflin.

Shapiro, H. Svi (1982). Education in capitalist society: towards a reconsideration of the state in education policy. *Teachers College Record* 83(4): 515–517.

Sheldon, B. (1986). Social work effectiveness experiments: review and implications. *British Journal of Social Work* 16: 223–242.

Sheldon, B. (1984). Evaluation with one eye closed: the empiricist agenda in social work research—a reply to Peter Raynor. *British Journal of Social Work* 14: 635–637.

Sheldon, B. (1983). The use of single case experimental designs in social work research. *British Journal of Social Work* 13: 477–500.

Sheldon, B. (1982). A measure of success. *Social Work Today* 13: 8–11.

Sheldon, B. (1978a). Letter to the editor. *British Journal of Social Work* 8: 219–220.

Sheldon, B. (1978b). Theory and practice in social work. *British Journal of Social Work: 8: 1–22.*

Sherman, Robert R. and Webb, Rodman B., eds. (1986). Qualitative Research. Special issue of the *Journal of Thought* 21(3, Fall).

Shils, Edward (1978). The order of learning in the United States from 1865 to 1920: the ascendancy of universities. *Minerva* 16(2): 159–195.

Shirom, Arie (1983). Toward a theory of organizational development interventions in unionized work settings. *Human Relations* 36(8): 743–764.

Showalter, E. (1977). *A Literature of Their Own.* Princeton, NJ: Princeton University Press.

Skrtic, T. M., Guba, E. G., and Knowlton, H. E. (1985). *Interorganizational Special Education Programming in Rural Areas: Technical Report on a Multi-site Naturalistic Field Study.* Washington, DC: National Institute of Education.

Smircich, L. (1986). Behind the debate over the validity of alternative paradigm research. Paper presented at the annual meeting of the American Educational Research Association, San Francisco.

Smircich, L., and Calas, M. B. (1987). Organizational culture: a critical assessment. In

F. M. Jablin, L. L. Putnam, K. H. Roberts, and L. W. Porter (eds.), *Handbook of Organizational Communication*, pp. 228–263. Newbury Park, CA: Sage.

Smith, David (1987). The limits of positivism in social work research. *British Journal of Social Work* 17: 401–416.

Smith, John K., and Heshusius, Lous (1986). Closing down the conversation: the end of the quantitative-qualitative debate among educational inquirers. *Educational Researcher* 5(1): 4–12.

Smith, L. N., and Kleine, P. G. (1986). Qualitative research and evaluation: triangulation and multimethods reconsidered. In D. D. Williams (ed.), *Naturalistic Evaluation. New Directions for Program Evaluation*, No. 30. San Francisco: Jossey-Bass.

Smith, Mary Lee (1987). Publishing qualitative research. *American Educational Research Journal* 224: 173–183.

Smith, Mary Lee (1982). Benefit of naturalistic methods in research in science education. *Journal of Research in Scientific Education* 19: 627–638.

Smith, Mary Lee (1981). Naturalistic research. *The Personnel and Guidance Journal* 59(9): 585–589.

Smith, Richard (1979). Myth and ritual in teaching education. In M. R. Pusey and R. E. Young (eds.), *Control and Knowledge: The Mediation of Power in Institutionalized and Educational Settings*. Canberra: Education Research Unit, Australian National University.

Smith, Richard (1980). Skepticism and qualitative research. *Education and Urban Society* 12(3): 383–398.

Snitow, Ann, Stansell, Christine, and Thompson, Sharon, eds. (1983). *Powers of Desire: The Politics of Sexuality*. New York: Monthly Review Press.

Southern, R. W. (1953). *The Making of the Middle Ages*. New Haven, CT: Yale University Press.

Spector, Barbara S. (1984). Qualitative research: data analysis framework generating grounded theory applicable to the crisis in science education. *Journal of Research in Science Teaching* 21(5): 459–467.

Spindler, George, and Spindler, Louis (1985). Ethnography: an anthropological view. *Educational Horizons* 63(4): 154–157.

Spivak, G. C. (1987). *In Other Worlds: Essays in Cultural Politics*. New York: Methuen.

Stafford, J. Martin (1981). Marxism, neutrality and education. *Journal of Philosophy of Education* 15(2): 161–166.

Stainback, Susan, and Stainback, William (1984a). Broadening the research pespective in special education. *Exceptional Children* 9: 400–409.

Stainback, Susan, and Stainback, William (1984b). Methodological considerations in qualitative research. *Journal of the Association for the Severely Handciapped* 9: 330–334.

Stainback, Susan, and Stainback, William (1985). Quantitative and qualitative methodologies: Competitive or complementary? A response to Simpson and Eaves. *Exceptional Children* 51(4): 330–334.

Stake, Robert E. (1978). Should educational evaluation be more objective or more subjective? More subjective! Paper presented at the annual meeting of the American Educational Research Association, Toronto, Ontario, Canada, April 11–15.

Stevens, B. J. (1984). *Nursing Theory: Analysis, Application, Evauation* (2nd. ed.). Boston: Little Brown.

Sullivan, Richard E. (1960). *Heirs of the Roman Empire*. Ithaca, NY: Cornell University Press.

Sungaila, Helen M. (1979). Let's choose everything: a response to "The Theory Problem." *Journal of Educational Administration* 17(1, May): 87–91.

Swanson, Janice M., and Chenitz, Carol W. (1982). Why qualitative research in nursing? *Nursing Outlook*, 30(4): 241–245.

Swartzberg, Sharan (1978). Letter to the editor. *American Journal of Occupational Therapy* 32: 329.

Tawney, R. H. (1926). *Religion and the Rise of Capitalism*. New York: Mentor Books.

Taylor, James B. (1977). Toward alternative forms of social work research: The case for naturalistic methods. *Journal of Social Welfare* 23: 119–126.

Thelin, John R. (1986). The search for good research: looking for "science" in all the wrong places. *The Review of Higher Education* 10(2, Winter): 151–158.

Thomas, D. A., and Alderfer, C. P. (1989). The influence of race on career dynamics: theory and research on minority career experiences. In M. Arthur, D. Hall, and B. Lawrence (eds.), *Handbook of Career Theory*. Cambridge, England: University Press.

Tibbetts, Paul (1975). On a proposed paradigm shift in the social sciences. *Philosophy and Social Science* 5: 289–297.

Tranel, Daniel D. (1981). A lesson from the physicists. *Personnel and Guidance Journal* 59: 452–429.

Tronto, J. (1987). Beyond gender difference to a theory of care. *Signs* 12(4): 644–663.

Tunnell, Gilbert B. (1977). Three dimensions of naturalness: an expanded definition of field research. *Psychological Bulletin* 84: 426–512.

Tuthill, Doug, and Ashton, Patricia (1983). Improving educational research through the development of educational paradigms. *Educational Researcher* 12(10): 6–14.

Underground Grammarian (1986). The lady with the lump: I can stand out the war with any man. *IMAGE* 18(3): 123.

Unger, Rhoda Kesler (1983). Through the looking glass: no wonderland yet. *Psychology of Women Quarterly* 8(1): 9–32.

Van Maanen, John (1979a). The fact of fiction in organizational ethnography. *Administrative Science Quarterly* 24: 539–550.

Van Maanen, John, ed. (1979b). Qualitative methodology. Special issue of *Administrative Science Quarterly* 24(December).

Van Manen, Max (1980). Doing phenomenological research and writing: an introduction. Monograph No. 7. Alberta, Canada: University of Alberta.

Walberg, Herbert J., Schiller, Diane, and Haertel, Geneva D. (1979). The quiet revolution in educational research. *Educational Researcher*, 8(9): 179–183.

Wax, Murray, and Wax, Rosalie. (1980). Anthropological fieldwork: comments on its values and limitations. *Journal of Thought* 15 (3, Fall): 1–10.

Weber, Max (1958). *The Protestant Ethic and the Spirit of Capitalism*. New York: Charles Scribner's Sons.

Weber, Robert Phillip (1984). Computer-aided content analysis: a short primer. *Qualitative Sociology* 7(1,2, Spring/Summer): 126–147.

Weedon, C. (1987). *Feminist Practice and Poststructuralist Theory*. Oxford: Basil Blackwell.

Weick, Karl (1985). Sources of order in underorganized systems: themes in recent organizational theory. Y. S. Lincoln (ed.), *Organizational Theory and Inquiry: the Paradigm Revolution*. Newbury Park, CA: Sage.

Weick, Karl E. (1976). Educational organizations as loosely coupled systems. *Administrative Science Quarterly* 21: 1–19.

Weiner, Stephen S. (1986). Shipyards in the desert. *The Review of Higher Education* 10(2): 159–164.

Weingartner, Charles (1982). Educational research: the romance of quantification. *Et cetera: A Review of General Sematics* 39(2): 109–128.

Welch, Wayne W. (1983). Experimental inquiry and naturalistic inquiry: an evaluation. *Journal of Research in Science Teaching* 20: 95–103.

White, Morton (1965). *Foundations of Historical Knowledge*. New York: Harper & Row.

Willems, E. P., and Raush, H. L. (1969). *Naturalistic Viewpoints in Psychological Research*. New York: Holt, Reinhart & Winston.

Williamson, John B., Karp, David A., Dalphin, John R., and Gray, Paul S. (1981). *The Research Craft: An Introduction to Social Research Methods* (2nd ed). Boston: Little Brown.

Willower, Donald J. (1981). Educational administration: some philosophical and other considerations. *Journal of Educational Administration* 19(Summer): 115–139.

Wilson, Stephen (1977). The use of ethnographic techniques in educational research. *Review of Educational Research* 47(Winter): 245–265.

Windsor, Ann (1987). Nursing students' perception of clinical experience. *Journal of Nursing Education* 26: 150–154.

Winkler, Karen J. (1986). A historian criticizes value-free scholarship, cites need for moral judgment in research. *Chronicle of Higher Education* 31(17): 10–11.

Winkler, Karen J. (1985). Questioning the science in social science, scholars signal a turn to interpretation. *The Chronicle of Higher Education* 26: 5–9.

Wolcott, Harry F. (1985). On ethnographic intent. *Educational Administration Quarterly* 21(3): 187–203.

Wolcott, Harry F. (1975). Criteria for an ethnographic approach to research in schools. *Human Organizations* 34: 111–128.

Wood, Robert E. (1983). Conflict theory as pedagogy. *Teaching Sociology* 10(4): 463–485.

Yerxa, Elizabeth J. (1984). Evaluation versus research: Outcomes or knowledge? *American Journal of Occupational Therapy* 38: 407–408.

Yerxa, Elizabeth J. (1981). Basic or applied? A developmental assessment of occupational therapy research in 1981. *American Journal of Occupational Therapy* 38: 407–408.

Yin, Robert K. (1984). *Case Study Research: Design and Methods*. Beverly Hills, CA: Sage.

Young-Bruehl, E. (1987). The education of women as philosophers. *Signs* 12: 207–221.

Zukav, Gary (1979). *The Dancing Wu Li Masters: An Overview of the New Physics*. New York: Bantam Books.

Zurmuehlen, Martin (1980). Affirmation and study: phenomenology in doctoral research. *Review of Research in Visual Arts Education* 12: 1–12.

Effects of Academic Labor Markets on Academic Careers

Ted I. K. Youn
School of Education
Boston College

This review examines the literature on academic labor markets and academic careers. While we find a modest body on the subject in social research in labor markets and careers, intellectual interchange among disciplines has been fragmentary. Various disciplines have adopted different units of analysis and have employed different levels of generality and abstraction. Social science research has not developed any explicit conceptualizations to relate careers, formal organizations, and labor markets (see extensive discussion of this general problem in Spenner, Otts, and Call, 1982). One notes, for example, that studies in social psychology consistently treated careers only as elements of individual choice and personal development over life stages. The work of Super (1957), Holland (1973), Levinson (1978), and Miller et al. (1979) argues that careers are individual-level phenomena. Psychological perspectives on careers have generally ignored effects of labor markets on careers.

Treatments of careers and markets in economics and sociology, on the other hand, have been dominated by the economic theory of human capital and the sociological theory of status attainment and stratification. Both perspectives, particularly in the decade of the 1960s, explain careers and income attainments in terms of individual endowments, ability, and investments, and both treat careers as a matter of individual achievement. Most individuals, however, are employed not in a one-on-one situation by an employer, but rather in an organization whose structure and institutional arrangements have some impact on mobility and income attainment. Furthermore, these structural aspects of job and mobility are profoundly affected by the conditions of labor markets. Positional inequality in careers generated by firms, organizations, industries, and the economy has been traditionally excluded by both the theory of human capital and the theory of status attainment.

The author is grateful for comments provided by David W. Breneman, W. Lee Hansen, Michael McPherson, Richard H. Hall, and Rachel Rosenfeld. Alan E. Bayer's helpful suggestions for an earlier draft are gratefully recognized.

In the mid-1970s, there was a slow but discernible shift in the direction of studies pursued by researchers studying labor markets and careers. In broad terms, the shift involved increasing attention to structural and institutional arrangements that may shape wages, job histories, and mobility in workplaces by integrating sociological and economic conceptions of labor markets and careers. Early signs of this development may be found in the emergence of the institutional-economic perspective on labor markets, notably in the work of Doeringer and Piore (1971), Gordon et al. (1972), and Williamson (1975), followed by the work by structuralist sociologists such as Baron and Bielby (1980), Granovetter (1981), Spilerman (1977), and Spenner et al. (1982). The contributions most notably serve to sensitize researchers to the role of formal organizations, particularly stressing the interdependence of formal organizations and their institutional environments in explaining careers and mobility. Hierarchy, either within or among organizations, causes stratified and differentiated labor market outcomes and processes.

This review reflects the general direction of this shift in recent studies of the economics and sociology of labor markets, careers, and organizations; and it synthesizes literature which is relevant to the effects of academic labor markets on careers.

Reviewing several major developments, we can organize these studies into five general categories. The development of these perspectives takes into account the institutional and structural correlates that explain labor market processes and outcomes in higher education. The categories are:

1. Demographic trend analysis
2. Human capital theory
3. Screening model
4. Institutional ascription model
5. Structural perspectives on careers and markets

This chapter reviews several general propositions that seem appropriate in synthesizing these perspectives.

To classify perspectives and traditions of thought may oversimplify reality, but classification aids exposition of the different lines of research and abstraction. My remarks on trends in and preoccupations of recent work through these categories merely represent an organization of convenience. Hence, the classification does not necessarily imply mutually exclusive approaches to analysis.

DEMOGRAPHIC TREND ANALYSIS

One of the early comprehensive attempts to analyze trends in the employment of educated labor forces was carried out by Folger, Astin, and Bayer (1970). Their study was primarily concerned with the more general questions of future utilization patterns, and supply and demand. Specifically, Folger and his colleagues examined the nature of supply and demand imbalances among highly educated workers in tracing flows of populations through levels of education and provided detailed analysis of adjustments that are likely to be made to rectify imbalances between the supply of and the demand for college teaching positions.

While Folger and his colleagues were more interested in broad issues of America's educated labor forces, a series of articles published in the late 1960s and the late 1970s by Allan M. Cartter were more directly concerned with patterns of employment of Ph.D.'s who were to teach in colleges and universities.

Cartter's studies (1965, 1966, 1971, 1972, 1974, 1976) are, again, based on demography and emphasize the changing size of a national cohort of college-age students in predicting future doctoral outputs and the need for Ph.D.'s to teach in colleges and universities.

Cartter's approach relies on linear extrapolation from enrollment levels in higher education, as Folger and his colleagues have done. He establishes that both supply of and demand for Ph.D.'s bulged in the 1960s when the baby boom population enrolled in universities and colleges (Cartter, 1974). For a decade, academic demand for Ph.D.'s exceeded supply and wages rose accordingly. Expanding undergraduate enrollments generated demand for faculty, which in turn encouraged larger graduate enrollments.

According to Cartter, while a relatively fixed portion of university-aged students will become Ph.D.'s, they concentrate in certain fields in response to market trends. Students commonly pursue graduate and professional education only if they are interested in the specific fields, and if there are jobs available in those fields. At advanced levels of education, the market-responsive model clears the market and, therefore, serves as a successful mechanism for balancing supply and demand.

As to factors that determine the level of demand for Ph.D.'s, Cartter argues that demand for Ph.D.'s is also generated by research and development (R&D) expenditures, but that greater demand comes from colleges and universities that need Ph.D.'s to teach undergraduates, whose numbers are determined largely by demographic trends. The technology of education generates a coefficient that, when coupled with the size of undergraduate enrollments in a given period, determines the demand for Ph.D.'s. Thus, Cartter's method is often referred to as a *fixed-coefficient* model.

Cartter's projections, as many young academics learned to their dismay, were remarkably accurate. The labor market for new doctorates in most fields turned sour in the early 1970s.

The criticism of this demographic analysis, particularly of studies by Cartter, came from two sources. First, one group of critics (Freeman, 1971; Freeman and

Breneman, 1974) argued that the enormous imbalance between supply and demand that Cartter projected would not occur, for students would respond rationally by seeking other occupations not requiring the Ph.D. A similar line of criticism applied to the study by Folger, Astin, and Bayer, as their analysis tended to underestimate the role of individuals in making career choices when they faced either shortages or oversupply of educated workers. The argument has its roots in the human capital theory, which stated that individuals would opt for alternative ways of investment and, therefore, that the rate-of-return approach to estimating the future would be more appropriate (Hansen, 1967; Ashenfelter and Mooney, 1968).

The second source of criticism came from several studies that examined the way academic institutions responded to labor market changes (Breneman, 1974; Moffat, 1976; Youn, 1981; Youn, 1989).

Breneman (1976), for example, argued that the Cartter studies ignored the role that academic departments play in governing the supply of new doctorates. In a detailed investigation of the doctoral output of 28 departments at Berkeley covering the 21-year period (1947–1968), Breneman demonstrated the dramatic differences in Ph.D. output among departments, differences far greater than departmental graduate enrollments would suggest. The analysis led to a view of academic departments as prestige-maximizing entities, with definite objectives regarding the number of graduate students to enroll and to receive the degree. This research, completed in 1970, was published in 1976 by the National Bureau of Economic Research, edited by Fromkin, et al. in the volume *Education as an Industry*.

Studies by Moffat (1976) and Youn (1981, 1989) pointed out that Cartter's studies failed to explain the mobility of Ph.D.'s among various institutional groups and, therefore, that a more systematic analysis of how the academic occupational structure works over time was needed.

Cartter's (1976) explanation for the mobility of Ph.D.'s among the institutional groups was shown in the relationship between graduate schools and employing institutions:

> First, it is evident that Ph.D.'s from any given class of graduate schools tend to spread themselves out through the job market, but principally in a downward direction. Second, regardless of the labor market tightness or looseness, institutions tend to hire from the same array of graduate schools. Hiring probably is influenced by school ties of present faculty and personal relationships built up over the years between graduate departments and employing institutions. (p. 203–204)

Cartter (1976) then proposed that:

> One way of viewing the difference in market effects is to measure the proportion of doctorate recipients who take first teaching positions in institutions of superior, equal, or lower prestige than their Ph.D. granting school. (p. 203)

What Cartter refers to as "market effects" on the production and employment of Ph.D.'s in different institutional sectors raises several questions: Is the rate of movement over time from Ph.D. producing to employing institutions constant or changing? What might be the relationship between "market effects" and different academic careers? If institutions tend to hire from the same array of graduate schools, what are the consequences of such "self-recruitment" processes? Later, these questions were dealt with by studies which subscribed to the institutional screening perspective, particularly among sociologists.

THE HUMAN CAPITAL THEORY

In economics, the theory of human capital explains how endowments such as ability and schooling translate into returns in the marketplace, and how an individual's attributes and background generate educational, occupational, and economic attainment at different points in the life course (Becker, 1964; Mincer, 1971; Rees and Schultz, 1970). Early economic studies of academic professionals examined the effects of graduate education on earnings (Ashenfelter and Mooney, 1968; Hansen, 1967; Ashenfelter, 1969; Scott, 1979; Ault, Rutman, and Stevenson, 1979) or the extent of relationships between scholarly productivity and earnings (Hansen, Weisbrod, and Strauss, 1978; Tuckman and Hagemann, 1976).

These economic analyses generally conclude that returns to graduate education are fairly substantial, even though there are differences among fields. Furthermore, scholarly productivity does explain earnings among academics. While an additional unit of research productivity yields a substantial increase in annual earnings, such earnings tend to decline over the career cycle at an increased rate with the number of publications (Hansen et al., 1978).

A more comprehensive economic analysis of academic markets was carried out by Richard Freeman (1971, 1975, 1976). Freeman explains postwar developments in the high-level employment market on the basis of price. The theory of price, according to Freeman, explains the allocation of resources by means of wage differentials. In his analysis of research physicists (1975), Freeman treats the labor market as national, with the demand for physicists coming from universities, government, and private industry, and the supply consisting of young men and women, each choosing a particular career and committing to as many as ten years of university training. Labor markets for the highly educated differ from other job markets in the length of training time required. This training lag means that the supply of Ph.D.'s cannot adjust quickly to changes in demand, which results in a "boom and bust cobweb cycle phenomenon," (1976, p. 64). A shortage of graduates results in higher wages, which attract an increased number of graduate students to the field. Five or more years later these students enter the market, driving wages downward, reducing the quality of placements, and causing prospective students to shift into different fields. Enrollments drop, and five years later there is again a supply shortage, leading to a wage increase.

Empirically, Freeman (1971) demonstrates that, beginning in 1968, there was a sudden decline in the growth rate of first-year graduate enrollments in all fields. At that time, he wrote, there was an unemployment rate of 5.4%, out-mobility of 3.0% for scientists under 30 years of age, and a drastic decline in the growth rate of starting salaries for Ph.D. scientists. Freeman argues that from 1964 to 1969 starting salaries for physicists showed an annual increase (controlling for inflation) of 11.7%, and from 1969 to 1973 the physics labor market witnessed a significant fall in real wages. By 1970 physics earnings over all male professional earnings dropped to the level of 1954, the pre-*Sputnik* era. Physics seems to have experienced the most dramatic decline among the science and engineering fields, but the pattern applied to all fields.

Changes in the academic labor market are described, therefore, in a recursive model that balances wages, enrollments, and Ph.D. outputs over time. Freeman's model assumes that changes in total science Ph.D. output were a function of changes in R&D expenditures, GNP, previous Ph.D. cohort size, starting salaries in alternative occupations, stipends, and the stock of available baccalaureates. (Several methodological points were disputed among economic studies. See James P. Smith and Finis Welch, 1978.)

Economic studies (in the neoclassical tradition), such as those by Freeman, focused on the workings of the labor market and the interplay between supply and demand to determine individual earnings. Put another way, the neoclassical perspective posits a marginal productivity theory of distribution which assumes perfect competition, complete knowledge, and rationality. Therefore, the theory points to wage competition as the central force driving the labor market. This particular tradition also assumes that people generally come into the labor market with definite, preexisting skills, or lack of skills, and that they compete against one another on the basis of wages. According to this theory, education and training are crucial because they generate the skills that people bring into the market. As a highly skilled person raises his or her productivity, he or she also raises earnings.

While there had been emerging criticisms of human capital models from radical and Marxist economic theorists who challenged this orthodox theory from the perspective of historically rooted class-based conflicts between workers and employers (Boweles and Gintis, 1975; Marglin, 1976), sociologists challenged human capital models with different conclusions (Granovetter, 1977; Baron and Bielby, 1980; Berg, 1981). While the human capital theory posits that labor markets offer open opportunity and workers' wages are largely a function of ability, education, and training, sociologists regard wages as heavily constrained by institutional inflexibility rather than by the skills and merit of the worker. The prevailing economic analysis usually ignores institutional structures and occupation as intervening variables (Stolzenberg, 1975). For sociologists, occupations are the key to understanding earnings or other workings of the labor market. The forces that determine an individual's occupational attainment affect earnings (Granovetter, 1981). Structural properties such as rigid career ladders and early career attainments are imposed by the nature of the occupation itself.

The influence of occupational categories is most apparent in measuring career mobility between occupations. Occupational segmentation generates relatively impermeable barriers to mobility between different occupational boundaries (Spaeth, 1979; Tolbert, 1982).

In a way, occupational categories are analogous to an array of institutions differentially ranked in the academic system. In other words, the logic used to determine occupational segmentation between professional, managerial, and manual work is similar to the logic that discretely separates academic research work at elite research institutions from teaching at two-year or technical institutions (Youn, 1989). Thus, there are relatively impermeable barriers between research and teaching sectors. While the rate of mobility between these sectors may be facilitated in early career periods, later career mobility among academics may be constrained by institutional barriers.

Sociological critics generally do not underestimate the importance of an individual's ability, skills, and personal characteristics in determining one's success and failure. But they also argue that ideologies vary from one institutional setting to another, and institutional structures of occupation and work organizations weaken individual choice and competition and thus contribute to the persistence of inequality among workers. The general idea of institutional sorting and the notion of occupational impediments to workers' mobility have led to an alternative perspective to human capital theory, the "job competition" model.

THE SCREENING OR "JOB COMPETITION" MODEL

This approach is almost an obvious antithesis to the theory of marginal productivity of distribution postulated by the theory of human capital. It argues that labor markets are rarely competitive and that institutional impediments create market imperfections (Reder, 1955; Berg, 1971). Contrary to the conventional theory of marginal productivity, alternative distributional mechanisms must be introduced, based on market imperfections that actually exist.

The institutional screening model or "job competition" model has also been called *credentialism* or *queuing theory* and involves the idea of *vestibules* in the labor market. The central idea is that a given degree or field is valuable because of the advantage it offers in a job market where training is differentiated in terms of "quality" (Niland, 1972; Stiglitz, 1975; Wyer and Conrad, 1984). Proponents of the screening model (Niland, 1972; Adkins, 1974; Moffat, 1976; Wyer and Conrad, 1984) argue that social factors, such as institutional prestige, origin, or organizational location, induce higher aspirations in the college-going population and hence determine enrollment and outputs in graduate education.

Screening-model advocates argue that jobs are also differentiated according to their quality and attractiveness, regardless of the existing labor market situation. Change in the demand for higher education leads to job shifting among Ph.D.'s—that is, some less qualified Ph.D.'s would be absorbed into new types of jobs, such as two-year-college teaching. In effect this would upgrade the credentials required for certain occupations (Thurow, 1972, 1975, 1976). Since it emphasizes an upgrading of credentials, this approach can be characterized as "job competition," in which a Ph.D.'s place in a queue is based largely upon the quality of his or her education.

According to this approach, the prestige and resources of a field and a particular graduate department determine its appeal to students, who believe that high-prestige degrees will help them obtain better jobs. A Ph.D. student with a high-prestige education merely displace another student with less desirable institutional origins from a job for which the latter may be equally qualified (Niland, 1972).

Advocates of the "job competition" theory, in contrast to the orthodox "wage competition" theory, argue that (1) the number and type of job slots are *technologically determined*; (2) the workers' skills and their wages are nearly irrelevant in determining the number and type of job positions actually filled; (3) wages are, in fact, claimed to be rigid, and "queues" of workers at relatively fixed wages constitute the supply of labor; and (4) hiring employers use screening devices based on the attractiveness of individual workers.

Based on this theory, several relevant conclusions can be drawn on the general state of academic markets and higher education in America. First, the distribution of academic job opportunities is determined partly by the character of technological progress, which generates specific jobs in certain proportions. Society's demands for certain types of knowledge, as well as technical changes since World War II, have profoundly affected research-oriented personnel in universities. The post-*Sputnik* upsurge of scientific development and public policy changes brought a massive change in institutions of higher education.

Second, institutional habits and customs influence academic wage rates. Wages are generally inflexible in entry-level academic jobs. Thus, skills, ability, and other qualifications for a given job will have a minimal effect on wages. Academic jobs are segmented by a variety of institutional factors. Thus, academic workers, by and large, seem to operate in *labor markets* that offer different working conditions, different opportunities, and different institutional norms to govern incentives.

In the "wage competition" model, according to Thurow (1975), wages fluctuate in the short run to clear the market, while in the long run, wage changes precipitate shifts in supply and demand curves. In the case of the "job competition" model, Thurow contends (1975), changes in hiring standards and required training help to clear markets. Only after a substantial period of disequilibrium in relative wages do changes occur. According to the "job competition" model, the academic labor market can clear its disequilibrium by inducing more credential requirements (Ph.D. requirements) and additional (postdoctoral) training.

Finally, in Ph.D. labor markets, supply is constituted by the "queue" of the highly trained workers. An individual's prospects are determined by her or his relative position in the academic labor queue (i.e., prestige of the Ph.D.-granting institution) or labeling of individuals (Stiglitz, 1975) and distribution of job opportunities in academic labor markets. As Thurow observes, the most preferred workers (Ph.D.'s from the most prestigious institutions, in this case) get the best institutional offers. These preferred workers may receive wages that are not related to their productivity but to the rank order of their institutional positions (Lazear and Rosen, 1981). In this context, an academic job is best thought of as "a lifetime sequence of jobs rather than as a specific job with a specific employer with specific skills" (Thurow, 1975, p. 76), and the basic allocative process depends on institutional screening.

The idea of the labor market "queue" also raises the possibility of uses of signals given by job seekers and evaluations of attractiveness of job seekers (Spence, 1973; Wyer and Conrad, 1984). Academic job seekers from less prestigious origin adopt a signal that represents a particular membership, while job seekers from more attractive origins obviously provide a signal which may have a different set of employer's expectations. The greater the correspondence between the signals (as interpreted by the prospective employers) and the employee's later productivity, the greater the efficiency of the labor market.

INSTITUTIONAL ASCRIPTION MODEL

Several sociological studies of scientists' careers in academic markets analyze the relationship between scientific productivity and institutional prestige (departmental prestige). Although they differ in research design, data, measures of scientific or scholarly productivity, and measures of institutional prestige and location, these studies consistently report a positive relationship between scientific productivity and departmental prestige (Caplow and McGee, 1958; Berelson, 1960; Crane, 1965, 1970; Hargens and Hagstrom, 1967; Hagstrom and Hargens, 1968; Hargens, 1969; Cole and Cole, 1973; Burke, 1988).

In reviewing major studies in the field, we find two explanations for the relationship between institutional position and productivity. One suggests that more prestigious departments select more productive scientists for their faculties;

that is to say, productivity is causally prior to institutional position. The alternative proposes that being at a more prestigious department or institution facilitates greater productivity.

The first argument is promulgated by Storer (1966) and Cole and Cole (1973), whose studies are based on Merton's (1973) notion of the normative structure of the social system of science. Merton argues that science is governed by norms of universalism, according to which scientific achievement determines careers. Studies by Hargens and Hagstrom (1967), Storer (1966), and Cole and Cole (1973) show that a scientist's productivity has as strong an effect on academic appointment as does the ranking of the scientist's doctoral department.

Taking the second position, Diana Crane's study (1970) concludes that the prestige of one's doctorate has more influence on being selected by a prestigious position than productivity does. "Despite the system's normative commitment to universalistic criteria," she argues, "they are not utilized in practice" (p. 961), suggesting that ascriptive rules may explain the academic reward system. Studies by J. S. Long (1978), Long, Allison, and McGinnis (1979), Long and McGinnis (1981), and B. Reskin (1979) support Crane's thesis. Long's careful analysis of careers in biochemistry challenges the contention that academic positions are allocated exclusively or largely on the basis of scientific productivity. The study by Long and his colleagues (1979) finds that the effect of departmental location on individual productivity is strong, while the effect of productivity on the allocation of academic positions is weak. The prestige of a scientist's first teaching position is influenced by ascriptive processes or particularistic rules. Doctoral prestige has the strongest impact on the prestige of first position, even though it may have a smaller impact on future productivity. Preemployment productivity among scientists has little impact on the prestige of the first position. Furthermore, the study finds that the effect of departmental prestige on productivity increases steadily over time.

As the debate over achievement vs. ascription continued, Reskin (1979) introduced another source of ascriptive effects. Her work is concerned primarily with the influence of sponsorship on students' careers. She concludes that in the academic stratification system, ascriptive rules play an important role. (The institutional versions of ascriptive rules are the prestige of doctoral origins and the first job, and the eminence of sponsorship.) Sponsorship by eminent scientists and scholars at the initial career stage furthers the later careers of academic scientists. Reskin concludes that institutional ascription, not achievement, explains successful careers. Similarly, a study by Cameron and Blackburn (1981) reports that sponsorship variables affect the nature of first job placement and access to other resources such as research grants, opportunities for collaboration, and involvement in networks. Thus, sponsorship by eminent senior colleagues explains the extent of academic career success.

Several important points are made by the institutional ascription model. First, studies in this vein conclude that academic or scientific career mobility does not resemble an open-opportunity model. Academic job seekers' decisions are constrained by institutional attributes such as doctoral prestige, the prestige of the hiring department, the eminence of sponsorship, and the nature of the hiring organization. The academic stratification system does not promote a perfectly competitive system where individual members are valued on the basis of universalism. Social ties that determine career mobility in academia work in more particularistic ways.

Secondly, the location of the initial job has an important effect on future success. The prestige of the first career position is determined largely by the prestige of the graduate institution. Even preemployment productivity has little impact on the location of the first job.

While these studies aid understanding of the theoretical problems of academic stratification, they are mostly concerned only with elite academic scientists in particular fields. They ignore problems faced by academics who are recruited by teaching institutions or other organizations in the system of higher education. The ascription model presents a picture of a meritocratic social system in higher education where institutional rules continue to breed inequality of opportunity.

Then, does the extent of ascription increase as job market conditions change? In tighter markets, will job seekers depend more upon ascriptive rules?

THE STRUCTURAL PERSPECTIVE ON CAREERS AND LABOR MARKETS

In the mid-1970s the growing concern among social scientists with problems of social inequality and poverty led to the introduction of radical and structural perspectives to the study of labor markets (Gordon, 1972; Doeringer and Piore, 1971; Harrison, 1971; Reich et al., 1973; Rumberger and Carnoy, 1980; Bluestone, 1968). While the conventional status attainment theory and the neoclassical theory of human capital treat social inequality as evidence of differences among individuals in terms of endowments possessed and returns expected in the marketplace, the emerging radical and structural perspective focuses on the larger structural and institutional mechanisms that might cause inequality among social positions (Kerr, 1954; Kalleberg and Sørensen, 1979; Tolbert, Patrick, and Beck, 1980; Baron, 1984; Stolzenberg, 1975; Spilerman, 1977). Researchers have increasingly recognized that rewards are attached to organizational positions and that organizations differ systematically in their allocative process and rewards. A class of organizations within any particular social system forms a distinct stratification system. The American higher education system has its activities separated into different types of institutions. These institutions, "deliberately or otherwise" (Clark, 1983), are ordered into hierarchies. Hierarchy divides labor markets into discretely separate entities (Edwards, 1979; Gordon, Edwards, and Reich, 1982; Youn, 1981; Youn, 1989; 1988). One such structural mechanism is the formal organization, or firm, which relates to the complex nature of labor markets.

Jobs fall into one of two discretely related labor markets—internal or external. Internal labor markets impose administrative rules and procedures which determine the allocation of labor for jobs, while external markets allocate labor to jobs on the basis of direct economic relationships, such as competition. Hence, the dual labor market hypothesis explains differences among individuals and social inequality in a social system.

The dual labor market hypothesis led to useful exchanges between labor economics and sociological analyses of occupations. A career is no longer viewed as merely a matter of individual achievement. Depending on a person's location on the job ladder, career opportunities are set beyond personal control. The extent of labor market segmentation shapes career outcomes (Kalleberg and Sørensen, 1979; Youn, 1989). Hence, structurally formed career lines are created and maintained by labor market complexities (Spilerman, 1977). The institutional environment encompassing a worker's career origins shapes opportunity structures and thereby constrains and channels subsequent career outcomes.

Important contributions arising from the exchanges between sociological studies and radical economic literature in the mid and the late 1970s include the knowledge that social structure and institutional arrangements shape careers and an understanding of how labor markets interact with careers.

Yet, in social science research, substantial disagreements exist on the conceptualization and measurement of sectors and labor markets (see Baron and Bielby, 1980, for the debates). Some say that the structuralist perspective and radical economic theory ignore the role of personal factors and individual choice in careers and attainments (see Cain's discussion—Cain, 1976). Nevertheless, some basic propositions set out by structuralists and radical/institutional economists are useful in understanding the nature of academic careers and their relationship to academic labor markets. The individual choice model pursued by orthodox economic studies falls far short of explaining the more institutional and sectoral characteristics of academic labor markets, as well as the complex interactions between academic organizations (firms) and labor markets.

SUMMARY

Having thus reviewed a number of perspectives, I can now offer some general statements on the nature of academic markets and careers. Even though these generalizations represent areas of controversy, they should help us understand the nature of academic careers and labor markets.

Effects of Academic Hierarchies on Market Stratification.
Over 3,000 American universities and colleges in varying degrees have activities arranged into different status hierarchies. Hierarchies create differentiated and stratified labor markets.

First, a vertical differentiation of institutions evolves in two distinct tasks: advancing knowledge through research and educating students through teaching. At the top of the hierarchy, leading research institutions command greater prestige while promoting a more universalistic orientation toward research. At the lower rung of the status ladder, two-year and junior colleges place greater emphasis on localized rewards for successful teaching.

Secondly, this institutional hierarchy based on organizational tasks may be subdivided into further categories whether they are public or private, secular or religious, and so on. Each subdivision of institutions is arranged into a vertical differentiation. Each subdivision thus breeds divided or segmented labor markets.

Hierarchy within an institution leads to internal labor markets for tenure-track positions, non-tenure-track positions, and part-time positions (Roemer and Schmitz, 1982; Tuckman and Pickerill, 1988).

This subdivision of organizational labor markets limits mobility chances (Rosenfeld and Jones, 1988). Thus, it creates problems of exit and reentry into academia.

While Cartter's (1976) analysis fails to incorporate the nature of academic organizations into the fixed-coefficient model, orthodox economic studies typically argue that the variables under investigation—income and prices, for example—are worth studying on their own merits. The model Freeman proposes assumes either that unmeasured variables, such as organizational or other institutional attributes, do not change, or that they change without affecting the expected values of variables that are under investigation (see also Cain, 1976 for a similar argument). Indeed, this controversy renders the issue more empirical than theoretical.

The "job competition" model of the screening perspective recognizes that the types of job positions available affect labor market outcomes. Thus, an academic's location may affect his or her chance of being attractive in different types of markets. The screening model fails to indicate, however, that organizations impinge on labor market outcomes. Instead, emphasis is placed on the individual who competes in a queue for various academic jobs (Niland, 1972; Youn, 1989).

Studies by the sociologists of science recognize the importance of institutional ascription, such as the prestige of the graduate department, and its effects on mobility and career success. These studies are often involved in case studies of elite scientists and, therefore, are unable to incorporate a more dynamic relationship between different organizations and their markets.

Structuralists argue—euphemistically referring to "bringing the firms back in" (Baron and Bielby, 1980)—that organizational hierarchy and process should be incorporated into empirical analysis of economic segmentation and work. Yet, models for measuring structural effects on individual attainment or covariation among occupational and industrial characteristics remain incomplete.

Effects of Labor Market Outcomes.

More recent studies indicate that multiple career outcomes are possible as a result of the multiple nature of academic markets (Rosenfeld and Jones, 1987; Youn, 1981). Sectors that affect mobility and career success have distinct boundaries; an academic can presumably start out in a research career and either continue there or move to an academic teaching career (Rosenfeld, 1984; Youn and Zelterman, 1986) but may not be able to move from a teaching career to a research career at a major research institution (Parsons and Platt, 1973).

The degree of differentiation among academic organizations (Clark, 1983) and the degree of differentiation among academic fields suggest a multiplicity of overlapping markets—markets for research and graduate training organizations, for undergraduate teaching, for two-year college teaching (Brown, 1967; Clark, 1966; Cohen and Brawer, 1977), and so on (Smelser and Content, 1980; Youn and Zelterman, 1986; Youn, 1989). Relatively impermeable barriers to mobility between teaching and research seem to exist. Among academic fields, constraints on mobility seemed to be even greater between and among academic fields.

Thus, one could conclude empirically that the persistence of inequality of opportunity among academics in the educational system exists and could ask whether relative differences in the distribution of earnings may continue.

Generally, orthodox economists find little empirical support for the dual-market theories of status or mobility, and most empirical analyses produce no support for immobility across the occupational boundaries (Leigh, 1976). Freeman's studies (1971, 1975, 1976) argue that there is evidence of interfield mobility as well as intersectoral mobility when the level of demand decreases, while no interorganizational mobility has been suggested. The screening model suggests little or no evidence of immobility among jobs or sectors in academia.

Structuralists and institutional economists argued for generalization about outcomes of labor markets, however—namely, evidence of immobility between different segments (Tolbert et al., 1980; Bluestone, 1968; Osterman, 1975).

Effects of Entry Job on Career Lines.

Several studies (Long, 1978; Long et al., 1979; Reskin, 1979) argue that in the academic stratification system, the prestige of an academic's first job depends a great deal on institutional ascription, such as doctoral prestige and doctoral sponsorship. Even predoctoral productivity matters little to career success. Even though the point was not stressed by Long et al. (1979) and Reskin (1979), an extension of this argument raises the possibility that an initial position in an organization may be subject to internal labor markets. That is, entry jobs or entry portals lead into predetermined progression systems. Entering a research career may affect the option of continuing in research or moving to a teaching career, but entering a teaching career may not easily lead to a research career (Youn and Zelterman, 1986). There exists also the possibility of two career lines (Spilerman, 1977), which are-age specific and organization-specific. The research career line may be susceptible to the level of scholarly productivity and other institutionalized norms, while success in a teaching career line may be determined by organizational and bureaucratic rules.

A recent study of mobility among academic scientists by Allison and Long (1987) concludes that the prestige of the job destination is determined by the prestige of the prior job, suggesting that having a research-oriented position would likely lead to another research position. A similar conclusion is also made in a paper by Youn and Zelterman (1986) that the idea of orderly and sequential career lines may not work in academia.

The natural question is: If organizational prestige is subject to allocative rules, how much can career attainment depend on individual productivity and earnings?

Effects of Temporal Changes on Labor Markets and Careers.

Expansion and slowdown in the growth of the educational system over time raise important questions regarding the nature of career mobility and structural changes in markets (Freeman, 1975; Smelser, 1974; Smelser and Content, 1980; Youn, 1981, 1984). When the level of demand changes substantially, a number of complex institutional changes may follow (Breneman, 1976; Smith and Karlesky, 1977). For instance, the change from a period of expansion to a period of decline often increases the effect of the institutional ascription and, thus, increases the probability of downward distribution. Change from one period to another often increases the degree of market rigidity, and with it the degree of career segmentation between research and teaching. The study by Smelser and Content (1980) points out that the social structural base of the academic profession that is created in a period of expansion of higher education became a source of inflexibility when that phase gave way to a period of reduced growth. The structural base that a growing system needed to perform to capacity then faced a problem of excess capacity. This problem, in turn, raised a number of other questions regarding the political dimension of the academic recruitment system and the role of political actors in making decisions in academic organizations (Smelser, 1974; Trow, 1974).

Finally, a number of provocative research issues remain unstudied, for examplee: Does the change over time affect shifts in demand among disciplines? Does the temporal change widen salary differentials among fields? The answers to these questions may not be found by relying solely on either the structuralist model or the individual choice model. Individual earnings and career attainment in higher education may be explained by social and economic changes which explain the shift in demand and supply.

This chapter has reviewed the empirical corpus of literature on the subject matter and summarized several propositions that help to explain the relationship between academic labor markets and academic careers. Even though our basic intent is not to argue that one perspective or theory should replace the others, this chapter shows that there is evidence of a shift toward more structural explanations in studies of academic careers and markets.

Our examination of the levels and units of analysis adopted by the various approaches suggests areas where different perspectives may overlap or diverge. This chapter argues that research on academic careers and markets would benefit by incorporating the organizational structure and process of higher education into empirical analyses of economic segmentation and work.

REFERENCES

Adkins, Douglas L. (1974). The American educated labor force: an empirical look at theories of its formation and composition. In M. Gordon (ed.), *Higher Education and the Labor Market* New York: McGraw-Hill.

Allison, Paul D., and Long, J. Scott (1987). Mobility of scientists. *American Sociological Review* 53: 643–652.

Ashenfelter, Orley (1969). Some evidence on the private returns to graduate education. *Southern Economics Journal* 35(3): 247–256.

Ashenfelter, Orley, and Mooney, Joseph D. (1968). Graduate education, ability and earnings. *Review of Economics and Statistics* 49(1): 78–86.

Ault, David E., Rutman, Gilbert, and Stevenson, Thomas (1979). Mobility in the labor market for academic economists. *American Economic Review* 69: 148–153.

Baldwin, R. G., and Blackburn, R. T. (1981). The academic career as a developmental process: implications for higher education. *Journal of Higher Education* 52: 598–614.

Barbezat, Debra (1988). Gender differences in the academic reward system. In D. W. Breneman, and T. I. K. Youn, (eds.), *Academic Labor Markets and Careers*. New York: Stanford Series in Education and Public Policy.

Baron, James N. (1984). Organizational perspectives on stratification. *Annual Review of Sociology* 10: 37–69.

Baron, J. N., and Bielby, William (1980). Bringing the firms back in: stratification, segmentation, and the organization of work. *American Sociological Review* 45: 737–765.

Bayer, Alan E. (1968). The effect of international interchange of high-level manpower in the U.S. *Social Forces* 46: 465–477.

Becker, Gary S. (1964). *Human Capital*. New York: Columbia University Press.

Berelson, Bernard (1960). *Graduate Education in U.S.* New York: McGraw-Hill.

Berg, Ivar (1971) *Education and Jobs: The Great Training Robbery*. Boston: Beacon Press.

Berg, Ivar (1981). *Sociological Perspectives on Labor Markets*. New York: Academic Press.

Bluestone, Barry (1968). The tripartite economy: labor markets and the working poor. *Poverty and Human Resources* (July/August), pp. 2–41.

Boweles, Samuel, and Gintis, Herbert (1975). *Schooling in Capitalist America*. New York: Basic Books.

Breneman, David W. (1974). *Graduate School Adjustments to the New Depression in Higher Learning*. Washington, DC: National Board on Graduate Education.

Breneman, David W. (1976). The Ph.D. production process. In J. T. Fromkin, Tamison, D. T. and Radner, Roy (eds.), *Education as an Industry* National Bureau of Economic Research. Cambridge, MA: Ballinger.

Breneman, David W. (1977). Effects of recent trends in graduate education on university research capability in physics, chemistry, and mathematics. In B. L. Smith and J. Karlesky (eds.), *The State of Academic Science*. New York: Change Press.

Breneman, David W., and Youn, Ted I. K., (eds.) (1988). *Academic Labor Markets and Careers*. Philadelphia, PA: Stanford Series in Education and Public Policy, The Falmer Press.

Brown, David G. (1967). *The Mobile Professors*. Washington, DC: American Council on Education.

Burke, Dolores L. (1988) *A New Academic Marketplace*. New York: Greenwood Press.

Cain, Glen (1976). The challenge of segmented labor market theories of orthodox theory: a survey. *Journal of Economic Literature* (December), pp. 1215–1257.

Cameron, S. W., and Blackburn, R. T. (1981). Sponsorship and academic career success. *Journal of Higher Education* 52: 369–378.

Caplow, Theodore, and McGee, Reece (1958). *The Academic Marketplace*. Garden City, NY: Doubleday.

Cartter, Allan M. (1965). The supply and demand of college teachers. *American Statistical Association*, Social Statistics Proceedings, pp. 70–80.

Cartter, Allan M. (1966). *An Assessment of Quality in Education*. Washington, DC: American Council on Education.

Cartter, Allan M. (1971). Scientific manpower trends for 1970–1980. *Science* 172: 132–140.

Cartter, Allan M. (1972). Faculty needs and resources in american higher education. *Annals of the American Academy of Science* 404:71–87.

Cartter, Allan M. (1974). The academic labor market. In M. S. Gordon (ed.), *Higher Education and the Labor Market*. New York: McGraw-Hill.

Cartter, Allan M. (1976). *Ph.D.'s and the Academic Labor Market*. New York: McGraw-Hill.

Clark, B. R. (1966). The mass college. In Vollmer, Howard M., and Mills, Donald L. (eds.), *Professionalization*. New York: Prentice-Hall.

Clark, B. R. (1983). *The Higher Education System: Academic Organization in Cross-National Perspective*. Berkeley: University of California Press.

Clark, B. R. (1987). *The Academic Life: Small Worlds, Different Worlds*. Princeton, NJ: Princeton University Press.

Cohen, A., and Brawer, F. (1977). *A Two-Year College Instructor Today*. New York: Praeger Press.

Cole, Jonathan R., and Cole, Stephen (1973). *Social Stratification in Science*. Chicago: University of Chicago Press.

Cole, Stephen, and Cole, Jonathan R. (1967). Scientific output and recognition: a study in the operation of the reward system in science. *American Sociological Review* 32: 377–390.

Crane, Diana (1965). Scientists at major and minor universities: a study in productivity and recognition. *American Sociological Review* 30: 699–714.

Crane, Diana (1970). The academic marketplace revisited. *American Journal of Sociology* 7: 953–964.

Doeringer, Peter B., and Piore, M. J. (1971). *Internal Labor Markets and Manpower Analysis*. Lexington, MA: Heath Lexington Books.

Edwards, Richard (1979). *Contested Terrain: The Transformation of Workplace in the Twentieth Century*. New York: Basic Books.

Folger, J. K., Astin, Helen S., and Bayer, Alan E. (1970). *Human Resources and Higher Education: Staff Report of the Commission on Human Resources and Advanced Education*. New York: Russell Sage Foundation.

Freeman, Richard B. (1971). *The Market for College-Trained Manpower: A Study in the Economics of Career Choice*. Cambridge, MA: Harvard University Press.

Freeman, Richard B., and Breneman, D. W. (1975). *Forecasting the Ph.D. Labor Market: Pitfalls for Policy*. Washington, DC: National Board on Graduate Education.

Freeman, Richard B. (1975). Supply and salary adjustments to the changing science manpower market: physics 1948–73. *American Economic Review* 65:27–39.

Freeman, Richard B. (1976). *The Overeducated American*. New York: Academic Press.

Fromkin, J. T., Tamison, D. T., and Radner, Roy (eds.) (1976). *Education as an Industry*. National Bureau of Economic Research, Cambridge, MA: Ballinger

Gordon, David M. (1972). *Theories of Poverty and Unemployment: Orthodox, Radical and Dual Labor Market Perspectives*. Lexington, MA: Heath Lexington Books.

Gordon, David M., Edwards, R., and Reich, M. (1982). *Segmented Work, Divided Workers*. Cambridge, MA: Cambridge University Press.

Granovetter, Mark. Review of Mincer's Schooling, experience and earnings *Harvard Educational Review*. 46(February): 123–127.

Granovetter, Mark (1974) Review of Mincer's Schooling, experience and earnings. *Sociological Quarterly* 18:608–612.

Granovetter, Mark (1981). Toward a sociological theory of income differences. In I. Berg (ed.), *Sociological Perspectives on Labor Markets*. New York: Academic Press.

Hagstrom, W. O., and Hargens, Lowell L. (1968). Mobility theory in the sociology of science. Paper presented at the Cornell Conference on Human Mobility, Ithaca (September).

Hansen, W. Lee (1967). The economics of scientific and engineering manpower. *Journal of Human Resources* 2(Spring): 191–215.

Hansen, W. Lee, Weisbrod, B. A., and Strauss, R. P. (1978). Modeling the earnings and research productivity of academic economists. *Journal of Political Economy* 86: 729–741.

Hargens, Lowell L. (1969). Patterns of mobility of new Ph.D.'s among american academic institutions. *Sociology of Education* 42:18–37.

Hargens, Lowell L., and Farr, G. M. (1973). An examination of recent hypotheses about institutional inbreeding. *American Journal of Sociology* 78: 1381–1402.

Hargens, Lowell L., and Hagstrom, Warren O. (1967). Sponsored and contest mobility of American academic scientists. *Sociology of Education* 40: 24–38.

Harrison, Bennett (ed.) (1954). *Education, Training and the Urban Ghetto*. Baltimore: Johns Hopkins University Press.

Holland, J. L. (1973). *Makling Vocational Choices: A Theory of Careers*. Englewood Cliffs, NJ: Prentice-Hall.

Kalleberg, Arne L., and Sørensen, Aage B. (1979). The sociology of labor markets. In *Annual Review of Sociology*, Vol. 5, edited by Alex Inkeles et al. Palo Alto, CA.

Kerr, Clark (1954). The Balkanization of labor markets. In E. Wright Bakke et al. (eds.), *Labor Mobility and Economic Opportunity*. Cambridge, MA: MIT Press.

Kohn, Melvin L., and Schooler, Carmi (1973). Occupational experience and psychological functioning: an assessment of reciprocal effects. *American Sociological Review* 38: 97–118.

Kohn, Melvin L., and Schooler, Carmi (1978). The reciprocal effects of substantive complexity of work and intellectual flexibility: a longitudinal assessment. *American Journal of Sociology* 84: 24–52.

Lazear, Edward P., and Rosen, S. (1981). Rank-order tournaments as optimum labor contracts. *Journal of Political Economy* 89: 135–148.

Leigh, Duane E. (1976). Occupational advancement in the late 1960's: an indirect test of the dual labor market hypothesis. *Journal of Human Resources* 11(Spring): 155–171.

Levinson, Daniel J. (1978). *The Seasons of a Man's Life*. New York: Knopf.

Long, J. Scott (1978). Productivity and academic position in the scientific career. *American Sociological Review* 43: 889–908.

Long, J. Scott, Allison, P. D., and McGinnis, R. (1979). Entrance into the academic career. *American Sociological Review* 44: 816–830.

Long, J. Scott, and McGinnis, R. (1981). Organizational context and scientific productivity. *American Sociological Review* 46: 422–442.

Marglin, Stephen A. (1976). What do bosses do? The origins and functions of hierarchy in capitalist production. *Review of Radical Political Economy (Summer)*, pp. 60–112.

McGee, R. (1960). The function of institutional inbreeding. *American Journal of Sociology* 65: 483–488.

Merton, Robert K. (1973). *The Sociology of Science*. Chicago: University of Chicago Press.

Miller, Joanne, Schooler, Carmi, Kohn, Melvin, and Miller, Karen (1979). Women and work: the psychological effects of occupational conditions. *American Journal of Sociology* 85: 66–94.

Mincer, Jacob (1971). *Schooling, Age, and Earnings*. New York: National Bureau of Economic Research.

Moffat, Linda (1976). Departmental prestige and doctoral production: an analysis of the structure of graduate education in physics from 1964 to 1972. Unpublished doctoral dissertation, Cornell University, Ithaca, NY.

National Board of Graduate Education (1975). *Outlook and Opportunities for Graduate Education*. Washington, DC.

Niland, J. R. (1972). Allocation of Ph.D. manpower in the academic labor market. *Industrial Relations* 2: 141–156.

Osterman, Paul (1975). An empirical study of labor market segmentation. *Industrial Labor Relations Review* 28: 508–523.

Parsons, Tallcott, and Platt, G. M. (1973). *The American University*. Cambridge, MA: Harvard University Press.

Reder, Melvin W. (1955). The theory of occupational wage differentials. *American Economic Review* 45(December): 833–852.

Rees, A., and Shultz, G. (1970). *Workers and Wages in an Urban Labor Market*. Chicago: University of Chicago Press.

Reich, Michael, et al. (1973). A theory of labor market segmentation. *American Economic Review* 62(2, May): 359–365.

Reskin, Barbara (1979). Academic sponsorship and scientist careers. *Sociology of Education* 52: 129–146.

Roemer, R., and Schmitz, J. E. (1982). Academic employment as day labor: the dual labor market in higher education. *Journal of Higher Education* 59: 516–531.

Rosenfeld, Rachel (1984). Academic career mobility for women and men psychologists. In V. Haas and C. Peiruci (eds.) *Scientific and Engineering Professions*. Ann Arbor: University of Michigan Press.

Rosenfeld, Rachel A., and Jones, Jo Ann (1987). Institutional mobility among academics. *Sociology of Education* 59: 212–226.

Rosenfeld, Rachel A., and Jones, Jo Ann (1988). Exit and reentry in higher education. In D. W. Breneman, and T. I. K. Youn, (eds.) *Academic Labor Markets and Careers*. New York: Stanford Series in Education and Public Policy.

Rumberger, Russell W., and Carnoy, Martin (1980). Segmentation in the U.S. labour markets: its effects on mobility and earnings of whites and blacks. *Cambridge Journal of Economics* 4: 117–132.

Scott, C. D. (1979). The market for Ph.D. economists: the academic sector. *American Economic Review* 69: 137–141.

Smelser, Neil J. (1974). Growth, structural change, and conflict in California public higher education, 1950–70. In Smelser, N. J., and Almond, G. (eds.), *Public Higher Education in California*. Berkeley: University of California Press.

Smelser, Neil J., and Content, Robin (1980). *The Changing Academic Market: General Trends and a Berkeley Case Study*. Berkeley: University of California Press.

Smith, B. L. R., and Karlesky, J. J. (1977). *The State of Academic Science: The Universities in the Nation's Research Effort*. New York: Change Magazine Press.

Smith, J. P., and Welch, Finis (1978) Overeducated American? *Proceedings of the National Academy of Education* Washington, DC: Vol. 5, pp. 49–83.

Spaeth, J. L. (1979). Vertical differentiation among occupations. *American Sociological Review* 49: 746–762.

Spence, Michael, A. (1973). Job market signaling. *Quarterly Journal of Economics*. 83: 355–374.

Spenner, Kenneth I., Otto, L. B., and Call, V. R. A. C. (1982). *Career Lines and Careers. Lexington, MA: D. C. Heath and Co.*

Spilerman, Seymour (1977). Careers, labor market structure and socioeconomic achievement. *American Journal of Sociology* 83: 551–593.

Stiglitz, J. R. (1975). The theory of screening, education and the distribution of income. *American Economic Review* 65: 315–342.

Stolzenberg, R. M. (1975). Occupations, labor markets and the process of wage attainments. *American Sociological Review* 40: 645–665.

Storer, Norman W. (1966). *The Social System of Science*. New York: Holt Rinehart & Winston.

Super, D. E. (1957). *The Psychology of Careers*. New York: Harper & Row.

Thurow, Lester C., and Lucas, Robert E. B. (1972). *The American Distribution of Income: A Structural Problem*. Joint Economic Committee Print, 92nd Congress, 2nd Session.

Thurow, Lester C. (1975). *Generating Inequality*. New York: Basic Books.

Thurow, Lester C. (1976). Education and economic equality. *The Public Interest 28: 66–81*.

Tolbert, Charles M., Patrick, M., and Beck, E. M. (1980). The structure of economic segmentation: a dual economy approach. *American Journal of Sociology* 80: 1–10.

Tolbert, Charles M. (1982). Industrial segmentation and men's career mobility. *American Sociological Review* 47: 457–476.

Trow, Martin (1974). Problems in the transition from elite to mass higher education. *Policies for Higher Education*. Paris, France: Organization for Economic Cooperation and Development.

Tuckman, Howard, and Hagemann, R. (1976). An analysis of reward structure in two disciplines. *Journal of Higher Education* 26–39.

Tuckman, Howard, and Pickerill, Karen L. (1988). Part-time faculty and part-time academic careers. In D. W. Breneman, and T. I. K. Youn, (eds.), *Academic Labor Markets and Careers*. Philadelphia, PA: Stanford Series in Education and Public Policy, The Falmer Press.

Williamson, Oliver E. (1975). *Markets and Hierarchies*. New York: Free Press.

Wyer, Jean C., and Conrad, Clifton F. (1984). Institutional origin: labor market signaling in higher education. *Review of Higher Education* 7: 95–109.

Youn, Ted I. K. (1981). The careers of young Ph.D.'s: temporal change and institutional effects. Unpublished Ph.D. dissertation, Yale University.

Youn, Ted I. K. (1984). Changing academic markets: effects of the expansion and contraction of higher education. Paper presented at the Annual Meeting of the American Sociological Association.

Youn, Ted I. K., and Zelterman, Daniel (1986). Academic career mobility in multiple labor markets. A paper presented at the Annual Meeting of the American Sociological Association. (To be published in *Work and Occupations: An International Sociological Journal*.)

Youn, Ted I. K. (1988) Patterns of institutional self-recruitment of young Ph.D's: Effects of academic markets on career mobility. *Research in Higher Education. 29:195–218.*

Youn, Ted I. K. (1989) *Career Mobility in Academic Hierarchies*. Forthcoming.

Faculty Evaluation and Faculty Development in Higher Education

John A. Centra
Syracuse University

Faculty members are being evaluated and developed now more than at any time in the history of American higher education. In the past fifteen to twenty years, formalized systems that attempt to evaluate the performance of faculty members in their various roles—as teachers, as researchers and scholars, or as people who provide service to their institutions, governments, professions, or communities—have become much more commonplace. Faculty development too has expanded in the past twenty years or so. More than half of the colleges and universities in the United States established "programs" to facilitate the development of their staffs in the 1970s and 1980s (Centra, 1976; Erickson, 1986).

Why this current emphasis? What were the social, economic, and historical factors that contributed to formalizing and extending both faculty evaluation and faculty development programs? This chapter will examine these questions and more. The specific practices now in use and what the research evidence is for selected methods will be discussed. Some future directions and needed research will also be examined.

Given the extensive research literature in these areas, particularly in faculty evaluation where, for example, the ERIC system contains over 1,200 listings alone in the past 20 years dealing with student ratings of instruction, the discussion in this chapter will rely heavily on reviews of research and on key studies.

HISTORICAL PERSPECTIVE

Although teaching and research are considered the major functions of faculty members, during the first two centuries of American higher education—that is up until the Germanic model of university research was introduced in the last half of the nineteenth century—faculty were expected only to teach and counsel

155

students. The lecture and recitation were the primary methods of teaching in colonial America and any evaluation of faculty effectiveness was incidental (Brubacher and Rudy, 1976). The recitation varied between a highly developed Socratic dialogue between tutor and student, to a verbatim recital by the student of Latin, Greek, or other prose (ibid.). At the end of the year, a committee of the trustees and the president observed as the teacher asked each student questions based on the year's recitations. This exercise was hardly an assessment of the teacher's effectiveness or the student's knowledge for that matter because teachers tended to put easy or leading questions to their students (Smallwood, 1935, cited in Rudolph, 1977, p. 146).

By the mid-1800s written examinations had largely replaced oral examinations and these were more revealing of both the course and the instructional quality. The exams were usually given at the end of the sophomore and senior years, with all students answering the same questions (Brubacher and Rudy, 1976). Because teachers graded the tests related to their courses, the examination results were not an unbiased measure of teaching outcomes. Charles Eliot, the president of Harvard, decried the fact that the teaching and examining function resided in the same person, a condition that still exists except for licensing and comprehensive examinations and a few introductory level courses. Today, as a century ago, end-of-course test scores or grades seldom reflect teacher effectiveness, and systems of faculty evaluation do not rely on such information alone.

The 40-year period following the Civil War was a time of great change in American higher education and in what professors did; in part this was due to the influence of the German university (Veysey, 1973). Teaching changed with the introduction of two new methods, the seminar and the laboratory, and with a shift in the purpose of the lecture. According to the German model, the lecture should be less of a reading and more of a means of informing students about the latest research; the lecture should also help students organize information from many sources and motivate them through the enthusiasm professors have for their specialty (Brubacher and Rudy, 1976). These notions are still used today to judge a lecture, with students, colleagues, or various administrators serving as judges.

Another change imported from Germany was the expectation that professors would conduct research and scholarly inquiry. The Ph.D. degree, first awarded in the United States in 1861, certified research competence (ibid.). Scholarly societies and journals, university presses, and the sabbatical leave were established to promote a new purpose of American higher education: the advancement of knowledge. From this time on professors in the universities, and eventually in increasing numbers of colleges, were expected to expand the frontiers of knowledge as well as their students' minds and morals. The purpose of higher education had changed and so had the basis for faculty evaluation. Publications and grant-getting increasingly became a critical criteria for tenure and promotions at more and more institutions.

The decades following the Civil War saw another change that was to have a major influence on faculty evaluation: the establishment of the academic department as a major source of power. From this time on departments increasingly influenced the curriculum as well as the hiring and advancement of their colleagues. Thus, the current emphasis on publications and the critical role that departments play in faculty evaluation have their roots in the "academic revolution" that started during the last several decades of the 19th century and accelerated in the 20th century (Jencks and Riesman, 1968).

CURRENT PRACTICES

As mentioned above, faculty evaluation has become much more formal and systematic in the past fifteen to twenty years. Legal considerations are one of the reasons for this recent change. Although the law does not dictate what specific methods institutions should use to assess faculty members, it is clear on the need for colleges to use job-related and nondiscriminatory practices in making personnel decisions, and that institutions apply the principles of due process (Centra, 1979). Other reasons for the recent change include a declining rate of enrollment growth coupled with budget restraints (thus forcing institutions to make distinctions among generally competent instructors), and pressure from students, parents, and legislators to upgrade instruction. The student activism of the late 1960s following student perceptions of themselves as consumers of higher education, in particular, helped to foster the use of student evaluations of instruction. Almost every college or university in the United States uses student evaluations of instruction in some way: some for faculty self-improvement, others for personnel decisions.

Colleges and universities that historically were committed to teaching are now emphasizing research productivity more in their reward system (Creswell, 1986). Research on characteristics of productive researchers (Creswell, 1985) and how best to assess scholarship and research have been the subject of many studies in recent years, several of which are discussed below.

ASSESSING TEACHING

Student evaluations, along with colleague evaluations, self-evaluation, and evaluations by committees and administrators, are the major sources of information used in assessing teaching. The remainder of this section summarizes briefly some key research findings for the first three sources: students, colleagues, and self-evaluations.

Before turning to the research findings, a word needs to be said about how good teaching has been described or defined. Theory has not played a major role in deliberations about good teaching and how it should be evaluated. The views of key groups, on the other hand, have been critical in these deliberations.

Surveys of faculty members, students, administrators, and alumni have, for example, resulted in remarkably similar qualities of good teaching. Good course organization, effective communication skills, clarity, and rapport with students are among the top ranked qualities of each of the groups (Wotruba and Wright, 1975). These qualities, in turn, are frequently reflected in student and faculty teacher rating questionnaires and form the basis for evaluation systems (Centra et al., 1987). Thus, when research studies, such as many of those summarized below, demonstrate that colleagues and students rank teachers at a college similarly, it is probably due in part to a common view of what good teaching is. In short, consensus has played a major role in identifying qualities of effective teaching and in evaluating individual performance.

Research on teaching in higher education, as at other levels of education, has addressed three main questions: How do teachers behave? Why do they behave as they do? And what are the effects of their behavior? (Dunkin and Barnes, 1987; Gage, 1963). As this body of research continues to grow, a better understanding of what effective teaching is and how best to evaluate and improve it should follow.

Student Evaluations

Although research evidence supporting the use of student evaluations dates back over fifty years to the work of H. H. Remmers (1934) at Purdue, studies done in recent years have been able to resolve a number of major critical issues. The findings of this recent research have been generally supportive and have contributed to the use of the evaluations in faculty personnel decisions. Initially the evaluations were used by individual teachers for course and instructional improvement, often referred to as a formative use, but as the positive research evidence mounted, and as the need for "objective" information on classroom teaching has increased, student evaluations have been recommended or required for summative (tenure, promotion, merit) purposes.

Institutions that use student rating forms for formative or summative purposes have relied on at least three approaches to collecting the information. Some, possibly the majority, have developed their own set of items or have adapted forms developed elsewhere. These colleges may either machine score the forms or may allow individual faculty members or departments to hand score the numerical responses (occasionally individual faculty members or departments will develop and administer their own form). A second approach is to adopt one of the systems developed at another institution. Several large institutions have developed instruments or systems to evaluate instruction. One such system features a computerized catalog of items that allows instructors to select items appropriate to their approach to teaching. Purdue's Cafeteria System and the Instructor and Course Evaluation System (ICES) developed at the University of

Illinois are examples of the computer-based catalog approach (Centra, 1979; Miller, 1987). The ICES system includes over 400 items classified by content (e.g., course management, instructional environment) and by level of specificity (global, general concept, specific). A third choice for institutions is to elect one of the commercial forms available. The IDEA form, developed at the Center for Faculty Evaluation and Development at Kansas State University, and the SIR form, developed at Educational Testing Service, are the two best known and widely used forms (Centra, 1979; Miller, 1987).

A brief summary of the research evidence on student evaluations follows.

Reliability and Stability
Numerous studies have shown that the internal consistency of ratings, that is, the extent of student agreement on ratings within a class, are at an acceptable level providing enough students have made ratings (Feldman, 1977; Centra, 1979). The reliability coefficients are typically close to .90 for twenty student raters, and just above .80 for fifteen raters. For personnel decisions, some studies indicated that the number of courses needed to provide a sound judgment of an individual's teaching effectiveness is five or more, assuming at least fifteen raters in each class (Gilmore, Kane, and Naccarato, 1978). Another aspect of reliability is the stability of ratings over time. Longitudinal studies over a five week period (Centra, 1973b), or a year (Overall and Marsh, 1980), indicated a fairly good level of stability between repeated ratings of the same teachers.

Dimensions
Hundreds of factor analyses of rating items have been conducted over the years and the factors that emerged naturally depended on the items included. Certain factors, however, have been repeated in study after study: Course Organization/ Planning; Student-Instructor Interaction (sometimes divided into Individual and Group Interaction); Communication Skills, or Presentation Clarity; Workload, or Course Demands; and Examinations/Grading (see, for example, summaries by Feldman, 1988, Centra, 1979; Marsh 1984b). Other factors less frequently identified include Student Involvement; Assignments/Readings; and Instructor Enthususiam/Dynamism. These factor analytic studies not only support the construct validity of student evaluations, but the factors also have been useful in summarizing item responses for teacher or administrator use.

Potential Biasing Effects
The question of whether student evaluations reflect teacher behavior or whether they reflect extraneous course, teacher, or student variables has been addressed in numerous research studies. A bias, in this instance, would be present if any of the variables studied had a significant effect on students' ratings but did not also

affect other indicators of teacher effectiveness. Among the variables studied have been instructor rank, instructor or student personality, instructor or student gender, student college year, class size, expected (or actual) grade, reason for taking a course, purpose of ratings, and academic discipline. Reviews of these studies by Doyle (1975), McKeachie (1979), Centra (1979), Feldman (1978), Marsh (1984a), Murray (1985), Aleamoni (1981), and others indicate relatively small biasing effects. Small classes (i.e., under 15) generally receive slightly higher ratings but one might argue that they also can provide a better teaching environment (i.e., more individual attention) and hence produce better learning as well as better ratings.

A major concern of faculty members is the influence of grades on ratings and the possibility that students will reward easy-grading teachers with higher ratings. Although there are likely instances when this does occur, there is no evidence that "leniency bias" produces a systematic and constant effect that has any practical significance (Marsh, 1984b).

The well-known Dr. Fox studies also investigated a potential biasing effect on student evaluations—specifically whether instructor expressiveness had an overriding influence on the ratings. The initial study by Naftulin, Ware, and Donnelly (1973) discredited the validity of student ratings by demonstrating that an expressive teacher was rated highly in spite of the inaccurate content being taught (educational "seduction" was their term for the finding). Later, more sophisticated studies by Abrami, Leventhal, and Perry (1982), and by Marsh and Ware (1982) found that variations in expressiveness and content were reflected in ratings of teacher enthusiasm and organization, respectively, as they should be. Students learned more when *both* expressiveness and content were present.

The effect of teacher personality on student evaluations is complex because, as Dunkin and Biddle (1974) point out in their model of classroom teaching, teacher personality traits ("presage" variables) can be expected to affect classroom behaviors ("process" variables) which in turn determine student evaluations of teaching ("product" variables). One path analytic study supports this rationale but the model and variations of it should be the basis for further research before a firm conclusion can be reached (Erdle, Murray, and Rushton, 1985).

Validity: Multisection Studies

Perhaps the most widely accepted criterion of effective teaching is student learning. A criterion-related approach to the validity of student evaluations uses an assessment of student learning at the end of the course and relates this to ratings that students give the teacher. Higher rated teachers should also have better student achievement results. Multisection courses with common final examinations have been employed by researchers to investigate the relationship, with mean student ratings and mean student achievement in each course as the units of analyses. Ideally, as in two studies at a Canadian university, students are also assigned at random to each section (Sullivan and Skanes, 1974; Centra, 1977b). The results of these and some 70 multisection validity studies as summarized in a meta-analysis by Cohen (1981) were supportive: correlations were in the .40 to .50 range for many of the factors as well as for the global evaluation of teaching. Slightly lower correlations for the Faculty-Student Interaction factor and near-zero correlations for the Workload or Course Demands factor were also found. These results, along with those which reported good agreement between trained observers' ratings of teacher behavior and student ratings of the same behavior provide strong support for the validity of student evaluations (Murray, 1985; Erdle and Murray, 1986).

Utility
The utility of student evaluations—how useful they are in improving instruction, and whether they provide useful information in personnel decisions—is also a critical issue. The theoretical underpinning for expecting change in teacher behavior is provided by dissonance or imbalance theories (Heider, 1958; Festinger, 1957). Specifically, if the feedback provided by students is new and valued by teachers, then teachers can be expected to change their behavior. Cohen's (1980) meta-analysis and Marsh's (1984b) review of feedback studies concluded that student evaluations do provide teachers with feedback that can lead to improvement in instruction, albeit modest improvement. But when augmented by an effective intervention, such as an external consultant, that improvement has been greater. Murray (1985) found that improvement was more likely if training procedures focused on specific, observable behaviors rather than generalities. Research on the importance of student evalutions in tenure and promotion is more limited. Leventhal, et al. (1981) and Salthouse, McKeachie, and Lin (1978) studied student ratings at research universities and found that student evaluations had little effect on personnel decisions over and above a department chair's report. The extent to which the student ratings may have influenced department chairs was not ascertained. A later study by Lin, McKeachie, and Tucker (1984), however, found that a combination of numerical data and student comments on teaching effectiveness did influence decisions when candidates had moderate research productivity.

Self-Evaluations
A faculty member's description of his or her teaching and research activities is an important part of any personnel review. The question is whether self-evaluations as opposed to self-descriptions should have any weight in an activity report. A further question is whether self-evaluations can contribute to improve-

ment in performance. The research evidence points to a negative response to the first question and a positive reply to the second.

Self-ratings of overall teaching effectiveness differed significantly from colleague, administrator, or student ratings, according to a study by Blackburn and Clark (1975) that was conducted at a small college. In that study, all but self-ratings showed substantial overlap with each other. Several studies have compared self-ratings of teaching with student ratings. Centra (1973a) found relatively low correlations between the two (about .21), but Marsh, Overall, and Kessler (1979) and Marsh (1982) found a correlation of about .45. Marsh also reported generally small differences in mean responses between students ratings and faculty self-ratings, a finding that also conflicted with the Centra (1973a) study. One explanation for the variation in findings is that ratings by students in a previous semester may have caused convergence during a later semester when the Marsh studies were conducted, as in fact was found in a study by Braskamp and Caulley (1978). In other words, student ratings improved after a semester's use and self-evaluations may have become more realistic.

While the above findings would cast doubt on the use of self-ratings for salary, tenure, or promotion purposes (in fact, under such conditions, self-ratings might be even more inflated), the same studies included findings that supported their use for formative uses. Teachers were usually aware of the areas of teaching in which they were strong (or weak) in the sense that students identified a similar ranking of rating factors. Thus self-ratings or self-analysis could be useful in conjunction with consultations or in helping faculty members select the most appropriate materials or workshops for teaching improvement.

Colleague Evaluations

Colleague assessments are essential in judging research and scholarship performance but how they should be used in judging teaching is more uncertain. When colleague evaluations are based entirely on classroom observations, they will likely have low interrater agreement (i.e., faculty members give each other generally high ratings and do not always concur in what they observe; Centra, 1975). Training and an extensive observation schedule would increase the reliability but it's not realistic to expect faculty members to spend the time required in these activities. When colleagues' evaluations are based on something other than, or in addition to, classroom observations, they tend to have better reliabilities and to correlate reasonably well with student evaluations (Blackburn and Clark, 1975; Guthrie, 1954; Maslow and Zimmerman, 1956). Root (1987) studied ratings by a six-person executive committee that had undergone some brief basic training in order to establish a common understanding of the ratings. The committee agreed substantially in their ratings of faculty members on teaching, research, and service, with the strongest interrater reliabilities in research (.97) followed by teaching (.90) and service (.90). The correlations between ratings in teaching, research, and service were low (e.g., .19 for research × teaching), indicating that performance in each of the areas tends to be independent. An alternative explanation is that "compensatory adjustments" were made by the raters so that they would rate someone high in one area to compensate for a low rating in another area, thus spreading out salary increments for which the ratings were used. The Root study was based on only one year's data so more analyses of this kind are needed; but the results would encourage colleges to use ad hoc committees of colleagues to judge teaching, as some now do. The committees should be expected to base their judgments on more than just classroom observations (i.e., course materials, reports from current and ex-students, and the like). In the interest of going beyond student rating forms, evaluations systems need to consider ways of collecting reliable and valid assessments from colleagues.

Further study and policy analysis are also needed for the relatively recent emphasis on the use of evaluation in post-tenure review. Some institutions currently require tenured faculty to repeat a tenure-type review periodically, generally every three to five years (Licata, 1986). At the present time, institutions that require these reviews use them largely to help improve faculty performance. But depending on legal and other considerations, they may in the future be used increasingly to document inadequate performance for the removal of a particular staff member or to make staff reduction decisions during retrenchment.

Licata's (1986) review on post-tenure evaluation indicated that the procedures and criteria used vary somewhat from institution to institution, but they often parallel those used for the original decision on whether to confer tenure. From the limited research dealing specifically with post-tenure evalution, Licata recommended:

1. The purpose for the evaluation (i.e., informative or summative) should drive all other aspects of the evaluation plan.
2. Faculty must be involved in the design of the plan.
3. Faculty and administrators should agree upon the specifics of the plan.
4. The need for flexibility and individualization in a post-tenure evaluation plan should not be overlooked (e.g., priorities may change as individuals age).
5. Faculty development programs should be linked to a post-tenure evaluation system.
6. Innovative approaches to post-tenure evaluation and institutional planning are needed (e.g., the faculty growth contract). (pp. 67–68)

ASSESSMENT OF RESEARCH

The importance given to research and scholarship in evaluating faculty members will, of course, depend on institutional type and purpose. Moreover, what is acceptable performance varies not only by institution but by discipline. A survey of department chairs indicated, for example, that journal articles and grants received are especially critical to the evaluation of natural science faculty members (Centra, 1977a).

The criteria for evaluating research and scholarship performance include both quantity and quality dimensions. Examples of the quantity dimensions include the number of:

Articles in professional journals;
Books as sole or senior author;
Monographs or book chapters;
Papers at professional meetings;
Books as junior author or editor.

The quality of scholarly research is generally judged by peers at the institutions, peers at other institutions, and by various administrators. Honors or awards from the profession, grants, and being a referee or editor of a professional journal are also considered.

A relatively new method of assessing quality is to note the number of times a person's publications have been cited in subsequent literature. The citation indices published through the Institute for Scientific Information (Indices in the Sciences, Social Sciences and Humanities) allow a systematic account of citations (Garfield, 1979). Although principally used for literature searches, the indices are being increasingly used by personnel committees, particulary when tenure or upper level promotions are being considered.

But there are problems in the use of citations as performance indicators, as Cole and Cole (1967) and Braxton and Bayer (1986) point out. Among these are the differences in citations by disciplines, citations that may be critical rather than positive, and the possibility that the significance of work produced may not be recognized by contemporaries.

Another way of accounting for quality is to give extra weight to articles in highly rated journals. Braxton and Bayer (1986) discussed various ways in which journals might be weighted, including the use of peer ratings of journals and an "impact" factor based on the average number of citations received by the journal.

Quality and quantity of research and scholarship are related but the extent of the relationship indicates that both should be looked at in assessing performance. In studies where citation counts, as a measure of quality, were related to the number of articles published, Cole and Cole (1967) found a correlation of .72 for a sample of physicists. Slightly lower correlations were reported for other disciplines by Meltzer (1956), and by Schrader (1978) who noted a correlation of .60 for a sample of psychology Ph.D's.

In addition to the advancement of knowledge, research is often said to stimulate faculty members' thinking and to help keep them abreast of their field. This in turn should make them more effective teachers. The research evidence, however, provides only marginal support for this rationale. Feldman's (1987) review of the many studies that have compared research productivity (as assessed by number of articles, citations, and other ways) and teaching effectiveness (as assessed by students) concluded that only a small positive correlation exists between the two variables. The average correlation was .12 for 29 studies; for individual studies the association was often not statistically significant. Although a relationship of this magnitude would not support the belief that research enhances teaching (or vice versa), some have also argued that research performance at least does not appear to detract from classroom teaching (Centra, 1983). An alternative hypothesis by Feldman, citing a point made by Black (1972), is that effective teachers who are also productive researchers might be even more effective as teachers if they did less research; Feldman's subsequent analyses of possible mediating factors (such as time spent in research and teaching), however, did not support the hypothesis.

An issue yet to be dealt with is how computer software as well as other instructional materials produced by teachers should be treated in summative evaluations. Faculty members are not always given credit for the computer software they produce, materials which may in fact have far-reaching effects in instruction (Chronicle of Higher Education, 1987).

Summary

This section has reviewed the major issues and findings in the evaluation of teaching and research performance, the two areas that receive the major emphasis in faculty evaluation. A survey of department chairs indicated that only 2% considered public or community service a critical factor in evaluating faculty (Centra, 1977a).

In both teaching and research, it is clear that no one method or source provides a complete picture of performance. The research evidence has underscored the strengths of each method and the relationships among them. Faculty evaluation is an inexact science applied to a sensitive area and as such can be expected to stimulate further research and discussion. Some future issues and research needs conclude this section.

Future Needs and Issues

Student Evaluations

Although the research evidence on student evaluations is generally supportive and probably accounts in part for their increased use, some issues still need further study.

1. Do student evaluations limit a teacher's approach to instruction because of the items included on most rating forms? Some critics claim that the evaluations reflect and support a conservative or traditional role of the teacher as information-giver and the student as receiver (Wilson, T. 1987). Murray (1987), on the other hand, argues that innovation is more common today than it was prior to the wide use of student ratings, and that highly rated teachers are more likely to use nontraditional methods than are teachers receiving lower ratings.

2. Are there systematic subgroup differences among students that have special significance for designing and improving instruction? Centra and Linn (1976) discovered various "points of view" within separate classes by using inverse factor analysis. These differing perspectives on instruction were moderately related to such known student characteristics as gender and grades, although not consistently across classes. These findings underscore the importance of the context of student evaluations (i.e., the particular course) in interpreting the meaning of the evaluations. Any number of other student characteristics, such as learning style, might also be related to differing points of view on instruction and deserve further study.

3. Are there other forms of student feedback to instructors that might prove more useful than graphic rating scales for diagnosing and improving instruction? Although Ory, Braskamp, and Pieper (1980) found similarities in the results obtained from written remarks, interviews, and rating scale data, the impact and use of the results could differ for teachers. Centra (1987) has experimented with use of electronic mail in providing anonymous student-teacher feedback throughout the semester. The results have been promising, especially in larger classes in which other forms of communication fail to inform.

4. Scriven (1978) has raised the issue of merit vs. value in personnel decisions. Further policy research is needed in how an individual's value to the institution and other factors not directly related to merit are or should be considered in decision making.

5. How does teaching in the performing and fine arts differ from traditional classroom instruction and how should students and others evaluate this instruction? Many courses in these areas are individualized or emphasize small group instruction; student evaluations should focus on a different set of factors than those from lecture or discussion courses.

Self and Colleague Evaluations

In comparison to student evaluations, little research has been conducted on either self or colleague evaluations of instruction. Some questions that might be addressed follow.

1. How can self-evaluations be coupled with student evaluations or video replays to be effective in instructional diagnosis and improvement? Viewing

oneself in a microteaching situation is being used to increase self-awareness but little systematic research has been reported on its effects for improving college teaching.

2. How do the various sources of evaluation information relate to student learning measures? Needed are multimethod studies in which self-evaluations or self-reports, colleague evaluations, student evaluations, and objective measures of student learning in a course are analyzed, possibly through multimethod factor analysis.

3. In the interest of going beyond the use of student evaluations, especially in tenure and promotion decisions, how can colleague evaluations be made economically and reliably? Can colleagues be "trained" in a relatively short period of time to make valid evaluative judgments? The Root (1987) study, cited earlier, investigated evaluations of teaching, research, and service by colleagues after a brief training stint. Further research along this line is needed.

4. Although the use of colleague evaluations may provide a more complete evaluation picture, might it also lead to faculty distrust and reduced effectiveness? More attention needs to be paid to the effects of instructional evaluation systems on the general morale and colleagiability of faculty members.

5. How do beginning teachers incorporate informal as well as formal evaluative information in adjusting what they do in the classroom? Qualitative research might best be used initially to examine this question.

6. Are there collaborative arrangements among faculty members that might prove effective for formative purposes? The use of dyads and triads, in which faculty members visit each other's classes and review course materials in a cooperative venture, has shown some promise for improving instruction (Grasha, 1977).

Assessment of Research

A major issue in the assessment of research or scholarly productivity is in the measurement of quality. Can quality be judged fairly across the different disciplines? How should productivity be measured in the performing arts and other similar areas? What weight should institutions give to the preparation of computer software and other instructional materials produced by teachers? These and related questions are perhaps more policy than researchable issues, but they need to be addressed if fair personnel decisions are to be made.

FACULTY DEVELOPMENT

Historical Perspective

The faculty development "movement" is now about 20 years old. Faculty development practices certainly existed previously but they were not well articulated nor very comprehensive (Miller and Wilson, 1963; Many, Ellis, and Abrams, 1969; Eble, 1971). The sabbatical leave, for example, dates back to the late 1800s but it was a single practice directed generally at facilitating a faculty member's writing and research.

A 1960 survey of 214 southern colleges by Miller and Wilson (1963) identified a few widely used practices designed to orient new faculty members to an institution or to help update faculty members, such as precollege workshops, financial assistance for attendance at professional meetings, and occasional department conferences on teaching. But the authors concluded that there was a dearth of well-articulated, comprehensively designed *programs* for faculty development. A briefer survey, conducted in the late 1960s with a broader sample of institutions, reached a similar conclusion (Many, et al., 1969). Still further evidence for this finding emerged from the results of a questionnaire study done as part of the AAUP Project to Improve College Teaching: Eble (1971) reported that faculty members at some 150 schools stated almost unanimously that their institutions did not have *effective* faculty development programs. Nevertheless, a handful of institutions, mainly universities, did establish faculty development (or educational development) programs in the mid to late 1960's (Alexander and Yelon, 1972; Crow et al., 1976).

A combination of factors in the late 1960s and early 1970s led to an upsurge in programs and practices. A declining number of students and financial resources led to a decrease in faculty mobility, which meant that institutions needed to renew their existing staffs. The disenchantment with the quality of teaching expressed by students and public dissatisfaction with the competence of college graduates ignited a need to upgrade teaching in particular. A widely read monograph titled *Faculty Development in a Time of Retrenchment* highlighted the need and importance of faculty development (Group for Human Development in Higher Education, 1974).

Programs that blossomed in the 1970s included those that promoted faculty growth in such areas as personal skills (personal development), others that focused on course design (instructional development), and many that attempted to renew or assist faculty in their varied roles. This last description probably comes closest to defining the all-encompassing purpose of faculty development as it evolved in the late 1970s. In practice, however, at most institutions faculty development focused almost exclusively on teaching improvement. Abedor and Sachs (1984), for example, defined it as a process that "emphasizes activities which increase the faculty members' knowledge, skills, sensitivities, and instructional techniques so that they are better able to fulfill their teaching responsibilities" (p. 395). There is little question that teaching improvement has been the major focus of most faculty development efforts, but programs have also included such activities as career counseling and professional writing improvement programs (Boice, 1982). Gaff (1975) and Berquist and Phillips

(1975) also described organizational development as an aspect of faculty development. All in all, one or more of the following may be part of an institution's faculty development program.

1. *Instructional Development*. Specialists provide assistance in course design, curriculum development, media, instructional technology, and testing.

2. *Personal Development*. Seminars and individual sessions with faculty members emphasize the development of interpersonal skills and growth of the faculty as individuals. Career development and life planning skills could also be subsumed here.

3. *Organizational Development*. Practices such as team building and managerial development are used to improve the institutional environment for teaching and decision making. The needs, priorities, and organizational structure of an institution are considered (Gaff, 1975).

4. *Professional Development*. A more recent term that includes the development of faculty members as researchers, as providers of service, and as teachers. The professional organization for people interested in faculty development, the Professional and Organizational Development Network in Higher Education (POD), reflects this broader mission for faculty development.

By the mid-1970s, one survey estimated that slightly over half of the postsecondary institutions in the United States provided a "program" of faculty development (Centra, 1976). Some of these consisted of only a few traditional practices but others were full-fledged programs with full-time directors. Although many institutions curtailed or shut down their programs in the next decade due to mounting budget constraints, apparently many new programs were created. A 1984 survey sponsored by the Professional and Organizational Network in Higher Education found that the overall proportion of institutions with faculty development programs was about the same as it had been a decade earlier (Erickson, 1985). There were, however, fewer units with a full-time faculty development director in 1984 than a decade earlier. More typically, deans or other administrators had assumed responsibility for faculty development along with their other duties.

An International Movement

The conditions that led to the growth of faculty development programs in the late 1960s and early 1970s in the United States were present in other Western countries as well. An international review published in 1979 described programs in twelve countries (Teather, 1979). The titles of some of the chapters in the book illustrate the different emphases and concerns at the time among the countries:

Canada, an emphasis on instructional development.
New Zealand, working with teachers toward course improvement.

The Indian Subcontinent, a problem of resources.
Sweden, strong central provision complementing local initiatives.
Switzerland, largely noninstitutionalized instructional development activities.
The Netherlands, tertiary teacher training as a growth industry.

It's apparent from the above titles that the major focus of programs was instructional improvement. This has also been the focus of an annual international conference, Improving University Teaching, which was first held in the mid-1970s. Sponsored by the University of Maryland, the conference is still held in a different country each year.

The Effectiveness of Faculty Development Programs and Practices

A literature search conducted on ERIC and other abstracts yielded 393 references to faculty development between 1965 and 1985 (Bland and Schmitz, 1986). Many of these were articles or papers describing programs or approaches at an individual institution. Only a handful of publications had addressed the all-important issue of the impact of programs on individual participants or their institutions. These studies have typically surveyed or interviewed faculty members and/or program coordinators; some included site visits by teams of experts. Very seldom have measures of student learning been used, even when such measures would be expected to reflect the ultimate criterion of a program. This omission is understandable. As Eble and McKeachie (1985) point out, the many factors that influence student learning in a course or field make it unlikely that a single faculty development program will produce a measurable and causal effect on learning measures.

Nevertheless, increased student learning may be the key to changing teacher behavior. If one considers that the three major purposes of a faculty development program that seeks to improve teaching are (1) change in the classroom practices of teachers, (2) change in their beliefs and attitudes, and (3) change in student learning outcomes, the question is: In what temporal sequence are these purposes most likely to occur (Guskey, 1986)? Some faculty programs attempt to change teachers' beliefs and attitudes first, in the hopes that such changes will bring about changes in teaching practices and in student learning. But the research evidence suggests that change in teachers' beliefs and attitude are more likely the result rather than the cause of improvement in student learning (Guskey, 1986). Faculty development programs might therefore concentrate on changing those teaching practices that result in changes in student learning, rather than focusing on faculty members' beliefs and attitudes. The latter changes will only take place if teachers see that a practice enhances student learning in their courses (Guskey, 1986).

Studies of Practices

A survey of 756 two- and four-year institutions by Centra (1976) listed 45 development practices, to which program coordinators indicated the extent of use and their judgment of the effectiveness of each practice at their institutions. Among the institution-wide practices seen as effective by close to two-thirds of the respondents were grants for projects to improve instruction or to develop new approaches to courses or teaching, sabbatical leaves, and travel grants. Least effective among the institution-wide practices were annual awards to faculty for teaching excellence and the circulation of a development newsletter on campus. Both practices have considerable visibility and signal an institution's intent to reward or publicize good teaching; but the majority of coordinators did not see them as having a major impact at their institutions.

Coordinators also had varying views about the different instructional analysis or assessment practices. The analysis of in-class videotapes was seen as one of the more effective practices though it was used infrequently by faculty. Another practice rated effective, but little used, was the professional and personal development plan (growth contract). Systematic ratings by students were widely used to improve instruction but were seen as only moderately effective. The coordinators also rated formal or informal assessments by colleagues as less effective than either consulting with expert faculty or master teachers.

From a list of ten topics that might be the focus of workshops, seminars, or similar presentation, respondents indicated that those dealing with specific techniques of instruction and with new knowledge in a field were among the best attended and most effective. Workshops that explored general issues or trends in education were judged as least effective.

A final category of practices involved specialists providing assistance to faculty members. One of the more widely used and effective was assistance in employing audiovisual aids in instruction. Instructional development specialists were present at only a third of the institutions but were rated as effective or very effective at the vast majority.

More recent studies have continued to shed light on the effectiveness of particular practices. Grants for teaching improvement or research projects, sabbaticals, and travel awards were highly rated by respondents in the Blackburn et al., (1980) study as well as the Siegel (1980) study. But the Levinson-Rose and Menges (1981) analysis questioned how much these practices actually affect instruction, even though they may be preferred by faculty members.

Released time as a means of increasing faculty writing and research productivity was questioned in a study by Boice (1987). Based on data from faculty at four institutions, Boice found that faculty given released time usually persist in old habits, and that new faculty did not benefit from a released-time program. Although Boice studied the effect on research productivity, his major conclusion would seem to be applicable to teaching improvement as well: ''released time applied passively, without encouraging new work habits and changed institutional attitudes, may be doomed to inefficiency. Without clear goals and supports for using released time, the practice does not seem likely to achieve its ideals" (p. 324).

The role of department chairs in faculty development was studied through a naturalistic analysis by Creswell et al. (1987). Interviews with effective department chairs provided a catalog of different approaches that the chairs used with faculty members' particular types of problem situations (e.g., "deadwood," nurturing rising young stars).

Creswell et al. proposed a matrix of faculty situations and contextual factors to help guide further qualitative or quantitative analyses. The cells in the matrix suggested further research on questions such as:

1. Do the faculty situations vary depending on whether the assistance is initiated by faculty or department chairs?
2. Do the faculty situations or approaches vary by discipline areas?
3. Do the faculty situations or approaches vary by institutional type? (pp. 24–25)

Instructional development and curriculum development projects have continued to receive favorable judgments in more recent studies. Both Gaff and Morstain's (1978) study of sixteen institutions participating in a special teaching improvement project and Eble and McKeachie's (1985) evaluation of the programs supported by the Bush Foundation in the Midwest rated these development projects as effective. Workshops and seminars were also judged favorably by Eble and McKeachie, quite possibly because the institutions in their study generally focused on specific topics. The Eble and McKeachie study is the largest and most recent evaluation of faculty development programs. Forty-one of the forty-five colleges in Minnesota, North Dakota, and South Dakota which received Bush Foundation support participated. The site visits, interviews, and survey data resulted in several recommendations for establishing effective faculty development programs. In addition to those mentioned above, they recommended (pp. 203–205):

Faculty ownership: Programs will be more effective if faculty members feel that the program is theirs.

Administrative support: Effective programs require strong administrative support.

"Single-focus" vs. "cafeteria" approaches: Avoid both extremes. Single-focus programs were not rated highly but neither were programs that offered a smorgasbord of activities without attention to how they related to each other. (p. 214)

Follow-up activities: Follow-up meetings, refresher training, and public reports to the faculty are likely to help provide a lasting impact.

Faculty preferences: Faculty preferences for released time, travel, sabbaticals, and the like are probably not the most cost-effective approaches, particularly if some impact on teaching and student learning is a goal. Instructional development and curricular change projects have more promise.

Faculty Career Stages

Some researchers have argued that many faculty development approaches do not take into account the differing needs of individual professors at different stages of their careers (Blackburn, Behymer, and Hall, 1978; Baldwin, 1984; see also Clark and Lewis, 1988, for a review of faculty career development as an indicator of faculty vitality). Others have stated that success in faculty development depends on the depth of knowledge about faculty attitudes, motivation, and other characteristics (Wergin, Mason, and Munson, 1976). Clearly, faculty members need different kinds of support at different times in their careers, and college administrators as well as faculty development coordinators need to keep this in mind in working with individuals. Younger faculty, for example, may profit from workshops and seminars, whereas senior faculty seem to prefer individual growth opportunities (Baldwin and Blackburn, 1981). With increasing age, many professors also become more interested in teaching than in research (Fulton and Trow, 1974). So the issue may not simply be which practices work best, but which practices work best for individuals at different stages of their careers.

Nevertheless past research has shown that faculty who need faculty development most frequently do not take part in institutional programs (Gaff, 1975; Centra, 1976). While this group is probably a very small portion of any given faculty, some critics would argue that a faculty development program has failed if it has not reached these individuals. For some people, an important purpose of faculty development is to remediate individuals who are inadequate in some way through mandatory activities if necessary. Many faculty development practitioners, however, reject this clinical or "diseased patient" approach; they argue that a program should be built on "winners" and on those faculty members looking to experiment and improve (Erickson, 1986).

Clark and Lewis (1988) have discussed how individual career vitality and organizational vitality are interrelated. Early retirement strategies, they conclude, may result in a modest degree of change but institutions must devise plans to enhance the vitality of those who will remain at the institution for years to come. Strategies "premised on shared individual and organizational responsibility—are the most realistic, feasible, and compatible with the professional ethos" (Clark and Lewis, 1988). Moreover, similar to Creswell et al. (1987), they argue that additional research is needed on the interactions between the career development of faculty members and the institutional conditions affecting individual performance.

CONCLUDING REMARKS AND FUTURE NEEDS

The student personnel/student development movement began almost seventy years ago and has grown into an array of counseling, placement, and other student services that can be found on campuses across the country. By comparison, faculty development is still in its early stages. On many campuses its growth and effectiveness has waxed and waned during the past two decades, depending on uncertain external or internal funding and on the limited commitment of faculty or administrator supporters. The research to date indicates that there are a variety of effective ways to improve teaching and to help renew or train faculty members. Which practices are most cost effective and how best to involve faculty members in appropriate activities at different stages of their careers are among the future issues that need to be addressed.

REFERENCES

Abedor, A. J., and Sachs, S. G. (1984). Faculty development, organizational development, and instructional development: Choosing an orientation. In R. K. Bass and G. R. Dills (eds.), *Instructional Development, The State of the Art*, Vol. 2, pp. 394–403. Dubuque: Kendall/Hunt.

Abrami, P. C., Leventhal, L., and Perry, R. P. (1982). Educational seduction. *Review of Educational Research* 52: 446–464.

Aleamoni, L. M. (1981). Student ratings of instruction. In J. Millman (ed.), *Handbook of Teacher Evaluation*, pp. 110–145. Beverly Hills, CA: Sage.

Alexander, A. T., and Yelon, S. L. (1972). *Instructional Development Agencies in Higher Education*. East Lansing, MI: Continuing Education Service.

Baldwin, R. G. (1984). The changing development needs of an aging professoriate. In C. M. N. Mehrotra (ed.), *Teaching and Aging*. In *New Directions for Teaching and Learning, Vol. 19*. San Francisco: Jossey-Bass, September.

Baldwin, R. G., and Blackburn, R. T. (1981). The academic career as a developmental process: implications for higher education. *Journal of Higher Education* 52(6): 598–614.

Berquist, W. H., and Phillips, S. R. (1975). Components of an effective faculty development program. *Journal of Higher Education* 46(2): 177–211.

Black, S. (1972). Interactions between teaching and research. *Universities Quarterly* 26(3): 348–352.

Blackburn, R. T., Behymar, C. E., and Hall, D.R. (1978). Research note: correlates of faculty publications. *Sociology of Education* 51(2): pp. 132–141.

Blackburn, R. T., and Clark, M. J. (1975). An assessment of faculty performance: Some correlations between administrators, colleagues, student, and self-ratings, *Sociology of Education* 48: 242–256.

Blackburn, R. T., Pellino, G., Boberg, A., and O'Connell, C. (1980). Are institutional improvement programs off-target? In *Improving Teaching and Institutional Quality. Current Issues in Higher Education*, No. 1. Washington, DC: American Association for Higher Education.

Bland, C. J., and Schmitz, C. C. (1986). Faculty vitality on review: retrospect and prospect. American Educational Research Conference, San Francisco.

Boice, R. (1982). Increasing the writing productivity of "blocked" academicians. *Behavior Research and Therapy* 20: 197–207.

Boice, R. (1987). Is released time an effective component of faculty development programs. *Research in Higher Education* 26(3): 311–326.

Braskamp, L. A., and Caulley, D. (1978). *Student Rating and Instructor Self-Ratings and Their Relationship to Student Achievement*. Urbana-Champaign: Measurement and Research Division, University of Illinois.

Braxton, J. M., and Bayer, A. M. (1986). Assessing faculty scholarly performance. In *Measuring Faculty Research Performance. New Directions for Institutional Research*, J. Crewell (ed.) 50(June): 25–42.

Brubacher, J. S., and Rudy, W. (1976). *Higher Education in Transition*. New York: Harper & Row.

Centra, J. A. (1987). Faculty evaluation: past practices, future directions. Presented at the Second National Conference on Faculty Evaluation and Development, Kansas State University, April 1–3.

Centra, J. A. (1983). Research productivity and teaching effectiveness. *Research in Higher Education* 18(4): 379–389.

Centra, J. A. (1979). *Determining Faculty Effectiveness*. San Francisco: Jossey-Bass.

Centra, J. A. (1977a). How universities evaluate faculty performance: a survey of department heads. GREB Research Report No. 75–5bR. Princeton, NJ: Educational Testing Services.

Centra, J. A. (1977b). Student ratings of instruction and their relationship to student learning. *American Educational Research Journal* 14(1): 17–24.

Centra, J. A. (1976). Faculty development practices in U.S. colleges and universities. Project Report 76–30. Princeton, NJ: Educational Testing Services.

Centra, J. A. (1975). Colleagues as raters of classroom instruction. *Journal of Higher Education*. 46: 327–337.

Centra, J. A. (1973a). Self-ratings of college teachers: a comparison with student ratings. *Journal of Educational Measurement* 10(4): 287–295.

Centra, J. A. (1973b). Effectiveness of student feedback in modifying college instruction. *Journal of Educational Psychology* 65(3): 395–401.

Centra, J. A., and Linn, R. L. (1976). Student points of view in ratings of college instruction, *Educational and Psychological Measurement* 36: 693–703.

Centra, J. A., Froh, R., Gray, P., and Lambert, L. (1987). *Evaluating Teaching for Tenure and Promotion*. Syracuse, NY: Syracuse University, Center for Instructional Development.

Chronicle of Higher Education (1987). Software for teaching given little credit for tenure review, Vol. 33, No. 27, p. 1.

Clark, S. M. and Lewis, D. R. (1988). Faculty vitality: context concerns and prospects. In John C. Smart (ed.) *Higher Education: Handbook of Theory and Research*, Vol. IV, New York: Agathon Press.

Cohen, P. A. (1981). Student ratings of instruction and student achievement: a meta-analysis of multisection validity studies. *Review of Educational Research* 51: 281–309.

Cohen, P. A. (1980). Effectiveness of student rating feedback for improving college instruction: a meta-analysis. *Research in Higher Education* 13(4): 321–341.

Cole, S., and Cole, J. R. (1967). Scientific output and recognition: a study in the operation of the reward system in science. *American Sociological Review* 32(3): 377–399.

Creswell, J. W., ed. (1986). *New Directions in Institutional Research*, No. 5. San Francisco: Jossey-Bass.

Creswell, J. W. (1985). *Faculty Research Performance*. Report #4. ASHE-ERIC Higher Education Reports.

Creswell, J. W., Wheeler, D. W., Seagren, A. T., Vavrus, L., Grady, M., Wilhite, M., and Egly, N. (1987). The faculty development role of department chairs: a naturalistic analysis. Paper given at the Association for the Study of Higher Education, Baltimore, November.

Crow, M. L., Milton, D., Moomaw, W. E., and O'Connell, W. R., Jr. (1976). *Faculty Development Centers in Southern Universities*. Atlanta: Southern Regional Education Board.

Doyle, K. O. (1975). *Student Evaluation of Instruction*. Lexington, MA: Lexington Books.

Dunkin, M. J., and Barnes, J. (1987). Research on teaching in higher education. In M. C. Wittrock (ed.), *Handbook of Research on Teaching* (3rd ed.). New York: Macmillan.

Dunkin, M. J., and Biddle, B. J. (1974). *The Study of Teaching*. New York: Holt, Rinehart & Winston.

Eble, K. E., and McKeachie, N. J. (1985). *Improving Undergraduate Education Through Faculty Development*. San Francisco: Jossey-Bass.

Eble, K. E. (1971). *Career Development of the Effective College Teacher. Washington, DC: American Association of University Professors.*

Erdle, S., and Murray, H. G. (1986). Interfaculty differences in classroom teaching behaviors and their relationship to student instructional ratings. *Research in Higher Education* 24(2): 115–127.

Erdle, S., Murray, H. G., and Rushton, J. P. (1985). Personality, classroom behavior and student ratings of college teaching effectiveness: a path analysis. *Journal of Educational Psychology* 77(4): 394–407.

Erickson, B. L. (1986). Faculty development at four-year colleges and universities: lessons learned in faculty evaluation and development. Proceedings of 1986 conference, Center for Faculty Evaluation and Development. Kansas State University, Manhattan, Kansas.

Erickson, G. R. (1985). An overview of the 1985 POD survey of faculty development practices. Available from the Instructional Development Program. University of Rhode Island, Kingston.

Feldman, K. A. (1988). Effective college teaching from the students and facultty's view: matched or mismatched priorities. *Research in Higher Education*. 28(4): 291–344.

Feldman, K. A. (1987). Research productivity and scholarly accomplishment of college teachers as related to their instructional effectiveness: a review and exploration. *Research in Higher Education* 26(3): 227–298.

Feldman, K. A. (1978). Course characteristics and college students' ratings of their teachers and courses: what we know and what we don't. *Research in Higher Education* 9(3): 199–242.

Feldman, K. A. (1977). Consistency and variability among college students in rating their teachers and courses: a review and analysis. *Research in Higher Education* 6(3): 233.

Festinger, L. (1957). *Theory of Cognitive Dissonnance*. Stanford, CA: Stanford University Press.

Fulton, O., and Trow, M. (1974). Research activity in American higher education. *Sociology of Education* 47(Winter): 29–73.

Gaff, J. G., and Morstain, B. R. (1978). Evaluating the outcomes. In J. G. Gaff (ed.), *New Directions for Higher Education: Institutional Renewal Through the Improvement of Teaching*, Vol. 24. San Francisco: Jossey-Bass.

Gaff, J. G. (1975). *Toward Faculty Renewal: Advances in Faculty, Instruction, and Organizational Development*. San Francisco: Jossey-Bass.

Gage, N. L. (1963). *Handbook of Research on Teaching*. Chicago: Rand McNally.

Garfield, E. (1979). *Citation Indexing: Its Theory and Application in Science, Technology and Humanities*. New York: Wiley.

Gilmore, G. M., Kane, M. T., and Naccarato, R. W. (1978). The generalizability of student ratings of instruction: estimation of teacher and course components. *Journal of Educational Measurement* 15(1): 11–13.

Grasha, A. P. (1977). *Assessing and Developing Faculty Performance: Principles and Models*. Cincinnati: Communication and Education Associates.

Group for Human Development in Higher Education (1974). FACULTY DEVELOPMENT IN A TIME OF RETRENCHMENT. New Rochelle, NY: Change.

Guskey, T. R. (1986). Staff development and the process of teacher change. *Educational Researcher* 15(5, May): 5–12.

Guthrie, E. R. (1954). *The Evaluation of Teaching: A Progress Report*. Seattle: University of Washington Press.

Heider, F. (1958). *The Psychology of Interpersonal Relationships*. New York: Wiley.

Jencks, C., and Riesman, D. (1968). *The Academic Revolution*. Garden City, NY: Doubleday.

Leventhal, L., Perry, R. P., Abrami, P. D., Turcotte, S. J. C., and Kane, B. (1981). Experimental investigation of tenure/promotion in American and Canadian universities. Paper presented at the annual meeting of the American Educational Research Association.

Levinson-Rose, J., and Menges, R. J. (1981). Improving college teaching: a critical review of research. *Review of Educational Research*. 51: 403–434.

Licata, C. M. (1986). *Post-Tenure Faculty Evaluation*. ASHE-ERIC Higher Education Reports No. 11.

Lin, Y., McKeachie, W. J., and Tucker, D. G. (1984). The use of student ratings in promotion decision, *Journal of Higher Education* 55(5): 583–589.

Many, W. A., Ellis, J. R., and Abrams, P. (1969). *In-Service Education in American Senior Colleges and Universities: A Status Report*. DeKalb: College of Education, Northern Illinois University.

Marsh, H. W., Overall, J. U., and Kessler, S. P. (1979). Validity of student evaluations of instructional effectiveness: a comparison of faculty self-evaluations and evaluations by their students. *Journal of Educational Psychology* 71: 149–160.

Marsh, H. W., and Ware, J. E. (1982). Effects of expressiveness, content coverage, and incentive on multidimensional student rating scales: new interpretations of the Dr. Fox Effect. *Journal of Educational Psychology* 74(1): 126–134.

Marsh, H. W. (1984a). The influence of student, course and instructor characteristics on evaluations of university teaching. *American Educational Research Journal* 17: 219–237.

Marsh, H. W. (1984b). Student evaluations of university teaching: dimensionality, reliability, validity, potential biases, and utility. *Journal of Educational Psychology* 76: 707–754.

Marsh, H. W. (1982). Validity of students' evaluations of college teaching: a multitrait-multimethod analysis. *Journal of Educational Psychology* 74: 264–279.

Maslow, A. H., and Zimmerman, W. (1956). College teaching ability, scholarly activity, and personality. *Journal of Educational Psychology* 47: 185–189.

McKeachie, W. J. (1979). Student ratings of faculty: a reprise. *Academe* 65(6): 384–397.

Meltzer, L. (1956). Scientific productivity in organizational settings. *Journal of Social Issues* 12(3): 32–40.

Miller, R. I. (1987). *Evaluating Faculty for Promotion and Tenure.* San Francisco: Jossey-Bass.

Miller, W. S., and Wilson, K. W. (1963). *Faculty Development Procedures in Small Colleges.* Atlanta, Southern Regional Education Board.

Murray, H. G. (1987). Impact of student instructional ratings on quality of teacher education. Paper presented at the annual meeting of American Educational Research Association, Washington, DC.

Murray, H. G. (1985). Classroom teaching behaviors related to college teaching effectiveness. In J. C. Donald and A. M. Sullivan (eds.), *Using Research to Improve Teaching. New Directions for Teaching and Learning.* Vol. 23. San Francisco: Jossey-Bass.

Naftulin, D. H., Ware, J. E., and Donnelly, F. A. (1973). The Doctor Fox lecture: a paradigm of educational seduction. *Journal of Medical Education* 48(7): 630–635.

Ory, J. C., Braskamp, L. A., and Pieper, D. M. (1980). Congruency of student evaluative information collected by three methods. *Journal of Educational Psychology* 72: 181–185.

Overall, J. J., and Marsh, H. W. (1980). Students' evaluations of instruction: a longitudinal study of their stability. *Journal of Educational Psychology* 72: 321–325.

Remmers, H. H. (1934). Reliability and halo-effect of high school and college students' judgments of their teachers. *Journal of Applied Psychology* 18: 619–630.

Root, L. (1987). Faculty evaluation: reliability of peer assessments of research, teaching and service. *Research in Higher Education* 26(1): 71–84.

Rudolph, F. (1977). *Curriculum: A History of the American Undergraduate Course of Study Since 1636.* San Francisco: Jossey-Bass.

Salthouse, T. A., McKeachie, W. J., and Lin., Y. G. (1978). An experimental investigation of factors affecting university promotions decisions. *Journal of Higher Education* 49: 177–183.

Schrader, W. B. (1978). *W. B. Admissions Test Scores as Predictors of Career Achievement in Psychology.* GREB No. 76-1R. Princeton, NJ: Educational Testing Services.

Scriven, M. (1978). Value vs. merit. *Evaluation News,* No. 8, 1–3.

Siegel, M. E. (1980). Empirical findings on faculty development programs. In W. C. Nelsen and M. E. Siegel (eds.), *Effective Approaches to Faculty Development.* Washington, DC: Association of American Colleges.

Smallwood, M. L. (1935). *An Historical Study of Examinations and Grading Systems in Early American Universities.* Cambridge, MA: Harvard University Press.

Sullivan, A. M., and Skanes, G. R. (1974). Validity of student evaluation of teaching and the characteristics of successful instructors. *Journal of Educational Psychology* 66: 584–590.

Teather, D. C. B., (ed.) (1979). *Staff Development in Higher Education.* New York: Nichols Publishing.

Theall, M. (1986). *Components of the TCEP System.* Boston: Northeastern University.

Veysey, L. (1973). Stability and experiment in the American undergraduate curriculum. pp. 1–63. *Content and Contest Essays on College Education,* McGraw-Hill.

Wergin, J. R., Mason, E. J., and Munson, P. J. (1976). The practice of faculty development. *The Journal of Higher Education* 47(3): 289–308.

Wilson, R. C. (1987). *The Personal Teaching Improvement Guides Program: A User's Manual.* Berkeley: University of California.

Wilson, T. (1987). Pedagogical justice and student evaluation of teaching forms: a critical perspective. Paper presented at American Educational Research Association, Washington, DC.

Wotruba, T. R., and Wright, P. L. (1975). How to develop a teacher-rating instrument: a research approach. *Journal of Higher Education.* 46(6): 653–663.

Higher Education's Odd Couple: Campus Archives and the Office of Institutional Research

John R. Thelin
The College of William and Mary

and

Marsha V. Krotseng
The University of Hartford

PLANNING BY THE NUMBERS

Ours is the age of numbers. Nowhere is this more true than in the planning and management associated with the complex organizations of colleges and universities. The two staples of contemporary campus planning—enrollments and budgets—certainly call for a numerical grasp. *Accountability*, by definition, implies the capacity to count, whether it be dollars or students. During the past two decades the two major statistical data bases, known as HEGIS (Higher Education General Information Systems) and its successor, IPEDS (Integrated Postsecondary Education Data System), have become the lifeblood of our contemporary effort to report the condition and character of higher education. Institutional research in higher education has evolved as a systematic activity whose credo is that measurement goes hand in glove with management. Following Folger's (1983) example, institutional research is defined here ''broadly to include those studies, policy analyses, and information collections that assist college administrators to understand and deal with both the internal operations and external environment of their institution'' (p. 78).

The need for numbers as a fact of organizational life is not without its problems, namely, a false sense of precision and a danger of information overload. That there sometimes is confusion or bewilderment accompanying this reliance on quantitative data is not merely a sign of ''math anxiety'' or an avoidance excuse by those who ''do not like statistics.'' Rather, it is a warning sounded by sophisticated social and behavioral scientists who themselves are involved in the application of research to policies and practices. Consider the memorable incident associated with David Stockman, director of the federal

180

government's Office of Management and Budget during the early years of President Ronald Reagan's administration: after perusing the federal budget, of which he was a primary architect, Stockman concluded in an interview with a reporter for *The Atlantic Monthly*, "None of us really understands what's going on with all these numbers" (Greider, 1981, pp. 27, 28). Or as Harvard economist Martin Feldstein said in 1983 when he assumed the role of chairman of the Council of Economic Advisors and joined his first work session on the proposed budget draft, "They don't actually believe this mumbo-jumbo do they?" Stockman (1986) cautioned Feldstein that, "It's too late to think logically. The time has come to start thinking hard" (p. 362).

But is this necessarily sound advice for higher education research? It is not "too late" for us to think logically or to work thoughtfully to improve research about colleges and universities. Enhancement of institutional research can come from several directions. One partial solution is to gather more and better numbers; and, indeed, recent reports from Washington, D.C., herald the federal government's increased commitment to collection of educational statistics (Vobejda, 1988). In fact, organizations and individuals "appear to be constantly needing or requesting" additional data, although Feldman and March (1981) attest that these entities "often collect more information than they use or can reasonably expect to use" (p. 174). Second, scholars can devise increasingly sophisticated statistical tests—metaphorically, a sharpening of "research tools." This is precisely the welcomed refinement that comes from, for example, a recent work such as *Applying Statistics in Institutional Research* (Yancey, 1988). And the periodic self-examination of institutional research as a professional activity through the Association of Institutional Research (AIR) and its regional affiliates, as well as via professional literature such as Jossey-Bass's "New Directions in Institutional Research" series, provides an antidote of sorts to complacence (Lindquist, 1981). These responses, however, may be characterized as "playing from strength," i.e., developing or polishing existing, central approaches to institutional research.

There is another intriguing approach: the venture of a profession that plays from weakness, i.e., turns attention from time to time to its peripheral dimensions. An example of this might be as follows: the statistical analyses that characterize institutional research in higher education can gain in credibility and sophistication if increased attention is paid to the *context* of data, rather than to the data themselves. It is to the interpretation, analysis, and insights fostered by the various numbers colleges collect that we direct our attention. Our underlying concerns are as follows:

Institutional statistics make more sense when extended over time and space— from single snapshots into cinema, from single words into sentences and paragraphs.

Numerical data make more sense when placed in the context of "third factors" (Cipolla, 1970).

In "research" about institutional behavior, data do not "speak for themselves"—and information ought be connected to the concepts and theories of scholarly disciplines. This level of forethought is the difference between typing and writing, between collecting and analyzing.

Without these *caveats* the task of data collection runs the risk of becoming an end in itself. Educational institutions, especially in their relations with government agencies, run the risk of "drowning in data" and being preoccupied with paperwork (Loepp, 1988). Our contention is that the office of institutional research can best be seen and used not only as a tool in getting immediate answers to questions, but also as a source of institutional *memory* for connecting past, present, and future (cf. Fincher, 1987). Indeed, "any institutional planning effort requires information on the institution's past, its present situation, its environment, and forecasts of its future condition" (Lasher and Firnberg, 1983, p. 98). Given this conception, the office of institutional research has on many campuses an overlooked partner: another source of institutional memory, namely, the campus archives. Our chapter, then, can best be seen as an exercise in matchmaking, an orchestrated mating dance to bring together this "odd couple" of institutional memory—the archives and the office of institutional research—with the aim of providing improved interpretation of college and university condition and behavior. Hoaglin and associates (1982) have shown the significance of such archival information for secondary analyses of a collection of studies for answering new policy questions.

Our position is that statistical analysis is established as central to higher education institutional research—and that this is both understandable and not without limits and problems. Our second premise is that imaginative triangulation with archival records and historical sources might invigorate and strengthen the collection and analysis of higher education statistics. This claim will be more evident if one first understands the process of institutional research. What follows is a profile of the round-of-life of a typical campus office of institutional research.

THE OFFICE OF INSTITUTIONAL RESEARCH: A YEAR IN THE LIFE

An urgent telephone call summons the director of institutional research to the university president's office. The state senate bill that would alter the tuition and fee structure for all public institutions of higher learning has suddenly gained new momentum.

"Please prepare an assessment of its potential impact on our enrollment and revenue pictures by this afternoon," directs the chief executive. "I have a meeting in the state capital tomorrow and need some 'hard data' to build a convincing case."

Meanwhile, the assistant director of institutional research is busy fielding an intriguing array of questions ranging from the familiar to the novel: a faculty member seeks advice in constructing a self-study survey instrument; a doctoral candidate inquires about access to information used in compiling the university's annual "student characteristics" report; a campus administrator from a nearby state expresses interest in the institution's exemplary assessment program; a department chair requests some figures as background for budget prepation; and an inquisitive alumna queries, "Can it be true that 20% of our student body comes from Texas?"

Given this assortment of constituents and concerns, life in an involved office of institutional research is anything but routine. In fact, the best generalization to describe the "typical" day of an institutional researcher is that there can be no generalization; each day is unusual. Institutional research offices learn to "expect the unexpected"—even queries about the capacity of the campus water filtration plant. Yet, while lacking a set daily routine, institutional researchers do dance to a distinct annual rhythm whose tune is set largely by state and federal data-reporting requirements.

In keeping with this rhythm, offices of institutional research and planning maintain a wealth of information—as well as a touch of mystique. What really happens to all those data? Where do they come from? Where do they go? Much of the information is generated from records customarily created by other university offices, including those of the registrar, personnel, business affairs, student financial aid, and various deans and department chairs. And virtually every month, representatives of either the federal Integrated Postsecondary Education Data System (IPEDS, formerly HEGIS) or the state governing or coordinating board expect transmittal of certain vital reports.

For example, in mid to late summer the state board may request such information as "degrees granted" from the preceding spring, "degrees to be conferred" at the close of the summer term, and a profile of characteristics of currently enrolled students. A number of such reports are characteristically due in July as the board staff prepares final summaries of activities for the previous academic session and enters a new fiscal year. The opening of each semester will herald two additional peak periods in the institutional research cycle: institutional enrollment and course enrollment and student characteristics are among the reports sought in September; January deadlines call for information on fall semester student outcomes or course grades.

Just after the institutional researcher has satisfied the state board's September requirements, IPEDS injects a set of national surveys requesting data on faculty salaries as well as enrollment by student characteristics and programs or levels.

By mid-November IPEDS seeks additional estimates, including degrees awarded, current fund revenues, current fund expenditures and transfers, full-time faculty, and tuition and fees. In the interim, the research staff stays busy coordinating a host of other state reports in such diverse areas as student aid, National Direct Student Loan default rates, space utilization, National Teachers Examination scores, library holdings, and finance.

Simultaneously, the institutional researcher becomes engaged in a number of ongoing studies that support these external data requirements and—more significantly—provide for effective institutional planning. Following consultation with numerous officials, both on and off campus, the office arrives at enrollment projections by late fall and then turns to budget analysis (depending on the timing of the state's legislative session). Other ongoing analyses review the following: characteristics of entering freshmen, including their average SAT or ACT scores; faculty characteristics; performance of transfer students; distribution of grades by department; and, survey responses by non-returning students. Superimposed on these continuing activities are distinct day-to-day issues and questions; filling out surveys sent by other institutions, professional associations, or agencies; and special projects assigned by the university president.

A thoughtfully constructed institutional profile or fact book offers a ready snapshot of the institutional research year. This publication, frequently edited in early summer for distribution at the outset of the fall semester, concisely and graphically answers the question, "What do institutional researchers do?" Various sections highlight many of the aforementioned studies, including those of entering students (their geographical diversity, intended majors, and transfer credits); academic operations (e.g., grade distributions, student credit hour production, and classroom utilization); faculty characteristics (their average salaries, tenure status, and rank distributions); and institutional support (educational and general revenues and expenditures). Indeed, it is the "publication and dissemination of a factbook [that] demonstrates to much of the rest of the campus that the Institutional Research component is . . . active" (Nichols, Howard, and Sharp, 1987, p. 102).

This professional activity moved toward the campus foreground in 1984 following the inclusion of "Institutional Effectiveness" among accreditation criteria of the Southern Association of Colleges and Schools (SACS) and, more recently, with bold state and national mandates for student outcomes assessments. Proposals buried in the Reagan administration's final budget linked federal campus-based financial aid to student outcomes and hence, ultimately, to the institutional research effort. Under such legislation, colleges and universities "would have to establish a series of 'student-outcome objectives' to measure how much their students had learned, how many students had graduated, and how many had obtained jobs. Institutions that did well in meeting goals they had set in those areas would receive more money" (Wilson, 1988, p. A26). Applying slightly different tactics, the Commonwealth of Virginia incorporated funds for the measurment of student and institutional progress in its 1988-1990 biennial budget. Public institutions replied almost immediately by advertising position openings for "student assessment specialists" or by elevating the status of institutional research on their campuses: "Because institutional research can provide significant information in all phases of a college or university program, it [has become] an essential element in planning and evaluating the institution's success in carrying out its purpose" (Southern Association of Colleges and Schools, 1984, p. 11).

This enhanced emphasis on institutional research as central to the university's effectiveness tends to echo the reasons for the establishment of such offices in the first place: "During the late 1950s and 1960s, the practice of institutional research grew with the blessings of many institutional presidents and executive officers" in response to "growth, expansion, and the need for more and better information" in postsecondary education (Peterson, 1985, p. 5). Thus, while the historic roots of the *practice* of institutional research have even been traced back to Yale of the early 1700s, institutional research as a systematic, bona fide *profession* and campus fixture is barely three decades old. Little wonder, then, that to the institutional researcher, the term *historical data* conjures memories of the "golden age" of the 1960s.

BEYOND BUSINESS AS USUAL: HISTORICAL HEGIS

Given this composite profile of a university office of institutional research, a few salient points stand out in bold relief. First, unless serious attention is directed to long-term planning, the institutional research staff appears reactive, forced to respond to directives from other offices and agencies, and must respond to directives from other offices and agencies. Second, an inordinate amount of professional time is devoted to gathering statistics, performing established tests and presentations. Third, institutional research studies are driven by the data the offices are mandated to collect. Fourth, the annual round of life is such that compliance with demand for customary reports leaves little opportunity for "venture capital" research or innovation. Fifth, the press for answers to immediate questions tends to make analyses present-minded and short-run. Such syndromes are understandable but leave the nagging question: Do these reports and activities constitute "research"? Here are some queries that suggest some reservations about the maturation of institutional research:

Is there a lack of disciplinary perspective for key concepts or theoretical frameworks and lack of opportunity to generate hypotheses and inquiries? We have reasonable doubt that there is any assurance that the major insights, concepts, and analytic frameworks of such disciplines as history, sociology, economics, and political science guide how we analyze institutional information.

The crucial corollary is the question: Is there a danger that institutional research, with its perennial reporting requirements, crystallizes into "business as usual"—when such not need be the case?

How might alliance with the campus archives help the office of institutional research resolve such problems—and rescue itself from the tedium of "business as usual"? One strategy is to consider the fundamental housekeeping question: What happens to "old" HEGIS data? The question was raised about a decade ago by Lunney (1979), who reported that most offices made little use of old records once the current year's data were compiled and reported to other offices and agencies. In a similar vein, the April 1987 American Educational Research Association's journal, *Educational Researcher*, featured an interesting article, "The Fate of the Files," indicating that university institutes and research centers often discard old records and primary sources shortly after publication of reports or summaries; and even when the original data are stored, they remain virtually unexamined within the office or institute (Nespor, 1987). In basic economic terms, Miller (1980) contends that *no* institutional evaluation or report should be "filed and forgotten," especially "considering the investment of thousands of hours and dollars and the importance of keeping the institution abreast of its problems" (p. 426). Herein lies the best prospect for connecting contemporary institutional research effort with some historic or changing conception of life within the institution: the notion of *Historical* HEGIS.

Static, isolated data make little sense for analysis. One needs a "run" of comparable statistics in order to plot patterns over time or to construct ratios that provide measures of institutional performance. The problem is twofold: as suggested above, when HEGIS data do exist for earlier years, emphasis is on storage rather than active use. The problem is compounded further because comprehensive, compatible statistics do not extend very far back in time. At best, HEGIS data in a few selected categories go back to the early 1970s—and even this is problematic as there have been substantial changes in reporting format and categories of collection. But to solve this problem, perhaps statistics could be compiled for earlier years via fresh gleanings of archival materials. This is no less than a case for institutions to devote some effort to collecting *post hoc* HEGIS data. It could involve making use of old HEGIS records as well as analyzing primary sources and documents to construct HEGIS data from the distant past.

A pilot study by one of the coauthors set out to demonstrate this approach in the area of research on student enrollment and retention (Thelin, 1984). Current concern over dropout rates and allegedly low percentages of degree completion led to the question: How does our contemporary student performance match with those of students at the turn of the century? Analysis of annual enrollment reports over the forty-year period 1880–1920 at six selected institutions led to some surprising findings. First, there was substantial evidence of transfers and dropouts—contrary to the notion of the traditional four-year cohesive experience. Second, although there was great difference from institution to institution, it was not uncommon to find in the early 1900s a dropout rate of almost 50% between freshman and senior year. One historic institution consistently showed a degree completion rate of less than 20%. Another college claimed to be a "four-year degree-granting" institution when, in fact, about three-fourths of its students voluntarily left the college in good academic standing at the end of the sophomore year in order to pursue teaching careers—with little intention of returning to complete the bachelor's degree (Thelin, 1984). Comparable research strategy could be applied to areas where we now use ratios and indicators: institutional finance, library holdings, degrees completed, expenditures per student. To offer another potentially valuable model, O'Keefe's (1987) examination of costs and expenditures at six well-known institutions of higher education in 1976 and 1986 might also be applied to data of an earlier era, although his work clearly illustrates some of the formidable perils associated with comparative study of financial issues.

The appeal of "historical HEGIS" is that it enhances the notion of *longitudinal study*. By way of comparison, consider the case of Alexander Astin's annual profile of American college freshman values and attitudes, a model of behavioral science research awaited by scholars and administrators each year. Important to note is that Astin's annual report has gained in potency and influence because now it provides a *historical* dimension, recently published as *The American Freshman: Twenty Year Trends* (Astin, Green, and Korn, 1987). It is this transformation from a relatively static profile of a single year to an extended series of interacting profiles that suggests how institutional research can fuse history with the social and behavioral sciences.

CLIOMETRICS AND THE CAMPUS CONDITION

Historical HEGIS is best seen as an obvious facet of a larger research design: *cliometrics*—literally, "historical statistics." The attractiveness of the approach is that it can be extended to connect present data to either the immediate past or distant eras. Its danger as one goes back in time is the fallacy of anachronism, i.e., the assumption that our familiar present-day practices and categories make sense to another era. This situation serves to reinforce our earlier emphasis on the importance of taking account of *context* in the analysis of institutional statistics.

The limit of our discussion is that even if one is willing to accept the marriage proposal of historical archives and institutional research, there are scant good examples to guide subsequent research. The most basic obstacle is that few archives have maintained comprehensive statistics on institutional characteristics. Harvard University is exceptional, thanks in large measure to the university archivist and to the long-term commitment of economist Seymour Harris. Harris's *The Economics of Harvard* (1970) stands as a remarkable reference work for tracking over three hundred years of trends and patterns in virtually every conceivable dimension of organizational life—from fund-raising to faculty tenure. But more often than not, one who ventures into cliometrics finds, at best, partial victories. For example, at the University of Kentucky the Bureau of Institutional Records compiled and published a fine summary of university finances, with attention to sources of income listed for each year from the late 19th century into the post–World War II era; strangely, however, there were no comparable listings for expenditures—hence, the analyst is left with tantalizing yet grossly incomplete materials for ratio analysis over time.

Fortunately, there are some excellent models of synthesis. The indefatigible Seymour Harris went beyond his own institution, Harvard, to lead a project for the Carnegie Commission on Higher Education that led to a massive compendium of historical statistics on national trends in higher education (Harris, 1972). The limit of this work, obviously, is that scholars do not have access to the *disaggregated* data from which Harris constructed his composite profiles. Colin Burke (1982) devoted over a decade to a fresh compilation and examination of statistics on college operations and college attendance in the 19th century—a herculean task that resulted in a major revision of our conception of institutional mortality prior to the age of the modern university. In contrasting scope to Burke's nationwide profile, the best example of "micro" historical reconstruction of institutional operations and finances from a distant era is Margaret Foster's study of the economics of colonial Harvard, *Out of Smalle Beginings* (1962). Surprisingly, this spawned few comparable works for other institutions, probably because such scholarship demands extraordinary finesse in the disciplines of both social history and economics.

The unavoidable fact is that extending the statistical data base back in time will require reliance on secondary and primary sources from the archives and other agencies, sometimes including census data (e.g., Kiecolt and Nathan, 1985). One relatively easy approach is to make use of the annual reports published in college catalogs. Until fairly recently, catalogs were comprehensive documents that often included summaries of enrollments, budgets, and so on. Similarly, student yearbooks used to have for each graduating senior elaborate information on such matters as date of birth, secondary school, choice of major, activities, and so on (Barry, 1975). These lend themselves to systematic compilation of demographic and financial profiles, respectively.

But there are degrees of reliability and accuracy. Dependence on published enrollment summaries might be consistent over time if the same format is used by an institution in its annual catalogs. Less clear is whether the summaries carry the accuracy or refinement we expect today in our data collection. One recent study of enrollment and attrition trends in the early 1900s contrasted two data collection methods: reliance on published annual summaries of class-by-class numbers and actual cohort tracking of an entering freshman class on a name-by-name basis over five years, relying on the primary source of annual student rosters. The resultant statistical profiles of student persistence and degree completion were substantially different: the presidential summaries gave a misleading representation of about 15%–20% overstatement, whereas the name-by-name tracking that went back to original rosters showed a higher dropout rate and a significantly lower rate of bachelor's degree completion (Thelin, 1984). Neither study was "wrong" but, rather, illustrates that, then as now, more sophisticated, careful data collection and analysis require greater time and resources. One caveat is that *post hoc* data collection is time-consuming, sometimes improbable. For example, sending an opinion survey to members of the Class of 1895 today is not likely to elicit a high response rate, although it might give credence to Voltaire's quip that "history is a pack of lies that the dead play on the living." In most cases, historical HEGIS will depend on reconstruction from records and documents.

The fusion of historical research and sources with contemporary records remains relatively underdeveloped for the study of a crucial dimension of higher education: campus subcultures and the actual patterns of student life within the campus experience. Twenty years ago Burton Clark and Martin Trow (1967) provided a useful model and typology. Yet all too often their typology has been either ignored or untested, accepted as a static mold. In fact, it is an invitation for each institution to draw its own profiles and to trace its processes of institutional life over time. To develop this strand of institutional understanding will require not only historical perspective but also reliance on ethnography and approaches developed by anthropologists. Recently historian Helen Horowitz's *Campus Life* (1987) has presented a new synthesis of the configurations of undergraduate culture over two hundred years. But the interesting (and perplexing) part of her excellent study is multiple: first, it is a composite study that tells little about the distinctive patterns at particular institutions; second, data on the 19th and early 20th centuries are more descriptive than materials from our own era. The residual message is that colleges and universities are laggard in monitoring their distinctive cultural life.

To test out this bold claim, it is useful to compare the reports and data of an office of institutional research with the campus profiles presented in such popular publications as *The Yale Daily News' Insider's Guide to the Colleges* or Edward Fiske's *New York Times Selective Guide to Colleges* (1982). The popular publications provide prospective students and their parents with candid, graphic insights and clues into the "hidden curriculum," the best places to get pizza, courses to avoid, professors to seek, and so on. And in the case of Fiske's report, colleges are rated (not unlike restaurants) according to "four-star" criteria in such timely or vital areas as academics, the student body, housing, food, social life, and extracurricular activities. The usual response of college authorities is to bask in the glow of a high rating, or at another extreme, to denounce the inside guides if perchance their own campus receives a low rating for academics, or simply to be oblivious to the imagery. If, indeed, the popular inside guides are superficial, the ball bounces back to the college administration's court: "What do institutions know and publish that is truly perceptive about their campus and its ethnography?" Sadly, the answer is "very little." The recent demand for assessment of student outcomes has caught most colleges woefully unprepared. In fact, state officials sometimes are hungry for data assessing educational progress over time, and institutional researchers, with a bit of foresight and imagination, could have been positioned to serve up a bounteous feast (Krotseng, 1988). This research void becomes still more glaring when one jumps from outcomes to the more subtle nuances of the experience and life within the campus.

Here mention of Astin's freshman profiles is again useful. Astin relies heavily on attitudinal surveys in which entering freshmen complete inventories and questionnaires. Important as such data are, they offer only a glimpse at the actions and patterns of behavior that accompany self-reported student values. And there is the potential limit that what freshmen say about themselves differs from how they actually behave. In short, when data on students do exist, they usually are survey data. To understand the campus condition—and the dynamics of student-faculty life within an organization—one ultimately ought to have unobtrusive measures. These are the kinds of reconstructed and observed data one associates with such disciplines as history and anthropology. Commenting on the use of subjective data, Miller (1980) contends that "it is better to be generally right than precisely wrong. Objective data are important, yet considerable variation exists in the availability and quality of such evidence. . . . The lack of 'hard' data should not deter careful and systematic decision making about important institutional matters" (p. 425). However, the rich subjective data are in short supply. Testimony of sorts to this void is that in recent years the demand for "assessment" of college performance has left most campuses scrambling to assemble new instruments, new surveys—ironically, though, at commencement speeches and in view books, deans and presidents have no qualms about waxing eloquent about the characteristics of campus life. In fact, most such claims are spoken "without fear—and without research." How might institutional research amend this situation?

The prospects and possibilities get a bit better when we look at the recent efforts within offices of institutional research. At the University of California in 1980 an example of institutional research that combines historical methods with contemporary statistical records is thus: we carry around an image of the "typical college student" and the "real college experience"—in that "Joe College" and "Betty Coed" spend four years as full-time residential students, each selects a major field in the sophomore or junior year. Interesting, but is it accurate? A fascinating study at Berkeley relies on data dealing with course registrations, course drop-add data, and enrollment patterns to signal a transformation of the college experience. For example, freshmen are dropping and failing more courses, taking longer to complete the degree, and—by voting with their feet—shifting inordinate resources to lower division instruction, increasing the amount of time spent on repeating courses and offering remedial courses. The institutional resource pyramid has been turned upside down, and—one suspects—the four-year round-of-life has been altered (University of California, 1980; Schoch, 1980; Thelin, 1986b, 1987, pp. 156–157).

Here are the raw data by which to offer a new sketch of the rhythm of college life. The ultimate task for the institutional researcher is to make sense out of the disparate statistics so as to graphically capture the shape or even the personality of the institution over time. In *Images of Organization* (1986), Gareth Morgan shows how one might "read" an institution, an analytic process that includes sifting data to describe the particular campus as if it were, for example, a certain animal. A college that is overextended in eight directions might be seen as an octopus. Or a campus that conveniently changes its mission statement in light of external resources could be accurately depicted as a chameleon (Thelin, 1986a). Other institutions will have even more drastic alterations—as they, for example, accommodate returning students and part-time students. Yet this ethnography and personality of campus life seldom crops up either in our institutional research reports or in our "house histories" of colleges and universities. There is an image lag—in that we tend by default to cling to a traditional notion of "college life." More disconcerting, as noted in the earlier discussion of retention rates, is the suggestion that the image does not always hold up well historically!

Another promising case comes from Rutgers, where anthropologist Michael Moffat (1985) has been studying undergraduate rites of passage. Rejecting the attitudinal survey approach, Moffat has relied on participant-observation data, self-reporting forms and daily logs of time, and archival memoirs of students. He has ingeniously probed the question: Are students today studying more or less than their counterparts from earlier epochs? The added appeal of this study is that it provides a contemporary "Rutgers variation" on the concept of the "hidden curriculum" (Snyder, 1970). Moffat found reliance on survey data to be risky on two counts: first, students respond according to what they *should* be doing (namely, giving lip service to the dean's convocation wisdom about "two hours of study for every hour in class"), or they simply have no good accounting or recall. The ethnographic and historical research approach allowed the researcher to spot subcultures, varying studying styles and guises, and to come up with reasonable estimates of about three hours of study per day. Careful checking of student diaries from the 19th and early 20th centuries, with careful distinctions of time spent, suggests a surprising finding: students of the earlier eras were preocuppied with being conscientious students, but often this was an expression of concern that they ought be studying more—rather than testimony to the fact that they did study the ideal of six hours per day!

The residual point is that each institution has its own pattern to describe and decode. Howard London's (1978a,b) studies of subcultures at an urban community college suggest a world of a "hidden curriculum" markedly different than that described by Benson Snyder (1971) in his study of MIT of the mid-1960s. And a study of community colleges by the California Postsecondary Education Commission (1981) indicates a silent transformation in the character and composition of community college student bodies (a virtual disappearance of the student who intends to transfer to the four-year college), with a bifurcation between two markedly different student groups: remedial, low-income students and, at the other extreme, highly educated, affluent students who are "education-wise" and who return again and again to the community college to upgrade skills and to use education to enhance careers and recreation. Such are the transformations in the subcultures of student life that ultimately shape the institution—yet that unfortunately are not often studied or monitored by institutional research because they require systematic tracking over several years. Fortunately, a few individual scholars have responded to this void, as suggested by Townsend's (1986) manifesto for studying the historical saga and heritage of the community college as part of its present identity and mission.

One potential impetus for fusion of history, literary analysis, and anthropology into the institutional research effort may come from the nascent "student assessment" mandate now required by many accrediting associations and state legislatures. The following passage indicates how this fertilization across scholarly disciplines might take place:

> The Tennessee Performance Funding Project depended heavily on the leadership of the campus pilot project directors. These directors came from a variety of academic disciplines. Few of them had previous experience in program evaluation.
>
> One of the major outcomes of this statewide evaluation activity was the personal development of the project directors at each campus, and the many faculty working with them. They had opportunity to step outside their own academic field and to engage in a new line of inquiry. They had opportunity to probe new literature related to goal formulation, data acquisition, data analysis and evaluation.
>
> Physicists learned about the Delphi Technique. Historians examined standardized instruments for assessing general education competencies. Accountants studied the Institutional Goals Inventory. Sociologists reviewed the jury approach to the evaluation of data. And they all struggled with the interpersonal and management-of-change questions which they faced on their home campuses. (Bogue, 1980, pp. 82–83).

FROM MICRO TO MACRO: BEYOND THE CAMPUS TO POLICY ISSUES

One impediment to institutional investment in historical HEGIS is that studies will be seen as interesting yet not especially pertinent to the business of running an institution. At first glance this is true. But when one considers the domain of public policy, cliometrics may well have been a useful, worthwhile, and modest investment for colleges. This is so because discussions and debates of public policy at the state and federal level are in part informational and interpretive skirmishes, not to mention extended campaigns. In matters of federal funding, consider recent contentions by Secretary of Education William J. Bennett. On several occasions Bennett primed the public and Congress for proposed cuts in higher education funding on the basis that colleges are expensive, wasteful, and inefficient (Bowen, 1985). Colleges and universities usually rushed to respond to such charges—overlooking an effective approach: Bennett's indictments carried the assumption that there was some golden era where graduation rates and college costs were "better" than the current ones. In a similar vein, private colleges and universities were especially susceptible to popular criticism when a research report sponsored by the United States Department of Education suggested in August 1987 that private colleges cost more than public institutions to educate an undergraduate student. Responses came from national associations and scattered individual scholars (Wilson, 1987; Thelin, 1985), but most individual institutions were not well prepared to respond to the issue one way or the other. Without historical data which were synchronized with contemporary records, colleges could not really answer systematically even facile indictments. Had they been able to muster quickly comparisons of 1985 with, e.g., 1880 and 1930 and 1960, they might have been able to refute and defuse rash indictments, rather than invoke polemics or be confined to current data. Furthermore, a great deal of significant public policy is predicated on heritage and custom. In California, for example, the policy of "low tuition" and "no tuition" manifests a historic commitment to expanding access. But is this an artifact of a belief that does not work? Independent colleges and universities have relied on historical data to counter that custom—to show that low tuition has historically had little to do with diversity or modest-income access in student enrollments (Odell and Thelin, 1980).

A final area where institutions will be pressed to explain their past as well as present will be in litigation. For over ten years the University of California, for example, has been defendant in a suit that hinges on the ability (or inability) of the university to present a "societal impact statement." A decade ago, the university's first response was that although it could an provide an economic impact analysis, it was poorly prepared to present a systematic study of its societal impact (Thelin, 1982, pp. 14–15; Busch and Lacy, 1983; Sinclair, 1988). Whether this was an avoidance ploy or a frank admission of research limits, it does illustrate the potential importance of maintaining a sophisticated social and historical grasp of institutional behavior.

CONCLUSIONS

Why have the campus archives and the office of institutional research traditionally avoided each other? The best explanation is that although both are central to the "knowledge industry," each unit characterizes a markedly different section of the organizational brain. Institutional researchers are apt to say that archivists cannot count. Archivists, in turn, would respond that the institutional research office suffers from amnesia, as it has no memory. The appeal of historical HEGIS is that it provides a strategy by which to overcome the false dichotomy of "quantitative" versus "qualitative" research (Kuhns and Martorana, 1982). But healing this schism within the campus structure will not come easily or without effort.

Adoption of cliometrics and historical HEGIS strategies requires two shifts in thinking: one requisite is for institutional researchers to consider such disciplines as history and anthropology as having legitimacy as "applied research" endeavors. We are, for example, uncomfortable with the idea of anthropologists doing fieldwork in contemporary America but do not mind their studying the peculiar customs of a primitive, distant culture (Miner, 1956). Interesting to note is that the highly pragmatic fields of health care and product marketing have jumped ahead of colleges and universities, in recognizing (and hiring) anthropologists and ethnographers for their organizational research effort (Rathje, 1979; Heller, 1988). Economists and sociologists who study public policy issues increasingly look to microeconomics for clues to considering social context (Hemenway, 1978; Rich, 1981; Hoaglin, et al., 1982; Allen, 1978). For archivists and historians, recognition as an "applied researcher" requires that campus decision-makers acknowledge historical analysis as what might be termed a useful past in which documents are decoded and put into temporal context (e.g., Botstein, 1986), not merely an exercise devoted to the arcane description of a distant, disconnected past. In the domain of long-range planning, George Keller and Malcolm Moos's study of the University of Maryland, *The Post Land Grant University* (Moos, 1981) is exemplary in its synthesis of state and regional history, the national history of higher education, the nuances of state political conditions, and demographic data with specific institutional statistics.

Interoffice innovation is, of course, a two-way street. Hence, the second alteration necessary for a new institutional research synthesis is that historians and archivists will have to accept the notion of cooperation with institutional researchers who must digest, process, and respond to immediate questions in a timely manner. As with all marriages, this will require a period of adjustment. Earlier we chided college officials and institutional researchers for their tendency to be unable or unwilling to respond to the candid profiles of their campus published in popular consumer guides. Important to note is that institutional historians of colleges and universities, too, have usually shied away from candid, critical scrutiny, especially of the campus life in the recent past and the present. Nor have historians made use of the kinds of statistical profiles readily available from institutional research offices. One noteworthy exception that stands as a model of analysis of contemporary student life comes from historian Paul

Conkin's concluding chapter in his history of Vanderbilt University, *Gone with the Ivy* (1985). The biggest conceptual change necessary is for those of us who analyze information about colleges and universities, especially at newer institutions, to recognize that we are witnesses to "history in our own time." The accumulation of annual data chronicles a heritage and history that are significant and as yet remain largely underappreciated and unwritten.

REFERENCES

Allen, T. H. (1878). *New Methods in Social Science Research: Policy Sciences and Futures Research*. New York: Praeger.

Astin, A. W., Green, K. C., and Korn, W. S. (1987). *The American Freshman: Twenty Year Trends, 1966 to 1985*. Los Angeles: Higher Education Research Institute of the University of California, Los Angeles and the Cooperative Institutional Research program of the American Council on Education.

Barry, J. (1975). Archives. *Brown Alumni Monthly* (11, November): 17–20.

Bogue, E. G. (1980). State agency approaches to academic program evaluation. In E. C. Craven, (ed.), *New Directions for Institutional Research*, No. 27. San Francisco: Jossey-Bass.

. . . a book at school to write most every thing in. (1971). *Harvard Bulletin*. 73(9, March 22): 48.

Botstein, L. (1986). What has been learned so far: a cheap ticket to a fine college. *Harper's Magazine* (November), 76–77.

Bowen, E. (1985). The campus value line: college prices outstrip inflation in a seller's market. *Time* 126(8, August 26): 52.

Burke, C. (1982). *American Collegiate Populations: A Test of the Traditional View* New York: New York University Press.

Busch, L., and Lacy, W. B. (1983). *Science, Agriculture, and the Politics of Research*. Boulder, CO: Westview Publishers.

California Postsecondary Education Commission (1981). *Missions and Functions of the California Community Colleges*. Sacramento.

Cipolla, C. (1970). *Literacy and Development in the West*. Baltimore: Penguin.

Clark, B. and Trow, M. (1967). *Determinant of College Student Subcultures*. Berkeley, CA: Center for Research and Development in Higher Education.

Conkin, P. K. (1985). *Gone with the Ivy: A Biography of Vanderbilt University*. Knoxville: University of Tennessee Press.

Feldman, M. S., and March, J. G. (1981). Information in organizations as signal and symbol. *Administrative Science Quarterly* 26: 171–186.

Fetterman, D. M., and Pitman, M. A., eds. (1986). *Educational Evaluation: Ethnography in Theory, Practice, and Politics*. Beverly Hills, CA: Sage.

Finch, J. (1986). *Research and Policy: The Uses of Qualitative Methods in Social and Educational Research*. London and Philadelphia: Falmer.

Fincher, C. (1987). Improving institutional memory. *Research in Higher Education* 26(4): 431–435.

Firnberg, J. W., and Lasher, W. F., eds. (1983). *The Politics and Pragmatics of Institutional Research*. San Francisco: Jossey-Bass.

Folger, J. (1983). Institutional research, politics, and the federal government. In J. W. Firnbeg and W. F. Lasher (eds.), *The Politics and Pragmatics of Institutional Research, pp. 77–87. San Francisco: Jossey-Bass*.

Foster, M. S. (1962). *Out of Smalle Beginings . . ."*: *An Economic History of Harvard College in the Puritan Period, 1636 to 1712*. Cambridge: Belknap Press of Harvard University Press.

Greider, W. (1981). The education of David Stockman: sometimes reality has a sobering effect. *The Atlantic Monthly* 248(6, December): 27–40.

Harris, S. (1970). *The Economics of Harvard*. New York: McGraw-Hill.

Harris, S. (1972). *A Statistical Portrait of Higher Education*. New York: McGraw-Hill for the Carnegie Commission on Higher Education.

Heller, S. (1988). From selling Rambo to supermarket studies, anthropologists are finding more non-academic jobs. *The Chronicle of Higher Education* (June 1), p. A24.

Hemenway, D. (1978). *Prices and Choices: Microeconomic Vignettes*. Cambridge, MA: Ballinger.

Hoaglin, D. C., Light, R. J., McPeek, B., Mosteller, F., and Soto, M. (1982). *Data for Decisions: Information Strategies for Policymakers*. Lanham, MD: University Press of America.

Kiecolt, K. J., and Nathan, L. E. (1985). *Secondary Analysis of Survey Data*. Beverly Hills, CA: Sage.

Kissler, G. R. (1980). *Report of the Task Group on Retention and Transfer*. Berkeley: Office of the Academic Vice President, University of California.

Krotseng, M. V. (1988). From statehouse to statistics: Linking "Education Governors" with institutional research. Phoenix, AZ: Association for Institutional Research Annual Forum, May.

Kuhns, E., and Martorana, S. V., eds. (1982). *Qualitative Methods for Institutional Research*. San Francisco: Jossey-Bass.

Lasher, W. F., and Firnberg, J. W. (1983). The future of institutional research. In J. W. Firnberg and W. F. Lasher (eds.), *The Politics and Pragmatics of Institutional Research*, pp. 89–100. San Francisco: Jossey-Bass.

Lindquist, J., ed. (1981). *Increasing the Use of Institutional Research*. San Francisco: Jossey-Bass.

Loepp, D. (1988). Two tons of paperwork weigh heavy on officials. *Hampton Roads (Virginia) Daily Press* (March 2), pp. B1, B4.

London, H. B. (1978a). *The Culture of a Community College*. New York: Praeger.

London, H. B. (1978b). The perils of opportunity: the working-class community college student in sociological perspective. In H. S. Sacks, (ed.), *Hurdles: The Admissions Dilemma in American Higher Education*, pp. 145–192. New York: Atheneum.

Lunney, G. (1979). *About That Data Base Which Is Hiding in the Closet*. Southern Association for Institutional Research Conference, October.

Miller, R. I. (1980). Appraising institutional performance. In P. Jedamus and M. W. Peterson (eds.), *Improving Academic Management*, pp. 406–431. San Francisco: Jossey-Bass.

Miner, H. (1956). Body ritual among the Nacirema. *American Anthropologist* 58: 503–507.

Moffat, M. (1985). Coming of age in New Brunswick. *Rutgers Alumni Magazine*. 65(1, September): 7–9.

Moos, Malcolm (1981). *The Post-Land Grant University: the University of Maryland Report*. Adelphi: The University of Maryland.

Morgan, G. (1986). *Images of Organizations*. Beverly Hills, CA: Sage.

Nespor, J. (1987). The fate of the files. *Educational Researcher* 16(3, April): 12–15, 18–19.

Nichols, J. O., Howard, R. D., and Sharp, B. H. (1987). The institutional factbook: key to perception of institutional research and information dissemination on campus. In J. A. Muffo and G. W. McLaughlin (eds.), *A Primer on Institutional Research*, pp. 101–112. Tallahassee, FL: Association for Institutional Research.

Odell, M., and Thelin, J. (1980). *Keeping Pace: Trends in Federal and State Financial Aid for Students in California's Independent Colleges and Universities, 1975–76 to 1980–81*. Santa Ana, CA: Association of Independent California Colleges and Universities.

O'Keefe, M. (1987). Where does the money really go? *Change* 19(6): 12–34.

Peterson, M. W. (1985). Institutional research: an evolutionary perspective. In M. W. Peterson and M. Corcoran (eds.), *Institutional Research in Transition*, pp. 5–15. San Francisco: Jossey-Bass.

Rathje, W. (1979). The telltale garbage of Tucson. *Early Man* (Winter): 19–21.

Rich, R. F. (1981). *Social Science Information and Public Policy Making: The Interaction Between Bureaucratic Politics and the Use of Survey Data*. San Francisco: Jossey-Bass.

Schoch, R. (1980). As Cal enters the '80s, there'll be some changes made. *California Monthly*. 90(3): 1, 23.

Sinclair, W. (1988). The agri-biz bonanza: how your tax dollars produced the cubical tomato. *Washington Post* (January 10), pp. C1, C4.

Snyder, B. R. (1970). *The Hidden Curriculum*. New York: Knopf.

Southern Association of Colleges and Schools (1984). *Criteria for Accreditation*. Atlanta.

Stockman, D. A. (1986). *The Triumph of Politics: Why the Reagan Revolution Failed*. New York: Harper & Row.

Thelin, J. (1982). *Higher Education and Its Useful Past: Applied History in Research and Planning*. Cambridge, MA: Schenkman.

Thelin, J. (1984). Cliometrics and the colleges: the campus condition, 1890 to 1910. *Research in Higher Education*. 21(4). pp. 425–437.

Thelin, J. (1985). Why college costs so much. *The Wall Street Journal*. (December 11), p. 32.

Thelin, J. (1986a). The campus as chameleon: rethinking organizational behavior and public policy. In J. C. Smart (ed.), *Higher Education: Handbook of Theory and Research*. Vol. 2. pp. 103–108. New York: Agathon Press.

Thelin, J. (1986b). The search for good research: looking for ''science'' in all the wrong places. *The Review of Higher Education* 10(2): 151–158.

To, L. D. (1987). *Estimating the Cost of a Bachelor's Degree: An Institutional Cost Analysis*. Washington, DC: Office of Educational Research and Improvement, U.S. Department of Education.

Townsend, B. (1986). Past as prologue: seeds of an institution's identity. *Community, Technical, and Junior College Journal*. 57(1, August/September): 46–50.

University of California (1980). *University Planning Statement: 1980*. Berkeley: University of California, Office of the President.

Vobejda, B. (1988). U.S. to fill statistics gap in education. *The Washington Post*. (May 3).

Wilson, R. (1987). Education Department's finding that private colleges spend more than public institutions sets off brouhaha. *Chronicle of Higher Education* (September 2), pp. A59, A67.

Wilson, R. (1988). Reagan seeks a record $8.8-billion for aid to students. *Chronicle of Higher Education* (February 24), pp. A23, A26.

Yancey, B. D. (1988). *Applying Statistics in Institutional Research*. San Francisco: Jossey-Bass.

Student Financial Aid and Institutional Behavior: How Institutions Use and Benefit from Student Aid

Michael S. McPherson,
Williams College

Alan P. Wagner,
Organisation for Economic Cooperation and Development

and

Nancy A. Willie-Schiff,
New York State Education Department

On a spring day in 1985, David Stockman, then Director of the Office of Management and Budget, delivered himself of some observations on the motives and character of farmers and college presidents. College presidents, he averred, "Say that they care about students, but all they really care about is financing their budgets." It's understandable that a member of the Reagan administration would view budget balancing as a somewhat unseemly activity but, that aside, Stockman spoke an important truth: Student aid has plainly become an important means by which colleges and universities seek to meet their budgets.

As important as this source of support has become, however, the ways in which student aid enters the resource allocation decisions of colleges and universities remain relatively little studied. Most of the policy interest in and research on the effects of student aid have centered on decisions of students and their families about whether and where to enroll in postsecondary education. This emphasis on student behavior has often carried a tacit, sometimes even explicit, assumption that colleges and universities do not respond to changes in the nature of enrollment demand, including changes occasioned by shifts in the volume and form of externally funded student aid. It seems much more plausible to assume that institutions *do* respond. Within each institution, administrators often do weigh the possible effect on enrollment of changes in posted tuition rates and in packages of institutionally awarded aid. Due to the relatively large volume of student aid provided through third parties (most particularly, the federal government), there is a related question of the extent to which such externally provided financial support also directly benefits college and university budgets.

The purpose of this paper is to offer, in a preliminary way, a rationale and framework for examining how institutions use and benefit from student financial aid. Based on this general framework, the paper takes up two principal questions:

1. How do institutions, in practice, set tuition and package institutionally awarded financial aid in response to demand?
2. How important is federal student aid as a source of budgetary support for colleges and universities?

Definitive answers to these questions are not provided. Rather, the discussion and analysis of the questions help to further frame and explore a line of research which can yield important implications for improved institutional practices and a better understanding of the effects of alternate public policies. Although research in this area continues to accumulate, more work on the links between student financial aid and institutional behavior is clearly warranted if the purposes, uses, and effects of student financial aid are to be fully understood.

STUDENT AID AND INSTITUTIONAL BEHAVIOR

The interest in institutional resource allocation decisions, including the allocation of student financial aid, is not new. Various institutional planning models have been employed to track and to project the allocation of resources within particular institutions (see, e.g., Hopkins and Massy, 1981). Several analytical studies have focused on the allocation of student aid at individual institutions (Miller, 1975; Ehrenberg and Sherman, 1984) or within homogeneous groups of institutions (Spies, 1978; Zemsky and Oedel, 1984; Basch, 1987). By design, differences in responses to incentives and constraints across identified groups of institutions are excluded in most of these studies. Although much of the related analytical work with a national focus is useful, it is limited and somewhat dated (College Scholarship Service, 1971; Carlson, 1974, 1975; Wagner and Rice, 1977; Barnes and Neufeld, 1980; Manski and Wise, 1983).

For our purposes, the effects of various incentives and constraints on the institution's resource allocation decisions can be best derived from a microeconomic approach to institutional behavior. The framework corresponds with the approach developed and expanded by Miller (1975), Wagner and Rice (1977), Hopkins and Massy (1981), Ehrenberg and Sherman (1984), and Berg and

Hoenack (1985). The outlines and implications of such an approach can be briefly described as follows.

Conceptually, the institution can be viewed as attempting to enroll specific numbers of students of a given type in striving to meet its goals. In practice, the first step in this process is appplication/admissions. Applicants are accepted in accordance with stated admissions policies (minimum academic standards, maximum out-of-state enrollments, etc.). Of the admitted applicants, some proportion will actually enroll. This proportion is conventionally referred to as the yield, or "show-up" rate. The "show-up" rate really represents an aggregate demand relationship for potential students (from each of the defined student pools). As part of the price of an enrollment, posted tuition rates are weighed by students and their families against the anticipated net benefits from enrollment in making their enrollment decisions.

The institution may seek to affect the numbers applying and enrolling by changing recruitment activities to increase (decrease) the numbers applying from identified groups, modifying admissions criteria to increase (decrease) the numbers accepted from identified groups, or altering tuition rates or the amount and type of institutionally awarded financial aid to reduce the price paid by students and their families. While it cannot predict how any single student will respond, each institution probably can estimate how changes in tuition and/or in the financial aid package—its amount and its composition in grant, work, or loans—will affect the yield from a particular group of potential students. The magnitude of these effects has been examined and critiqued in a number of enrollment demand studies (for a review of the accumulated research, see Leslie and Brinkman, 1987).

Pricing strategies—fine tuning packages of institutionally awarded aid to maximize enrollments (from identified groups) at the least cost or boosting posted tuition to capture increased revenue from families/students and third party payers—are geared to the magnitudes of demand elasticities. For example, if the elasticity of demand within pools of highly valued potential students is relatively low, the costs of obtaining sufficient numbers from these pools through the use of institutionally awarded aid may be too large (relative to the contributions the students, once enrolled, will make). The (institutional) subsidy necessary to encourage additional enrollments, plus incremental instructional and student support costs, would need to be weighed against additional revenues and benefits provided by more students from the highly valued pools in order to determine whether such inducements should be offered.[1]

The presence of third party payers (such as the federal government) reduces the price paid for all who are eligible and potentially expands the size of the pools applying for admission. The institution can respond by reducing funds allocated to student aid from institutional sources, thereby freeing up funds for other purposes (including improvements in quality). The institution can also respond by raising its posted tuition rate, thereby capturing larger revenues from both students/families and third party payers. However, the success of this latter "high tuition" strategy also depends on the responsiveness of potential students—most particularly those who are not eligible for externally provided financial aid. These applicants will face higher costs (net of financial aid). Some will opt for relatively lower priced institutions. Others will elect nonschool options. Other things equal, the greater the propensity of such students to change their choices in these ways (i.e., the higher the elasticity of demand), the larger the loss to the institution in terms of revenue forgone and additional benefits associated with their enrollments.

Finally, it is important to note here that institutions differ in the use of recruitment, admissions, or pricing strategies. Public institutions, generally, have less discretion in altering admissions criteria or setting tuition rates than do private institutions. Among private colleges and universities, institutions with applications (qualified under current admissions criteria) exceeding places may alter different practices or policies than other institutions with an insufficient number of qualified applications. In these cases, differences in institutional (enrollment) goals and constraints on institutional policies and practices strongly influence the strategies actually adopted. Clearly, these differences need to be taken into account (see, e.g., McPherson, 1986; Basch, 1987).

INSTITUTIONAL DISCRETION IN AWARDING AID

Almost every college or university controls the allocation of some student aid funds. Such aid includes awards financed through institutional sources (e.g., tuition or endowment income) or financed by third parties (e.g., federal campus-based aid or private gifts). With the latter sources, institutions are permitted some discretion in the selection of the recipient and in the amounts awarded. Institutionally awarded aid accounts for about one-fourth of the total. These funds are usually allocated according to "need," defined as the budgeted costs of attendance *less* some contribution expected from the student/family. Of institutionally awarded student aid in 1983–1984, an estimated 65% to 70% was allocated on the basis of need. The proportion of institutionally funded aid allocated according to need was about 60%.[2] This emphasis on need-based criteria dates to the 1950s when college administrators, fearful of a growing competition for students with financial aid and tuition discounts, agreed to provide aid to a student only if he/she required more than the centrally calculated expected family contribution to meet his/her costs of attendance. When financial aid awards are limited to defined "need," colleges compete for students based on programs of study, quality, and other attributes rather than through financial inducements. However, reviews of stated policies and the results of institutional practices indicate that institutions may be departing from the cartel-like arrangement.

The Scope for the Manipulation of Need Analysis

One way institutions depart from common financial aid treatment is through the manipulation of need analysis itself—student expense budget, expected contribution, and financial aid packaging within need.

Budgets

Most institutions develop estimates of the costs of attendance (tuition and fees, room and board, books and supplies, transportation, incidentals) for groups of students likely to incur similar expenses during the academic year. The adequacy (or generosity) of these budgets may differ among student types and from institution to institution. For example, Van Dusen, Jacobson, and Wagner (1974) found that budgets used for self-supporting students tended to be less than the amounts these students typically spent during the school year, while dependent student budgets corresponded rather closely to expenses actually incurred by students in this group. The same study uncovered wide and apparently unexplainable differences in similar nontuition costs of attendance within the same metropolitan area. More recent studies have uncovered similar, if not as pronounced, differences. Based on a 1986–1987 comparison of expenditures for books, supplies, commuting, and other miscellaneous costs, actual expenses reported by students living off campus exceeded student expense budgets in average amounts ranging from almost nothing to over $600 depending on the type of institution attended (Korb et al., 1988). Differences in the adequacy (or generosity) of budgets among student types and across institutions potentially lead to calculations of need which provide larger and relatively more favorable student aid packages for some types of students at an individual college or for all students at some colleges.

Expected Contributions

The need analysis services and the federal government have served to enforce a cartel-like "pricing" agreement among most colleges and universities by generating or approving standard expected contributions. However, need analysis calculations and results are frequently reviewed and adjusted according to policies in place at individual colleges. In 1985–1986, some 68% of all institutions reviewed the standard calculation. Of those institutions reviewing and adjusting need analysis results, the average proportion of expected contributions actually changed exceeded 30% (Higginbotham, Davis, and Van Dusen, 1986). This proportion is up from the approximate 20% of cases changed through the 1970s. In 1985–1986, about 46% of the changes represented increases, while 27% of the changes represented decreases, in the centrally calculated parents' contribution. In both directions, the average change approached $500. Regardless of the direction, these data indicate the willingness of colleges and universities to depart from a centrally calculated and common determination of the expected contribution. The potential effect of these changes is to alter the estimate of need (and the amount of aid necessary to meet need) in ways that favor some students and some institutions.

Packaging

Once need, however defined, is estimated, college and university policies differ in the manner in which need is met. Institutional policies may call for aiding the neediest first or spreading the available aid among all eligible applicants. Similarly, packaging practices may provide grant assistance to the neediest first or allow all eligible applicants to receive some gift aid. According to a 1978–1979 survey of financial aid administrators at a sample of institutions, postsecondary educational institutions employ a variety of practices. No single packaging policy is utilized by more than 41% of all colleges. The distribution of packaging policies is displayed in Table 1, where practices most favorable to the neediest students are shown toward the left and those resulting in less targeting (of total or grant aid) are placed to the right. The information provided by administrators indicated that about 40% have adopted policies which ensure that the neediest will receive larger grants (29.9% using the grant/self-help ratio and 11% using a fixed self-help amount). An equal percentage had policies which correspond to a "floating grant amount" approach, in that grant amounts vary according to a number of criteria (including ability). Interestingly enough, four-year colleges and universities were more likely to have implemented policies which favored the neediest students than two-year or proprietary institutions.

By 1985–1986, many of these differences in financial aid packaging remained. According to Higginbotham et al. (1986), 59% of all institutions used equity packaging (which favors needy students); 41% did not. Nearly half (48%) had policies which ensured more gift aid would be directed toward low income students. Some 31% of all institutions had packaging policies which favored bright students (57% of private four-year institutions reported such policies). And, 10% packaged aid according to the competition—a kind of "see me last" approach.

Colleges and universities also adopt more specific policies which alter the size and composition of financial aid made available through institutional channels. One example of these more specific policies is the treatment of outside, private awards in the packaging of aid. To the extent they know about these awards, colleges and universities may reduce the amounts provided through the institution. The most favorable treatment would reduce only self-help aid (work and loans), and some 42% of all institutions adhered to this policy in 1978–1979. Alternatively, 29% reduced the institution's grant award from discretionary

TABLE 1. Stated Packaging Policies by Institution Type and Control: 1978–1979

	Total	Grant aid/ self-help ratio	Fixed self-help amount	Fixed grant amount	Floating grant amount	No set rules
		Percentage of institutions				
TOTAL	100.0%	29.9	11.0	3.1	40.8	15.2
Four-Year						
Public	100.0%	41.5	12.2	7.2	30.3	8.9
Private	100.0%	33.8	16.0	2.4	35.9	11.9
Two-Year						
Public	100.0%	19.6	10.0	0.0	50.9	19.5
Private	100.0%	33.2	11.9	0.0	54.9	0.0
Proprietary	100.0%	11.4	0.0	0.0	54.6	34.0

Key to practices:

"Grant aid/self-help ratio" equalizes the ratio of grants to self-help support for all students.

"Fixed self-help amount" awards a fixed amount of work, loans, or both before any grant aid is provided.

"Fixed grant amount" awards a fixed amount of grant aid for all students before any self-help is provided.

"Floating grant amount" awards grant aid, with the amounts differing across a range of criteria, including ability.

"No set rules" operates at institutions that evaluate applicants for aid on a case-by-case basis.

Source: Estimated from Applied Management Sciences, Inc. *Study of Program Management Procedures in the Basic Grant and Campus-Based Programs, Final Report. Volume 1. The Institutional Administration of Student Financial Aid Programs,* 1980a (Tables 9.1 and 9.2).

sources. The remaining institutions reduced both grants and self-help aid (Applied Management Sciences, 1980a). By 1982–1983, roughly the same proportion of institutions reduced self-help aid, but a somewhat smaller percentage indicated that they reduced the grant component only (Van Dusen and Higgenbotham, 1984). This shift indicates a more permissive treatment of outside, private awards in that those bringing in such support will, other things equal, receive a relatively larger grant component in their aid packages.

Another Look at the Effects of Student Characteristics on Packaging
In spite of the scope for institutional discretion for allocating aid *within* the framework of a need-based system, "need" as defined through centrally

determined rules and modified by the institution remains the only available basis on which to assess the distribution of institutionally awarded aid. Prior research dating back to the 1960s has largely suggested that undergraduates' financial need characteristics are poor predictors of the receipt of such aid. The multivariate work reported below represents an attempt to extend the earlier work in several ways in search of a consistent set of results. In contrast to the earlier work, the data set employed here is more recent, more detailed, and more reliable.

The Model

The conceptual approach has been generally described above. In its empirical formulation, the model of how student characteristics affect the distribution of institutionally awarded aid is applied to two questions: (1) How do student characteristics, net of individual institutional contexts, influence the probability of receiving such aid? and (2) Among those who receive institutionally awarded aid, how do student characteristics, net of individual institutional contexts, affect the amount of aid received?

The estimating equation for student-level data may be expressed as:

$$p(R) = f(P, D, C, e)$$

where $p(R)$ is the probability of an applicant receiving institutionally awarded aid; P is the set of student characteristics of principal interest; D is the set of student/family attributes which are used as controls; C is a set of variables representing differences among individual institutions; and e is a measure of other factors not included in the model.

Several associations are inferred from the general model. The central hypotheses center on three key student/family characteristics. The receipt and amount of institutionally awarded aid are presumed to be associated with such student characteristics as demonstrated need, academic ability, and minority group status. Other student characteristics are included as controls (enrollment status, gender, attendance status, dependency status, and family capacity-to-pay).

Implicit in this formulation is the assumption that all institutions have the same preferences and that all types of students respond to aid offers from all institutions in the same way, thereby creating consistent behavior patterns across institutions. To account for institutional differences in goals, strategies, and markets, a dummy variable for each institution is included.[3]

The Data

The data were collected in 1978–1979 as part of a major survey effort undertaken by the Office of Program, Budget, and Evaluation (OPBE) in the U.S. Office of

Education, called the Study of the Impact of Student Financial Aid Programs (SISFAP). The survey design involved random selection of half-time or more undergraduate students at a sample of institutions eligible to participate in federal student aid programs, stratified by type, control, selectivity, size, cost, state effort, and program offerings. The survey effort elicited financial aid record information from the financial aid office for each student and demographic, academic, and financial aid information from the students, themselves. Participation rates were high for institutions and students (Applied Management Sciences, 1979).

Analyses of the responses to individual items in the survey prompted OPBE to create a merged file, containing information from both financial aid records and student surveys. The merged file excluded cases for which information on key student attributes were missing (sex, year in school, dependency status, income enrollment status, and receipt of BEOG). The merged file contains 12,687 cases, about 60% of the student questionnaires and about 80% of the financial aid records. From the merged file, an analysis file, containing student and financial aid office responses for 7,787 student aid applicants known to aid administrators at collegiate institutions only, was created for use in this study.

Measurement
Although the distribution of all institutionally awarded aid—grants and self-help—is of interest, only institutionally awarded grant aid is used as the dependent variable in the equations. Such aid is defined to include the following:

- Supplemental Educational Opportunity Grants (SEOG)
- Institutional Need-Based Grants
- Institutional Ability-Based Grants
- Other Institutional Grants
- Athletic Scholarships
- Tuition Remissions
- Private Grants

These categories do not precisely describe the institutionally awarded grant aid of interest. Athletic scholarships tend to be awarded outside of financial aid offices as are tuition remissions and many private grants. Nonetheless, these comprise relatively small shares of the total amount of institutionally awarded grants recorded in financial aid offices (see Table 2).

Most of the independent variables are defined conventionally, as shown in Table 3. Means and standard deviations are provided in the Appendix. Alternate measures of variables (differences from institutional averages) and functional forms (logit for the receipt equations) were conducted, with virtually no

TABLE 2. The Size and Distribution of Institutionally Awarded Grants in Four-Year Colleges and Universities: 1978–1979

	Public 4-year	Private 4-year
	(Unweighted)	
Distribution by type	100%	100%
SEOG	54	44
Institutional		
Need-based	4	1
Ability-based	16	22
Athletic	2	3
Other	2	3
Remission	12	14
Private	10	14
	(Weighted)	
Total awards	533,718	448,634
Unduplicated recipients	498,996	367,049

Source: SISFAP Merged Analysis File.

differences in results. The results from the raw data, ordinary least squares regressions, are reported here.

Results of Student-Level Equations

The student-level (OLS) equations are shown in Tables 4 and 5. As shown there, the variables included in the equation account for a relatively small proportion of the variance (adjusted R^2 of .12 and .19 for public four-year and private four-year institutions, respectively). Perhaps more important, when the variables were entered sequentially (key student characteristics, controls, and institutional dummy variables), the institutional variables were found to account for most of the explained variance.

Generally, need and student ability (i.e., high school grades) were both associated with the probability of receiving institutionally awarded grant aid, although the effects are quite small. A $1,000 increase in need, all else equal, was associated with a 7.1 percentage point increase in the likelihood of receiving an award for applicants at public four-year institutions and a 5.5 percentage point increase for applicants at private four-year institutions. A 10-point increase in high school grades, at the mean, was associated with a 5 percentage point increase in the probability of receiving institutionally awarded aid. Student characteristics were also associated with the size of the institutionally awarded grant, among those receiving such an award, but again the estimated effects are

TABLE 3. Definition of Variables for Student-Level Model

Variable	Measure
Receipt of aid	1 = non-zero sum of dollars from 7 categories of institutionally awarded grant aid; 0 = zero sum from 7 categories of institutionally awarded grant aid.
Amount of aid	For recipients of institutionally awarded aid, sum of dollars from 7 categories.
Demonstrated need	Expense budget *less* expected family contribution, BEOG award, and state grant award.
Academic merit	High school grade point average (0 to 100).
Minority status	1 = nonwhite; 0 = white.
Enrollment status	1 = entering; 0 = continuing or transfer.
Gender	1 = male; 0 = female.
Course load	1 = full-time; 0 = part-time.
Dependency status	1 = dependent; 0 = independent.
Family capacity-to-pay	Size of BEOG award (0 to 1,600)
Institutional context	Set of dummy variables, one for each institution in the data base (47 public 4-year; 48 private 4-year).

Source: SISFAP Merged Analysis File.

very small. A $1,000 increase in need, all else equal, was associated with institutional grant awards $80 higher at public four-year institutions and $69 higher at private four-year institutions.

On the basis of the analyses shown here, it must be concluded that wide use of standardized need analysis and rule-driven entitlement programs did not impose homogeneity onto institutional financial aid practices. The modest, if significant association between need and the allocation of institutionally awarded grant aid, the significance of the institutional dummy variables, and the weak explanatory power of the equations all suggest that institutional aid practices apparently differ widely and do not necessarily complement the purposes of tax supported, rule-driven grant and loan programs (if the principal purpose of these programs is to encourage the allocation of all student aid to the neediest students).

Results of Institution-Level Equations
In order to explain the change in the probability of receiving an institutionally awarded grant that was associated with each institutional setting, the coefficients of the set of dummy variables from the student-level equations were regressed on

TABLE 4. Determinants of the Allocation of Institutionally Awarded Grands in Public 4-Year Institutions: 1978–1979

Explanatory variables	Dependent variables	
	Receipt	Amount
Need	.071*	80*
Minority status (1 = nonwhite)	−.043	35
Academic merit	.005**	−3
Enrollment status (1 = continuing)	.064**	127*
Course load (1 = full-time)	−.168**	−20
Gender (1 = male)	.002	7
Dependency status (1 = dependent)	.121*	1
Family capacity-to-pay	.054**	86**
I1	−.404*	−532*
I2	−.093	−242**
I3	−.645*	0
I4	−.016	477
I5	−.358*	−127
I6	−.116	271**
I7	−.187	39
I8	−.516*	−120
I9	.000	0
I10	−.172	−18
I11	−.246**	−610*
I12	.053	−37
I13	−.539*	0
I14	−.007	−103
I15	−.114	−218**
I16	−.508*	0
I17	−.407**	−340
I18	−.131	−21
I19	−.420*	−1
I20	−.261*	−128
I21	−.329*	−315**
I22	−.150	330**
I23	−.490	0
I24	−.413	−256
I25	.219	31
I26	−.141	96
I27	−.231**	−163
I28	.000	0
I29	−.277	−118

continued

TABLE 4. Determinants of the Allocation of Institutionally Awarded Grants in Public 4-Year Institutions: 1978–1979 (Continued)

Explanatory variables	Dependent variables	
	Receipt	Amount
I30	−.015	−179
I31	.219**	−54
I32	−.308*	−215
I33	−.347*	−304**
I34	−.414*	−213
I35	−.039	−277**
I36	−.343**	−227
I37	−.285*	−138
I38	−.451*	223
I39	−.501*	712**
I40	−.346*	57
I41	−.097	11
I42	−.328*	21
I43	.125	−93
I44	−.154	−94
I45	−.272*	70
I46	.000	0
I47	−.017	215
Constant	.039	822*
R^2	.125	.238
(n)	(1,007)	(303)

*significance $P < .01$
**significance $P < .10$
Source: SISFAP Merged Analysis File.

institution-level independent variables. Although findings from institutional surveys over the years have suggested relationships between institutional features and their packaging practices, the only multivariate modeling effort yielded inconclusive results about the packaging of federal campus-based aid (Applied Management Sciences, 1980b). Consequently, the specification of the institution-level equations represents a tentative, first step guided principally by judgment and theoretical considerations.

The complete set of institution-level variables is shown in Table 6. Four influences on institutional packaging decisions are posited. First, institutions of similar *mission* should package in the same way. Differences in mission are presumed to be reflected by enrollment scale, undergraduates as a share of total

TABLE 5. Determinants of the Allocation of Institutionally Awarded Grants at Private 4-Year Institutions: 1978–1979

Explanatory variables	Dependent variables	
	Receipt	Amount
Need	.055*	69*
Minority status (1 = nonwhite)	−.025	70
Academic merit	.005*	13*
Enrollment status (1 = continuing)	.025	17
Course load (1 = full-time)	.274*	−17
Gender (1 = male)	.013	141*
Dependency status (1 = dependent)	.048	32
Family capacity-to-pay	.096*	44
I1	−.377**	−521**
I2	−.511*	−747**
I3	.008	−229
I4	−.623*	385
I5	.000	0
I6	−.513*	−145
I7	−.603*	−539**
I8	−.158	−168
I9	.887*	0
I10	−.120	−49
I11	−.397**	1
I12	−.275	− 357
I13	−.448*	572**
I14	−.611*	−437
I15	−.854*	−166
I16	−.199	583*
I17	−.282	−249
I18	−.844*	−468
I19	−.487*	−565**
I20	−.956*	0
I21	−.674*	−121
I22	−.364**	76
I23	−.965*	0
I24	−.452*	−392
I25	−.620*	−368
I26	−.531**	−483
I27	−.645*	−851**
I28	−.637	−98
I29	−.161	271

continued

TABLE 5. Determinants of the Allocation of Institutionally Awarded Grants at Private 4-Year Institutions: 1978–1979 (Continued)

Explanatory variables	Dependent variables	
	Receipt	Amount
I30	−.423**	−194
I31	−.434**	354
I32	−.002	−501**
I33	−.303**	−224
I34	−.312**	−221
I35	−.590*	−636*
I36	−.594*	−329
I37	−.455*	−356
I38	−.460*	−420
I39	−.547*	−124
I40	−.055	104
I41	−.468*	13
I42	−.373**	−29
I43	.106	−851
I44	−.683*	−565
I45	−.313**	−263
I46	−.285	−370
I47	−.472*	−335
I48	−.902*	0
Constant	−.069	−212
R^2	.193	.242
(n)	(1,330)	(646)

*significance $P < .01$
**significance $P < .10$
Source: SISFAP Merged Analysis File.

enrollment, and the predominant racial/ethnic composition of the student body. Second, institutions of similar *fiscal condition* should package in the same way. Here, measures of endowment, tuition, and expenditures are presumed to reflect this influence. Third, institutions enrolling comparable *student bodies* should package in the same way. In this case, the proportion of needy students and the relative academic ability of those enrolled may be taken as an indication of student body characteristics. Finally, an institution's *market position*, measured as rates of acceptance or attendance, may lead to differences in packaging.

When submitted to ordinary least squares estimation, only the equations for public four-year institutions yielded valid results. For the private four-year

TABLE 6. Definition of Variables for Institution-Level Model

Variable	Measure
Enrollment	Total headcount enrollment.
% undergraduate	Percentage undergraduate.
Race	Race/ethnicity of 60% or more of student body; 1 = non-white; 0 = white.
Tuition	Tuition and required fees.
Unit expenditures	Expenditures per weighted (FTE). Weights (from Bowen, 1980) are: lower division undergraduate = 1.0; upper division undergraduate = 1.5; graduate and first-professional = 2.5.
Unit endowment	Endowment per weighted FTE.
Unit aid	Total restricted and unrestricted institutional funds allocated for scholarships and grants per full-time enrollment.
Average SAT	Average SAT in 1976.
Average family financial condition	Average expected family contribution.
Aid rate	Aid recipients per needy applicant.
Acceptance rate	Acceptances per application.
Show-up rate	Enrollments per acceptance.

Source: SISFAP Merged Analysis File.

equation, the available degrees of freedom are small relative to the unadjusted R^2. As shown in Table 7, however, few of the institution-level characteristics appeared to be associated with differences in the probability of receiving an institutionally awarded grant at public four-year colleges and universities. Many of the attributes are highly collinear, reducing the statistical significance of the parameter estimates. Interestingly, both the acceptance rate and show-up rate were marginally significant (at the .20 level). If the inverse relationship between show-up rate and institutionally awarded aid can be accepted, it implies that such aid was being used as a price discount to bolster enrollments, independent of the characteristics of aid applicants.

Student Aid as Institutional Aid

The scope for, and apparent exercise of, discretion in tuition setting and in the packaging of student financial aid raises a related set of questions on the role of externally provided financial aid funds—primarily those made available through federal programs—as a source of budgetary support for colleges and universities. How much federal aid actually finds its way into institutional budgets? Is there

TABLE 7. Determinants of Institutional Effects on Institutionally Awarded
Grants at Public 4-Year Institutions: 1978–1979

Explanatory variables	Receipt
Enrollment	.000
% undergraduate	−.391
Race	.431
Tuition	.000
Unit expenditures	−.046
Unit endowment	.000
Unit aid	.000
Average SAT	.000
Average family financial condition	.112
Aid rate	.126
Acceptance rate	.085***
Show-up rate	−.403***
Constant	.054
Adjusted R^2	.334
F	2.294
(n)	(32)

**significance $P < .1$
***significance $P < .2$
Source: SISFRAP Merged Analysis File.

any justification for providing such institutional support? And, is student aid the best vehicle for serving these purposes?

The last two questions, in effect about federal *institutional* aid, used to be on the national agenda in a major way. In the late 1960s, when Congress began contemplating a major increase in federal support for higher education, the higher education community was divided between supporters of student aid and of formula-based instutional aid. The latter was motivated by serious concerns about the financial viability of small private colleges and about the fiscal capacity of states to sustain the large burdens created by the expansion of public colleges and universities. When Congress passed the Education Amendments of 1972 which instituted the Basic Educational Opportunity Grant (later renamed Pell), proposals for direct institutional aid were close competitors.[4] In adopting the student aid strategy, Congress clearly thought that such an approach would meet at least partly the goals the institutional aid strategy aimed at as well.[5]

In the years since 1972, however, the conception of the roles and purposes of federal support for undergraduate education have narrowed to questions of access and choice, particularly for low income students. On the rare occasions when writers on student aid have recognized its potential role in institutional finance, they have a nearly instinctive tendency to view that role with dismay, as a regrettable (if not alarming) diversion of funds provided by taxpayers from their proper purpose. The analogy that leaps to mind is that of General Dynamics or some other defense contractor lining its managers' or shareholders' pockets with money that was supposed to purchase weapons. Before undertaking a closer examination of the magnitudes involved, it is important to develop in a preliminary way why this analogy is misleading and probably inappropriate.

The weakness of the analogy lies in the fact that higher education is not produced (for the most part) by profit-seeking firms. When the government procures weapons from a defense contractor, we want them to get those weapons at the lowest possible cost. We are rightly disturbed when payments go instead to support the general budgets of defense firms or are larger than the amounts strictly necessary to get the work done. And the reason for this vigilance is clear. We know in a profit-seeking firm where excess revenues go: either to the owners in the form of higher dividends or more valuable shares of stock, or to the managers in the form of corporate jobs and taxpayer-supported perquisites.

But nonprofit suppliers—whether government owned or independent—are different. Obviously they may sometimes "skim" excess revenues, putting them into fancy offices for administrators or fancy salaries for faculty. This is precisely the argument advanced by the U.S. Department of Education (see, e.g., Snyder and Galambos, 1988). But, normally, when a college or university gets added resources, these resources are assumed to be spent for "education." More specifically, the resources go toward the broadly defined purposes for which the institution exists. Trustees, boards of regents, and such exist mainly to make sure that happens. Moreover, those educational purposes are understood, in the main, to be public purposes. That's why colleges and universities are exempt from taxes and citizens are encouraged to donate to them. Indeed, a simple mark of the disanalogy between Siwash U. and General Dynamics lies here: When is the last time someone remembered General Dynamics in a will?

None of this aims to prove that there can never be too much of this (arguably) good thing. It does suggest, however, that the reaction to any possible leakage of federal student aid money into general institutional budgets as a sign of waste or worse may be based on a very narrow view of the federal role in higher education.

Some Magnitudes

Just how much support is provided to institutions anyway? The question can best be approached in two stages. First, it will be helpful to document the magnitude of the federal student aid effort relative to both higher education revenues as a whole and relative to other federal expenditures on higher education (notably research). Then, second, the tricky, and in large part conjectural, task of sorting out the portion of federal student aid that winds up helping institutional budgets can be tackled. In this connection, it is important to keep in mind that some federal student aid spending pays for food, lodging, and books for students (and perhaps, as Secretary of Education Bennett has reminded us, for student cars and vacations as well). A good deal relieves parental budgets of spending they would otherwise have to undertake.

The Relative Importance of Federal Student Aid Effort

A survey of higher education budgets from the 1960s through the 1980s turns up several key facts.

First, a great deal of the growth in federal student aid during the 1970s was in "specially directed" aid programs funded outside the Deparment (then Office) of Education. From 1973 through 1977, the two principal programs of this kind—the Vietnam era GI Bill and payments to children of Social Security recipients—averaged out at more than 10% of all higher education revenues.[6] The principal U.S. Department of Education grant program (BEOG or Pell) never got as high as 5%.

Second, the expansion in the 1970s of "generally available" student aid provided through the Department (Office) of Education was largely matched by a reduction in federal spending on research at colleges and universities. In 1968, total federal spending on higher education equaled just under one-quarter of higher education revenues, and of that about two-thirds was research. In 1977, leaving aside the GI Bill and Social Security, federal spending again was just under 25% of higher education revenues but now two-thirds was student aid. By 1980, the costs of federal student aid had increased considerably as the Guaranteed Student Loan (GSL) program grew in size and cost. After 1981, federal spending on both university research and student aid has lagged behind growth in higher education costs and revenues.

Third, the shift of support from research to student aid in the 1970s produced an important change in which kinds of schools are being supported by federal spending. Federal research spending has always been concentrated on universities and indeed has been narrowly focused within that group on a limited set of "research universities." In the heyday of federal research spending in the late 1960s, this source of support was remarkably important. In 1968–1969, federal grants accounted for more than 40% of revenues at private universities, and 23% at public universities.[7] In that same year, the comparable figure for federal grant expenditures at public two-year colleges was less than 2%. By 1977–1978, research had become a less important source of funds—representing 30% rather than 40% of revenues at private universities. But, student aid had become more important and was much more equally spread among types of colleges and universities. Thus, in the Pell program (where data are best), Pell revenues amounted to about 3.5% of revenues at private universities but were more than 6% of revenues at public two-year colleges. An even more dramatic shift in the sectoral allocation of federal funds involves the "proprietary" sector—the profit-seeking "trade schools." It's not much of an exaggeration to say that this sector was called into existence by the development of need-based student aid programs for which proprietary school students could qualify. While data for the proprietary sector are comparable to those reported above on the overall sources of revenue for nonprofit institutions, it's instructive to note that the share of Pell revenues absorbed by students in the proprietary sector grew from 8.6% in 1974 to 12.3% in 1980 and by 1984 was over 20%.

These three points taken together paint a different picture of the history of the federal student aid effort. The "big dollars" in federal student aid in the 1970s fell outside the framework of need-based student financial aid, and those "specially directed" programs (the GI Bill and payments to children of Social Security recipients) were only rather indirectly related to the main goals of federal support for higher education. For other programs of research and student aid thought through and defended as higher education programs, the 1970s represented mainly a shift in the form of the federal effort—from research support to student financial aid—with no growth in the share of higher education revenues deriving from federal sources. This change in the form of support meant a substantial reallocation of federal revenues among types of institutions.

In the 1980s, to bring the story up to date, the "specially directed" aid windows have slammed shut. Federal expenditure for "generally available" aid has shifted importantly from grants to loan subsidies. And, federal research and student aid efforts have lagged behind growth in costs and revenues.

Estimates of the Shares to Institutions

How much federal student aid actually winds up easing higher education budgets? In working through this question, it's useful to distinguish three broad categories of federal student assistance: (1) the "campus-based" programs; (2) grants to students; and (3) loan guarantees and subsidies.[8] Of this total, only the "campus-based" money comes in the first instance onto college and university budgets. The rest goes in the first instance to students.

The "campus-based" money is provided to institutions to award to needy students. It may be used to subsidize campus jobs (College Work-Study), finance low interest loans (National Direct Student Loans or NDSLs), or to provide grants (Supplementary Educational Opportunity Grants) for needy students. Most colleges would use some of their own income for these purposes—student jobs and grant and loan assistance—whether or not they received federal assistance.

As long as the amounts the "feds" provide are less than what colleges would budget for the same purposes, the campus-based money is just like general purpose institutional aid. Thus, for example, an extra $100,000 in SEOGs for a school with a $1 million budget of its own resources for need-based grant assistance frees $100,000 from that budget. The school can put those freed-up resources to giving more grant aid than it otherwise would, to cutting the grass more frequently, or to buying books for the library—just as it could with unrestricted gift. Thus, a large share of campus-based aid serves to benefit institutional finances.

There are two reasons, though, why campus-based aid is not 100% institutional aid. First, some schools, especially in the public sector where fewer institutional resources are devoted to aid, may get more campus-based money in some categories than they would spend themselves on that category of aid. The amount of resources freed in that case just equals what the schools would otherwise spend, which falls short of the total federal allotment.

The second limit on the "fungibility" of campus-based aid derives from restrictions the federal government imposes on how the money may be spent. For instance, work-study money has to be used to subsidize jobs for needy students. A school may have a large budget for student employment but be unable to find qualified needy students available to fill some jobs. In that case, extra work-study money could not be used to place needy students in those jobs, so a dollar-for-dollar saving in the employment budget might not be possible. Despite these limitations, campus-based money is generally quite valuable to schools in budgetary terms, especially at private colleges.

How about the rest of the money—the grant and loan money that goes directly to students without any institutional discretion? Schools get added revenue from such aid to the extent that the aid either (1) induces the student (or her family) to spend more than he (they) would without the aid or (2) allows the school to spend less on the student (or charge her more) than it otherwise would. To the degree that these things don't happen, the aid winds up relieving the family's, rather than the institution's, budget.[9]

Finally, the benefit to a college or university from federal student aid programs may be less if it is induced to undertake added costs (its enrollment may expand, for instance). In an era of rapid growth in enrollments like the late 1960s, this may be an important issue. Indeed, the "cost of education allowances" in the 1972 Education Amendments were intended to respond to just such a situation. Policymakers and college officials were concerned that the objective of increasing the enrollments of low income students could be threatened by a lack of capacity within higher education generally and the implicitly high marginal costs their enrollments would impose. In circumstances such as these, the benefit to the institution's budget is net of the additional costs incurred as a result of the enrollments. These added costs are less likely to be important now, when excess capacity is the rule at most insitutions. Thus, the revenue implications of student aid can probably be viewed today as net revenue implications.

These points will make more sense if we consider some hypothetical cases. Three of the cases illustrate circumstances under which externally provided student aid helps a school's budget while the other two cases illustrate circumstances under which such aid has no effect.

Case 1. Joe Smedley, family income $15,000 per year, gets a $1,400 Pell grant, which induces him to enroll at a local community college rather than forgoing participation in postsecondary education altogether. Out of the Pell grant, Smedley pays his $600 tuition to the school—a revenue item the school otherwise would not get. Because the school has excess capacity, the costs of the added enrollment are trivial.

Case 2. Irene Marlitz, family income $32,000, would go to her local public university without aid. But a $2,500 GSL encourages her to go to a private college, paying $5,000 in tuition instead of the $2,000 the public college would charge. The total revenues of the higher education system go up by $3,000—a $5,000 gain to private colleges, a $2,000 loss to public institutions. Notice that in this case the gain in higher education revenues exceeds the amount of the federal loan (as well as the subsidy implicit in the terms of the loan).

Case 3. Lorna Doone, family income $18,000, is admitted to a highly selective private college. Because her SATs are double 800's, the college is prepared to offer her a generous full need scholarship worth $16,000 even if she cannot get federal aid. But, in fact, she gets a $1,500 Pell grant, causing the college to reduce its aid offer to $14,500 and releasing $1,500 for other purposes.

Case 4. Irene Marlitz's twin sister, Beth, likes the public university just fine. Staying at the university, she only qualifies for a $1,500 GSL which she is willing to accept. Her parents would have paid her $2,000 tuition, but she lets them off the hook. The parents are better off by $1,500; the higher education system doesn't see a nickel more.

Case 5 John Marker, family income $64,000, qualifies for a $2,000 GSL at a high cost private university. If subsidized federal loans were not available, the university would offer John only a market rate loan, backed by its endowment. Not making this loan is of no financial consequence to the school, so it doesn't benefit from the availability of the GSL. John's choice of school would be the same either way, so the benefit he gets from the GSL is simply the lower repayments the federal subsidy makes possible.

These cases help to clarify the general principles: Higher education generally gains revenue if federal aid gets students to enroll who otherwise would not (Case 1). An individual college or university will gain revenue if, for students who would be there anyway, the federal aid lets them cut back on the aid they would otherwise offer from their own resources (Case 3). An individual college or university also gains revenue if the federal aid encourages students who otherwise would not have enrolled at the institution to do so (Cases 1 and 2). And, in cases where students change their college choices because of aid, revenues may also be redistributed between institutions (Case 2).

The analysis also suggests some generalizations about the degree to which federal student aid benefits institutional budgets. First, campus-based aid will in general have more impact than direct aid to students, simply because institutional discretion makes campus-based aid more fungible (as described in the previous section, "Institutional Discretion in Awarding Aid"). Second, aid going to needier students will in general have a larger institutional impact than aid to less needy students, both because such aid is more likely to affect the students' behavior (bringing them to college or a more expensive college) and because such aid is more likely to replace aid the institution would otherwise allocate from its own resources. Third, the more of its own resources an institution spends on need-based aid, the more likely it is to benefit from federal aid, because it will have a better chance to release its own resources for other purposes.

Three interesting points follow from these generalizations. For one thing, it's easy to see why private colleges, which tend to have larger aid budgets and therefore have found federal aid more fungible, have seemed to feel they have a larger stake in the federal aid programs (and especially campus-based aid) than the public colleges. This is true, even though considerably more than half of all federal aid goes to students at public institutions. Second, it is interesting to note that there is a fair coincidence of purpose between the federal interest in targeting aid on needier students and the institution's interest in gaining budgetary help from aid. The political pressure to expand aid to "middle income" students (and higher) has not come from the colleges but from parents. This makes sense since, as the foregoing analysis suggests, it is they who principally benefit from it.

Finally, the generalizations lead to some tentative conclusions about the relative impact on college budgets of the different major types of federal student aid. Campus-based aid has a quite strong impact, especially at private colleges. Because it is well concentrated on high need students many of whom would either not enroll or else would receive institution-based aid to replace it, Pell grant aid has a fairly strong impact. GSLs subsidies probably have the least impact on institution budgets, because a larger share of the money goes to low or no need students whose behavior is likely unaffected by it and because GSL aid, if it were replaced by colleges, would likely be replaced by unsubsidized (or lightly subsidized) loans that don't cost colleges much. If this analysis is correct, it carries a quite important historical implication. The very rapid growth in GSLs in recent years along with the real decline in campus-based aid together imply that federal aid has become considerably less valuable in supporting college and university budgets than it used to be.

Although translating these qualitative implications into hard numbers is plainly quite hazardous, some conjectural calculations may at least be suggestive. Suppose we say, for the sake of concreteness, that 80% of campus-based aid, 50% of Pell aid, and 20% of GSL aid goes to help college and university budgets. Although on the basis of the above discussion the ranking is proabably right, the absolute numbers cannot be defended. For 1984, these numbers would imply that of $13 billion in federal aid awarded, about $4.5 billion, or a little more than a third, wound up as net additions to higher education budgets. The remaining two-thirds went to students and families, helping with their living expenses or just easing their finances. In 1975, total Office of Education aid was only $3 billion, but of that almost $1 billion was Pell (BEOG) and over $800 million was in campus-based programs.[10] Guaranteed loans were just 40% of federal aid awarded. According to the rationale just developed, an estimated $1.4 billion of federal student aid benefited institutional budgets, or about 46% of the total. In dollars of 1986 equivalent value, then, the 1975 federal aid contribution to institutional budgets amounted to $2.7 billion.

The estimated $4.5 billion finding its way into the general budgets of colleges and universities is not an overwhelming amount. States provide much more in direct operating subsidies. Still, it is on the same order of magnitude as annual revenues derived from charitable gifts and not much less than federal research support to colleges and universities.

Institutional Support and Federal Policy

How should we feel about this several billions of dollars in aid to institutions from the standpoint of federal policy? One response is that it is simply a regrettable necessity as a by-product of the federal effort to promote the legitimate goals of "access" and "choice" for students. Just as the defense budget helps contractors and Medicare helps doctors and hospitals, the generation of some institutional support from student aid is inescapable.

But, while some institutional support may be inescapable, is it altogether regrettable and something to be minimized? Suppose, for example, that federal grant aid to students at private colleges is cut back dramatically, as the Reagan administration has several times proposed. Suppose, further, that these institutions managed by rearranging their budgets to make up for most or all of the aid reductions to their students and potential students. Presumably they would do so by diverting endowment income and other operating income from library expenditures, graduate research in the humanities, faculty sabbaticals, building maintenance, and so on, to cover the loss of federal aid.[11] If this were the response, then there is a legitimate sense in which current federal student aid might be viewed as paying not for students but for all those items that would be cut back if aid were withdrawn. That is, a *part* of federal financial aid (about one-third of the total) would be functioning as general institutional support.

Would the loss of this support be bad? The answer to this question depends, first, on whether the federal government has a general interest in fostering the health and supporting the general operations of universities and colleges and, second, on whether student aid is an appropriate vehicle to ensure this interest.

The broader question of the federal interest was extensively debated in the late 1960s and early 1970s when the nature of the federal role in higher education was an important topic of scholarly and political discussion. Some economists argued at the time, and continue to argue, that there is no reason for general government subsidy of universities. We might call these economists' conception a "purchase of services" model. Higher education should run like any other business. It produces a number of products, of which the most prominent is educated students, but others are athletic spectacles and research. If federal or state governments have particular requirements such as research or expanded enrollments of disadvantaged students, they should buy those services in the market at minimum cost. From this standpoint, student aid should support institutions as little as possible.

Although the perspective has considerable force and certainly great influence as an intellectual framework, there are reasons for caution in applying it to higher education. First, aspects of financing higher education other than student aid depart considerably from these principles. The "purchase of services" logic would suggest that higher education should not have nonprofit status or tax exemptions. It would suggest that states should not provide operating subsidies to colleges. It would even cast doubt on the peer-reviewed grant system of funding research, in contrast to the contract-oriented system used for much nonacademic federal research.

Second, no other nation currently finances higher education in the economically "rational" way implied under the "purchase of services" approach. Traditionally, societies have found some way or ways of placing "buffers" between universities and the marketplace, through religious protection or combinations of governmental and charitable support. The point goes beyond the argument that some of the products of universities generate "externalities." That argument can be readily handled in the "purchase of services" model. Rather, the idea seems to be that universities should be financed and operated in a way that ensures some autonomy from immediate social demands, whether those demands are registered through private markets or through demands from governments for particular services. If this view has weight, it suggests that universities and colleges should have some sources of money that are not closely tied to the particular services they supply. These funds could be used, for example, to support research on topics that are at a particular moment out of fashion (currently, say, the humanities or pure mathematics). Similarly, colleges and universities should not be so dependent on student support that they lose the capacity to make independent judgments about curricular needs.

This perspective on higher education suggests the value of plural sources of funding and control. Indeed, it may argue for a measure of redundancy and slack in funding. This will, from the standpoint of the "purchase of services" model, appear messy and inefficient. It may, nevertheless, be desirable.

Merits of the Student Aid "Vehicle"

The foregoing only presents a rationale for federal support to institutions of higher education. But, if federal support of colleges and universities is justified, is student financial aid a good vehicle for providing some of it? The question requires comparisons among the available alternatives.

The most obvious alternative is some kind of formula-based institutional aid which provides support to institutions in proportion to the number of students they enroll, or degrees they produce, or some other formula. Such formulas, and their relative merits, were extensively discussed in the early 1970s. Formulas for allocating institutional support tend to be unwieldy and difficult to implement at the federal level. With thousands of institutions to serve, any such formula would have to be highly impersonal and minimally discretionary. No meaningful apparatus for qualitative judgment is conceivable.[12] Furthermore, it would be hard to design an impersonal mechanism that did not create perverse incentives: rewarding degrees encourages diploma mills; rewarding enrollments discourages high completion standards and encourages lengthy programs; and so on. Finally, it would be hard to design a mechanism that did not either sharply discourage entry of new institutions, as minimum age of institution or size restrictions would do, or overly encourage it, as straight capitation grants might do. None of these problems is necessarily unacceptable or insoluble, but it is clear that most mechanisms for distributing federal institutional aid have significant drawbacks.

Student aid as a vehicle for aiding institutions has some attractive features. By encouraging institutions to respond to the needs of disadvantaged students, the main incentives of this form of support have some appeal. It contains a built-in mechanism for accommodating the entry of new institutions (funds follow students). It also allows for the reallocation of aid among institutions and sectors as their relative fortunes change.

But the aid vehicle has some drawbacks. Ironically, as a means to provide support for institutions, too much money winds up with students. As estimated above, only about a third of the aid awarded actually benefits institutional budgets. Of course, student aid is primarily intended to support students. Yet, recent shifts in the forms of federal student aid imply that such support has become increasingly *less* valuable to institutions. While it is reassuring that the aid awards most valuable to institutions—ones that go to high need students—also fit best with other rationales that support student aid (e.g., fairness and wider opportunity), the rapid growth in loans accompanied by real declines in federal campus-based aid programs has not only eroded the targeting of federal aid but also reduced the value of such aid to institutions.

A second difficulty with student aid as a vehicle for supporting institutions is its tendency to encourage the entry of profit-seeking firms. This is a subtle matter. So long as student aid policy is viewed from the standpoint of responding directly to student needs (encouraging access and choice), there is little reason to restrict the use of aid to not-for-profit institutions. And, indeed, federal legislation has been amended to make it easier for students attending proprietary schools to qualify for financial aid. The result has been enormous growth in the proprietary sector, whose students now receive something over 20% of Pell grant aid and a similar fraction of the volume of Guaranteed Student Loans (Korb et al., 1988). This is acceptable from the standpoint of a "purchase of services" model. However, if a sizable proportion of externally provided student aid serves as general budgetary support for the institutions in which aid recipients enroll, the advantages of the student aid vehicle are clouded. As noted above, profit-seeking institutions tend to turn general budgetary support into profit, while nonprofit and government-run institutions tend to turn such support into further provision of services. It seems unlikely that Congress would ever have included proprietary institutions in a direct institutional aid formula on terms as generous as the student aid programs imply. Yet, it is quite difficult, despite some efforts in this direction, to develop and introduce differential treatment of profit-seeking and not-for-profit institutions.

CONCLUSIONS

While recent financing and demographic trends have increased the importance of student financial aid in institutional enrollment and revenue strategies, details about the pricing and financial aid packaging practices and policies of colleges and universities remain relatively sketchy and the extent to which externally provided financial aid eases institutional budgets remains unknown. Nonetheless, such evidence as exists suggests that the scope for institutional discretion in pricing and financial aid packaging is significant—even within the framework of a structured, centralized need analysis system. The potential for obtaining substantial institutional support from federal student aid programs would appear to be great.

Do institutions exercise discretion in pricing and aid packaging? The answer seems to be yes. Colleges and universities continue to depart from standardized need analysis procedures. Relative to the standard, uniform determination of need, different policies and practices would clearly favor (or disadvantage) some students. The result is that, quite apart from stated policies, student characteristics appear to be modestly associated with the allocation of institutionally awarded grant aid. While this conclusion is drawn from an analysis of the distribution of financial aid in the late 1970s, there is no reason to believe that colleges and universities are exercising *less* discretion in awarding discounts in today's competitive environment.

To what extent do colleges and universities benefit directly from the large federal stake in student financial aid? In one sense, higher education generally, and private research universities in particular, appear to have experienced reductions in all forms of federal support. The rapid growth in "generally available" federal student aid has not been enough to fully offset the decline in "specially directed" benefits to veterans and Social Security recipients and in federal funding for research. But, out of funds allocated through the major federal student aid programs, perhaps one-third of the total—an estimated $4.5 billion—ultimately benefits institutional budgets. These conclusions might be taken to suggest that the current distribution of financial aid to students is inappropriate. The allocation of institutionally awarded aid to students on criteria other than need potentially reduces access to and choice in higher education for students from lower income and disadvantaged households. To the extent they represent increased subsidies for students who would otherwise have enrolled, such awards certainly do not reinforce the presumed public interest in improved access, equity, and choice. From this perspective, tax supported student aid funds allocated by the institution (e.g., SEOG) as well as institutionally generated funds set aside for student aid discounts should be directed toward the neediest of potential students who, without such aid, would not enroll.

Alternatively, institutionally awarded student aid may be used to improve the academic environment for *all* students (by attracting a more heterogeneous group of students in terms of backgrounds, abilities and interests) or to sustain enrollments in specialized programs where marginal costs may be quite low. Moreover, to the extent externally provided financial aid frees up institutional resources for expenditures on quality improvements in faculty and facilities, such a "leakage" into institutional budgets may well be defensible as well.

Neither perspective appears to be entirely correct. That institutions apparently strive to meet an array of objectives simultaneously through pricing, aid discounts, and resource allocation strategies should not be surprising. However, changes in the volume and composition of the demand for enrollment, including those financed through externally provided student aid, alter the scope for and gains/losses from such strategies. In altering the potential trade-offs, third party donors are particularly well placed to influence the balance between quality and financial health on the one hand and access and choice goals on the other. Public policymakers and program administrators need to take this broader view of student aid's effects—on institutional responses—if public student aid programs are to be effective in promoting access and choice.

It has not been our intention to replace the usual demand-oriented perspective on student aid with an institutionally oriented perspective. Rather, we have attempted to introduce the institutional point of view with the belief that such a perspective is essential to obtain a more complete view of how student aid works and what it can do. Although the arguments and analyses presented here are crude and incomplete, they should be considered as initial steps in a promising and important line of research.

NOTES

1. Institutions may, of course, incur additional costs in accommodating increased enrollments generally or a different composition of enrollments (from identified groups, in identified fields). Recent empirical work suggests that, apart from the subsidies required to attract additional enrollments, the marginal costs of instruction are relatively low, for part-time students (Brinkman, 1985) and for undergraduates (Hoenack et al., 1986). See Berg and Hoenack (1985) for an evaluation of the marginal benefit/marginal cost calculation for graduate students at the University of Minnesota.

2. The estimates come from unpublished tabulations of the 1983–1984 Student Aid Recipient Surveys, carried out by the National Institute of Independent Colleges and Universities and the American Association of State Colleges and Universities. Only those funds monitored and allocated by institutional financial aid offices are included in the total. Thus, awards made by third parties (e.g., federal rule-driven programs such as Pell and GSL, private employer or community association scholarships) are excluded by definition. Awards made by the institution, but not monitored by the financial aid office (e.g., some tuition waivers for students, employees, and employee dependents), are also omitted. Some 65% of institution-ally *awarded* gift aid is allocated according to need in the public sector; the comparable share in the private sector is 70%. About two-thirds of institutionally *funded* gift aid in the private sector is awarded on the basis of need compared to a 30% share in the public sector.

3. The contextual analysis permits the examination of the effects of student charac-teristics apart from the effects of individual institutions (see Burstein, 1980, for a discussion of the rationale for and use of contextual analysis). The approach represents an extension of earlier studies which had failed to distinguish between individual (student) and contextual (institutional) effects.

4. Indeed, the amendments authorized an institutional aid program, "Cost of Educa-tion" allowances, keyed to the number of BEOG recipients an institutiton enrolled. This provision was never funded.

5. See Gladieux and Wolanin (1976) for a penetrating account of the legislative history that supports this point.

6. Revenues defined as educational and general revenues net of institutional student aid expenditures.

7. Most of these grants are for research, but published federal data do not permit the research component to be broken out for that year.

8. The relatively small National Direct Student Loan program might be classified under either (1) or (3). For the purposes of this discussion, it is included with the campus-based programs.

9. This formulation sounds quite zero-sum. What the school doesn't get, the family does, and conversely. This is true enough in accounting terms. Notice that when aid gets a student to a school she wouldn't otherwise attend, both the student and the school are likely to benefit.

10. All figures are amounts awarded, except for NDSL loans, where the government appropriation (which represents additions to schools' revolving accounts) is used.

11. If institutions drew down their endowments more rapidly to cover higher aid costs, they would in effect be reducing future expenditures on items like those listed in the text.

12. There is an interesting contrast here to the issue of state-level institutional aid or operating subsidy. Because any one state oversees fewer institutions and has, in

effect, the authority that comes with ownership, it's at least conceivable for states to exert strong qualitative judgment. Some do so much more actively and effectively (which are not the same) than others.

REFERENCES

Applied Management Sciences, Inc. (1979). *Study of Program Management Procedures in the Campus-Based and Basic Grant Programs.* Technical Report No. 1: Sample design, student survey yield, and bias. Washington, DC: U.S. Department of Health, Education and Welfare, Office of Evaluation and Dissemination.

Applied Management Sciences, Inc. (1980a). *Study of Program Management Procedures in the Campus-Based and Basic Grant Programs, Final Report,* Vol. 1: *The Institutional Administration of Student Financial Aid Programs (Final Report).* Washington, DC: U.S. Department of Education, Office of Program Evaluation.

Applied Management Sciences, Inc. (1980b). *Study of Program Management Procedures in the Campus-Based and Basic Grant Programs, Final Report.* Vol. 2: *Who Gets Financial Assistance, How Much, and Why? (Final Report).* Washington, DC: U.S. Department of Education, Office of Program Evaluation.

Barnes, Gary T., and Neufeld, John L. (1980). The predictability of college financial aid offers: evidence from the class of 1972. *Economic Inquiry* 18 (October): 667–91.

Basch, Donald L. (1987). Variation in student financial aid among New England private colleges: a conceptual and empirical analysis. *Proceedings of the Fourth Annual NASSGP/NCHELP Research Conference on Student Financial Aid Research,* Vol. 1. Albany: New York State Higher Education Services Corporation.

Berg, David J., and Hoenack, Stephen A. (1985). The implementation of cost-related tuition at the University of Minnesota. Paper prepared for the DePaul/Exxon Conference on Undergraduate Differential Pricing. Chicago: DePaul University.

Brinkman, Paul T. (1985). The financial impact of part-time enrollments on two-year colleges. *Journal of Higher Education* 56(May/June): 338–353.

Burstein, Leigh (1980). The role of levels of analysis in the specification of education effects. In Alan J. Thomas, and Robert Dreeban, (eds.), *Issues in Microanalysis,* pp. 119–90.

Carlson, Daryl (1974). Student price response coefficients for grants, loans, work-study aid, and tuition changes: an analysis of student surveys. Unpublished paper, Department of Agricultural Economics, University of California at Davis.

Carlson, Daryl (1975). *A Flow of Funds Model for Assessing the Impact of Alternative Student Aid Programs.* Research Memorandum EPRC 2158-28. Menlo Park, CA: Educational Policy Research Center, Stanford Research Institute.

College Scholarship Service (1971). *New Approaches to Student Financial Aid* (Cartter Panel). New York.

Ehrenberg, Ronald G., and Sherman, Daniel R. (1984). Optimal financial aid policies for a selective university. *Journal of Human Resources* 19(Spring): 202–30.

Gladieux, Lawrence E., and R. Wolanin, Thomas (1976). *Congress and the Colleges.* Lexington, MA: Lexington Books.

Higginbotham, Hal, Davis, Jerry S., and Van Dusen, William D. (1986). Survey of undergraduate financial aid policies and practices. Presentation at National Association of Student Financial Aid Administrators Annual Meeting, Dallas, July.

Hoenack, Stephen A., Weiler, William C., Goodman, Rebecca D., and Pierro, Daniel J. (1986). The marginal costs of instruction. *Research in Higher Education* 24: 335–418.

Hopkins, David S. P., and Massy, William F. (1981). *Planning Models for Colleges and Universities.* Stanford, CA: Stanford University Press.

Korb, Roslyn, Schantz, Nancy, Stowe, Peter, and Zimbler, Linda (1988). *Undergraduate Financing of Postsecondary Education: A Report of the 1987 National Postsecondary Student Aid Study*. Washington, DC: National Center for Education Statistics, U.S. Department of Education.

Leslie, Larry L., and Brinkman, Paul T. (1987). Student price response in higher education: the student demand studies. *Journal of Higher Education* 58(March/April): 181–204.

Manski, Charles F., and Wise, David A. (1983). *College Choice in America*. Cambridge: Harvard University Press.

McPherson, Michael S. (1986). Public enrollment, private enrollment, and student aid: a supply and demand analysis. *Proceedings of the Third Annual NASSGP/NCHELP Conference on Student Financial Aid Research*, Vol. 1. Springfield: Illinois State Scholarship Commission.

Miller, Leonard S. (1975). College admissions and financial aid policies as revealed by institutional practices: a progress report prepared for the TIMS XXII international meetings. Berkeley: School of Social Welfare, University of California.

Snyder, Thomas P., and Galambos, Eva C. (1988). *Higher Education Administrative Costs: Continuing the Study*. Washington, DC: Office of Educational Research and Improvement, U.S. Department of Education.

Spies, Richard R. (1978). *The Effect of Rising Costs on College Choice: A Study of the Application Decisions of High-Ability Students*. New York: College Entrance Examination Board.

Van Dusen, William D., and Higginbotham, Hal (1984). *Survey of Undergraduate Need Analysis Policies, Practices, and Procedures*. New York: College Entrance Examination Board.

Van Dusen, William D., Jacobson, Edmund, and Wagner, Alan (1974). Analyses of student costs of attendance. Paper prepared for the Office of Planning, Budgeting, and Evaluation, U.S. Office of Education. Washington, DC: College Entrance Examination Board.

Wagner, Alan P., and Rice, Lois D. (1977). *Student Financial Aid: Institutional Packaging and Family Expenditure Decisons*. Final Report. Washington, DC: The College Board.

Zemsky, Robert, and Oedel, Penney (1984). *The Structure of College Choice*. New York: College Entrance Examination Board.

APPENDIX

TABLE A1. Means and Standard Deviations of Variables Used in Student-Level Equations

	Public 4-year		Private 4-year	
	Mean	St. dev.	Mean	St. dev.
Receipt equations				
Receipt	.301	.459	.485	.500
Need	1.157	1.227	2.392	1.822
Minority status (1-nonwhite)	.274	.446	.248	.432
Academic merit	85.68	6.80	86.25	7.29
Enrollment status (1 = continuing)	.316	.465	.332	.471
Course load (1 = full-time)	.974	.159	.985	.122
Gender (1 = male)	.758	.429	.481	.500
Dependency status (1 = dependent)	.426	.495	.868	.034
Family capacity-to-pay	.618	.500	.520	.064
(n)	1,007		1,330	
Amount equations				
Amount	.574	.405	.927	.688
Need	1.415	1.278	1.743	2.634
Minority status (1 = nonwhite)	.257	.438	.294	.456
Academic merit	86.36	6.95	86.13	7.50
Enrollment status (1 = continuing)	.330	.471	.338	.473
Course load (1 = full-time)	.960	.195	.994	.079
Gender (1 = male)	.406	.492	.477	.500
Dependency status (1 = dependent)	.779	.416	.858	.350
Family capacity-to-pay	.638	.528	.618	.651
(n)	303		646	

Source: SISFAP Merged Analysis File.

**TABLE A2. Means and Standard Deviations of Variables Used in
Institution-Level Equations**

	Public 4-year	
	Mean	St. dev.
Receipt equation		
Coefficient	−.218	.211
Enrollment	10728	12591
% undergraduate	.86	.10
Race	.03	.18
Tuition	712	226
Unit expenditure	2889	1009
Unit endowment	268	546
Unit aid	231	215
Average SAT	939	103
Average family financial condition	1371	510
Aid rate	.89	.17
Acceptance rate	.93	.70
Show-up rate	.68	.17
(*n*)	32	

Source: SISFAP Merged Analysis File.

Understanding Student College Choice

Don Hossler
Indiana University

John Braxton
Syracuse University

and

Georgia Coopersmith
Syracuse University

INCREASED INTEREST IN STUDENT COLLEGE CHOICE

During the past three decades, a diverse set of demographic and public policy issues have fueled increased interest in student college choice. These issues include the emergence of the federal government as a significant source of student financial aid, the declining pool of high school graduates, and past declines in the postsecondary participation rates of black high school students. As a result of these trends, federal, state, and institutional policy-makers, as well as social science researchers, have become interested in understanding the factors that shape the decision to attend a postsecondary educational institution (PEI).

Public policy-makers at the state and federal level have a vested interest in understanding the factors that influence aggregate student enrollments. Both federal and state policy-makers use postsecondary participation rates as indices of economic competitiveness as well as overall quality of life. Although the relationship between education and economic competitiveness and quality of life is mulitivariate, the commonly held belief is that increased levels of education at the state level improve the quality of life for citizens and attract more business and industry.

As the result of increased state and federal investments in student financial aid, state and federal policy-makers can use research on student college choice to more effectively target financial aid dollars. In some states, policy-makers are also committed to maintaining vitality in both the public and private sectors of postsecondary education. A better understanding of student college choice can provide appropriate incentives to help achieve this goal.

Institutional policy-makers have sought to understand the phenomenon of student college choice in order to develop marketing strategies designed to attract the desired number of students. Selective institutions have used student college choice research to help them attract students with desirable academic and nonacademic characteristics.

Among researchers, interest in student college choice has its roots in econometric studies of student demand for higher education and the status attainment literature. More recently, investigators have attempted to answer more applied questions, such as: (1) What are the effects of financial aid upon access to postsecondary education? And (2) what factors determine the selection of one PEI over another?

Student college choice, however, should be of interest to both policy-makers and researchers for reasons that go beyond its relationship to aggregate postsecondary enrollments or the effects of attending college upon status attainment. Students' decisions to continue their formal education beyond high school, as well as where they attend, have important outcomes for society as well as the individual.

A wide range of benefits accrue to society as the result of a well-educated populace. The benefits include increased productivity (Denison, 1971; Schultz, 1961), lower welfare and crime rates (Erlich, 1975; Garfinkel and Haveman, 1977; Spiegleman, 1968), a higher rate of technological development, and greater participation in civic and community affairs (Bowen, 1977). Although scholars and policy-makers may differ on the amount of the costs which our society should bear to provide postsecondary education for its people, few would argue that society does not derive both economic and noneconomic benefits from a well-educated citizenry.

From the perspective of the individual, student college choice also has identifiable outcomes. Individuals incur costs and benefits not only by deciding to pursue a postsecondary education, but also by deciding what type of postsecondary educational institution they will attend. Jencks et al. (1972) found that college-educated males have a significant advantage over males with a high school education, even when ability and family background are controlled. Leslie and Brinkman (1986) compared the lifetime income of high school and college graduates and concluded that the individual rate of return for earning a bachelor's degree is 11.8% (p. 214). In addition, college-educated individuals have better employment fringe benefits and lower rates of health problems, and report being more satisfied with their lifestyle (Bowen, 1977). There are also individual outcomes related to the type of postsecondary education a student completes. Leslie and Brinkman (1986) concluded that graduates of four-year institutions received more financial benefits than those who attended two-year institutions, and students who attended more prestigious institutions appear to accrue more benefits than students attending less prestigious four-year PEIs (although this appears to be the result of a greater likelihood to attain more total years of postsecondary education).

Furthermore, student college choice may be linked with student attrition. The attrition literature suggests that there are linkages between the concept of student-institution fit and student persistence (Williams, 1984). Although the relationship between a student's understanding of postsecondary educational options and the student's subsequent persistence has not been empirically examined, logic would suggest that students who employ a more thorough college selection process are more likely to attend a PEI that matches their needs and interests. In a recent paper on student persistence, Attanasi (1986) concluded that "getting ready" behaviors that high school students engage in prior to postsecondary matriculation are related to student persistence (pp. 14–25). "Getting ready" behaviors include developing a college-going frame of mind and anticipating what college will be like. These "getting ready" behaviors may be similar to the final phase of college choice, where students weigh various postsecondary educational alternatives and choose one PEI on the basis of a cost-benefit analysis or perhaps an intuitive sense of "fit." Although the relationship between persistence and student college choice goes beyond the scope of this chapter, the linkages may be an area worthy of future research.

The literature on student college choice covers a wide range of topics that employ a diverse set of methodological approaches. Studies range from single institutional studies that investigate the information sources that potential postsecondary students find most useful in selecting a specific postsecondary educational institution to attend to causal models which examine the effects of student characteristics upon postsecondary educational attainment. In an attempt to bring order to the literature on student college choice, this chapter has been organized into the following three sections: The first section reviews the conceptual approaches that have been used to frame investigations of student college choice. This section will focus on econometric studies, status attainment research, and models of student college choice. The second section uses a three-stage model of student college choice to integrate the diverse research on factors that influence the decision to attend a postsecondary educational institution and the subsequent decision as to which postsecondary educational institution to attend. The last section presents a summary of empirical studies of student college choice and discusses future research questions and related methodological issues regarding student college choice.

For many students participation in higher education includes some form of advanced vocational training. Therefore, the terms *postsecondary education* and *postsecondary educational institutions*, rather than *college* or *university*, will be used in this chapter. These terms are intended to encompass certificate programs as well as two- and four-year degree programs housed in colleges, vocational institutions, and universities.

Defining Student College Choice

Although *student college choice* is the term frequently used to describe the process that results in students' decisions to continue their formal education at a PEI (D. Chapman, 1981; R. Chapman, 1979; Hossler and Gallagher, 1987; Jackson, 1982; Litten, 1982; Tierney, 1980a), the term has not been formally defined in the literature. In addition to *student college choice*, terms such as *college plans* (Baird, 1973), *educational goals* (Tillery and Kildegaard, 1973), and *the demand for higher education* (Campbell and Siegel, 1967) have also been used as descriptors by researchers who have investigated correlates of the decision to attend a PEI. Although the correlates of student college choice are easily identified, the choice process it is more difficult to study because student college choice is a longitudinal and cumulative process that begins at an early age and culminates in the decision to attend a PEI (Corrazini et al., 1972). In this chapter, the term *student college choice* will be used to describe the process that results in (1) making a decision to continue formal schooling after high school and (2) deciding which PEI to attend. We define student college choice as:

> a complex, multistage process during which an individual develops aspirations to continue formal education beyond high school, followed later by a decision to attend a specific college, university or institution of advanced vocational training.

PERSPECTIVES ON STUDENT COLLEGE CHOICE

Conceptual approaches to describing the college choice process are found in three categories of models which specify factors leading to college choice as well as the relationship among the factors: econometric, sociological, and combined (Jackson, 1982). Within each of these three categories, various conceptual approaches or models have also been developed and will be reviewed.

Econometric Models

Two strands of econometric models of college choice are present in the literature. One strand seeks to predict enrollments with institutions, states, and the nation as the units of analysis, while the other strand focuses on the individual student as a unit of analysis (Fuller, Manski, and Wise, 1982). To be conceptually consistent with the definition of student college choice used in this chapter, only those econometric models which seek to estimate the choice process of the individual student will receive attention. Within the strand of econometric literature, which focuses on the choices of individual students, two types of choices are modeled. One type of choice is between enrollment in a PEI or the pursuit of a noncollege alternative such as the military or a job (Kohn, Manski, and Mundel, 1976; Bishop, 1977; Fuller, Manski, and Wise, 1982; Manski and Wise, 1983; Nolfi, 1978), while the choice of a particular PEI from a set of PEIs is the second type of choice process (Radner and Miller, 1970; Kohn et al., 1976; R. Chapman, 1979).

Regardless of the type of choice addressed by the various models, all the models reviewed postulate a weighing of various factors to make a choice. To elaborate, an individual student will select a particular PEI if the perceived benefits of attendance outweigh the perceived benefits of attendance at other PEIs or a noncollege alternative. In other words, the individual student strives to maximize the expected utility of the choice to be made. This formulation specifies the relationships among the factors in each of the models presented. Although the type of choice and the specific factors posited to be influential may differ across the various econometric models, underlying formulations concerning the relationships among factors are the same.

College or Noncollege Choice
Five models have been advanced to describe factors posited to be influential in the process of choice between college attendance or a noncollege alternative (Kohn et al., 1976; Bishop, 1977; Nolfi, 1978; Fuller et al., 1982; Manski and Wise, 1983). Such models have also been termed *college-going models* (Kohn et al., 1976).

Expected costs are factors common to all of the college-going models. Expected costs include tuition, net tuition (tuition minus financial aid), room and board, and various living expenses. Earnings forgone due to college attendance are additional expected costs included in models advanced by Bishop (1977) and Fuller et al., (1982).

Future earnings expected either from college attendance (Bishop, 1977; Fuller et al., 1982) or from a noncollege alternative (Bishop, 1977; Nolfi, 1978) are additional economic factors. According to Fuller et al., (1982), expected or future earnings from college attendance are estimated by students through the value expected to accrue from receipt of a college degree. Various student background characteristics are factors also predicted to influence college-going behavior (Kohn et al., 1976; Bishop, 1977; Nolfi, 1978). Such family background characteristics as parental educational level (Kohn et al., 1976; Bishop, 1977), parental level of income (Kohn et al., 1976; Bishop, 1977; Nolfi, 1978), number of siblings, and parental occupation (Bishop, 1977) are among the student background characteristics included in some of these econometric models (Kohn et al., 1976; Bishop, 1977; Nolfi, 1978).

High school characteristics such as the proportion of graduates going to college or some other PEI (Nolfi et al., 1978) and high school quality (Bishop, 1977) are also factors predicted to affect college-going behavior. Aspirations of neighborhood peers are an additional factor identified (Bishop, 1977).

College characteristics are also assumed to affect college-going choice. The underlying assumption behind the inclusion of college characteristics in this type of college choice model is that individual students will make a choice between attending a PEI or a non-PEI based on the maximum utility or benefit received from the "most attractive" college available to the individual student (Kohn et al., 1976). Both Bishop (1977) and Kohn et al., (1976) include college characteristics in their models of college-going behavior.

Among the college characteristics adduced as influential in determining the maximum utility of the "most attractive" college available to the student are admissions standards (Bishop, 1977), the average ability of students attending the college, educational expenditures, breadth of institutional offerings, and the quality of campus life (Kohn et al., 1976).

Choice Among Colleges

The term *choice among colleges* refers to the selection of a particular college from a set of alternative colleges from which an individual student has received offerings of admission. Kohn et al., (1976) refer to this process as "college choice." Three econometric models of college choice will be discussed in this chapter subsection (Radner and Miller, 1970; Kohn et al., 1976; R. Chapman, 1979).

Like the models of college-going behavior, each of the three models of college choice also identifies costs as factors which influence the choice of one PEI over a set of alternative PEIs. Costs are influential in that students compare PEIs in their set of choices on the basis of their costs and perceived benefits (Kohn et al., 1976). Out-of-pocket expenses to attend different PEIs are one cost factor (Radner and Miller, 1970; R. Chapman, 1979), while tuition costs and net tuition for all possible PEIs are another factor considered to influence the selection process (Kohn et al., 1976). A ratio of college costs to parental income is an additional factor identified (Radner and Miller, 1970). This ratio suggests that if costs for attendance exceed parental discretionary income for a given PEI, then the probability of selecting that particular PEI decreases.

Such student background characteristics as parental income and student academic ability are also posited as factors in the college choice process (Radner and Miller, 1970; Kohn et al., 1976). Presumably such factors enter into the weighting process for alternative PEIs.

College characteristics are understandably included as factors effecting the choice of a PEI. The admission selectivity of a given PEI is identified by Radner and Miller (1970) and by Kohn et al., (1976) as an indicator of college quality, while academic reputation has been suggested by R. Chapman (1979). Quality dimensions are posited as significant, as students would prefer to attend a higher quality college (Kohn et al., 1976). However, at the same time, students would also prefer not to attend a PEI where average student ability is considerably higher than their own. Thus, this factor is accounted for by two of the econometric models of college choice (R. Chapman, 1979; Kohn, Manski, and Mundel, 1976).

In addition to admissions selectivity, the same array of college characteristics identified as important in the college-going model advanced by Kohn et al., (1976) is also postulated to be influential in their econometric model of college choice. Moreover, a range of college attributes such as the size/graduate orientation, masculinity/technical orientation, ruralness, fine arts orientation, and liberalness are also suggested as factors of importance in the college choice process by R. Chapman (1979).

Consumer Model of Choice
A more general model of college choice is offered by Young and Reyes (1987). They identify costs and risks as the principal factors. Moreover, this model is applicable to various stages of the college choice process. In this econometric model, costs are the use of personal resources to earn a degree. Both monetary efforts and nonmonetary effort are forms of personal resources or costs. Financial aid is classified as a type of monetary effort. Risks are also monetary and nonmonetary. A monetary risk revolves around the perceived value or benefit of receiving a college degree in relationship to its costs, whereas nonmonetary risks may be social or psychological. Failure to earn a degree is an example of a nonmonetary risk.

Although not directly stated by Young and Reyes, the choice of a PEI rather than a noncollege alternative requires that an individual student estimate a minimal degree of costs and risks associated with college enrollment. However, Young and Reyes do posit that if risks are perceived to be great, then the influence of cost is reduced.

Costs and risks are also related to stages of the college choice process derived from Kotler and Fox (1985). These stages are (1) need arousal, or when an initial interest in college is developed; (2) information gathering; (3) decision evaluation, or the narrowing down of choices to a particular set of choices; and (4) decision execution, or the choice of one PEI over another. Young and Reyes (1987) suggest that such nonmonetary costs and risks as parental and peer expectations are more influential in the need-arousal and information-gathering stages than are monetary costs. However, monetary costs become more influential in the decision to enroll in one PEI over another. At this stage, financial aid is predicted to play a significant role.

Sociological Models
Sociological models of college choice have focused on the identification and interrelationship of factors which influence aspirations for college attendance.

Aspirations for college are of interest to sociologists, as aspirations are an integral element in the status attainment process. The status attainment process is concerned with the role played by various factors in the allocation of individual positions or occupations of varying degrees of prestige or status (Sewell and Shah, 1978). Within this allocative process, the role of education is of central importance.

The derivative model of status attainment was developed by Blau and Duncan (1967). In this model, family socioeconomic background and student academic ability are predicted to have a joint positive effect on aspirations for college. Parental encouragement (Sewell and Shah, 1978) and the influence of significant others and high school academic performance (Sewell, Haller, and Portes, 1969; Sewell and Hauser, 1975) were factors subsequently added as refinements to the basic model. Significant others are the students' parents, teachers, and peers.

The influence of significant others and academic performance represent a linkage of social-psychological mechanisms with status attainment (Sewell et al., 1969). To elaborate, mental ability is assumed to affect academic performance in high school. High school performance and family socioeconomic status exert positive influences on the perceptions of significant others concerning the focal student. Aspirations for college are, in turn, affected by the influence of significant others. Significant others such as parents, teachers and friends influence student aspirations either as models or through the behavioral expectations they communicate.

Two additional perspectives on the shaping of aspirations for college are provided by Boyle (1966) and by Alwin and Otto (1977). Although both Boyle and Alwin and Otto focus on the role of high school context, the formulations of these two models are distinctly different and merit closer examination.

Boyle's model is complex and is best described by beginning with those factors predicted to have a direct influence on the shaping of aspirations for college. Two psychological factors—academic ability and motivation—are posited to directly affect college aspirations. Academic ability is largely determined by high school academic standards, which are, in turn, affected by the structural characteristics of the school and by the preparation and motivation of students. More specifically, the centralization or decentralization of autonomy of local school districts in the development of academic standards (standardized examinations) affects standards at the level of the individual high school. Put differently, variability in high school standards is a function of the extent to which autonomy is extended to the individual high school. The high school student body composition also influences the standards and practices of a high school. High schools vary in composition of their student bodies in terms of the preparation and motivations of students. Well-prepared and highly motivated students are more willing to expend effort in their course assignments and are more amenable to instruction. Student body composition also indirectly affects student motivations for college aspirations. The composition of a student body determines the peer group subcultures of a high school, which, in turn, influence the motivation of students to develop plans for attendance. Thus, Boyle's model addresses the influence of both between- and within-school factors on college aspirations.

The model advanced by Alwin and Otto (1977) also accounts for the effects of between- and within-school variables on the formulation of plans for postsecondary education. This model is comprised of two stages. In the first stage, three background characteristics and school context variables are predicted to indirectly affect college aspirations. Gender, socioeconomic level, and academic ability are the student characteristics, while average student socioeconomic background, average student ability, and the proportion of enrollment which is male are the contextual or between-school variables. These variables are exogenous, or not influenced by any other variables within the model, and are predicted to directly affect academic certification and social influences. These, in turn, directly influence aspirations for college. Grades and placement in a college preparatory curriculum are dimensions of academic certification.

In the second stage of this model, the effects of academic certification and social influences on college aspirations are outlined. While academic certification plays a direct role in shaping institutions, this variable also develops the expectations of significant others for the development of postsecondary educational plans. More specifically, such significant others as peers, teachers, and parents use students' high school performance as a basis for the formulation of expectations. Such significant others also take into account the socioeconomic background and academic ability of the student in the development of such expectations.

Moreover, it is also posited that students take into account their academic ability, previous academic achievements, and the expectations of significant others in the development of postsecondary educational plans. This model is depicted in Figure 1.Thus, Alwin and Otto (1977) like Sewell, Haller and Portes (1969) also point to the importance of significant others in influencing aspirations for college. However, the formulations regarding the influence of significant others are different.

Combined Models

Although both status-attainment and econometric models have focused on student decision-making in regard to college selection, neither of these conceptual approaches has provided satisfactory explanations of the *process* of college choice. Renewed interest in the subject has caused scholars to look again at both areas from an applied-research tradition in order to better understand consumer decision-making and recruitment efforts (Hanson and Litten, 1982). The new

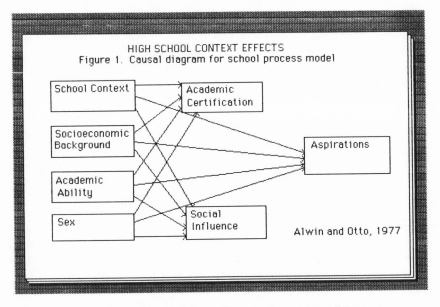

FIG. 1. Causal diagram for school process model

models, by extricating and combining the most powerful indicators in the decision-making process from previous models, provide a conceptual framework that hopes to predict the effects of policy-making interventions. These combined models, as befitting the longitudinal nature of the college choice process, are presented as sequential and as stages in the decision-making process. Institutional and market research have also made their contribution to the combined models by identifying the difference between student *perceptions* of institutional characteristics and objective institutional indicators and by showing the impact of institutional actions on college choice (i.e., recruitment, financial aid, and admissions activities).

Market research has studied the relationship between the type of student and the category of institution to which he or she applied (Zemsky and Oedel, 1983). Demographics, geographic origins, socioeconomic backgrounds, aptitude, and student interests have been analyzed in order to build a profile of the characteristics of students entering individual institutions. Looking for patterns, market research has found a homogeneity that seemingly cuts across all other variables; that is, the personal characteristics of the student—religious and political preferences, levels of sophistication and readiness for college—relate significantly to the existing student body of the college in which she or he enrolls (Clark et al., 1972; Zemsky and Oedel, 1983). From an institutional perspective, the choice process can be likened to a funnel, with a broad pool of prospective students at the top and a narrow pool of students who choose to enroll at the bottom (Litten, 1982).

As in the college-going models advanced by Kohn et al., (1976), Radner and Miller (1970), and R. Chapman (1979), market research indicates that students seek their set of colleges based on their perception of the college community; that is, they seek a college that most closely fits their social preference. These perspectives may be unrealistic. According to R. Chapman (1979), college-bound high school seniors, regardless of the institution they expect to attend, share a highly stereotyped, idealized image of college life, an image that may not be representative of any actual institution. Market research has identified the duality of a college market and the relationship between the structure of student choice and the structure of institutional comparisons—the forces shaping college-bound students' decisions and the institutional consequences of those decisions (Zemsky and Oedel, 1983, p. 25). As market research has shown, the importance of institutional identity in the college choice process, and these intervening variables, along with those from the status attainment and econometric models, has been incorporated in the combined models now examined.

The major distinction between the combined models and those of status attainment and econometric conceptualizations is that the combined models attempt to identify those factors affecting the decision-making process from a policy analysis perspective; that is, the models attempt to describe the various economic and social forces that affect decision making in order to find opportunities for intervention in the student college choice process. These forces include (1) constraints upon the decision that the researcher and policy-maker should be made aware of and (2) institutional activities that can be undertaken to achieve desired results (beneficial interventions). Because combined models approach the conceptual framework of college choice as applied research and therefore offer opportunities for intervention, they can be more useful to public and institutional policy analysts than could the earlier status-attainment and econometric models.

Two general categories of combined models have been proposed: a three-stage model (Hossler and Gallagher, 1987; Jackson, 1982; Hanson and Litten, 1982) and a multistage model that generally comprises between five and seven stages (Litten, 1982; Kotler, 1976; R. Chapman, 1984).[1] A careful study of both categories reveals much overlap and general consensus (Figure 2). In fact, the three-stage model can be viewed as a simplified, "collapsed" version of the other. Differences between the models lie in the description of the intervening variables and in how they define constraining and institution activity.

The elements of a causal model will be used to provide the framework for a comparative discussion of the combined models of college choice. Intervening variables are those between the independent and dependent variable arranged in stages (or in the terminology of behavioral science, they are the intermediant

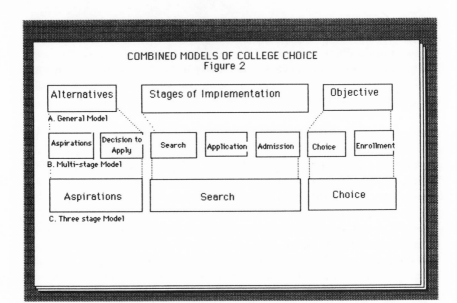

FIG. 2.

variables of a cause-and-effect sequence). The two types of variables alluded to are (1) constant variables, which include influential factors effecting the process over which the student has no control, and (2) adjunct variables, which consist of auxiliary action taken by the institution that can beneficially affect the outcome of the decision-making process. These combined models are in agreement in regard to the descriptors that make up the independent variables of the model, although a variety of terms are used to describe the characteristics that cause an individual to consider postsecondary education as a viable alternative following graduation from high school. These include "college aspirations" (Hanson and Litten, 1981; Jackson, 1982; Litten, 1982), which is the referent used to describe the desire to attend. The terminology's source comes out of the literature on status attainment and includes factors such as socioeconomic status, aptitude, high school performance, gender, and family background. *Predisposition* (Hossler and Gallagher, 1987) and *general expectations* (D. Chapman, 1981) are also terms that have been used to describe the same set of individual factors.

Kotler (1976) proposed seven stages of the college choice process in his market research theory: (1) decision to attend, (2) information seeking and receiving, (3) specific college inquiries, (4) applications, (5) admission, (6) college choice, and (7) registration. These stages have been retained in subsequent combined models, although most often several of these individual actions have been incorporated into broader categorical stages. Kotler's model correctly identifies many activities of the college selection process. It also reflects his market research orientation. For instance, by separating "information seeking" from "specific college inquiries," Kotler offers institutions an additional opportunity for interaction. In a later publication, Kotler and Fox (1985) propose that in the information seeking stage, people often form images of schools based on inaccurate or limited information. The image formed affects the student's choice of colleges to which he or she will make specific inquiries. Thus, the image of the college, realistic or not, has a strong influence on the later stages of selection.

D. Chapman (1981) proposed a model of college choice that attempts to identify important variables and influences affecting student college choice. Unlike the other combined models, Chapman's model does not comprise a series of behavioral stages. Rather, it shows the interrelationship of student characteristics with external forces that result in individual expectations of college life. As such, it may not be as useful for devising intervention strategies, but its clear description of influential factors helps to identify important variables.

The model includes SES, aptitude, level of educational aspiration, and high school performance under the general category of student characteristics. D. Chapman states that students not only enter PEIs at different rates due to their socioeconomic status, they also distribute themselves differently across various types of PEIs. Because many PEIs publish test scores and class rank of their entering class, students self-select colleges prior to application based upon their own assessment of aptitude, as indicated by high school performance (Chapman, 1981, p. 483). Student aspirations include both an estimate of their "prospects" and an expression of their hopes and desires for the future. Under the general heading of external influence, Chapman has included as subcategories significant persons, fixed college characteristics, and college communication efforts.

Research has shown that parents exert the most influence on college choice and that other significant influences can include counselors, peers, teachers, and college admissions officers. Fixed college characteristics are those that help to define the institution such as costs, campus environment, location, and program offerings. Together, these create the institutional image. Even though these characteristics are open to change, the image may remain fixed with students and counselors for a long period of time (ibid, p. 476). The market approach to college admissions believes that institutions can promote an image through their recruitment materials and thereby exert desirable influence on a targeted student population. College communication efforts are described as written publications and recruitment materials. The broad categories of student characteristics and external influences shape the individual's expectations of college life, which in turn influence that student's choice of colleges.

The variables that make up the student characteristics (SES, aptitude, level of aspiration, high school performance) have been described in full in the discussion of status attainment and need not be gone into again.

If the purpose of Chapman's model is to identify the variables important to college choice, Jackson's model (1982) is intended to test the strength of the relationships between variables in order to identify the most effective areas of intervention. Jackson proposes a three-phase model of college choice and describes these phases as (1) preference, (2) exclusion, and (3) evaluation. From the status attainment models, Jackson draws individual characteristics that result in educational and occupational aspirations which result in student preferences for postsecondary education. According to Jackson, the strongest correlate of student aspiration is high school achievement, which is affected by other variables. Next in strength is context, which includes peers, neighborhood, and school. The third correlate of student aspiration is family background. High school aspiration reflects not only a preference for certain options but also the perception of access and availability of certain options.

Jackson's analysis of econometric models suggests that alternatives (PEIs) are initially excluded because of geographic, economic, and academic considerations that act as constraints when they interact with student characteristics. Whereas most PEIs are appropriate for most students, it is the consideration of basic cost, programs and requirements, and location that creates a real difference. Location can add to basic expense when the costs of travel, residence, and out-of-state tuition are considered. Secondly, students don't have access to complete information on all possible college options, and they proceed in the choice process with only partial information. Students also come with their own exclusion criteria that are based on their expectations of financial resources and future economic performance. These conscientiously act as constraints on college choice, causing students to limit their range of options. Thus Jackson describes the processes of phase 2 as the exclusion phase.

The final phase includes the student's evaluation of options, the translation of his or her preferences into a rating scheme, the selection of a choice set, and ultimately, the decision to enroll in a particular college. Although the rating scheme by which students evaluate their choices is not well understood, Jackson contends that family background, academic experience, location, and college costs are most important to this model of student choice. Recruitment information, college characteristics, and job benefits are ranked as having moderate effects college choice. In this model, social context can claim only a weak effect.

In summary, Jackson ranks the effects of different variables found in the general three-stage model of student college choice in order to inform the design of enrollment strategies. This model is presented as a means for evaluating enrollment tactics.

Both Chapman and Jackson present a generalized model of the influence of college choice and their relationship to the outcomes of institutional policy-making in general terms. Litten (1982), Hanson and Litten (1982), R. Chapman (1984) and Hossler and Gallagher (1987), on the other hand, have attempted to

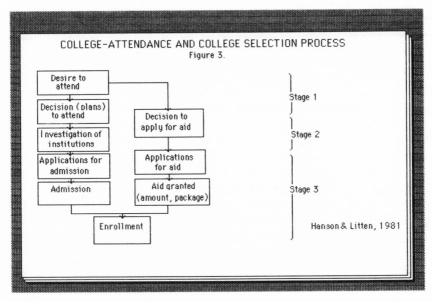

FIG. 3.

create models that show how the *process* of college choice is undertaken and how it is different for different people. The most effective marketing strategies address the needs of different target populations in specific ways, and therefore a model of college choice that takes into account how the college selection process is different for various groups provides important information for enrollment strategists (Litten, 1982). These multistep, combined models take into account the personal and family background and characteristics that have been borrowed from the status attainment models. Hanson and Litten's (1981) model was used to distinguish how the college selection process is different for men and for women. It also distinguishes between the parallel activities related to the application for college admission and application for financial aid (p. 74). In this model, the six steps of the admission process—(1) desire to attend, (2) decision to attend, (3) investigation of institutions, (4) application for admission, (5) admission, and (6) enrollment—have been organized as three stages (see Figure 3). Stage 1 incorporates the desire and decision to attend. The fact of gender is included as one of the predictors of college aspirations in the sociological models and is emphasized as a controlling variable in the Hanson and Litten model. Variables of self-esteem and self-assessment are seen as differing for men and women, thereby affecting educational aspirations (men have tended to be more self-confident). Stage 2 is described as the investigation stage, and parental influence, geographical location, financial considerations, and college environment have been shown to affect women more than men. Women have been more likely to apply for early decision and to apply earlier in general than men, a difference found later in Stage 3.

Litten later expands this model, drawing upon Chapman's broader, structural model. The "Expanded Model of the College Selection Process" (Litten, 1982, p. 388) draws upon variables from the status-attainment and econometric conceptual approaches. The social attributes of the high school, student performance as indicated by class rank, and high school curriculum are shown to affect student aspirations to attend or not to attend. Likewise, SES and personal attributes—such as academic ability, self-image, and the nature of the economic, political, and cultural environment—are all shown to affect the student's predisposition to attend. At the information-gathering stage, the influence of significant others (parents, peers, close friends) is influential. From market theory, variables of college action (recruitment, policies, publications, media) are demonstrated to have an effect on application. Finally, the college's action to grant or not to grant admission also influences the decision to enroll. Research applied to this model indicated that the timing of steps in the selection process is closely tied in to parental education, especially as it relates to how information on colleges is obtained. By drawing a line around the entire decision-making process, Litten's model illustrates that the control variables have a probable point of principle impact but that they continue to exert influence throughout the process. By developing an awareness of the individual differences in timing, policy-makers may be able to approach targeted groups with information appropriate to their different timetables (Litten, 1982).

R. Chapman (1984) proposes a five-stage theory of how students select a college and adds to the literature by further clarifying the basic terminology used to describe the various behavioral stages. In Chapman's model, the first stage is identified as "Presearch" behavior and is described as that period of time when a student first recognized "the possible need and desirability of a college education." This terminology is close enough to the "college aspirations" or "predisposition stage" of other models to be used interchangeably. By Chapman's definition, the second stage, "Search," is characterized by the active acquisition of alternative variables that characterize colleges, such as cost, quality of life, and academic programs. The search phase concludes when the student decides upon a set of colleges. The set is comprised of the colleges to which applications will be submitted and reveals a process of self-selection. Research has shown that students apply to those colleges they are likely to be admitted to; likewise, we must assume that the colleges in this set are at least minimally acceptable to them (R. Chapman, 1984). At the application decision, however (stage three), the possibility of financial aid is still an unknown but will effect the next stage, the choice decision. Choice is the decision to select one of several colleges to which the student has been admitted. It is at this point that actual, rather than perceived, college characteristics become of primary importance, along with the factors of financial aid. As with all other models, Chapman's model of the college choice process ends with matriculation, the actual action of enrolling in a college.

The conceptual models of college choice identify significant variables and show the sequence of the decision-making process. Of special interest to researchers and policy-makers are the control variables consisting of constraints (environmental factors or characteristics of the population) and adjuncts (auxiliary actions taken by policy-makers to enhance the process, such as pricing, programming, and recruitment materials). The concept of constraints comes from the economic models, which indicated that students first exclude and then evaluate alternatives. Econometric theory has also been used to predict the impact of change in public policy toward financial aid. Research on the relationship of financial aid and college choice has demonstrated that aid has a significant impact on college attendance and choice of college (R. Chapman, 1979; Fields and LeMay, 1973; Litten, 1986). Likewise, the perception of the out-of-pocket cost of attending a particular institution affects the selection decision (Kohn et al., 1976; Bishop, 1977; Nolfi, 1978; Fuller et al., 1982; Manski and Wise, 1983; Litten, 1986). The importance of identifying constraints, therefore, is that they are variables over which public and institutional policy-makers can exert some control. The combined models of college choice provide useful information for the development of enrollment tactics. By describing the relative strength of different variables, the models also provide the means whereby strategies can be evaluated for projected efficiency and effectiveness.

These three conceptual approaches can also be compared on the range of variables included and on their explanatory power. The combined models are the most inclusive of the three approaches, as a wide range of variables is predicted to influence the college choice process. Moreover, the combined models incorporate more than a single stage of the choice process. The econometric models also include a number of variables of presumed influence and focus on one of two stages in the choice process: college-going and choice behavior. The sociological models, however, include a limited number of variables and focus on only the aspiration stage of the choice process.

When the approaches are compared on their explanatory power, the combined models appear to be limited. Although the models of this category posit relationships between various variables, few assumptions and concepts which seek to explicate the linkages between influential variables are advanced, and those that are have not been investigated. While the econometric models offer the notion of maximum utility of the perceived benefits of one choice alternative over another, assumptions and linking concepts among variables are also lacking. The sociological models not only provide several alternative perspectives on the mechanisms for the development of aspirations of college choice but also move beyond statements of relationships to the advancement of assumptions and concepts which seek to explain these relationships. Thus, the sociological models appear to have the most explanatory power of the three conceptual approaches to the study of college choice.

Given these assessments, we suggest a need for further development of the econometric and the combined models of the college choice process. Such development should focus on enhancing the explanatory power of these conceptual approaches. However, as the combined models appear to be the most inclusive in terms of the stages and factors included, this category of approaches is perhaps the best candidate for further theoretical development. Specific suggestions for such theoretical development are subsequently discussed in this chapter.

A REVIEW OF RESEARCH ON STUDENT COLLEGE CHOICE

In addition to the theoretical work that provides a conceptual framework for this chapter, there are numerous studies that have examined various aspects of student college choice. The foci of these studies include the postsecondary aspirations of high school graduating classes, the relationship between high school guidance counseling and postsecondary plans, the impact of financial aid on postsecondary attendance rates, and institutional studies that attempt to determine which factors affect the decision to attend a specific PEI.

For this review, the three-stage model of student college choice proposed by Hossler and Gallagher (1987) will be used as the conceptual framework for organizing empirical investigations of college choice. Although, this model does not capture the complexities of the choice process that are present, for instance, in the model of Kotler (1985), it includes the major stages of the choice process. In addition, this model combines most of the variables found in both econometric and sociological models of student college choice. The model also suggests that institutional variables have an impact on student college choice. By employing a three-stage model, it is possible to bring some order to a diverse, and sometimes chaotic, set of empirical investigations. By employing a theoretical model to organize and review existing research on student college choice, it is possible to conduct a systematic analysis of methodological questions and theory development in the next section of this chapter. The model of Hossler and Gallagher (1987) is based on the work of R. Chapman (1984), Jackson (1982), and Litten (1982). This model of student college choice includes the following stages:

1. Predisposition—The "developmental phase in which students determine whether or not they would like to continue their formal education beyond high school."
2. Search—Searching for the attributes and values which characterize postsec-

ondary educational alternatives as well as learning about and identifying the right attributes to consider.

3. Choice—Formulating a choice (or application set) and deciding which institution to attend. (Hossler and Gallagher, 1987, p. 211)

In this chapter, each stage is examined separately and related research is reviewed. Although this approach integrates and extends our knowledge of student college choice, such an endeavor is not without conceptual and methodological problems.

A review of the research on student college choice quickly reveals that it has not been based upon a common set of theoretical assumptions. Most of the existing research has not been conceptualized in such a way that these studies can easily be categorized into the three-stage model that has been outlined. Many of the investigations, while grounded in concrete practical problems, lack any guiding theoretical constructs. As a result, many studies are based upon a unique set of assumptions. There is great variance in the survey instruments or interview protocols and the results of these college choice studies.

To clarify relationships among variables, available evidence has been carefully reviewed. In addition, causal ordering has been reported whenever such findings were available. Out of necessity, the format of the examination of each stage of student college choice is different. Because there are so many investigations which have examined the correlates of postsecondary enrollment and the demand for higher education, much is known about the factors that influence the predisposition stage of student college choice. The *correlates* of predisposition, as well as some of the *process characteristics* (timing, variability among different students, etc.) of predisposition can be discussed in detail.

Conversely, the search stage has received little attention. Little is known about how students go about collecting and evaluating information about PEIs before they select the institutions to which to apply. Therefore, the discussion of search in this chapter is limited to an examination of the process characteristics (timing and information sources).

The third stage, choice, has received considerable attention from individual institutions. These institutions have studied the correlates of choice in order to understand why students select one PEI over another. It is more difficult to arrive at generalizations similar to those arrived at when examining predisposition. Nevertheless, more is known about the choice stage than is known about the search stage.

Predisposition

During the predisposition phase of student college choice, students arrive at a tentative conclusion to continue, or not continue, their formal education after high school graduation. Since few studies of student college choice have been conducted using a college choice model, the predisposition section of this chapter draws primarily upon research that has examined correlates of postsecondary participation. From the perspective of a college choice model, studies that examine such variables as the relationship between SES, or levels of parental encouragement, and postsecondary enrollment provide insights into the factors that influence whether or not a student will attend a PEI. The array of variables that have been found to be correlated with a predisposition toward postsecondary attendance include:

1. Family socioeconomic status is positively associated with postsecondary participation (Corrazini et al., 1972; Ekstrom, 1985; Elsworth et al., 1982; Gilmour et al., 1978; Hause, 1969; Jackson, 1978; Manski and Wise, 1983; Perlman, 1973; Sewell et al., 1972; Sewell and Hauser, 1975; Tuttle, 1981; Yang, 1981).
2. Student academic ability and achievement are positively associated with postsecondary participation (Bishop, 1977; Carpenter and Fleishman, 1987; Hause, 1969; Jackson, 1986; Manski and Wise, 1983; Sewell and Hauser, 1975; Tillery, 1973; Tuttle, 1981; Yang, 1981).
3. Race and ethnicity are associated with postsecondary participation. Caucasians and Asians are more likely to participate, black and Hispanic students are less likely to participate (Hossler, 1984; Litten, 1982; Manski and Wise, 1983; Tuttle, 1981).
4. Gender has little impact on postsecondary participation (Carpenter and Fleishman, 1987; Elsworth, 1982; Hossler and Stage, 1987; Marini and Greenberger, 1978; Stage and Hossler, 1988).
5. Parental levels of education are positively associated with postsecondary participation (Carpenter and Fleishman, 1987; Gilmour et al., 1978; Hossler and Stage, 1988; Jackson, 1986; Solmon and Taubman, 1973; Trent and Medsker, 1967; Tuttle, 1981; Yang, 1981).
6. Family residence—urban or rural location—has differential effects on postsecondary participation (Anderson et al., 1972; Dahl, 1982; Lam and Hoffman, 1979).
7. Parental encouragement and support for postsecondary education are positively associated with postsecondary participation (Carpenter and Fleishman, 1987; Conklin and Dailey, 1981; Ekstrom, 1985; Gilmour et al., 1978; Hossler and Stage, 1988; *Parents, Programs and Pennsylvania Student Plans*, 1984; Russell, 1980).
8. Peer encouragement and support are positively associated with postsecondary participation (Carpenter and Fleishman, 1987; Coleman, 1966; Falsey and Heyns, 1984; Jackson, 1986; Russell, 1980; Tillery, 1973).
9. Encouragement from high school counselors and teachers are positively associated with postsecondary participation (Ekstrom, 1985; Falsey and

Heyns, 1984; Tillery, 1973; *Parents, Programs and Pennsylvania Student Plans*, 1984).

10. Student educational aspirations and career plans are positively associated with postsecondary participation (Carpenter and Fleishman, 1987; Dahl, 1982; Gilmour et al., 1978; Hilton, 1982; Jackson, 1978; *Parents, Programs and Pennsylvania Student Plans*, 1984; Peters, 1977; Trent and Medsker, 1968).

11. The quality of the high school and the academic track the student is enrolled during high school are positively associated with postsecondary participation (Alexander et al., 1978; Elsworth, 1982; Harnqvist, 1978; Falsey and Heyns, 1984; Kolstad, 1979; *Parents, Programs and Pennsylvania Student Plans*, 1984; Peters, 1977).

12. The labor market and increased rates of return[2] are positively associated with postsecondary participation (Adkins, 1975; Bishop, 1977; Campbell and Siegel, 1967; Chressanthis, 1986; Corrazini et al., 1972; Dresch and Waldenberg, 1978; Jackson, 1978; Mattila, 1982).

Although each of these variables has been correlated with a predisposition toward enrollment in a PEI, the strength of the association between these variables and predisposition is not consistent across all studies.

Socioeconomic Status

SES is positively associated with a predisposition to attend a PEI. A consistently positive relationship has been found between SES and postsecondary participation rates (Alexander et al., 1978; Corrazini et al., 1972; Ekstrom, 1985; Elsworth et al., 1982; Gilmour et al., 1978; Hause, 1969; Jackson, 1978; Perlman, 1973; Sewell et al., 1972; Tuttle, 1981; Yang, 1981). Elsworth et al. (1982) found that SES explained 9.3% of the variance in postsecondary participation rates among youth in Australia (p. 71). Tuttle (1981) reported that SES accounted for 6.8% of the explained variance in his study of students from the 1980 High School and Beyond study (HSB). The nature of the relationship between SES and predisposition, however, is not specified in all of these studies. In addition, there is some evidence that the impact of SES on predisposition may be different for men and women (Marini and Greenberger, 1978; Stage and Hossler, 1988). In a multivariate analysis of the correlates of postsecondary participation in Australia, Ekstrom (1985) concluded that SES (along with sex, age, and home location) explained most of the variance in participation rates. Gilmour et al. (1978), in a qualitative study of the postsecondary plans of high school seniors in Pennsylvania, reported that as the family income and educational level of parents increased, students started to think about their postsecondary plans earlier.

Not all studies, however, have found SES to play an important role in explaining postsecondary participation rates. Jackson (1986) conducted a comparison of the postsecondary participation rates from the National Longitudinal Study of 1972 (NLS) and the 1980 HSB. Using multiple-regression techniques, he found that SES, while significant, explained only 3.0% of the variance in postsecondary participation rates in the NLS sample and 4.4% of the variance in the HSB sample (Jackson 1986, p. 18). Yang (1981), in a longitudinal study of 1,714 high school seniors that employed multiple-regression techniques, found that SES did not add to the amount of explained variance when parental educational background and parental encouragement were also considered. Similarly, Leslie et al. (1977), in a study of 1,000 high school seniors in Pennsylvania that employed qualitative interview techniques and multiple-regression analysis, found that SES did not have a major impact on student plans to attend a PEI.

Despite the findings of Jackson (1986), Yang (1981), and Leslie et al. (1977), when causal modeling techniques are utilized SES does have a significant, although indirect effect on postsecondary participation. Manski and Wise (1983) used conditional logit analysis to examine the college choice decisions of 23,000 high school students who participated in the National Longitudinal Study of 1972. Their results indicated that SES was associated with the likelihood of postsecondary enrollment (or predisposition), but the effect was not strong. In a path-analytic study, Tuttle (1981), using HSB data, found that SES had an indirect effect through student ability/achievement on the predisposition stage. Tuttle's results suggest that although SES may not directly influence predisposition, SES does directly influence student achievement in high school, which in turn does exert a positive influence upon the predisposition stage. Similarly, Carpenter and Fleishman (1987) employed path analysis to study student college choice in Australia and reported that the effect of SES was indirect. The effects of SES on the predisposition of these students were mediated through parental encouragement and explained 15% of the variance in parental encouragement for college attendance (p. 94). In support of an indirect effect of SES on predisposition in a LISREL path-analytic study of the postsecondary aspirations of 2,495 high school juniors in Pennsylvania, Marini and Greenberger (1978) found that SES explained 8.9% more of the variance in ambition for boys. Conversely, SES explained 12.2% more of the variance in academic achievement for girls (p. 73).

A review of the findings suggests that SES does have an impact on predisposition; however, the impact may not be direct. Rather, SES has a positive effect upon the academic success of students, their educational aspirations, and the educational expectations they perceive that others have for them.

Student Ability
Trent and Medsker (1967) stated that "There is some question as to whether socioeconomic status or ability has the greater influence on the decision to attend

college'' (p. 3). Like SES, the empirical evidence supports the assertion that student ability is positively correlated with a predisposition toward postsecondary education (Bishop, 1977; Carpenter and Fleishman, 1987; Hause, 1969; Jackson, 1978, 1986; Manski and Wise, 1983; Mare, 1980; Peters, 1977; Rumberger, 1982; Tillery, 1973; Tuttle, 1981; Yang, 1981). While Elsworth (1982) did not find that ability added to the amount of variance explained by his path model, this is the only study reviewed that included a measure of ability or achievement and did not find a significant relationship between ability/ achievement and a predisposition toward postsecondary education. Manski and Wise (1983) found that high school GPA and SAT scores were the best predictors of who applied to college. In another analysis of NLS data, Peters (1977) concluded that high-ability high school students are eight times more likely to go to college than low-ability students (p. 9). Tillery (1973) reported similar findings. Jackson (1978) analyzed data from the National Longitudinal Study of 1972. He investigated the impact of financial aid on college choice using discriminant analysis. He found that academic standing improved his ability to predict college enrollment by 12% (p. 568). In a later comparative analysis of NLS and HSB data, Jackson (1986) reported that academic test scores explained 6.4% of the variance in postsecondary participation rates for the NLS sample and 8.1% of the variance for the HSB sample. Grades explained 4.2% of the variance in postsecondary participation rates for the NLS sample and 7.9% of the variance for the HSB sample (p. 18). Yang (1981), using multiple regression, also found that high school grades explained 15% of the variance in postsecondary aspirations and 12% of the variance in the actual attendance rates of high school students (p. 13).

Further support for the contribution of ability/academic achievement comes from Carpenter and Fleishman (1987) in their path-analytic study of Australian high school students. They found that academic achievement and ability had a direct effect on postsecondary participation. In addition they noted that achievement interacts with students' self-assessments of their postsecondary potential. They did not find a one-to-one correspondence between ability/achievement and postsecondary participation, however, because some students do not assess themselves realistically. In another path analysis that used HSB data, Tuttle (1981) found that grades explained 6.3% of the variance in the predisposition toward postsecondary education (p. 12). In a LISREL path-analytic study, Hossler and Stage (1988) also found that student ability was a good predictor of postsecondary aspirations.

The cumulative weight of the findings in these studies reviewed indicates that student ability and student achievement have a significant and direct impact upon the predisposition of high school students toward a postsecondary education. As ability and academic achievement rise, students are more likely to aspire to attend a PEI and they are more likely to follow through on their plans.

Ethnicity

Historically, black students and other minorities were less likely to attend a PEI (Hossler, 1984). Enrollment trends among minority students rose sharply, however, during the 1970s. Between 1966 and 1977 the numbers of black students enrolled in postsecondary education tripled (*Chronicle of Higher Education*, 1978). Through 1986, participation rates slowly declined; however, in 1986 the black student enrollments started to increase (Evangelauf, 1988, p. A33). Such trends make it difficult to anticipate the impact of race on the predisposition phase of college choice. The inclusion of studies that were conducted when the postsecondary participation rates of minority students was higher, or lower, would be misleading since the factors that influenced the participation rates of minority students have changed. In an attempt to try to capture the current impact of race on predisposition, this review has been limited to a sample of recent investigations.

Ekstrom (1985), in an analysis of HSB data, reported that the impact of race upon postsecondary participation rates disappeared when SES was controlled. Tuttle (1981) found similar results; he found that when SES was controlled, minority students of average ability had a 6% higher probability of attendance (p. 13). Manski and Wise (1983), using NLS data, found similar patterns among black students, as did Jackson (1986), who used both NLS and HSB data sets. Hossler and Stage (1987), in a descriptive study of the postsecondary plans of Indiana ninth-grade students, found that ninth-grade minority students reported thinking more about postsecondary education than white students; however, white students were 4% more likely to indicate that they planned to attend a PEI (p. 10).

Similarly, Brown (1982), who compared NLS and HSB data, arrived at some disturbing findings. He found that the numbers of black students aspiring to attend two- and four-year PEIs had increased between the 1972 NLS study and the 1980 HSB study. From an equity perspective, this suggests that although more black students are aspiring to attend PEIs, fewer are actually attending. Attempts to determine the impact of race on predisposition are like tracking a moving target. At the moment, current evidence suggests that any correlation between race and predisposition is the result of other background variables, such as SES, which may be associated with race. Nevertheless, the declining rates of postsecondary participation of black students, when viewed with the knowledge that black students may have higher aspiration rates, give reason to be concerned about access and choice for black students.

Gender

College enrollment patterns for women, like those for minority students, have been in a period of transition. While women have historically been underrepresented in PEIs, there are now more women than men enrolled (*Update*, 1986).The findings from recent studies on the role of gender in aspirations for postsecondary participation are contradictory. Two studies (Hossler and Stage, 1987; Stage and Hossler, 1988) used correlational statistics and LISREL path-analytic techniques to examine the postsecondary aspirations of ninth-grade students in Indiana. They found that women thought more about going to a PEI but received less family support. Carpenter and Fleishman (1987) and Elsworth (1982), who conducted their studies in Australia, found that gender had no impact on postsecondary aspirations and participation. In fact, Tuttle (1981) deleted gender from his path model because it was not significant in the correlation matrix. Based upon these findings the role of gender on predisposition is uncertain. While some evidence suggests that women may receive less encouragement to attend a PEI, the large increase in enrollment rates among women would suggest that gender no longer plays a major role in the predisposition stage of student college choice.

Parental Educational Levels

Several studies have found a relationship between the level of parental education and predisposition (Carpenter and Fleishman, 1987; Gilmour et al., 1978; Hossler and Stage, 1987, 1988; Jackson, 1986; Manski and Wise, 1983; Solmon and Taubman, 1973; Trent and Medsker, 1967; Stage and Hossler, 1988; Tuttle, 1981; Yang, 1981). Carpenter and Fleishman (1987) found a strong relationship between the father's education and postsecondary enrollment. In his study of NLS and HSB participants, Jackson (1986) concluded that each year of parental education increased the likelihood of the student attending a PEI by 6% (p. 13).

Yang (1981) followed 1,714 rural high school seniors during their senior year in high school and their first year in college. Using qualitative data and multivariate analysis, his results revealed that the father's education exerted a stronger influence than the mother's upon the aspiration levels of the students, but the mother's education exerted more influence on actual attendance rates. Gilmour et al. (1978) reported that students with parents who had a college education started thinking earlier about continuing their education after high school. Tuttle (1981), however, using path analysis to study HSB data, found that parental education was not significant in the correlation matrix and therefore deleted it from his path model.

In two separate analyses of a sample of Indiana high school students, employing LISREL, Hossler and Stage (1988) and Stage and Hossler (1988) looked at the effects of parental education upon the postsecondary plans of Indiana ninth-graders. The first study (Hossler and Stage, 1988) found that the combined level of parents' education had a positive indirect and direct effect upon students' educational plans. Parents' education explained 43.5% of the variance in the amount of parental encouragement that parents gave students to attend a PEI (an indirect effect), and in addition, parental education directly explained 9.5% of the variance in students' educational aspirations (p. 7). The second study (Stage and Hossler, 1988) indicated that the mother's level of education had a positive indirect effect upon the educational plans of both male and female students (mediated through parental encouragement), while the father's level of education had both a positive direct and indirect effect upon the postsecondary educational plans of male and female students (total effect was 7.0% for females and 7.6% for males (pp. 20, 21)). In addition, Hossler and Stage (1988) found that the level of parental education was the best predictor of the parents' educational expectations for their children as well as the best predictor of the students' GPAs (explained 34.7% of the variance, p. 7). These findings are similar to those of Manski and Wise (1983), who compared the application probabilities of students whose parents had less than a high school education with those of students whose parents had a college degree or more. Across income levels ranging from $6,000 to $18,000, they found that in most income brackets, students who had parents with a college education more than doubled the probability that they would apply for college (p. 88).

Overall, the evidence suggests that the level of parental education exerts a strong influence upon predisposition toward postsecondary education, more than either SES or student ability.

Family Residence Characteristics
There is some empirical evidence to support the assertion that the location of family residence affects postsecondary participation rates (Anderson et al., 1972; Astin and others, 1980; Dahl, 1982; Lam and Hoffman, 1979; Willingham, 1970). These studies of family residence typically focus upon the impact of living in an urban or rural location, and whether nearness to a PEI influences postsecondary participation rates. Anderson et al. (1972) used multiple-regression techniques to analyze SCOPE data (which included postsecondary participation rates from four states). They found that the relationship between distance and college attendance was complex and varied in different states and for students of different ability levels. Generally, students who lived within twenty miles of a PEI were more likely to enroll. The variance in the effects of PEI distance from home ranged from a low of no effect on high-ability men from Illinois to an increase in college-going rates of 22% for low-ability men in Illinois (p. 249). The amount of variance explained by nearness to a PEI was small. Astin and others (1980) and Willingham (1970) reported similar findings.

Anderson et al. (1972) also found that students who lived in urban areas were more likely to attend a PEI. More recently, Dahl (1982), employing discriminant analysis in a longitudinal study of Kentucky high school seniors noted that students who resided in urban areas were more likely to enroll in a PEI. Another study employing discriminant analysis (Lam and Hoffman, 1979), conducted at a single Canadian university, reported that students who lived in rural areas were less likely to enroll in a PEI.

Although the effects of residence characteristics were significant in each of these studies, they did not have a strong or even moderate effect upon a predisposition toward postsecondary education. When ability and SES were controlled, the effects of residence characteristics diminished.

Parental Encouragement
Investigations of student college choice have consistently found that the amount of parental encouragement and support for postsecondary education is related to the likelihood of attendance (Carpenter and Fleishman, 1987; Conklin and Dailey, 1981; Ekstrom, 1985; Gilmour et al., 1978; Hossler and Stage, 1988; Murphy, 1981; *Parents, Programs and Pennsylvania Student Plans*, 1984; Russell, 1980; Stage and Hossler, 1988; Soper, 1971; Tillery, 1973). Several descriptive studies have reported a significant positive relationship between parental expectations and the educational aspirations of high school students (Ekstrom, 1985; *Parents, Programs and Pennsylvania Student Plans*, 1984; Russell, 1980; Soper, 1971; Tillery, 1973). Murphy (1981), in a descriptive study of high school seniors and parents, noted that 42.6% of all students and 50% of all parents said that the idea of attending a PEI was first initiated by parents (p. 143). Hossler and Stage (1988), in their LISREL path model, found that parental encouragement for their students explained 18.2% of the variance in the postsecondary plans of Indiana ninth-graders and exerted the largest direct effect on students' plans.

Carpenter and Fleishman (1987) found that parental expectations did not directly influence the postsecondary enrollment decision. Parental expectations, however, did influence student's perceptions of subjective norms (perceptions of what students believed others thought they should do), which in turn were strongly related to postsecondary enrollment. Furthermore these authors' results demonstrated that as the level of parental encouragement increases, student achievement also increases. Conklin and Dailey (1981) used multiple-regression techniques to analyze data gathered from a longitudinal study of high school students from their sophomore to senior year. The sample included 2,700 students in southern New York State. They also found that as the level of parental encouragement increased, students were more likely to attend four-year PEIs and more selective PEIs. Sewell and Shah (1978) made an even stronger case for the importance of parental encouragement. Using data from NLS, they found that the amount of parental encouragement explained 37% of the variance in postsecondary aspirations (p. 12). Parental encouragement explained more of the variance than any other variable, including SES and student ability.

When these findings are considered in total, parental encouragement appears to play an important role in the predisposition phase. Parental level of education, combined with parental educational aspirations for their children, may be the best predictors of student postsecondary plans. Carpenter and Fleishman's (1987) finding—that as parental encouragement rises, so does student achievement—also raised possibilities of a reciprocal relationship between parental encouragement, achievement, and predisposition. That is, as students perform better in school, parents provide more encouragement, which in turn provides further motivation for students to further improve their performance.

Peer Support and Encouragement
In addition to parental encouragement, researchers have found a relationship between predisposition toward postsecondary education and the level of support and encouragement of peers (Carpenter and Fleishman, 1987; Coleman, 1966; Falsey and Heyns, 1984; Jackson, 1986; Russell, 1980; Tillery, 1973). Falsey and Heyns (1984) asserted that one of the outcomes of attending private schools is that students establish friendship patterns that result in more contact with students planning to attend PEIs. For students attending private schools, these patterns increase the likelihood that they will attend college. In a study of 13,000 high school students in Manitoba that did not use inferential statistics, Russell (1980) reported that the postsecondary aspirations of friends were cited as one of the most influential factors in determining students' postsecondary plans. Coleman (1966) and Tillery (1973) described similar findings. In his comparison of the NLS and HSB samples, Jackson (1986) found that the presence of college-going peers produced one of the strongest correlations when he attempted to isolate the most important determinants of postsecondary enrollment. Hossler and Stage (1987), however, employed correlational statistics to examine the relationship among postsecondary plans of Indiana ninth-graders and their peers. They found that those students who were not planning to attend a PEI more frequently consulted their peers. This may suggest that students who are not planning to attend college may be more likely to be influenced by their peers than those students who are planning to go to college. The results from these studies suggest that peers also influence the predisposition phase of student college choice. In total, however, the evidence indicates that peer support and encouragement are not strongly associated with predisposition.

Encouragement from High School Counselors and Teachers
Boyer's recent book, *College: The Undergraduate Experience* (1986), asserted that high school counselors and teachers need to work more with high school students so that the student college choice process will be more informed. Some empirical investigations have examined the influence of encouragement from

high school counselors and teachers on predisposition (Ekstrom, 1985; Falsey and Heyns, 1984; Lewis and Morrison, 1975; Tillery, 1973; *Parents, Programs and Pennsylvania Student Plans*, 1984). These investigations indicate that counselors and teachers have little impact on the postsecondary aspirations of students (Lewis and Morrison, 1975; Tillery, 1973; *Parents, Programs and Pennsylvania Student Plans*, 1984). Ekstrom (1985), Hossler and Stage (1987), and Lewis and Morrison (1975) did find that low-income and minority students were more likely to consult with counselors. Even among minority students, however, the actual percentage of students that relied on counselors was far below 50% (Hossler and Stage, 1987; Lewis and Morrison, 1975). These findings suggest that counselors and teachers have very little influence upon the predisposition stage of most high school students.

Student Career Plans and Aspirations
Research on the predisposition stage of student college choice indicates that the educational goals and career aspirations of high school students are positively related to enrollment in a PEI (Carpenter and Fleishman, 1987; Dahl, 1982; Gilmour et al., 1978; Hilton, 1982; Jackson, 1978; *Parents, Programs and Pennsylvania Student Plans*, 1984; Peters, 1977; Trent and Medsker, 1968). Several studies reported that over 80% of all high school students who indicate that they plan to enroll in a PEI follow through on their plans (Dahl, 1982; Hilton, 1982; Peters, 1977; Trent and Medsker, 1967). However, when causal models are developed, it appears that student aspirations are influenced by SES, student ability/achievement, and parental expectations (Carpenter and Fleishman 1987; Corazzini et al., 1972; Hossler and Stage, 1988). Thus, while student aspirations may be a good predictor of student outcomes, aspirations may simply reflect the effects of other variables.

School Quality and Academic Track
In addition to all of the variables examined thus far, some investigators have also concluded that the quality of the high school and placement in an academic track influence predisposition (Alexander, 1978; Elsworth, 1982; Falsey and Heyns, 1984; Kolstad, 1979; *Parents, Programs and Pennsylvania Student Plans*, 1984; Peters, 1977). The effects of school quality, however, are contradictory. Alexander (1978), Elsworth (1982) and Falsey and Heyns (1984) reported evidence suggesting that high school quality does effect predisposition. Elsworth's study (1982), however, was conducted in Australia and may not be generalizable to the United States. Falsey and Heyns's (1984) study focused upon the student outcomes of attending private high schools. Their findings may not be generalizable to all types of high schools. Alexander's (1978) study found that the social status of the high school was correlated with attendance at a PEI. Kolstad (1979),

however, used multiple-regression analysis with a sample drawn from NLS and concluded that when SES and other background characteristics are held constant, high school quality is only weakly correlated with enrollment in PEIs.

With respect to the high school curriculum, research suggests that being in an academic track has an impact on the predisposition phase (Jackson, 1986; Kolstad, 1979; *Parents, Programs and Pennsylvania Student Plans*, 1984; Peters, 1977). The Pennsylvania study, in fact, found that high school track was a better predictor of attendance in a PEI than grades. Similarly, Jackson (1986) found strong zero-order correlations between academic track and postsecondary enrollment. Kolstad (1979), however, reported that academic track did not exert much influence on postsecondary participation when background characteristics were controlled. Unfortunately, there were no path analytic models to indicate whether other variables have causal links with academic track. It appears that a student's academic track is correlated with the predisposition phase of student college choice, but the precise nature of the relationship between academic track and the decision to attend a PEI cannot be specified. Causal models, however, might be expected to show that SES, ability, and parental encouragement exert a strong influence upon the academic track that students are enrolled in during high school.

Effects of the Rate of Return and Labor Market
Economists as well as education researchers have also investigated the relationship between (1) the labor market, (2) the rate of return, and (3) postsecondary enrollments (Adkins, 1975; Bishop, 1977; Campbell and Siegel, 1967; Chressanthis, 1986; Corazzini et al., 1972; Dresch and Waldenberg, 1978; Jackson, 1978; Mattila, 1982). The questions driving these investigations are:

1. Do the employment opportunities for graduates of PEIs have any impact on decisions to go to a PEI? When the number of jobs for graduates of PEIs decline do postsecondary enrollments decline? When the number of jobs increases, do postsecondary enrollments increase?
2. Are students' decisions to continue their education beyond high school influenced by their perceptions of the rate of return?

In the aggregate, the answer is that the predisposition phase of college choice is not greatly influenced by either labor market activities or the rate of return. Adkins (1975), after comparing postsecondary enrollment trends since the Great Depression to trends in the labor market, stated that the postsecondary enrollments have increased steadily despite shifting trends in the labor market. Corazzini et al. (1972) concluded that during periods of high unemployment students are more likely to attend a PEI rather than be unemployed. Chressanthis (1986) and Hossler (1984) observed the same trend during the recession of the late 1970s.

TABLE 1. The Correlates of Predisposition

Variable	Strength of association
Ability/achievement	Strong
Academic track	Strong
Parental levels of education	Strong
Parental encouragement	Strong
Student aspirations	Strong
Peer encouragement	Moderate
Ethnicity	Weak
Family residence	Weak
Gender	Weak
High school counselors and teachers	Weak
Labor market and rate of return	Weak
SES	Weak
School quality	Weak

Changes in the rate of return also have little effect on the predisposition phase of college choice. Despite the well-documented decline in the rate of return during the 1970s (Bird, 1975; Dresch and Waldenberg, 1978; Freeman, 1976), aggregate postsecondary enrollments continued to increase. Mattila (1982) found that enrollment rates among men during the 1970s declined, and he attributed this to changes in draft laws and the declining rate of return. However, Bishop (1977) and Campbell and Siegel (1967) attempted to measure the effects of rate of return on the demand for higher education. Both studies concluded that high school students were either unaware of shifts in the rate of return or discounted future rates of return at such high levels that it had no effect on their postsecondary educational plans. The results of these econometric studies indicate that although some subpopulations of high school students (e.g., males) may be more responsive to economic inducements, in the aggregate, these inducements have little or no impact on the predisposition phase of most high school students.

This review of the correlates of the predisposition indicates that a number of factors influence the predisposition stage of student college choice. Table 1 summarizes the strength of the association between these factors and a positive predisposition toward postsecondary education.

Process Characteristics of Predisposition
In addition to the correlates of the predisposition stage, several process characteristics are also involved in the development of a predisposition toward postsecondary education. Gilmour et al. (1978) concluded that the decision to

attend a PEI is closely intertwined with the career-decision-making process. The two processes take place simultaneously. A predisposition toward postsecondary education is an evolving process that proceeds at differential rates for different students. Gilmour et al. (1978) noted that the sharpness, or certainty, of students' postsecondary plans varied greatly among students at the same grade level. For example, when studying two students at the same grade level, one student reported that she wanted to be a premed student at Duke or Stanford, the other student planned to go to a college to be "something better."

These distinctions in the certainty of students' plans are further demonstrated in Ekstrom's (1985) results. Among the students in the HSB study, 41% reported that they decided to attend a PEI by the sixth grade, 53% had decided by the eighth grade, and 61% had decided by the ninth grade (p. 15). Stewart et al. (1987), in a retrospective study conducted at Michigan State University, found that 80% of the students had made the decision to attend a PEI by the end of their junior year in high school (p. 13). Parrish (1979) investigated the postsecondary plans of high school juniors in one high school and reported that 59.8% of the students planned to attend a postsecondary institution and that 22.3% were undecided (p. 3).

Hossler and Stage (1987) found that although nearly 72% of the Indiana ninth-graders in their sample planned to attend a college or vocational institution (p. 8), few ninth-graders had thought beyond the predisposition phase. The ninth-grade questionnaire included a set of questions that asked them to indicate how far they wanted to travel to go to college, the size of the institution they wanted to attend, and whether they wanted to commute or live in campus housing. Most of the respondents were undecided. Students with parents who had more education or who were from high-SES families were more likely to have made some decision about these campus attributes, but over 50% of these students were also undecided (p. 18).

Jackson (1982) observed that the decision to consider attending a PEI was not final. He found that some students who initially planned to attend a PEI eventually decided not to continue their education after high school. The findings from this research review indicate that parents and peers provide information and counseling for students and help shape the predisposition stage. By the end of the junior year in high school, if not sooner, most students have formed their predisposition toward postsecondary education. During the predisposition stage, however, most students think of attending a PEI in global terms and lack specificity in their plans. Table 2 outlines the key process characteristics of the predisposition stage.

Search

Because so little attention has been given to the search stage of student college choice, the format of this section differs from that of the predisposition stage.

TABLE 2. The Process Characteristics of Predisposition

Duration	Early childhood to the 9th–10th grades
Related factors	Closely related to development of career plans
Specificity of plans	Vague, only certain they want to attend a PEI
Important influences	Parents

Rather than a detailed review of the correlates of the search stage, this section concentrates on a discussion of the process characteristics of this stage.

Timing

The junior year of high school is an eventful year for students in the college choice process. Most students have reached closure on the predisposition stage during the junior year and enter the search stage. Gilmour et al. (1978), in their study of high school students in six Pittsburgh high schools, found that 72% of the students in their sample developed a list of PEIs during their junior year (p. 15). Stewart et al. (1987) also found that 80% of the students who attended Michigan State University started investigating their postsecondary options during their junior year (p. 14).

Gilmour et al. (1978) also discovered that taking the PSAT often precipitated the development of a list of potential PEIs. During the early phase of the search process the list of PEIs included 3–6 institutions (p. 15). Gilmour et al.'s findings suggest that the search process nears completion by the summer of the junior year. They reported that during that summer, most students narrowed their list to 2–4 PEIs (p. 17). However, data collected by Lewis and Morrison (1975), in a series of interviews with high school seniors throughout their senior year in high school, indicated that for many students the search stage continued into the senior year. By October of their senior year, students reported that only 50% of all of the PEIs that they ultimately considered had been added to their list of potential schools. By the end of January, students had dropped 50% of the PEIs to which they were considering sending applications. The average number of schools considered by students before they began to eliminate institutions was 9.3; as students continued to evaluate institutions, 5.7 was the average number of schools dropped from consideration (p. 17).

Approximately 90% of all PEIs that were considered had been added by February (p. 12). In total, it appears that the junior year and the first months of the senior year in high school are the time frame during which most students move from the search stage to the choice stage of student college choice.

Information Sources

As the search stage started, Gilmour et al. reported that most students had only a casual awareness of PEIs. Some of the first sources they consulted were college guidebooks such as *Peterson's Guide*. Cibik (1982), in a study of high school seniors at a single high school, found that most students first learned of PEIs from friends (50.6%), a personal campus visit (12.7%), or campus publications (11.7%) (p. 101). Tierney (1980b) reported that low-SES students have fewer information sources than high-SES students. This seems to be indirectly supported by Ekstrom (1985), who noted differences in whom students consult when selecting a curriculum in high school. She found that students in general and vocational tracks are more likely only to talk to friends when selecting courses. Students in the college preparatory curriculum consult more sources such as parents, counselors, and friends. Litten (1982) has suggested that low-SES students are less likely to have college-educated parents as well as fewer contacts with well-educated role models. As a result these students are more likely to have access to less information about postsecondary education.

Cibik (1982, p. 100) also asked the high school students in her sample to identify their informational needs. Their information needs were:

Academic quality, 67.6%
Cost, 63.2%
Career availability, 55.4%
Qualification criteria for aid, 55.4%
Helpfulness and instructors, 50.2%

Lewis and Morrison (1975) found that the most frequently used sources of information were (in rank order) catalogs, campus visits, guidance counselors, students already enrolled in college, and admissions officers.

Although many observers have suggested that students are not well informed at any point of the college choice process (Jackson, 1982; Lewis and Morrison, 1975; Litten, 1982), the search stage can be characterized as an active, rather than passive, process. Lewis and Morrison (1975) reported that the search activities most frequently engaged in by high school seniors included (1) writing away for a catalog, (2) campus visits and interviews, (3) talking to guidance counselors, (4) using catalogs available in high schools, and (5) talking to students already in college. The two most frequent activities required students to initiate activities as opposed to using sources of convenience or passively waiting for information to come to them. Caution must be exercised in interpreting these results, however, because this study was conducted before the widespread use of mail marketing techniques (which are possible through the sales of prospective students' names by The College Board, American College Testing, and other

TABLE 3. The Process Characteristics of Search

Duration	9th–10th grades to fall of senior year
Nature of search behavior	Active, student-initiated
Information sources	Friends, campus visits, campus publications
Most important concerns	Institutional quality, degrees lead to careers, faculty

organizations). The use of mail marketing techniques may have made the search process more passive.

Limits on Search
During the search stage students establish limits on the process. Gilmour et al. (1978) observed that most of the students in their sample first established geographical and cost limits; then they determined which institutions offered programs of interest to them. Tierney (1980a) and Astin and others (1980), using larger data sets, also found that geography and cost are important considerations during the search stage.

Table 3 presents the key characteristics of the search stage of student college choice.

In total, little information is available about the search stage, and a number of questions remain. Other than the PSAT, are there other key events that influence the search stage? For students who are planning to enter a vocational institution or a two-year college, and who are less likely to take the PSAT, are there any key external events that affect the search stage? Little is known about how students discover the range of PEIs. How do students learn the names of institutions in order to decide which ones to consider? Do PEIs play any role in the search stage? Could they play any role in the search stage? Could state and federal agencies intervene by disseminating more information about financial aid or postsecondary educational opportunities? Although Gilmour et al. (1978), Lewis and Morrison (1975), and Cibik (1982) have suggested that college guides and institutional information are used during the search stage, caution should be exercised in interpreting these findings. Johnson and D. Chapman (1979) reported that many of the written materials PEIs use are above the reading level of most high school students. In addition, D. Chapman (1981) noted that students use most written material from PEIs to confirm decisions they have already made. If this is the case, how do students go about evaluating a range of PEIs?

Questions of equity and access are also important questions during the search stage. Ekstrom (1985), Gilmour et al. (1978) and Tierney (1980b) indicated that low-SES students, as well as students enrolled in vocational and general tracks, have fewer sources of information about PEIs. Miller (1983), in an examination of how PEIs use college SEARCH mailings,[3] reported that many colleges exclude students who reside in low-income zip code areas. This may further exacerbate the lack of information available to low-income students. Although researchers can speculate about the relationships between student characteristics and the search stage, investigations of the search stage are few. Multivariate studies of the search stage could greatly enhance our understanding of this important stage of student college choice.

Choice

Although the search stage of student college choice has not received a great deal of attention, the choice stage has attracted considerable attention. This stage includes (1) the selection of an application set of institutions, that is, the identification of the PEIs students actually apply to, as well as (2) the final matriculation decision. The research literature on the choice stage is dominated by single-institution studies, conducted either at individual high schools or individual PEIs. These studies typically examine the factors that influenced a student's decision to enroll in a specific PEI. There are some well-crafted studies that use larger samples to examine the selection of a PEI. However, they examine aggregate choice decisions such as the selection of a private PEI over a public PEI or the selection of a high-status PEI over a lower status PEI. Research on the choice stage employs a variety of univariate and multivariate statistical designs, as well as qualitative techniques. Missing, however, are studies that employ experimental designs that permit the utilization of causal modeling techniques.

This section on the choice stage will first examine the student correlates of choice. Some of the same variables, such as socioeconomic status or ability, will be used to organize the discussion of student correlates; however, there is little information available about the impact of variables such as gender, peer encouragement, high school quality, or labor market considerations on the choice stage. In this discussion of the choice stage, the institutional correlates of choice (of the institutional characteristics that are associated with selecting one type of public institution over another or in the decision to attend a specific PEI) will be discussed. These institutional characteristics include nonfinancial attributes (e.g., perceived quality and location) and financial attributes (e.g., tuition costs and financial aid). Finally, some of the process characteristics of the choice stage will be described.

Socioeconomic Status

Although different studies have reported conflicting results as they have attempted to determine the impact of SES on the choice stage, the weight of the evidence suggests that SES is related to both the cost and the quality of PEIs which students apply to and attend. Leslie et al. (1977) did not find a strong correlation between SES and the cost of the institution that students attended. Tierney (1980a, b) used multiple-regression analysis to analyze NLS data and a sample of high school seniors in Pennsylvania. In both studies he found that SES did not affect the cost of the institutions that students applied to, but it was related to institutional status. Lower SES students were less likely to apply to high-status institutions. Maguire and Lay (1981) used discriminant analysis to study the choice stage of applicants to Boston College; they found that low-SES students were just as likely to attend private institutions as high-SES students. Interestingly, Dahl's (1982) analysis of the choice stage for Kentucky high school seniors showed that low-income students were even more likely to choose private PEIs.

Hearn (1984), however, used multivariate techniques to analyze the college choice preferences in a longitudinal sample of students and reported that low-SES students were less likely to apply to high-status PEIs. Spies (1978) used multiple regression to analyze data from a sample of high-ability students. He discovered that middle- and low-income students were less likely to apply to high-status institutions. Maguire and Lay (1981) also found similar results. R. Chapman (1979) concluded that high-SES students are more interested in quality than the cost of attendance. Zemsky and Oedel (1983), in a study sponsored by The College Board, examined the PEI application patterns of students in the New England states. They found that high-income students were more likely to apply to PEIs that were out-of-state with more selective admissions standards. The cumulative evidence suggests that student SES does affect the choice stage of student college choice. High-SES students are more likely to apply to and attend selective PEIs. Surprisingly, however, SES does not seem to be associated with the cost of the PEIs students select.

Ability

Existing research on student ability suggests that it affects the choice stage of student college choice. Dahl (1982) found that high school graduates with the strongest academic credentials were the most likely to select an out-of-state PEI. They were also more likely to attend more selective PEIs. Hearn (1984) also reported that high-ability students were more likely to enroll in more selective institutions. The NLS data analyzed by Jackson (1978) revealed similar student choice patterns. Zemsky and Oedel (1983) found that student ability was directly related to the selectivity of the PEI students applied to as well as where the institutions were located. As student ability rose, the likelihood that students would apply to more selective, out-of-state PEIs also increased. In a single institution study, Maguire and Lay (1981) found that students with higher GPAs were more likely to apply to more selective institutions. Further, their results demonstrated that the preferences of students with high GPAs were more stable; these students were less likely to change their minds. In total, these studies indicate that student ability is positively associated with institutional selectivity. As student ability rises, the selectivity of the PEIs in a student's choice set also increases.

Ethnicity
Fewer studies have been conducted on the impact of ethnicity on the choice stage. In Hearn's (1984) study of this stage, which used longitudinal data from PSAT files, SAT/ACT files, and CIRP data, he found that black students were less likely to apply to more selective institutions. Stewart et al. (1987), in a descriptive study of freshmen at Michigan State University, reported that black students were more concerned about financial aid. He did not control, however, for student SES or ability. Based on these limited findings, we conclude that black students may be less inclined to apply to or enroll in selective PEIs and that they may be more concerned about financial aid and the cost of attendance. Although research has examined the choice stage for black students, little is known about this stage for other minority groups. This is an area that merits future study.

Parental Levels of Education
The research on this factor is limited. Litten et al. (1983) conducted an investigation into the postsecondary plans of high-ability students in six market regions (Baltimore/Washington, DC, Chicago, Dallas/Ft. Worth, Denver/ Boulder, Minneapolis/St. Paul, and San Francisco/Oakland) from which Carleton College attracted students. Using multidimensional scaling they analyzed the characteristics of different market segments in each market region. They found that levels of parental education were positively associated with a preference for private colleges. Gilmour et al. (1978) and Lewis and Morrison (1975), both of whom utilized interview techniques, found that students with college-educated parents applied earlier and to more PEIs. Gilmour et al. (1978) noted that they also made their decision to attend a specific institution earlier. Hearn (1984) concluded that parental education had a positive impact on attending more selective institutions. In total, these studies suggest that as levels of parental education increase, students enter and complete the choice stage earlier and are more likely to choose and attend selective institutions.

Family Residence Characteristics
Where students live may exert a small influence on the choice stage of student college choice. The most thorough discussion of the role of residence is found in

Anderson et al.'s (1972) analysis of student enrollment patterns in separate data sets. Anderson and his colleagues analyzed the postsecondary participation patterns of Wisconsin students between 1957 and 1964; and they also examined SCOPE data (from the states of California, Illinois, Massachusetts, and North Carolina) which contained information about the enrollment patterns of twelfth-graders in 1966. The authors employed multiple-regression techniques to analyze the data. They found a weak association between the presence of a local college option and college attendance. However, SES, parental level of education, student ability, and historical college enrollment patterns in various communities and regions had a larger effect upon enrollment rates than the presence of a nearby two- or four-year institution. Litten et al. (1983) and Lewis and Morrison (1975), as well as two single institution studies (Lay and Maguire, 1980; Muffo, 1987), reported that distance from home was negatively related to the likelihood of student application or enrollment. R. Chapman (1979) concluded that for students applying to Carnegie-Mellon University, distance was irrelevant. Maguire and Lay (1981) used multivariate techniques in their study of the application pool at Boston College and found that students who planned to attend a PEI near their homes were more likely to implement their plans. It appears that residence characteristics have a limited effect on choice. While multi-institution studies suggest that residence characteristics have a small impact, single-institution studies suggest that distance has a stronger effect. Factors such as institutional prestige, selectivity, and drawing power may explain the differences across institutions.

Parental Encouragement
The level of parental encouragement for students appears to be correlated with attendance at more selective institutions. Conklin and Dailey (1981) provide the most persuasive evidence of the importance of parental encouragement. Their findings showed that as the level of parental encouragement increased, the likelihood increased that students would (1) attend a PEI, (2) attend a four year PEI, and (3) attend a selective PEI. Keller and McKewon (1984), in a descriptive study of Maryland National Merit finalists, found that students who planned to enroll in private institutions reported more parental support for their educational plans. Welki and Novratil (1987), in a single-institution study that employed conditional logit analysis, also found that parental preference played an important role in the decision to attend the institution. Litten et al. (1983), in his six-market study of the Carleton College applicant pool, noted similarities between the postsecondary preferences of parents and students. The results, however, concluded that parents did not have an effect upon the final matriculation decision. This does not rule out the possibility that parents influenced students' decisions to consider attending selective institutions such as Carleton.

These studies suggest that parental encouragement plays a role in the choice stage; however, it would appear to be a subtle one which is not currently fully understood. Perhaps the most important parental role comes during the predisposition stage, when parental attitudes greatly influence student aspirations, and during the search stage, when parents may set some of the parameters on net cost and distance from home. During the actual choice stage, parents may not play a central role.

Peer Encouragement and Support
By the time students reach the choice stage, peers do not appear to have an impact. Jackson (1978), in his analysis of NLS data, did not find any relationship between peers and the actual matriculation decision. Gilmour et al. (1978), in his longitudinal study of high school seniors, also reported that peers did not play a role in the decision to attend a specific PEI.

High School Quality
Only one of the studies reviewed examined the relationship between school quality and the choice stage. Falsey and Heyns (1984) concluded that students enrolled in private schools are more likely to enroll in high-status PEIs. They did not control for background characteristics, however, and their findings may be the result of a higher proportion of high-ability and high-SES students attending private schools.

Institutional Attributes
Up to this point in this chapter, the unit of analysis has been the student. Student variables related to predisposition, search, and choice have been examined. This would suggest that PEIs have no impact on the student college choice process. In fact, PEIs have little impact on the predisposition phase. During the predisposition phase students have not sufficiently formulated their postsecondary plans, so that factors such as net cost, size of institution, distance from home, or reputation are not relevant factors. PEIs may, however, have an impact on the search stage; since this stage has not been studied, the effect of institutions on search is unknown. It is likely that students do begin to establish parameters for cost, distance from home, institutional size, specialized programs, and institutional selectivity during the search stage. These probably become important attributes during the search stage, but more research is needed to verify this. Nevertheless, by the time students reach the choice stage, it is clear that their plans are more fully developed and that institutional attributes are important determinants of where students enroll. There is sufficient research on the choice stage to examine some of these institutional attributes.

D. Chapman (1981) described factors such as two- and four-year institutions, academic reputation, size, public or private, and location as "fixed institutional characteristics." Since factors such as public and private, selectivity, and two- and four-year institutions are highly correlated with tuition levels, a discussion of cost is also included. This discussion of cost will focus both on the "list cost" (tuition and fees before financial aid had been awarded) and "net cost" (the cost of attending after financial aid has been awarded). In addition, there are what Hossler (1984) has described as "fluid institutional characteristics," which refer to marketing strategies, offering off-campus programs, and academic program changes designed to attract students. Many studies assert the efficacy of such strategies to attract more applicants and matriculants. For the purposes of this chapter, however, these studies have not been included. Most of these studies rely on anecdotal evidence or lack control groups that permit researchers to assess the effectiveness of such activities. In addition, the literature on this topic would move into a discussion of marketing which is beyond the scope of this chapter. This section will focus on two types of institutional attributes: nonfinancial attributes and financial attributes. Nonfinancial attributes include factors such as academic reputation and social life. Financial attributes include discussions of list and net cost.

Nonfinancial Attributes. A number of studies have been conducted that investigate the characteristics that students rate as most important when they decide to apply to or attend a PEI. Although the precise order of these characteristics varies from study to study, the most frequently mentioned characteristics are listed below in rank order:

1. Special academic programs (major area of study)
2. Tuition costs
3. Financial aid availability
4. General academic reputation/general quality
5. Location (distance from home)
6. Size
7. Social atmosphere

(Sources: Douglas et al., 1983; Bowers and Pugh, 1973; Dahl, 1982; Keller and McKewon, 1984; Konnert and Giese, 1987; Lay and Maguire, 1981; Litten, 1979; Litten et al., 1983; Stewart et al., 1987; R. Chapman and Jackson, 1987).

There are variations in the weighting of these factors by different student populations and for different PEIs. R. Chapman and Jackson (1987) investigated the choice stage of 2,000 academically talented students. Using conditional logit analysis to analyze the data, they concluded that institutional quality was the single most important determinant of the choice stage. Furthermore, they concluded that for high-ability students distance was irrelevant. In their six-market study of academically talented students, Litten et al. (1983) concluded that academic quality had the largest impact on the choice stage. They found, however, that nearness to home, lower costs, and smaller size were also preferred by students in the sample. Keller and McKewon's study of Maryland National Merit Finalists (1984) showed that students planning to attend out-of-state PEIs rated quality as the most important factor in selecting an institution. For students planning to attend an in-state PEI, costs were the most important factor. Leslie et al. (1977) studied the choice stage of 1,000 Pennsylvania high school seniors. They concluded that cost was the most important reason for selecting a PEI among low-income students.

In a study of the applicant pool at Boston College, Lay and Maguire (1980), using factor analysis, determined that the most important factors in deciding who came to Boston College were financial aid (negative), parental preferences, specific academic programs, size, location, and athletic and social activities. In a factor-analytic study of 231 athletes, Mathes and Gurney (1985) found that scholarship athletes placed more emphasis on the academic programs of the institution, while athletes in non-revenue-producing sports placed more emphasis on the coaching staff. In a study of athletes enrolled at colleges in a small college conference that did not award athletic scholarships, Konnert and Giese (1987) indicated that the opportunity to play intercollegiate sports was an important college selection factor for student athletes. Institutional quality and some measure of costs consistently appeared as the two most important reasons that students attend a specific PEI. However, these studies also reveal that there is great variation among students and types of institutions.

Moving beyond the effects of individual institutional attributes, Astin and others (1980) and Zemsky and Oedel (1983) revealed that state policies and the aggregate characteristics of PEIs in a region can influence the choice stage. In states with more generous state scholarship programs, Astin and others (1980) found high school students were more likely to enroll in private PEIs. In addition, students who resided in states with larger private PEI sectors were proportionately more likely enroll in private PEIs. Zemsky and Oedel (1983) also found that in states with a large and diverse range of PEIs, such as Massachusetts, high school students were less likely to attend an out-of-state PEI. It appears that the perceived availability of aid and presence of specific types of PEIs may raise the awareness levels of high school students about postsecondary educational options. Increased awareness may lead to higher attendance rates at all types of PEIs.

Financial Attributes. As already noted in the section on non-financial attributes, students do consider costs when selecting a college in which to enroll. In this section the effects that costs have upon the attendance patterns of different types of students and institutions will be examined. Student self-reports suggest that cost and financial aid are important considerations when applying to a PEI, or when selecting a PEI in which to enroll. Fenske et al. (1979) reviewed several previous studies they had conducted on recipients of Illinois State Scholarships. In 1976–1977, 40% of all of the respondents indicated that they would not have been able to attend the PEI they selected without a state scholarship. An additional 59% indicated that they would not have been able to attend at all without their state aid (pp. 149–151). Fenske et al. estimated that between 15% and 25% would have attended a public instead of a private PEI if they had not had state scholarships (p. 153). Leslie et al. (1977) indicated that only 25% of their sample of Pennsylvania seniors would not have attended any institution without aid. However, 43.5% of those who indicated that they were only able to enroll in a PEI because of aid were low-income students (p. 280). Lam and Hoffman (1979), in a single-institution study, found that students who did not enroll were more likely to report financial reasons as the cause for their nonattendance.

Although student self-reports suggest that financial aid influences the choice stage of student college choice, multivariate studies demonstrate that the relationship between cost and the choice stage is more complex. Dahl (1982) used discriminant analysis to examine the college enrollment patterns of high school graduates in Kentucky. He reported that those seniors who had planned to enroll but did not were more likely to indicate that low cost and financial aid were important factors in their decisions not to enroll. Hearn (1984), in his longitudinal study of high school students, found that the amount of variance in a student's choice of a PEI that was explained by institutional costs was not very high. Jackson (1978) analyzed NLS data using multiple regression and reported that the amount of aid only increased the likelihood of attending a specific institution by 8.5% (p. 566). Using High School and Beyond data in 1986, Jackson again reported similar results. R. Chapman and Jackson (1987) used conditional logit analysis to study the role of financial aid in the choice stage of academically talented students. They concluded that perceived quality has a greater impact on the choice stage than does the net cost. Their findings showed that on the average, the PEIs that students entered were more expensive than the institutions they did not attend. Furthermore, they found that it would have taken $4,000 in financial aid to move a second-choice institution to be the student's first choice, and $6,000 in financial aid to move a third-choice institution to first choice (p. 38). Freeman (1984), using a sample of students from private colleges in the Great Lakes region who had been awarded no-need merit-based aid, reported similar results.[4] Tierney (1980a) used multiple regression to examine the college choice patterns of 6,444 high school students included in the NLS data set. He found that as private institutions offered more aid, the likelihood of students' enrolling in a private PEI increased. Furthermore, he noted that as the tuition gap between public and private PEIs increased, students were more likely to enroll in a public institution.

An analysis of the impact of cost from the perspective of individual institutions, however, presents a somewhat different set of results. Supporting the findings already cited, R. Chapman (1979), who studied the applicant pool at Carnegie Mellon University, reported that cost had no effect on matriculation patterns. Lay and Maguire (1981), as well as Maguire and Lay (1981), in two investigations of the applicant pool at Boston College, found that the amount of aid did influence the matriculation decision of students. They found that better aid offers from competitor institutions resulted in 32% of their applicants' attending those institutions, even though they had rated Boston College as their first choice (p. 83). In a study of the applicant pool at Virginia Technical University, Muffo (1987) used multivariate techniques and concluded that high-ability nonmatriculants were more likely to report better financial aid offers from other institutions. This was especially true of high-ability black students. Litten et al. (1983) and Kehoe (1981) also found that students who (1) initially expressed interest in attending out-of-state PEIs and/or private PEIs, but who (2) also stated concerns about the cost of attendance, were more likely to decide to attend a less expensive private or in-state PEI. R. Chapman and Jackson (1987) indicated that when a high-ability student is undecided among two institutions, $1,000 in aid can shift a student's decision in favor of the awarding institution (p. 38).

By this point it should be evident that the relationship between cost and the choice stage is complex. In the aggregate, it appears that aid is not as important as student perceptions of quality. In fact, in the aggregate, net cost exerts only a modest influence on the choice stage. However, individual institutions do not function in the aggregate, and it appears that aid can make a difference to students who are undecided about two or more PEIs. The challenge for most PEIs is that they lack sufficient information about students to know in advance what the effect of financial aid will be. With the rising use of merit aid (Hossler, 1984), it appears that many institutions have decided to make Type I errors, erring on the side of awarding financial aid in order to attract students even though the additional funds may either not be needed or not be sufficient to move the institution to a first-choice institution. In addition, most of the evidence on the impact of financial aid at the institutional level focuses on high-ability students; little is known about the impact of financial aid upon less talented students.

In total, the choice stage of student college choice is a complex phenomenon which exhibits variation for among students and institutions. Table Four summarizes the correlates of the choice stage.

Process Characteristics of the Choice Stage
Although the correlates of the choice stage provide insights into this stage, the correlates do not adequately describe how students enter and complete it. The

TABLE 4. The Correlates of Choice

Student variables	Strength of association
Ability	Strong; high ability is associated with attending more selective PEIs
Parental encouragement	Strong; positively associated with attending more selective and 4-year PEIs
SES	Strong; positively associated with selectivity
Ethnicity	Moderate; blacks less likely to attend
Parental education	Moderate; students with college educated parents more likely to prefer private PEIs and high-status PEIs
Family residence	Uncertain
High school quality	Weak

Nonfinancial institutional variables	
Academic quality	Strong
Location	Moderate/strong
Financial aid availability	Moderate
Scope of postsecondary system in region	Moderate
Size	Weak
Social atmosphere	Weak

Financial institutional variables	
Net cost	Strong
Receipt of aid	Weak/moderate; depends on student preferences

choice stage has two phases. In the first phase students identify their application set of PEIs. In the second phase students select a PEI to attend. Two qualitative studies of high school seniors provide the most detailed information about this stage (Gilmour et al., 1978; Lewis and Morrison, 1975). The search stage of student college choice ends sometime between the end of the junior year in high school and January of the senior year for most high school students (Lewis and Morrison, 1975).

Stewart et al. (1987), in a retrospective study of freshmen attending Michigan State University, reported that 10% of the students made the decision regarding where they would enroll in their junior year, 70% made the decision sometime during their senior year, and 20% made the decision after their senior year (p. 14). The choice stage begins with a list of the PEIs student's are considering. Students consult a variety of sources while they are evaluating institutions to which to apply. At this point the role of parents and peers diminishes (Gilmour et al., 1978). Cibik (1982), in a descriptive study of high school seniors, found that students were more than twice as likely to report that they alone had the greatest impact on the choice stage (self, 59%; relatives, 21%) (p. 101). Ebberly (1987), however, in a retrospective investigation of freshmen attending Michigan. State University, indicated that students used the following sources of information in evaluating their application set: other college students (77%), friends (72%), high school counselors (70%), and family (61%) (p. 7). Lewis and Morrison (1975) reported that students use global constructs such as size and general quality, as well as specific criteria, such as the quality of the chemistry program, in evaluating PEIs. The reasons for some of the discrepancies reported among other indices are difficult to determine. Sample size and sample representativeness, as well as the types of questions asked, may account for the differences. More systematic research is needed in order to understand how students form and evaluate their application set.

Dahl's (1982) longitudinal study of Kentucky high school seniors, as well as Litten et al.'s (1983) six-market study, shed light on shifts in institutional preferences that take place during this evaluation process. Dahl's (1982) data enabled him to compare stated student preferences with where they actually enrolled. He observed that 75% of all students were involved in a shift among various sectors of postsecondary education (public, private, two-year, and four-year PEIs) in Kentucky (p. 15). Most changers stayed within their stated preference of two- or four-year institutions; however, they shifted either from public to private, from private to public, or from out-of-state to in-state PEIs. Approximately 66% of all changers shifted from the private sector to the public sector (p. 19). Thirty-three percent of the students who planned to enroll in a PEI out-of-state ended up enrolling in-state (p. 21). Only 13% of those students who planned to enroll in two-year PEIs shifted to another sector (p. 21). The public sector had the best holding power: 88.8% of all students who indicated that they planned to enroll in a public four-year institution followed through on those plans (p. 20). Litten et al. (1983) also found change in students' stated plans and actual enrollment patterns. They found that almost 50% of all students who had indicated a preference for private PEIs in February of their senior year expressed a preference for public PEIs by the summer (p. 102). They also reported an even larger group of changers who had shifted from a preference for highly selective institutions to less selective institutions. Although the time frames on the evaluation process are different as a result of the variance in when these data were gathered, Lewis and Morrison (1975) concluded that evaluation was continuous from early October to early April. After April the application set is established for most students.

The application period varies widely for students. Half of all students apply over a seven-week period, one-fourth of all students send in all of their

TABLE 5. The Process Characteristics of Choice

Duration	Fall of senior year to spring of senior year
Key influences	Students perceive choice as their own decision, and also recognize importance of parents and peers
Stability of choice	Moderate to high, though some shifting takes place
Application period	50% send in all applications in a 7-week period; there is great variability for the remaining 50%

applications at the same time, and 10% take 21 weeks to send in their applications (p. 22). Black students apply to more PEIs, are accepted by more PEIs, and are rejected by more PEIs. Women start the application process and end the process earlier than men. Jackson (1986) reports that over 90% of all college applicants are accepted by their top-choice institution; 97% are accepted to one of their top three choices (p. 7). By the end of May, most students have received their acceptance notifications and know where they are going to enroll (Lewis and Morrison, 1975).

As Table 5 demonstrates, the process characteristics of the choice stage appear to be the most logical and straightforward of the three stages. This may indeed be the case, or this may be because more attention has been paid to the process characteristics of this phase. Further research on the process characteristics of this stage, as well as the other two stages, is needed.

Student college choice is a complex phenomenon that has not yet been sufficiently researched using theoretical models and a systematic set of questions. There are a number of questions still to be examined regarding the process characteristics of choice. In addition, the role of financial aid and other institutional characteristics in student college choice is poorly understood. At the end of this chapter these questions will be examined. In the context of the research already reviewed, the next section of this chapter will examine methodological issues and questions of theory development.

SUGGESTED FURTHER DIRECTIONS

This chapter suggests (1) that a three-stage model of student college choice can be a useful conceptual approach for understanding the college choice process and (2) that it illuminates policy options at the federal, state, and institutional level. Although considerable research and numerous models pertaining to the college choice process are in the literature, much work remains to be done. Promising further directions fall into two categories: theory development and suggested further directions for research on the stages of predisposition, search, and choice.

TABLE 6. Important Correlates of Student College Choice

Variable	Predisposition	Search	Choice
Ability	Strong	Strong	Strong
Parental education	Strong	Moderate/strong	Moderate
Parental encouragement	Strong	Strong	Strong
SES	Weak	Moderate	Strong
Institutional characteristics	Weak/none	Weak/moderate	Moderate/strong

The suggested directions for each of these categories are presented in the following subsections.

Theory Development

As evidenced by the econometric, sociological, and combined models of college choice reviewed, considerable attention has been devoted to the identification of factors which may influence the choice process, as well as to the interrelationships among these factors. While these models serve to identify salient factors and their interrelationships, most of these models do not specify how each variable interacts within the model. Few of the combined models have undergone attempts to empirically validate them. The work of Boyle (1966) and Alwin and Otto (1977) is an exception. Both studies attempted to explain how family background characteristics interact with high school and community characteristics, as well as student grades and academic track, to influence the college aspirations of students. Needed are a set of concepts which would seek to explain the interrelationships among the various important factors in the college choice process. The extant models and empirical research reviewed might serve as a foundation for the assessment of concepts or theoretical frameworks obtained from various academic disciplines. Alternately, a grounded theory approach could be used to develop such a framework (Glaser and Strauss, 1967). Using naturalistic data-gathering methods, researchers could build a college choice model based upon observations of high school students.

Theory development might also follow the course of the construction of "middle-range" theories, rather than a general theory of college choice (Merton, 1957). To be specific, middle-range theories could be developed for each stage of the choice process. Some of the combined models examined in this chapter represent initial attempts at this. Middle-range theories for each stage are suggested, as the construction of a parsimonious general theory of college choice capable of empirical validation may be too difficult, if not an impossible task. For example, while parents may play an important role during the predisposition stage, they appear to be less important during the choice stage. In addition, institutional marketing activities have little effect on the predisposition stage, but their importance grows during the search and choice stages.

A "middle-range theory" for each stage of the college choice process should seek to identify the salient factors associated with the outcomes of each stage. At each stage, theory development should focus on policy implications. For instance, it may be that parental encouragement may still explain a large part of the variance at each stage of the process. If stage-based theories, however, only focus on parental encouragement at each stage this fails to identify other potential areas of intervention. If, however, theories and empirical validations of those theories attempt to hold parental encouragement and other background characteristics constant, then the influence of high school activities and curriculum and institutional marketing activities may be more readily observable.

Further Research Directions
Although much research has focused on identifying factors which influence aspirations or a predisposition toward college attendance, further research on this stage of the choice process is needed. Ethnicity has been found to exert a weak influence on predisposition, especially when SES is controlled. The structure of the development of predispositions toward college attendance, however, may be different for minority and majority students. If parents and teachers are less influential for minority students, are there other peers or role models who can serve as effective substitutes for these students? Thus, future research might focus on the development of separate causal models for each ethnic or minority group of interest. Such research would be of assistance in the development of public policy designed to increase the rate of postsecondary attendance of minority students.

As previously indicated, little is known about the correlates of the search stage of the college choice process. Research on this stage should focus on the role of parental education, SES, and student ability in the identification of attributes and valued characteristics which differentiate college alternatives. Moreover, the influence of the characteristics of PEIs in close proximity to the student's residence might also be considered in additional research on the search stage. A related question might also be to examine how ideal images or preferences for college characteristics develop during the search stage. Kotler and Fox (1985) provide a conceptual lead to the process of image formation. They suggest that during the search stage students form images of PEIs which are often based on incomplete information, yet these images influence both the search and choice stages.

Research on the processes involved in the search stage is also recommended. A variety of questions might guide such research. Additional research might seek to identify critical incidents other than taking the PSAT. Such research would build on the work of Lewis and Morrison (1975) and that of Gilmour et al. (1978), which revealed that taking the PSAT or application deadlines were critical incidents which influenced the college choice process. Academic track choices, which take place in the eighth or ninth grade for most high school students, are one possible critical incident. How do parents, counselors, etc., communicate their educational expectations to students? Other questions include: How do students find out about PEIs? How do they go about collecting information about them? How do they discover the relevant attributes to consider when evaluating PEIs?

Although considerable research has addressed factors which are influential in the choice stage of the college choice process, some additional topics of inquiry on this stage are suggested. The influence of institutional characteristics during the choice stage is a question that merits further examination. Of particular importance is the role of institutional image. The importance of the role of image has been identified by Silber et al. (1961) and by Clark et al. (1972) in the choice process. To date, however, image studies have been done at single institutions. As a result we are unable to determine how students both assess image and then weight these assessments to chose a specific PEI. To rigorously test the effect of image on the choice stage, a multiple-institution study including various types of PEIs with diverse images would need to be conducted.

One approach to assessing the influence of institutional image is suggested by the work of Kuntz (1987). In his research, Kuntz applied Coombs's (1964) "ideal point preference model" to the college choice stage. This application involved the comparison of images of PEIs held by students with their vision of an ideal college, the premise being that college preference is a function of the congruence between the ideal college and students' perceptions of a given set of PEI alternatives. The ideal point preference model could be used in assessing the role of institutional image not only in the development of a choice set of institutions, but also in the actual selection of a particular PEI.

Further research on the processes of the choice stage is also suggested. During the choice stage, how do students evaluate their application set? R. Chapman and Jackson (1987) reported that initial quality rankings at the start of the choice stage are the most important factor for high-ability students. Are these findings generalizable to all students? How much variance in the choice stage is explained by institutional marketing and financial aid practices?

In addition to these suggested research directions for the stages of the choice process, some more general topics of inquiry are in need of exploration. Research on the choice process has focused primarily on traditional-age students. Research on college choice for adult students is scarce and descriptive in nature. Given the increasing proportion of adult students enrolled in PEIs, there is clearly a need for more research on this topic. Similarly, little attention has been paid to the college choice process for community college students. Since adult students and students attending community colleges are more likely to be geographically bound, their choice stage may look very different. This population also merits study.

The full range of topics for further research outlined above can be addressed by the emergence of a systematic research line on student college choice. Longitudinal designs using a variety of institutional types should be the cornerstone for such research. Where quantitative approaches are appropriate for addressing this topic, simultaneous control of relevant factors (e.g., parental education, parental encouragement, student grades) should be used. Qualitative methodology may be particularly well suited for research on the process characteristics of each stage of college choice.

CONCLUSIONS

Student college choice is a complex phenomenon. It is not a single event, but the result of a process that begins at an early age for most students with a predisposition toward postsecondary education and ends in the selection of a PEI. For public policy-makers and institutional policy-makers questions of access, equity, and institutional vitality make student college choice a topic worthy of investigation. At each stage of the college choice process, a better understanding of college choice can facilitate more effective policy decisions. At the predisposition stage, the importance of parental encouragement indicates that any efforts to improve postsecondary participation rates should be targeted at parents as well as students. Furthermore, process research on predisposition reveals that most students have made their postsecondary plans by the end of the ninth or tenth grade. Thus, intervention programs need to begin early.

Research on the search stage indicates that developmental events such as taking the PSAT or academic tracking decisions influence the search stage. If public policy-makers wish to intervene during the search stage, the role of these events must be examined. More importantly, the dearth of research on the search stage makes it more difficult for policy-makers to develop intervention strategies. For instance, since little is known about how students identify potential PEIs and evaluate them, the effects of the marketing activities of individual PEIs are uncertain.

During the choice stage, institutional policy-makers can use an enhanced understanding of college choice to improve both marketing activities and student-institution fit. Research on the choice stage provides institutional policy-makers with a reverse lens that enables institutions to see themselves as students see them. This ability to see oneself through students' eyes could be used to recruit prospective students who are more likely to find that the institution meets their expectations.

With respect to marketing, institutional policy-makers can exert some influence by emphasizing quality and cost. Research on the process characteristics of the choice stage also reveals when students begin to apply to and evaluate PEIs. This can be useful information for institutional policy-makers. Nevertheless, many questions regarding the impact of institutional marketing efforts and financial-aid-awarding practices need further examination.

In addition to these applied questions a number of questions remain for the research community to address. This chapter points out the need for "middle-range" theories (Merton, 1957) that can be used to develop theoretical models for each stage of student college choice as well as models for different ethnic and other minority groups. In the search and choice stages, future studies should include large student sample sizes that examine the search and choice stages for multiple PEIs. Longitudinal studies which follow high school students from their early years in high school to their first year after high school would also be beneficial. Given the importance of parental encouragement, such studies should include the parents of the students. At the search and choice stages, causal modeling techniques should be employed that will enable researchers to untangle the interrelationships among a diverse set of variables.

Systematic, theory-driven research on college choice can enhance the accumulated knowledge on student college choice. It can lead to more effective policy decisions at the federal, state, and institutional levels. Students may also benefit from an improved understanding of college choice, which can lead to aid policies, high school guidance activities, and marketing activities that make college more accessible to students and that increase the likelihood of student fit. This would benefit the research community and policy-makers and extend our understanding of postsecondary institutions and students.

NOTES

1. As many as thirteen separate activities were identified by Lewis and Morrison (1975).
2. The income differential between high school graduates, usually computed over a lifetime. For example, an estimated rate of return of 10% indicates that when background characteristics are controlled, the typical college graduate earns 10% more over a lifetime when compared to the typical high school graduate.
3. SEARCH is a service marketed by The College Board in which the names and addresses of potential students are sold to PEIs. PEIs then send these students unsolicited information about themselves. Although ACT and other educational marketing firms also sell prospective student names, the term *search* has become synonymous with this approach to marketing.
4. R. G. Chapman and Jackson (1987) and Freeman (1984) used student samples that (were academically talented. There are no high-quality studies using students of average or below-average ability. As a result, the effects of no-need aid on less talented students are unknown.

REFERENCES

Adkins, D. L. (1975). *The Great American Degree Machine*. New York: McGraw-Hill.

Alexander, K., et al. (1978). *Status Composition and Educational Goals: An Attempt at Clarification*. Washington, DC: National Institute of Education. (ED 160 537)

Alwin, D. F., and Otto, L. B. (1977). Higher school context effects on aspirations. *Sociology of Education* 50: 259–273.

Anderson, C., Bowman, M. J., and Tinto, V. (1972). *Where Colleges Are and Who Attends*. New York: McGraw-Hill.

Astin, A., and others. (1980). *The Impact of Student Financial Aid Programs on Student College Choice*. Washington, DC: Office of Planning. (ED 187 368)

Attanasi, L. (1986). Getting in Mexican-American student's perceptions of their college-going behavior with implications for their freshman year persistence in the university. Paper presented at Annual Meeting of the Association for the Study of Higher Education, San Antonio, March.

Baird, L. L. (1973). *The Graduates: A Report on the Characteristics and Plans of College Seniors*. Princeton, NJ: Educational Testing Service.

Bird, C. (1975). *The Case Against College*. New York: David McKay.

Bishop, J. (1977). The effect of public policies on the demand for higher education. *Journal of Human Resources* 5(4): 285–307.

Blau, P. M. and Duncan, O. D. (1967). *The American Occupational Structure*. New York: Wiley.

Bowen, H. R. (1977). *Investment in Learning: Individual and Social Value of American Education*. San Francisco: Jossey-Bass.

Bowers, T. and Pugh, R. (1973). Factors underlying college choice by students and parents. *Journal of College Student Personnel* 220–224.

Boyer, E. L. (1987). *College: The Undergraduate Experience in America* New York: Harper & Row.

Boyle, R. P. (1966). The effect of the high school on student aspirations, *American Journal of Sociology* 71: 628–39.

Brown, K. G. (1982). Postsecondary plans of high-school seniors in 1972 and 1980: Implications for student quality. Presented at the AIR Forum, Denver, May. (ED 220 060)

Campbell, R., and Siegel, B. N. (1967). The demand for higher education in the United States, 1919–1964. *American Economic Review* 57: 453–499.

Carpenter, P. G., and Fleishman, J. A. (1987). Linking intentions and behavior: Australian students college plans and college attendance. *American Educational Research Journal: 24(1): 79–105*.

Chapman, D. W. (1981). A model of student college. *Journal of Higher Education* 52(5): 490–505.

Chapman, R. C. (1979). Pricing policy and the college choice process. *Research in Higher Education* 10: 37–57.

Chapman, R. C. (1984). Toward a theory of college selection: a model of college search and choice behavior. Unpublished manuscript, Alberta, Canada: University of Alberta.

Chapman, R. C., and Jackson, R. (1987). *College Choices of Academically Able Students: The Influence of No-Need Financial Aid and Other Factors*, Research Monograph No. 10. New York: The College Board.

Chressanthis, G. A. (1986). The impacts of tuition rate changes on college graduate head counts and credit hours over time and a case study. *Economics of Education* 5(2): 205–217.

Chronicle of Higher Education (1978). 16(5, November 13): 8.

Cibik, M. A. (1982). College information needs. *College and University* 57: 97–102.

Clark, B. R., Heist, P., McConnell, T. R., Trow, M. A., and Yonge, C. (1972). *Students and Colleges: Interaction and Change.* Berkeley, CA: Center for Research and Development in Higher Education.

Coelho, G. V., Hamburg, D. A., and Murphey, E. B. (1963). Coping strategies in a new learning environment: A study of the American college freshman. *Archives of General Psychiatry* 9: 433–443.

Coleman, J. S. (1966). Peer culture and education in modern society. In T. M. Newcomb and E. K. Wilson, (eds.), *College peer groups: Problems and Prospects for Research.* Chicago: Aldine.

Conklin, M. E., and Dailey, A. R. (1981). Does consistency of parental encouragement matter for secondary students? *Sociology of Education* 54: 254–262.

Coombs, C. H. (1982). *A Theory of Data* New York: Wiley.

Corazzini, A. J., et al. (1972). Determinants and Distributional aspects of enrollment in U.S. higher education. *Journal of Human Resources* 7: 26–38.

Dahl, R. W. (1982). College attendance and institutional choice. Results from the Kentucky longitudinal study. Paper presented at the Annual Forum of the Association of Institutional Research, Denver, June. (ED 220 227)

Denison, E. F. (1971). In R. W. Wykstra, (ed.) *Human Capital Formation and Manpower Development* New York: Free Press.

Douglas, P., et al. (1983). Factor in the choice of higher educational institutions by academically gifted seniors. *Journal of College Student Personnel* 24: 540–545.

Dresch, S. P., and Waldenberg, A. L. (1978). *Labor Market Incentives, Intellectual Competence, and College Attendance.* New Haven, CT: Institute for Demographic and Economic Studies.

Ebberly, C. G. (1987). Information sources used by high school seniors. Paper presented at the Annual Meeting of the American Association of Counseling and Development, New Orleans, March.

Ekstrom, R. B. (1985). *A Descriptive Study of Public High School Guidance: Report to the Commission for the Study of Precollegiate Guidance and Counseling.* Princeton, NJ: Educational Testing Service.

Elsworth, G., et al. (1982). *From High School to Tertiary Study: Transition to College and University in Victoria.* Hawthorn, Victoria: Australian Council on Education.

Erlich, I. (1975). On the relation between education and crime. In F. J. Juster (ed.), *Education, Income and Human Behavior.* New York, McGraw-Hill.

Falsey, B., and Heyns, B. (1984). The college channel: Private and public schools reconsidered. *Sociology of Education* 57: 111–122.

Fenske, R. H., Boyd, J., and Maxey, E. J. (1979). State financial aid to students: a trend analysis of access and choice of public or private college. *College and University* 54: 139–155.

Fields, C., and LeMay, M. (1973). Student financial aid: Effects on educational decisions and academic achievement. *Journal of College Student Personnel* 14: 425–429.

Freeman, R. (1976). *The Over-educated American.* New York: Academic Press.

Freeman, H. B. (1984). Impact of no-need scholarships on the matriculating decision of academically talented students. Paper presented at the Annual Meeting of the American Association of Higher Education, Chicago, March.

Fuller, W., Manski, C., and Wise, D. (1982). New evidence on the economic determinants of postsecondary schooling choices. *Journal of Human Resources* 17(4): 472–498.

Garfinkel, I., and Haveman, R. (1977). *Earnings Capacity, Poverty and Inequality.* Institute for Research on Poverty Monograph. New York: Basic Books.

Gilmour, J., et al. (1978). *How High School Students Select a College.* Pennsylvania State University. (ED 208 705)

Glaser, B. G., and Strauss, A. L. (1967). *The Discovery of Grounded Theory.* Chicago: Aldine.

Hanson, K. H., and Litten, L. H. (1982). Mapping the road to academia: A review of research on women, men, and the college-selection process. In P. Perun (ed.), *The Undergraduate Woman: Issues in Education.* Lexington, MA: Lexington Books.

Harnqvist, K. (1978). *Individual Demand for Education.* Analytical report. Paris, France: OECD. (ED 159 119)

Hause, J. C. (1969). Ability and schooling as determinants of lifetime earnings, or if you're so smart, why aren't you rich. *American Economic Review* 59: 289–298.

Hearn, J. (1984). The relative roles of academic ascribed and socioeconomic characteristics in college destinations. *Sociology of Education* 57: 22–30.

Hilton, T. L. (1982). *Persistence in Higher Education.* New York: The College Board.

Hossler, D. (1984). *Enrollment Management: An Integrated Approach.* New York: The College Board.

Hossler, D., and Gallagher, K. S. (1987). Studying student college choice: A three-phase model and the implications for policy-makers. *College and University* 2(3): 207–221.

Hossler, D., and Stage, F. (1987). *An Analysis of Student and Parent Data from the Pilot Year of the Indiana College Placement and Assessment Center.* Bloomington: Indiana College Placement and Assessment Center.

Hossler, D., and Stage, F. (1988). Family and high school experience factors' influence on the postsecondary plans of ninth grade students. Paper presented at the Annual Meeting of American Education Research Association, New Orleans, April.

Jackson, G. A. (1978). Financial aid and student enrollment. *Journal of Higher Education* 49: 548–574.

Jackson, G. A. (1982). Public efficiency and private choice in higher education. *Educational Evaluation and Policy Analysis* 4(2): 237–247.

Jackson, G. A. (1986). MISSA, the fall of Saigon, and college choice, 1972 to 1980. Paper presented at the Annual Meeting of the Association for the Study of Higher Education, San Diego, February.

Jencks, C., et al. (1972). *Inequality: A Reassessment of the Effects of Family and Schooling in America.* New York: Basic Books.

Johnson, R. H., and Chapman, D. W. (1979). An assessment of college recruitment literature: Does the high school senior understand it? Presented at Annual Forum of the Association of Institutional Research, San Diego, June. (ED 174 079)

Kehoe, J. J. (1981). Migrational choice patterns in financial aid policy making. *Research in Higher Education* 14(1): 57–69.

Keller, M. J., and McKewon, M. P. (1984). Factors contributing to postsecondary enrollments decisions of Maryland National Merit Scholarship Semifinalists. Paper presented at Annual Meeting of the Association for the Study of Higher Education, Chicago.

Kohn, M. G., Manski, C. F., and Mundel, D. (1976). An empirical investigation of factors influencing college going behaviors. *Annuals of Economic and Social Measurement* 5(4, Fall): 391–419.

Kolstad, A. J. (1979). The influence of high school type and curriculum on enrollment in higher education and postsecondary training. Paper presented at the Annual Meeting of the American Educational Research Association, San Francisco, April. (ED 173 627)

Konnert, W. and Giese, R. (1987). College choice factors of male athletes at private NCAA Division III institutions. *College and University* 63(1): 23–48.

Kotler, P. (1976). Applying marketing theory to college admissions. In *A Role for Marketing in College Admissions*. New York: The College Entrance Examination Board.

Kotler, P. and Fox, K. (1985). *Strategic Marketing for Educational Institutions*. Englewood Cliffs, NJ: Prentice-Hall.

Kuntz, S. S. (1987). A study of student's cognitive structure for colleges. Paper at the Annual Meeting of the American Educational Research Association, Washington, DC, April.

Lam, J., and Hoffman, D. (1979). The study of sequential student participation in University in a changing environment. Manitoba, Canada: Brandon University. (ED 198 785)

Lay, R., and MaGuire, J. (1980). Identifying the competition in higher education. *College and University* 56(1): 53–65.

Lay, R. and Maguire, J. (1981). Coordinating market and evaluation research on the admissions rating process. *Research in Higher Education* 14(1): 71–85.

Leslie, L. L., et al. (1977). The impact of need-based student aid upon the college attendance decision. *Journal of Education Finance* 2: 269–286.

Leslie, L. L., and Brinkman, P. T. (1986). Rates of return to higher education: An intensive examination. In J. Smart (ed.) *Higher Education: Handbook of Theory and Research* Vol. III. New York: Agathon Press.

Lewis, G. H., and Morrison, J. (1975). *A Longitudinal Study of College Selection* Tech. Report No. 2. Pittsburgh: School of Urban Public Affairs, Carnegie-Mellon University.

Litten, L. H. (1982). Different strokes in the applicant pool: some refinements in a model of student college choice. *Journal of Higher Education* 53(4): 383–402.

Litten, L. H. (1986). Perspectives on pricing. In D. Hossler (ed.), *Managing College Enrollments*, New Directions of Higher Education, No. 53. San Francisco: Jossey-Bass.

Litten, L. H., et al. (1983). *Applying Market Research in College Admissions*. New York: The College Board.

Maguire, J., and Lay, R. (1981). Modeling the college choice process. *College and University* 56(2): 123–139.

Manski, C. F., and Wise, D. A. (1983). *College Choice in America*. Cambridge, MA: Harvard University Press.

Mare, R. D. (1980). Social background composition and educational growth. *Demography* 16: 55–71.

Marini, M. M., and Greenberger, E. (1978). Sex differences in educational aspirations and expectations. *American Education Research Journal* 15(1): 67–79.

Mathes, S., and Gurney, G. (1985). Factors in student athletes' choices of colleges. *Journal of College Student Personnel* 26: 327–333.

Mattila, J. P. (1982). Determinants of male school enrollments: A time series analysis. *Review of Economics and Statistics* 64: 242–251.

Mayer, R. R., and Greenwood, E. (1980). *The Design of Social Policy Research* Englewood Cliffs, NJ: Prentice-Hall.

Merton, R. K. (1957). Priorities in scientific discovery. *American Sociological Review* 2: 635–659.

Miller, I. (1983). Higher education: The demography of opportunity. *Journal of College Admissions* 101: 10–13.

Miller, P. W., and Volker, P. A. (1985). On the determination of occupational attainment and mobility. *The Journal of Human Resources* 20(2): 197–213.

Muffo, J. A. (1987). Market segmentation in higher education: A case study. *Journal of Student Financial Aid* 17(3): 31–40.

Murphy, P. E. (1981). Consumer buying roles in college choice. *College and University* 57: 141–150.

Nolfi, G. J. (1978). *Experiences of Recent High School Graduates.* Lexington, MA: Lexington Books.

Parents, Programs and Pennsylvania Student Plans (1984). Harrisburg: Pennsylvania Association of Colleges and Universities.

Parrish, R. E. (1979). *Survey of Educational Goals: Ocean County High School Juniors and Seniors, Spring 1979*, Report 78-79-05. Toms River, NJ: Ocean County College. (ED 179–255)

Perlman, R. (1973). *The Economics of Education: Conceptual Problems and Policy Issues.* New York: McGraw-Hill.

Peters, W. B. (1977). *Fulfillment of Short-Term Educational Plans and Continuance in Education.* Washington, DC: National Center of Educational Statistics.

Powers, S., and Douglas, P. (1985). Gender differences in selecting of an institution of higher education: a discriminant analysis. *Psychological Reports* 56: 295–278.

Radner, R., and Miller, L. S. (1970). Demand and supply in U.S. higher education: a progress report. *American Economic Review* 30: 327–334.

Rumberger, R. W. (1982). Recent high school and college experiences of youth: Variations by sex, race and social class. *Youth and Society* 13: 449–470.

Russell, C. N. (1980). *Survey of Grade 12 Sudents' Postsecondary Plans and Aspirations.* Manitoba, Canada: Department of Education, September. (ED 201 225)

Schultz, T. W. (1961). Educational and economic growth. In N. B. Henry (ed.), *Social Forces Influencing American Education.* Chicago: National Society for the Study of Education.

Sewell, W. H., Haller, A. O., and Ohlendorf, G. (1971). The educational and early occupational status attainment process: replication and revision. *American Sociological Review* 35: 1014–1027.

Sewell, W. H., Haller, A. O., and Portes, A. (1969). The educational and early occupational attainment process. *American Sociological Review* 34: 82–92.

Sewell, W. H., and Hauser, R. M. (1975). *Education, Occupation and Earnings: Achievement in Early Career.* New York: Academic Press.

Sewell, W. H., and Shah, V. P. (1978). Social class, parental encouragement, and educational aspirations. *American Journal of Sociology* 3: 559–572.

Sewell, W. H., et al. (1972). The educational and early occupational status attainment process: replication and revision. *American Sociological Review* 40(1): 1014–1027.

Silber, E., et al. (1961). Competent adolescents coping with college decisions. *Archives of General Psychiatry* 5: 517–527.

Solmon, L. C., and Taubman, P. J. (1973). *Does College Matter?* New York: Academic Press.

Soper, E. L. (1971). *A Study of Factors Influencing the Postsecondary Educational Plans of Utah High School Students.* Washington, DC: National Center for Educational Statistics.

Spaeth, J. L. (1967). Occupational prestige expectations among male college graduates. *American Journal of Sociology* 73(5): 548–558.

Spiegleman, R. G. (1968). A benefit/cost model to evaluate educational programs. *Socio-economic Planning Sciences* 1: 443–460.

Spies, R. (1978). *The Effects of Rising Costs on College Choice. A Study of the Application Decision of High Ability Students.* New York: The College Board.

Stage, F., and Hossler, D. Differences in family influences on college attendance plans for male and female ninth graders. *Research in Higher Education* 30: 3.

Stewart, N. R., et al. (1987). Counselor impact on college choice. Paper presented at the Annual Meeting of the American Educational Research Association, Washington, DC.

Tierney, M. (1980a). Student college choice sets: Toward an empirical characterization. Paper presented at the Annual Meeting of the Association for the Study of Higher Education, Washington, DC, March.

Tierney, M. (1980b). The impact of financial aid on student demand for public/private higher education. *Journal of Higher Education* 51: 527–545.

Tillery, D. (1973). *Distribution and Differentiation of Youth: A Study of Transition from School to College.* Cambridge, MA: Ballinger.

Tillery, D., and Kildegaard, T. (1973). *Educational Goals, Attitudes and Behaviors: A Comparative Study of High School Seniors.* Cambridge, MA: Ballinger.

Trent, J., and Medsker, L. (1967). *Beyond High School: A Psychological Study of 10,000 High School Graduates.* San Francisco: Jossey-Bass.

Tuttle, R. (1981). *A Path Analytical Model of the College Going Decision.* Boone, NC: Appalachian State University. (ED 224 434)

Update. (1986, January). A report from the Washington Office of the College Board. Washington, DC: The College Board.

Welki, A. M., and Novratil, F. J. (1987). The role of applicant's perceptions in the choice of college. *College and University* 62(2): 147–160.

Williams, T. W. (1984). Recruiting graduates: Understanding student institutional fit. In D. Hossler (ed.), *Enrollment Management: An Integrated Approach.* New York: The College Board.

Willingham, W. W. (1970). *Free Access to Higher Education.* New York: The College Board.

Yang, S. W. (1981). Rural youth's decisions to attend college: aspirations and realizations. Paper presented at the Annual Meeting of the Rural Sociological Association, Guelph, Ontario, July. (ED 207 765)

Young, M. E., and Reyes, P. (1987). Conceptualizing enrollment behavior. *Journal of Student Financial Aid* 17(3): 41–49.

Zemsky, R., and Oedel, P. (1983). *The Structure of College Choice.* New York: The College Board.

Undergraduate Socialization: A Conceptual Approach

John C. Weidman
University of Pittsburgh

There has been a continuing interest in the study of the ways in which colleges affect the cognitive and affective lives of their students, during the years of enrollment (Pace, 1979; Chickering et al., 1981; Komarovsky, 1985; Katchadourian and Boli, 1985) as well as the years beyond college (Newcomb et al., 1967; Withey, 1971; Solmon and Taubman, 1973; Hyman, Wright, and Reed, 1975; Bowen, 1977; Winter, McClelland, and Stewart, 1981). The primary focus of the bulk of these works has been on identifying individual outcomes, both cognitive and affective, that can be attributed to college attendance. While often comprehensive in their treatment of research on college impact (e.g., Feldman and Newcomb, 1969; Astin, 1977), most of these works tend to focus on description of outcomes and do not deal explicitly with the development of comprehensive theoretical explanations for their occurrence or the building of conceptual frameworks. In part, this is because some of the more influential conceptualizations are fundamentally psychological and emphasize personality rather than social structural constraints (Feldman, 1972).

This pattern has continued into the current decade. In their systematic classification of research on college students during the period from 1969 to 1983, Kuh et al. (1986) found that only 10.8% of the articles published annually had a primary emphasis on theory development (i.e., establishing "causal relationships among sets of variables"). A mere 6.6% of the articles published annually dealt with concept integration (i.e., the production of "new knowledge about college students through analysis and integration of existing ideas"). These authors suggest that researchers have become comfortable with the extant

This is a revised version of a paper presented at the 1987 Annual Meeting of the Association for the Study of Higher Education, Baltimore, Maryland. The author is indebted to John Bean, Kenneth Feldman, Ludwig Huber, Patrick Terenzini, and Wagner Thielens for helpful comments on the manuscript, and to Charles Bidwell for stimulating consideration of many of the central notions upon which this conceptualization is based.

models of student development (e.g., Chickering, 1969) and that the difficulties of building new theoretical models outweigh the efficacy of relying on models that are already widely accepted.

Consequently, the purpose of the present chapter is to extend the body of research and thought on college impact by developing a comprehensive conceptual framework for understanding some salient elements of the socialization process as it occurs in higher education. The framework builds from both psychological and social structural conceptions, drawing upon sociological notions of the socialization process in adolescence and adulthood (e.g., Mortimer and Simmons, 1978; Brim, 1966) as well as more traditional approaches to addressing the importance of social structure in socialization and personality development (Hurrelmann, 1988). The background section traces briefly the pattern of research on college impact historically and identifies important sets of variables appearing in some of the more influential contemporary research on college impact. It is argued that this work, while specifying important variables and testing causal relationships among variables, could be more oriented toward theoretically explicating in a comprehensive fashion the underlying processes of college impact on students focusing particularly on nonintellective outcomes (e.g., Weidman, 1979, 1984). Because an extensive review of the cognitive dimensions of college impact has already been written (Pascarella, 1985a), this section is concerned primarily with affective dimensions of college impact, especially influences of college on students' values, personal goals, and aspirations. Important conceptual dimensions of the socialization process are discussed, paying particular attention to those characteristics of both individuals and institutions that are likely to enhance the influence of college on students.

A conceptual framework for understanding the undergraduate socialization process is developed in the third section of this chapter. The framework incorporates consideration of socializing influences experienced by undergraduates from a variety of sources, both within and external to the postsecondary educational institution. Particular emphasis is placed on social structural aspects of socialization, rather than on individual processes of dealing with socializing influences, not because the latter are any less important but because they are not under the control of postsecondary educational institutions and, hence, are not as "policy-relevant." More interpretive perspectives that focus more on the individual student's perceptions of the college environment (Huber, 1980) and less on structural aspects of socialization are incorporated, where appropriate, in developing the conceptualization. Attention is also paid to special student populations (e.g., women, minorities, and returning adults). The chapter concludes with a discussion of the implications of this conceptual framework for future research, for the design of collegiate institutions as agencies of socialization, and for students seeking to make informed choices about the types of colleges that are most appropriate for them.

BACKGROUND

At least one major study of the ways in which college students' lives are influenced during their years of enrollment has been published in each decade since the 1940s. Among the earliest was the study of young women attending Bennington College that was published by Theodore Newcomb (1943). As a social psychologist, Newcomb was interested in learning about the apparently liberalizing influence of attendance at the reputedly avant-garde Bennington College on the values of young women from Brahmin, decidedly conservative New England families. Interest in collegiate influences on undergraduates continued with research in the 1950s at another eastern women's college, the "Vassar studies," which were directed by another social psychologist, Nevitt Sanford. This work led to the publication of the first volume encompassing a broad spectrum of perspectives, many but not all based upon the Vassar research, on various aspects of the undergraduate experience (Sanford, 1962).

Another group of researchers, this time more sociologically oriented, was also doing related work during the 1950s on changes in undergraduates' orientations during college, the "Cornell Values Study." A major emphasis in this study was the study of changes in career choices and occupational values which built on the seminal work of one of the researchers, Morris Rosenberg (1957). Initially, the reports on this research suggested that the college experience had little, if any, influence on undergraduates' values (Jacob, 1957). The fully elaborated report (Goldsen et al., 1960) did, however, show specific types of college-related value changes.

During the 1960s research on college impact burgeoned, and by the end of the decade, the first systematic review and synthesis of this work was published by another sociologist, Kenneth Feldman, and his mentor, Theodore Newcomb. The Feldman and Newcomb (1969) book provided, for the first time, a sociologically oriented review of the then-extant college-impact literature. Also of great significance was the major theoretical analysis of college student development published by the psychologist Arthur Chickering (1969). More recently, Chickering (1981) has edited a lengthy volume updating such predecessors as Sanford (1962) and Feldman and Newcomb (1969).

Somewhat less well known than the works that have thus far been mentioned is a series of studies that were published in the 1960s by sociologists at the National Opinion Research Center (NORC) of the University of Chicago. Several lines of research are particularly noteworthy. The first involved a large national survey of June 1961 college graduates and focused on various aspects of their collegiate experience. James Davis (1964, 1965) published two volumes that explored the major and career choices of undergraduates along with their aspirations for postcollegiate careers. Not surprisingly, some of the items from the Cornell Values Study appeared on this survey. A second is represented in research on Catholic colleges written by Father Andrew Greeley (1967). A third is a survey study of virtually all of the undergraduates attending a single, small, liberal arts college in the Midwest published by Walter Wallace (1966).

In addition, NORC sponsored the publication of a set of papers dealing with various aspects of peer relationships among college students that was edited by two of the participants in a pair of 1959–1960 conferences at which they were originally presented, Theodore Newcomb and Everett Wilson (1966). Given the sponsorship by a survey research center, it is expectable that several chapters in this volume dealt with methodological issues in the study of college students. There were also, however, several conceptual chapters, among them one by Burton Clark and Martin Trow in which they presented their fourfold typology of college student subcultures (academic, collegiate, nonconformist, and vocational).

Finally, one of the most influential lines of empirical research on college students began with the inauguration in 1966 of a national survey of entering college freshmen by Alexander Astin, then at the American Council on Education. This annual survey has continued to the present and has been used for numerous empirical studies, quite a few of which are incorporated into Astin (1977). Not only did Astin maintain his own survey program, but he also joined forces in 1969 with Martin Trow under funding from the Carnegie Foundation for a follow-up of respondents to his first four freshman surveys, the results of which were published in a volume edited by Trow (1975).

Contemporary research on college impact has tended to draw upon conceptual frameworks (e.g., Chickering, 1969; Tinto, 1975; Astin, 1977; Weidman, 1984; Smart, 1986; Smart and Pascarella, 1986) that include at least four general sets of variables: (1) student background characteristics; (2) college characteristics; (3) measures of students' linkages to the college environment; and (4) indicators of "college effects." The first set of variables, students' background characteristics when they enter college, includes, for example, (a) social status indicators such as parental income and education, sex, and race; (b) ability and achievement indicators such as test scores and high school class rank; and (c) indicators of personal orientations such as career choices, values, goals, and aspirations prior to matriculation.

Characteristics of the collegiate environment experienced by students can be exemplified by (a) organizational variables such as type of control, size, and quality; (b) indicators of the academic environment such as curricular emphases, the student's major, and expectations held by faculty for student performance in class; and (c) indicators of the extracurricular environment such as residence arrangements, availability of campus organizations, and both formal and informal student activities. The third set, indicators of students' linkages to the organizational, academic, and extracurricular dimensions of the college environment, includes (a) interaction with faculty and peers; (b) amount of time spent studying; (c) involvement in campus life; and (d) both social and academic integration. Finally, "college effect" variables include values, career choices, and personal goals. In longitudinal studies, data on these variables tend to be collected upon entrance to college and then at some later point during the undergraduate years. Studies reflect wide variation in the time interval between college entrance and the subsequent data collection points (ranging from once or twice during college to many times, and sometimes even extending into the postcollege adult years).

When data on the same college effect variables are collected in succeeding years, the most recently collected data become the dependent variables, with previous measures then becoming additional independent variables since current status is generally dependent upon one's previous status on a particular indicator. Appropriately operationalized, these four sets of variables can provide a reasonably accurate portrait of several important aspects of the longitudinal process of college impact.

Research so conceived is especially useful for identifying the types of college effects that occur, the types of students likely to be affected by college attendance, the academic and extracurricular dimensions of colleges that are related to observed effects, and the types of student involvement in campus life that are associated with various dimensions of college impact.

This sort of approach does little, however, to clarify and explain in any systematic fashion the reasons why effects occur. Authors seldom develop and adequately operationalize a conceptual framework to explain the relationships among the variables. Rather, they rely either on intuitive use of *post hoc* conceptual frameworks or on reference to personal experience.

An intuitive approach provides a convenient opportunity for researchers to build an agenda for future research since explanations tend to incorporate unmeasured variables that are posited to be necessary for a fuller understanding of the college effects under investigation. It does not, however, necessarily lead to a systematic understanding of the underlying social processes that bring about college impact. If knowledge of how colleges influence their students is to be extended, researchers on college impact should begin to pay closer attention to identifying and operationalizing the specific social and interpersonal mechanisms that transmit and mediate the influences of the college environment. These conceptual variables can then guide empirical research.

In the next section of the chapter, several conceptual dimensions of the socialization process that are especially important for explaining college impact are discussed. These dimensions are then used to develop a comprehensive framework for understanding undergraduate socialization.

THE SOCIALIZATION PROCESS

Brim (1966) defines socialization as "the process by which persons acquire the knowledge, skills, and dispositions that make them more or less effective members of their society" (p. 3). While society may be viewed as a generalized social structure composed of smaller units (e.g., families, friends, organizations) within which people behave, it can also be thought of as being composed of groups, "each having a distinct subculture" (Clausen, 1968, p. 4). Hence, socialization involves the acquisition and maintenance of membership in salient groups (e.g., familial, occupational, organizational) as well as society at large. Consequently, socialization can always usefully be considered from the perspective of the society (or its constituent groups) as well as the individual. In order to understand socialization more clearly, it is important to identify social patterns of influence affecting individuals and groups. This is done in the present chapter by focusing on the part played by social relationships in the establishment and maintenance of expectations for appropriate member behavior (i.e., norms) and group integration. Dimensions of general socialization theory are then extended to the specific case of undergraduate socialization.

Norms and Social Integration

From the societal perspective, "socialization efforts are designed to lead the new member to adhere to the norms of the larger society or of the particular group into which he is being incorporated and to commit him to its future" (Clausen, 1968, p. 6). Norms are important for understanding the process of socialization because, according to Hawkes (1975), "a norm may be conceived loosely as a rule, a standard, or a prescription for behavior . . . that is in some way enforced . . ." (p. 888). Norms provide the basic standards for the regulations of individual behavior in groups as well as in the larger society (Hawkes, 1975, p. 888). Social integration, from this perspective, refers to the extent to which the society or subunit (e.g., institution, organization, group) is characterized by a shared acceptance of common norms that are reflected in solidary, cohesive, and reasonably stable patterns of relationships among its constituent parts (Parsons, Shils, and Olds, 1951, pp. 202–204).

From the perspective of the individual, socialization involves learning the appropriate (i.e., normative) modes of "social behavior and/or role enactment" within the groups in which membership is desired (Mortimer and Simmons, 1978, p. 422). *Role*, in this sense, refers to the "dynamic aspects" (Linton, 1936, p. 14) of positions or statuses in the group "and may be defined by the expectations (the rights, privileges, and obligations) to which any incumbent of the role must adhere" (Getzels, 1963, p. 311). *Social integration*, from the perspective of the individual, refers to the extent to which an individual's behavior in groups is characterized by willing acceptance of group norms and solidary relationships with other members. In terms of socialization, the more fully integrated an individual is into a group, the greater is that group's capacity for ensuring a reasonably high level of normative compliance among members.

This is not to say, however, that socialization is a completely deterministic process over which the individual being socialized has little or no control. On the contrary, as individuals mature and move toward the assumption of adult roles, there can be considerable flexibility both in the expectations held of new role incumbents and in the variety of ways in which roles may be fulfilled acceptably (Mortimer and Simmons, 1978, p. 424). This suggests the importance of incorporating both objective and subjective dimensions when explaining the socialization process (Hurrelmann, 1988). Futhermore, as individuals move toward adulthood, participation in the settings in which socialization occurs tends to be increasingly voluntary. Hence, individuals who do not find the normative expectations in a setting to their liking or who are not welcomed by members may attempt to seek other settings which are more commensurate with personal orientations.

Reference Groups and Social Relationships

An important step in understanding undergraduate socialization is to identify those sources of influences that are likely to be the most salient for particular students. Reference group theory is especially useful for identifying potentially important sources of socializing influences. According to Kemper (1968, p. 32) a reference group can be a person, group, or collectivity that an individual takes into account when selecting a particular course of action from among several alternatives or "in making a judgement about a problematic issue."

A particularly salient social mechanism for the transmission and processing of socializing influences in reference groups is interpersonal relationships, especially, but not limited to, those which involve close friendships (Shibutani, 1955, p. 568). According to Brim (1966), this process can be described as follows: "the individual learns the behavior appropriate to his position in a group through interaction with others who hold normative beliefs about what his role should be, and who reward or punish him for correct or incorrect actions" (p. 9).

Anticipatory Socialization

General pressures of at least two sorts operate simultaneously during college. First, students frequently have to make choices concerning their activities after completion of college. Second, students need to identify and then to prepare for attaining desirable goals. This process is called *anticipatory socialization*, i.e., "the acquisition of values and orientations found in statuses and groups in which one is not yet engaged but which one is likely to enter" (Merton, 1968, pp. 438–439). Anticipatory socialization prepares individuals for future positions, although much of the preparation is, according to Merton (1968), "implicit, unwitting, and informal" (p. 439).

For many undergraduates, one of the main tasks during college is to make decisions (some certainly more tentative than others) about the type of career or career preparation to pursue upon graduation. Students attempt to determine not only their own suitability for various occupations (both in terms of academic skills and perceived job demands) but also the reactions of significant others to their choices. Colleges, in addition to providing the education and credentials necessary for access to professional, managerial, and upper white-collar occupations, also provide experiences and resources for students to develop more generalized orientations toward work and leisure activities. In this sense, the undergraduate college serves as a context for anticipatory occupational socialization involving the concomitant influences of students' values and occupational aspirations because, according to Rosenberg (1957), "in addition to people choosing an occupation in order to satisfy a value, they may choose a value because they consider it appropriate for the occupational status they expect to fill in the future" (p. 24). The choice of an academic major is a central component of this process.

Temporal Aspects of Socialization

These processes of socialization do not apply only to the late-adolescence/early-adulthood period of life that is characteristic of most undergraduates. Socialization is considered to be a lifelong process that occurs as individuals adapt themselves to a variety of changing circumstances (Bragg, 1976, p. 6), not the least of which are changes in career demands, family responsibilities, and possibly even the employment structure. There are differences, however, in the basic content of socialization (ranging from the regulation of biological drives to specific group norms), the contexts in which socialization occurs (ranging from the dependent status of the child to the organizational settings of adulthood), and the responses of individuals (ranging from the very malleable child to the change-resistant adult) to socializing influences (Mortimer and Simmons, 1978, p. 423). During college, the passage of four years in the life of a late adolescent can result in considerable maturation that may influence receptivity to socialization influences. In fact, going through college as a late adolescent has been shown to have several similarities to a "rite of passage" (Tinto, 1987; Van Gennep, 1960; Kett, 1977). Collegiate institutions are, however, enrolling increasing numbers of undergraduates who are not late adolescents but "nontraditional," adult students who have a very different adaptation to make, including things like juggling family demands or financial exigencies (Bean and Metzner, 1985; Weidman and White, 1985; Metzner and Bean, 1987). They also tend to have much clearer personal and career goals than late adolescent undergraduates. Hence, studies of undergraduate socialization should take into account differences in the age and developmental stages of students.

A second consideration has to do with the duration of influence. Curtis (1974) has shown, for instance, that the socialization potential of an educational institution increases with the amount of time that a student spends enrolled. The sequential nature of certain types of socialization processes is also important. As formulated by Thornton and Nardi (1975), taking on a role can be described as moving through four stages: anticipatory, formal, informal, and personal. In each stage, there is "interaction between individuals and external expectations, including individuals' attempts to influence the expectations of others as well as others' attempts to influence individuals" (Thornton and Nardi, 1975, p. 873).

The first of these stages corresponds to anticipatory socialization. The formal stage occurs when the individual begins to assume the specific demands of the role, meeting the group's official or proclaimed expectations of the role. The informal stage occurs when the individual learns the unofficial or informal expectations for the role and adapts behavior accordingly. In the personal stage, the individual reconciles the formal and informal expectations with personal orientations, assumes full membership in the group, and begins to participate in the group's processes of shaping the expectations that will be held subsequently for new role incumbents.

Summary

Three components of the socialization process are particularly salient for the study of college impact: (1) individual, group, and organizational sources of socializing influences; (2) social processes (both inter- and intrapersonal interaction, social integration) through which these sources of socializing influences are encountered and responded to by students; and (3) resultant socialization outcomes in various college settings. This approach to understanding undergraduate socialization suggests two basic questions about the socialization of individuals in an organizational environment. One pertains to social interaction: What are the interpersonal processes through which individuals are socialized? The other pertains to organizational structure: What are the various characteristics of higher education institutions as socializing organizations that exert influences on students? The importance of considering both individual and organizational characteristics in studying socialization can be explained as follows: "Just as individuals may become differently socialized because of differences in past experience, motivations, and capacities, so may they become differently socialized because of differences in the structure of the social settings in which they interact" (Wheeler, 1966, p. 54).

The essence of this approach as it applies to the relationships among individual and organizational variables in the study of undergraduate socialization can be summarized as follows: Just as students differ in their patterns of interaction and personal orientations upon entrance, colleges differ in their structuring, intentionally or not, of both normative contexts such as student residences and classrooms, and of opportunities for social interaction among college students, faculty, and staff. Furthermore, because socialization occurs over a period of time and is a cumulative process, the relative importance of both settings and significant others may change during the course of the undergraduate years. Hence, it is essential that conceptualizations of undergraduate socialization incorporate the longitudinal aspects of change and stability over four (and often more) years.

The following sections of this chapter elaborate a conceptual framework and apply it to different aspects of undergraduate socialization. Consideration is given to the special problems of women, minorities, and nontraditional students as well as to those aspects of undergraduate socialization that persist through the life course.

UNDERGRADUATE SOCIALIZATION: A CONCEPTUAL FRAMEWORK

Figure 1 shows the conceptual framework developed for this chapter. The framework is intended to contribute to theoretical understanding of collegiate impact and, more generally, to understanding of socialization in organizations. Underlying this framework, on one level, are concerns for the situational and individual developmental constraints on the choices made by participants in an organizational environment. On another level, the framework explores a set of socialization processes, concentrating largely on the impact of normative contexts and interpersonal relations among an organization's members. It includes consideration of the joint socializing impacts of (1) student background, (2) the normative influences exerted by the academic and social structure of the college through the mechanisms of both inter- and intrapersonal processes, and (3) the mediating impacts of both parental socialization and non-college reference groups during college despite influences brought to bear upon students by participation in the more immediate campus social structure.

The framework is not, however, intended to be exhaustive. Dimensions and variables other than those which appear could be included, depending upon the particular interests of researchers. The framework is based primarily upon the author's own research (Weidman, 1984, 1989; Weidman and Friedmann, 1984; Weidman and White, 1985) as well as the conceptual work of Chickering (1969), Tinto (1975, 1987), and Astin (1977, 1984).

Briefly, the model was designed with several general considerations in mind. As has already been mentioned, it is concerned primarily with noncognitive *Socialization Outcomes*. Of considerable importance among these outcomes is career choice, a process which involves not simply the selection of a career field but also an assessment of the implications of particular occupations for "a style of life and a place in the community status system" (Beardsley and O'Dowd, 1962, pp. 606–607). With respect to *Student Background Characteristics*, the sociological literature on status attainment has demonstrated the necessity of

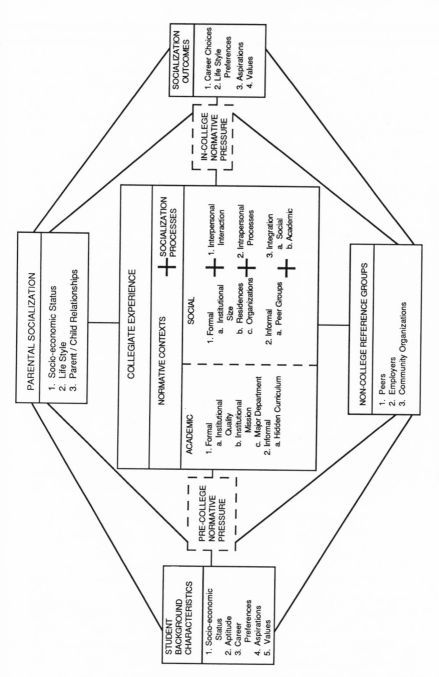

FIGURE 1. A CONCEPTUAL MODEL OF UNDERGRADUATE SOCIALIZATION

including family socioeconomic status, academic aptitude or ability, and aspirations in studies of occupational attainment because such background characteristics have been shown consistently to be related to outcomes (Alexander and Eckland, 1975; Hauser, Tsai, and Sewell, 1983). Astin (1977) also demonstrates the importance of including student background in studies of college impact.

The selection of conceptions for inclusion in the *Collegiate Experience* box is based largely on the work of Chickering (1969), who identifies six dimensions of college life that influence student development: (1) clarity and consistency of institutional objectives; (2) institutional size; (3) curriculum, teaching, and evaluation; (4) residence hall arrangements; (5) faculty and administration interaction with students; and (6) friends, groups, and student culture. Tinto's (1975, 1987) work suggests the importance of dividing *Normative Contexts* into an "academic" and a "social" component. Further differentiation into a "formal" and an "informal" part is suggested by Sanford (1962, p. 40). The within-in box boundaries do not have solid lines because they are assumed to be rather fluid.

With respect to *Socialization Processes*, the large "pluses" are used to indicate that normative influences can be transmitted to students through several mechanisms. In the conceptual model of dropout from higher education developed by Tinto (1975), goal commitments, aspirations, and values held at entrance to postsecondary education are posited to affect students' academic performances (grades and intellectual development) and social life (peer-group and faculty interactions) within the institution. Students' decisions to continue or drop out reflect the extent of their "academic integration" and "social integration" within the institution. This integration, in turn, influences subsequent institutional goal commitments as well as assessments of the personal importance of those commitments. Such subjective assessments of experiences in college (e.g., satisfaction, fulfillment of expectations) may be said to reflect "intrapersonal processes" (Weidman and White, 1985).

Because typical educational institutions are not encapsulated environments, it is reasonable to assume that performance in college may be affected by the student's ability to cope with problems at home and other community settings (Weidman and Friedmann, 1984; Weidman and White, 1985; Bean and Metzner, 1985). Atkin's (1982) finding that dropout among first-year college students is related to concern with "family/personal problems" also supports this extension of the framework, as does Tinto's (1982) acknowledgement that his model did not "seek to directly address the impact of financial stress or other forces external to the institution's immediate environment (e.g., external peer groups in an urban environment)" (p. 688). Hence, the present conceptual framework includes consideration of *Noncollege Reference Groups*. In addition, it includes *Parental Socialization* (Weidman, 1984) because it is assumed that such influences are present throughout the college years, even for those students who are independent householders.

In Figure 1, dotted lines appear around the two *Normative Pressure* boxes because they represent influences that tend to be either unmeasured or inaccurately measured in research on undergraduate socialization. Generally, this type of influence is inferred from patterns of joint covariation among variables constituting the college context. That is, inferences about the direction and intensity of normative pressures to which a student is exposed are based on observed relationships among characteristics of their collegiate experience and interpersonal linkages, especially interaction with faculty and peers and other types of participation in formal and informal aspects of college life. The model suggests that, in order to understand "normative pressure" more fully, persisting influences of both "parental socialization" and "noncollege reference groups" must be taken into consideration.

Finally, the dimensions of the model shown in Figure 1 are assumed to be linked in a bidirectional, as opposed to a unidirectional, causal fashion. It is assumed that there is a reciprocity of influences on undergraduates such that, during the college years, various dimensions can have greater or lesser importance for socialization, depending upon the outcomes considered as well as the particular stage both of students' lives and of their undergraduate experience.

To summarize the general conceptual framework, undergraduate socialization can be conceived of as a series of processes whereby the student: (1) enters college as a freshman with certain values, aspirations, and other personal goals; (2) is exposed to various socializing influences while attending college, including normative pressures exerted via (a) social relationships with college faculty and peers, (b) parental pressures, and (c) involvement with noncollege reference groups; (3) assesses the salience of the various normative pressures encountered for attaining personal goals; and (4) changes or maintains those values, aspirations, and personal goals that were held at college entrance. In the following sections, the dimensions of the framework are described in more detail. Specific attention is also paid to illustrating some of the more important linkages among dimensions.

Parental Socialization

Explicit in this framework is the recognition that the college campus does not, for most undergraduates, constitute a totally encapsulated environment. Parents, for example, influence the career preferences and orientations that students bring with them at college entrance (Winch and Gordon, 1974; Bengston, 1975). Furthermore, since the effects of parental socialization are so very likely to persist during the course of the student's college years, parental pressures and expectations may serve to mediate the impact of college experiences. Consequently, if the susceptibility of students to the socializing influences of the campus environment is to be determined, it is also necessary to assess the importance of parent-child relationships. Two questions are suggested by this approach: How are various aspects of parental socialization and lifestyles related to the persistence and change of undergraduates' orientations and preferences? How do aspects of the collegiate experience and parental socialization interact with one another in influencing the student during college?

In studies of career development, parental influences have been continuously identified as important contributing factors (Borow, 1966). Sociological research consistently shows that occupational attainment is related to such measures of parental social status as occupational prestige and educational attainment (Blau and Duncan, 1967; Alexander and Eckland, 1975). Other studies indicate that occupational values concerning autonomy in work are associated with a middle-social-class position as measured by educational and occupational status, and that these values are transmitted by parents to their offspring (Kohn, 1977; Morgan, Alwin, and Griffin, 1979; Mortimer, 1974, 1976).

Parental influences appear to be somewhat more important for the precollege socialization of black than white students. For black undergraduates, mothers tend to be very important influences on both college and career choices (Smith, 1981).

While there are strong correlations between such variables as parental lifestyle and career orientations of college freshmen (Weidman, 1984) and parental expectations for freshmen and college persistence (Bank, Slavings, and Biddle, 1986), there is also evidence that parental influences decline in importance during college so that by senior year the correlations between parental characteristics and career choices are no longer significant (Weidman, 1984). This suggests an important temporal dimension to parental influence, with parents decreasing in importance during the college years, especially for those undergraduates who leave their parents' homes to attend college.

It should also be noted, however, that finding no significant parental influences on the career choices of college seniors (Weidman, 1984) may be an artifact of the measures used which were based on students' self-reports of parental characteristics, expectations, and behavior. Studies (Davies and Kandel, 1981; Looker and Pineo, 1983) suggest that adolescents may systematically underestimate the importance of parental influences on aspirations. These authors demonstrate the importance of obtaining information about their attitudes and behavior directly from parents instead of relying solely on reports by adolescents of their parents' influence.

Noncollege Reference Groups

In addition to relationships with parents, undergraduates are likely to maintain ties of various sorts to significant others outside the collegiate environment. In the case of nontraditional students, especially those older than their early twenties, there may be the competing demands of employers and the students' own families at home (i.e., spouses and children) as well (Simpson, 1979; Bean and Metzner, 1985; Weidman and White, 1985). There may also be ties to churches and community organizations that can shape responses to collegiate influences. The support of noncollege significant others, including friends and other relatives (e.g., aunts and uncles, siblings, cousins, in-laws), is also important for older students (Bean, 1985; Weidman and White, 1985) as well as for minority students (Thomas, 1981; Nora, 1987) who have to cope with many competing expectations and, hence, are exposed to potentially conflicting normative pressures.

Student Background Characteristics
Characteristics of individuals that tend to be correlated with specific types of outcomes must be included in any conceptualization of the undergraduate socialization process. The contribution of student background characteristics to understanding college impact is investigated in at least three primary sources of literature: (a) research examining the broad spectrum of college effects on students (Feldman and Newcomb, 1969; Astin, 1977); (b) research on dropouts from higher education (Tinto, 1975; Pantages and Creedon, 1978; Lenning, 1982; Pascarella and Terenzini, 1980; Pascarella and Chapman, 1983); and (c) research on the sociology of status attainment (Sewell, Haller, and Portes, 1969; Sewell, Haller, and Ohlendorf, 1970; Alexander and Eckland, 1975; Jencks, Crouse, and Mueser, 1983; Hauser, et al. 1983). Figure 1 includes five examples of background characteristics which are not meant to be an exhaustive list, but rather illustrate categories that appear frequently in research. Socioeconomic status generally refers to the parents of the students and is most often measured by some combination of the parents' annual income, educational attainment, and occupational prestige (e.g., Duncan, 1961). Parents' education has been shown to exert a particularly strong influence on the college choices of black students (Litten, 1982).

Aptitude is an indicator of the student's academic ability and is most often measured by standardized test scores (e.g., SAT or ACT). Preferences, aspirations, and values held by students prior to college enrollment form the perspectives and expectations held by students prior to enrollment and shape their encounters with the higher education institution, especially early in the undergraduate years. These orientations also may be shaped by the collegiate experience and subsequently shape postcollege attainment. In fact, respondents to a large National Opinion Research Center sample of college graduates stated that their entering plans were a more important influence on ultimate career choice than their in-college grades (Spaeth and Greeley, 1970, pp. 171–172).

Precollege Normative Pressure

Parental socialization, the influence of significant others who are not part of the collegiate environment, and students' background characteristics combine to become crucial determinants of the student's susceptibility to institutional influences early in college. This same combination also influences the patterns of coping that students use to meet the new demands of college. It is assumed that the student entering college as a freshman cannot be considered to be a *tabula rasa*. Rather, prior experiences with family and significant others who are not members of the college community continue to generate normative pressures that shape students' expectations of and responses to their new environment.

Collegiate Experience

Socialization in college may be thought of as a process that "entails a continuing interaction between the individual and those who seek to influence him" (Clausen, 1968, p. 3). Socialization, in this sense, "does imply that the individual is induced in some measure to conform willingly to the ways of . . . the particular groups to which he belongs" (ibid. p. 4). Undergraduate socialization can thus be viewed as a process that results from the student's interaction with other members of the college community in groups or other settings characterized by varying degrees of normative pressure.

This portion of the conceptual framework draws heavily from the seminal structural-functional analysis of American universities by Parsons and Platt (1973). Specifically, the framework focuses on two aspects of their argument as it relates to undergraduate socialization. One has to do with what they term the "moral authority of institutions" (Parsons and Platt, 1973, p. 167). This refers to the normative order (including its mission as well as normative expectations of faculty and staff for students) of the college or university as a potent agent of socialization. The various aspects of a collegiate institution's normative order may then be studied by identifying social contexts (e.g., colleges or particular college groups) that are characterized by especially strong expectations for students. In Chickering's (1969) terms, the greater the "clarity and consistency of objectives," the stronger the normative consensus among members of a particular institution, organizational unit, or group within the institution. The second aspect of the Parsons and Platt (1973) discussion has to do with interpersonal relationships among various members of academic settings. According to Parsons and Platt, these interpersonal attachments make an important contribution to the members' social integration within the college.

Furthermore, interpersonal relationships contributing to the social integration of students into the academic system are related not only to the attainment of institutional goals but also to the personal goals of individual students (Tinto, 1975). Close, personal relationships among members of normative contexts contribute materially to the transmission and internalization of normative influences by members (Moore, 1969). Hence, in studying college student socialization, it is important to explore the impacts of normative contexts as well as the ways in which interpersonal relationships among members serve to either reinforce or counteract the normative influences exerted within various specific contexts (Lacy, 1978).

Following Tinto (1975), Figure 1 divides *Normative Contexts* into an *Academic* and a *Social* dimension. The academic dimension refers to those aspects of the collegiate environment that contribute explicitly to the fulfillment of educational objectives (as stated in the institutional mission), including such things as allocation of resources for and organization of instruction, and student selection in the admissions process. The social dimension refers to the ways in which opportunities for interaction among members are organized and clustered within the institution. The academic and social dimensions are further subdivided into "formal" and "informal" components, as suggested by Sanford (1962, p. 49). Formal structures are those designed to achieve the various stated objectives of the organization, generally built around a system of written rules and procedures. Informal structures tend to evolve as individuals adapt their own personal needs and expectations to the demands of the formal structure. Informal structures are characteristically more fluid and organized according to implicit rather than explicit rules and procedures. To understand undergraduate socialization, both the formal and informal aspects of normative contexts need to be investigated along with their relationships to one another.

Normative Contexts: Academic

Institutional and within-institution program quality, though fraught with problems of definition and measurement (Conrad and Blackburn, 1985), continues to be of considerable interest to scholars, policy makers, and consumers of higher education. The "frog-pond effect" (Davis, 1966; Reitz, 1975) suggests that college selectivity decreases students' preferences for seeking educationally high-level careers, largely because the competition between highly able students is greater than in less selective institutions. Other studies (Bassis, 1977; Drew and Astin, 1972), however, found positive effects of selectivity on aspirations and self-evaluations.

More selective institutions tend also to emphasize providing students with a broad liberal education rather than being narrowly job-focused, and thus are more likely to reflect normative pressures that encourage the development of values and aspirations that encompass broader facets of adult life (e.g., use of leisure time, cultural preferences, participation in community affairs) than simply career and income. Solmon and Wachtel (1975) found institutional quality as measured by levels of resource allocation to be positively associated with postcollege career income. Institutional reputation or prestige, often used as the primary measure in studies of quality, has also been shown to be related to both college completion and access to elite careers (Kamens, 1974).

The mission of an institution of higher education provides the statement of institutional purpose that drives resource allocation and establishes educational objectives (Meyer, 1970, 1972). The mission provides a frame of reference both for the student in choosing a particular college and for other external constituencies, especially employers, interested in making judgments about the qualifications of graduates. Institutional mission may also be reflected in affiliation with a religious denomination (Greeley, 1967). The nature of the socializing environment in religiously affiliated institutions can be characterized as follows:

> Studies have indicated that religious-affiliated colleges present the kind of setting that is most conducive to change of any sort. They are small, allowing for more personalized interaction of students and faculty. They have a higher degree of homogeneity in student social background than most colleges. They have a high degree of normative integration, and structural characteristics (residentiality) that support that integration. (Anderson, 1985, p. 323).

A particularly important locus of both faculty and peer influences on students is the academic department (Hearn, 1980; Hearn and Olzak, 1981; Weidman, 1979, 1984). Practically all postfreshman students have some affiliation with an academic department, since it tends to be the organizational unit through which degree requirements are formulated and certification of their successful completion is made. Vreeland and Bidwell (1966) assert that the department "has relatively well-defined goals and expectations for students, and commands powerful normative and utilitarian sanctions" (p. 238). These authors argue that the socializing impacts of the department are determined by the expressed goals of the faculty for undergraduate education, which, in turn, determine faculty behavior and expectations for students. They identify three areas of faculty emphasis or goals for undergraduate education: providing a broad, liberal education; providing occupational training; and mixed goals, where both are emphasized.

The academic department can be a powerful source of normative influences on student majors, in large part because of the faculty's ability to differentially reward students for their performance in courses, through both the assignment of grades and the encouragement of social interaction (Parsons and Platt, 1973, p. 179). Faculty evaluation of student's performances in class-related activities as well as in other settings can be a significant influence on students' goals and aspirations. In fact, for influences on students' career orientations within the department, major field faculty appear to be more important than major field peers (Phelan, 1979; Weidman, 1984). This may vary, however, by the level of the student. Freshmen, for instance, appear to be more susceptible to peer than faculty influence (Bean, 1985; Bank et al., 1986; Biddle, Bank, and Slavings, 1986). As students pass through the college years faculty may become more salient agents of socialization. It is likely that faculty influence is strengthened by faculty members' increasing contribution to the process of anticipatory socialization for significant adult roles as students concentrate on work in their major fields (Weidman, 1984). There is also evidence that differences in the orientations of students across major fields actually become sharper during the college years, thus suggesting that there are potent socializing influences exerted by major departments (Feldman and Weiler, 1976).

It is also important to remember that the department is part of a larger organization. Consequently, there may be socializing effects of interaction in nondepartmental settings within the college that either add an increment to or even cancel out the department's influences.

On the informal side, the "hidden curriculum" (Snyder, 1971) of higher education can also be a powerful source of influence on students. This term refers to the unspoken and unwritten rules defining faculty expectations for students' academic performance. Do tests, for instance, actually reflect what faculty say is important? Similarly, it could also refer to the unwritten rules of academic behavior as well as to other informal norms about what is acceptable as defined by students (Becker, Geer, and Hughes, 1968).

Normative Contexts: Social
Another important dimension here is the formal extracurricular structure of the college. Presumably, those students who participate actively in extracurricular activities may be more likely than their nonparticipant counterparts to look to peers or college staff who supervise the extracurricular activities rather than to departmental faculty as normative referents. It is also possible that the norms held by the extracurricular staff and peers differ from those held by departmental peers and faculty.

The spatial location, especially on- vs. off-campus, of reference groups can also affect their potential for socialization. The importance for socialization of participation in on-campus activities has been described by Vreeland and Bidwell (1965) as contributing to the power of the college to influence students because "the broader the scope of the student's involvement with the college, the more accessible he is to intervention and the more diverse the mechanisms that can be employed (especially mechanisms of indirect manipulation)" (p. 235). Consequently, limited student involvement with on-campus reference groups is likely to reduce the impact of normaive pressures exerted by a college. This has clear implications for examining differential socialization in residential and commuter institutions (Chickering, 1974; Pascarella, 1984).

There is also a relationship between the social climate of a living group and members' academic performance (Schrager, 1986). According to Blimling (1988), living in on-campus residence halls tends to increase students' satisfaction with college, increase participation in extracurricular activities, and improve retention.

It is, however, important to differentiate membership groups from reference groups. For instance, it is inappropriate to assume that students from the same residence will necessarily constitute each other's reference group(s). In a classic study of college women, Siegel and Siegel (1957) manipulated choice of residence location by deliberately assigning subjects to nonpreferred locations. The authors discovered that attitude change was greatest when subjects adopted "the imposed, initially non-preferred membership group as their reference group" (p. 364).

Socialization Processes: Interpersonal Interaction
An important determinant of the socialization potential of social relationships is the degree of intensity of feelings and other affective attachments between the people involved, namely, their sentiments (Homans, 1950, pp. 37–40). Another critical aspect of interaction is its frequency. The more frequently an individual interacts with specific others, the more he or she is exposed to their attitudes, values, and opinions. Furthermore, as Homans (1961, p. 182) argues, there is often a direct relationship between frequency of interaction with another person and liking that person. Homans (1961, p. 187) does not, however, assert this proposition without a qualification, which is that sentiments exchanged may be so negative that frequent interaction may lead to aversion rather than attraction between those involved. These notions of frequency and sentimental intensity of interaction are basic components underlying this conceptual framework. It is assumed that interaction involving frequent, primary relationships is more likely to have socializing impacts than interaction involving infrequent, impersonal relationships.

An emphasis on norms and social relationships in the academic department has been incorporated into this model for several reasons. First, primary social relationships have already been discussed as contributing to the social integration of and, consequently, to the potential normative pressure exerted on members by groups. Second, as Shibutani (1955) asserted, "socialization is a product of a gradual accumulation of experiences with certain people, particularly those with whom we stand in primary relations" (p. 568). Finally, both students and faculty tend to feel that the most enduring academic impacts of college attendance result from social interaction between faculty and students outside the formal classroom setting (Thielens, 1966; Wilson et al., 1975; Pascarella, 1980; Winteler, 1981). Availability of these opportunities may be a significant enhancer of collegiate influences on students.

Socialization Processes: Intrapersonal Processes

Another aspect of the student's collegiate experience included in this framework involves his or her subjective assessment of that experience. As one critic of the structural-functional interpretation of socialization has argued (Wrong, 1961), socialization encompasses both the transmission of norms and the individual processing of normative influences that result in the development of unique personal orientations to social contexts. Not surprisingly, there is a considerable literature dealing with the related phenomenon of "person-environment interaction" at college (Stern, 1970; Walsh, 1973; Moos, 1979). The general question raised by this approach is: How do the individual's perceptions of participation in various segments of the collegiate environment affect the socialization potential of the college? Put in a somewhat different way, the concern is with assessing whether or not favorable student attitudes about various aspects of the collegiate experience enhance the college's impact.

Several dimensions of students' perceptions of their colleges are of interest here. One is student satisfaction with college. In their extensive literature review, Feldman and Newcomb (1969, pp. 94–95) cited four studies of student satisfaction with college that suggest some variability in student satisfaction at different points during college. Sophomores reported the lowest levels (60% satisfied) and seniors reported the highest levels (more than 80% satisfied). This suggests that seniors have accommodated themselves better to the demands and expectations of their college, quite possibly reflecting the socializing influence of the campus over time. Another dimension that enhances the institution's socialization potential is the students' images of college, especially when they encompass subjective assessments of the college's contribution to the attainment of personal goals (Weidman and Krus, 1979).The student's perceived "fit" or subjective assessment of his or her degree of social integration into the life of the institution is a related dimension of interest in the conceptual framework.

Socialization Processes: Integration

Tinto (1975) described social integration into campus life as being due primarily to interaction with college faculty, administration, and peers as well as participation in extracurricular activities. He suggested that these relationships resulted in varying degrees of affiliation of the student with the college "that modify his educational and institutional commitments" (p. 107). There also continues to be a considerable amount of empirical research using Tinto's model (Ethington and Smart, 1986; Terenzini et al., 1985; Terenzini and Wright, 1986). Perhaps not surprisingly, patterns of results are somewhat different for studies of minority students than they are for studies of white students (Fox, 1986; Nora, 1987).

Social integration, particularly as it relates to primary social relationships with faculty and peers in the transmission of normative influences, has already been discussed. However, there are several other implications of social integration for student socialization. With respect to students' assessments of impersonal treatment on campus, the expectation is that the less favorable the student is in his or her perceptions of the college environment, the less likely that student is to be socialized toward the norms of the college. In addition, students' subjective assessments concerning suitability for careers and their willingness to participate in the formal occupational structure of society are important. There is an expectation that those students who question their ability to develop meaningful careers will also shy away from aspiring to high-status, demanding occupations.

Academic integration refers to the extent to which students accept faculty expectations for their academic performance as legitimate and behave accordingly. Most studies have tended to use grades as a primary indicator of academic integration, but it is certainly not uncommon for those students whose grades are not outstanding to perceive expectations to be appropriate and to embody academic norms.

In-College Normative Pressure

An examination of the socializing effects of normative pressure, expressed as either change or reinforcement of values, and transmitted by departmental members through primary social relationships is of considerable importance. It should also be noted that, while change in student orientations is often an expected outcome, reinforcement of already present student orientations may just as legitimately be expected (Feldman, 1969). Therefore, it is important to pay attention to the absence of observed change as well as significant change during college because both may imply college impact.

This approach parallels the work of Vreeland and Bidwell (1966, pp. 241–242), who posit three conditions that contribute to socialization of students toward departmental norms: faculty interest in undergraduate teaching; student/ faculty interaction measured on two dimensions, intimacy and frequency; and faculty and student norms that are "consistent and reinforcing." One way to determine faculty and student norms is to examine the goals of each for attaining such outcomes of a college education as vocational training, development of values, learning an academic discipline, intellectual enlightenment, or general education. The similarity between faculty and student educational goals can provide important information about the potential effect of faculty norms on either maintenance or change in students' incoming orientations.

Vreeland and Bidwell (1966, p. 254) suggest that the departmental faculty's collective conception of goals for undergraduate education conditions the faculty's conception of the instructional task. This, more than specific subject-matter content, determines the social organization of departmental student-faculty interaction. These authors systematize the structure of departmental faculty influence by dividing faculty goals for undergraduate education into two categories: technical and moral. Technical goals concern occupational preparation and the intellectual structure of an academic discipline. Moral goals concern the ethical practice of an occupation and the broadening or humanizing effects of education. According to this formulation, the expressed goals of faculty for undergraduate education determine faculty behavior and expectations, which, in turn, determine the socializing effects of the department.

Concerning the direction of impact, Vreeland and Bidwell (1966) suggest not only that different patterns of change occur as a function of faculty conceptions of the instructional process, but also that some values are more likely than others to be influenced by either technical or moral goals. Student values concerned with extrinsic rewards of occupational participation (income, status, recognition from colleagues) would be more likely to be influenced positively by technical rather than moral goals. Values concerned with individual creativity or interpersonal relationships, on the other hand, would be more amenable to positive influence by moral rather than technical goals.

Intensity of influence can refer both to the overall importance among faculty of a particular goal and to the consistency of faculty sentiments, i.e., the extent of agreement among faculty on the goals for undergraduate instruction. Consequently, in assessing potential departmental impact, both the general importance of a particular instructional goal and the level of consensus among faculty on the goal's importance should be assessed. Vreeland and Bidwell (1966) classified academic departments at Harvard according to the degree of consensus among faculty on moral and technical goals. Departments having high faculty consensus on technical goals included physics, chemistry, Germanic and Slavic languages, engineering, music, mathematics, astronomy, psychology, and philosophy. Departments having high faculty consensus on moral goals included architectural science, classics, government, economics, history, and fine arts. Departments having low consensus because various faculty members held different goals included romance languages, biology, anthropology, English, geology, and social relations.

A different approach to the analysis of the normative pressures exerted in various academic departments is the Environmental Assessment Technique (EAT) developed by Astin and Holland (1961; Astin, 1963; Holland, 1966). Taking research on the psychology of vocational choice as his basepoint, Holland (1966) developed a scheme classifying occupations in terms of six personality types: realistic, intellectual, social, conventional, enterprising, and artistic. Using these six modal types, Holland (1966, 1985) classified the normative pressures of major field environments according to the vocational preferences and personality orientations of the people in them. Some majors assigned to each of the types include the following: realistic-agriculture, industrial arts, engineering, and forestry; intellectual—mathematics, philosophy, physical science, and anthropology; social—education, nursing, psychology, American civilization, sociology, and social work; conventional—accounting, economics, finance, and business education; enterprising—history, international relations, political science, industrial relations, business administration, and management; and artistic—art and music education, fine and applied arts, English and journalism, and foreign languages and literature.

The usefulness of Holland's classification has also been verified cross-culturally in a study of environments in both British and Canadian universities (Richards, 1974). More recently, Smart (1985) used the Holland typology to study the extent to which major field environments reinforce students' values. He affirms the importance of focusing on organizationally and normatively well-defined units within the larger institution when studying college effects. Again, it should be pointed out that there are racial differences in major choice, especially among males, with whites more likely to choose "intellectual" majors and blacks more likely to choose "enterprising" majors (Braddock, 1981).

In the foregoing discussion of departmental climates, some general patterns appear that are useful in developing an understanding of undergraduate influence processes. Humanities departments tend to be populated by faculty and students who are concerned with intellectual activities, creative endeavors, and the development of values and ethical standards. Occupational value orientations among humanities majors tend to cluster in the area of intrinsic rewards rather than extrinsic rewards, with a moderate "people" orientation. Science and mathematics departments, while also high on members' intellectual orientations, are likely to be high on career orientation and occupational training as well. These areas will probably be relatively high on students' orientations toward both intrinsic and extrinsic rewards, with relatively low "people" orientations. Compared with other science departments, engineering departments are likely to have students somewhat lower on intrinsic reward orientation, somewhat higher on extrinsic reward orientation, and about the same on "people" orientation. Majors in the social sciences, particularly economics and political science, appear to have the highest extrinsic reward and people orientations, and the lowest intrinsic reward orientations. Faculty tend to be less favorably oriented to the pursuit of extrinsic rewards than students, especially in the humanities and social sciences, where little direct occupational training is provided and large numbers of graduates enter occupations unrelated to their majors.

Socialization Outcomes

The outcomes listed in Figure 1 are a few of the more important ones that have been of continuing concern to higher education scholars, especially as they reflect outcomes that are important both for adult life following college and for their potential contribution to societal well-being (Davis, 1965; Spaeth and Greeley, 1970; Bowen, 1977). While the continuing interest in research on status attainment among sociologists has already been noted, there is also something of a resurgence of interest in the higher education literature that investigates the effects of colleges on occupational attainment (e.g., Smart and Pascarella, 1986; Smart, 1986).

Patterns and Trends

It could be argued that the outcomes of undergraduate socialization during any particular time period are as much a function of the characteristics, values, and aspirations of the students as they are of the socialization processes that occur during college. Certainly, there is considerable documentation of the changes in career orientations over the past few decades, with a general increase in students' interest in obtaining specific occupational skills in college rather than a broad, liberal arts education (Hoge, 1976; Levine, 1980). While this trend holds for both sexes, women have made even greater changes in their career orientations then men, with women now aspiring to combine careers with marriage and family responsibilities (Regan and Roland, 1982). There are also rather different patterns of career socialization for women than for men (Bressler and Wendell, 1980; Perun, 1982; Eisenhart, 1985; Eccles, 1986).

Rather different patterns of college experiences also have been documented for minority students (Willie and Cunnigen, 1981; Thomas, 1981; Astin, 1982; Nettles, Thoeny, and Gosman, 1986). Racial tensions on predominantly white campuses were documented by Peterson et al. (1978) which apparently have surfaced again in the late 1980s. Problems of social and academic integration have also been well documented for minority students (Fox, 1986; Nora, 1987). This suggests that it is necessary to adapt conceptual frameworks to the differing patterns of socialization that may be represented among specific ethnic and gender groups.

Persistence over the Life Course

On another level, there is some limited evidence about the persistence of changes in values that occur during college. Interestingly, most of these studies have focused on political values and/or activities (Newcomb et al., 1967; DeMartini, 1983; Wieder and Zimmerman, 1976; Fendrich, 1976). A key factor in the maintenance of political activism after college appears to be the extent to which those views and behavior are supported by significant others, especially husbands of Bennington women (Newcomb et al., 1967) and employers. A study of students who attended universities in one of the major centers of civil rights protest during the early 1960s posited the following explanation for the persistence of white student activism:

Those adults who have remained free of the occupational commitments to money, status, and security continue to be political activists. Activists have pursued careers in work environments that either tolerate or encourage commitment to values different from the traditional extrinsic rewards (Fendrich, 1976, p. 96)

DeMartini (1983), in reviewing seven studies of white activists, also concludes that "maintenance of dissident political values is consistent with full integration into adult social roles" (p. 214). Black activists in the Fendrich (1976) study were similar to white activists in that those who valued extrinsic rewards the least were also more active in protest politics. The main racial difference was that black activism tended to focus almost exclusively on "the one-issue politics of advancing the race" (p. 97).

Finally, for those college activists whose fundamental values were learned from parents, the persistence of these values into adulthood can be construed to be an extension of the parental socialization process (DeMartini, 1983). In the case of more extreme behavior such as movement into the student counterculture, students withdraw from participation in major conventional roles, often separating from both parents and college in favor of peer support (Wieder and Zimmerman, 1976).

DISCUSSION AND POLICY IMPLICATIONS

The emphasis in the foregoing has been on the conceptual aspects of the complex processes of undergraduate socialization. To test empirically the framework that has been developed would require that variables be identified and then operationalized so that they can be measured. While that responsibility lies with the researcher, interested readers can see Lenning (1983) or Endo and Bittner (1985) for long lists of potential variables and Pascarella (1985a) for a discussion of some of the measurement problems involved in operationalizing variables. In addition, appropriate statistical techniques would have to be chosen because the model represents multidirectional processes rather than unidirectional causality.

There is, however, one measurement concern of particular importance. Throughout the discussion, it has been emphasized that the characteristics of specific normative contexts should be related as directly as possible to the student, preferably by identifying a linking mechanism of socialization. One of the best examples of a study that accomplished this linking is the study of undergraduates at a small, midwestern, liberal arts college that was done by Wallace (1966). He used sociometric techniques to quantify each undergraduate's "interpersonal environment," aggregating the questionnaire responses from each individual on campus who was named as being a friend of the student. Large sample survey research is not, however, always amenable to such techniques, especially since confidentiality of responses is often of great concern. It may then be necessary to settle for more general measures of membership group attachments based on friendship or interaction not tied to specific individuals.

The research by Holland (1985) and Smart (1985) suggests very strongly that the distribution of majors within an institution is an important factor in shaping the pattern of influence exerted by the institution. Currently, as colleges jump on the bandwagon and expand majors in business and career-oriented technical fields, there are consequences for the normative pressure on students. When normative pressures gravitate against the liberal arts, the character of an institution can very well change. The framework presented here calls attention to the various normative pressures exerted by different types of majors.

There is also evidence suggesting that first institutional impressions, beginning with freshman orientation, are very important for the anticipatory socialization of undergraduates (Pascarella, Terenzini, and Wolfle, 1986). Consequently, it is in the best interests of colleges to structure orientations in ways that maximize the development of student commitments to the institution, including providing an early opportunity for interaction with faculty.

Finally, the temptation should be resisted to assume that a framework dealing with affective dimensions of undergraduate socialization has no relevance for studies of the "value added" by college to cognitive knowledge and skills. In fact, academic learning can (and should) be reinforced by the sorts of participation in normative contexts that have been discussed. It is unfortunate that much of the current research on student academic learning relies on rather simplistic theories of student learning that tend to exclude the range of variables represented in the framework developed for this chapter.

REFERENCES

Alexander, K. L., and Eckland, B.K. (1975). Basic attainment processes: a replication and extension. *Sociology of Education* 48: 457–495.

Anderson, K. L. (1985). College characteristics and change in students' occupational values: socialization in American colleges. *Work and Occupations* 12: 307–328.

Astin, A. W. (1963). Further validation of the Environmental Assessment Technique. *Journal of Educational Psychology* 54: 217–226.

Astin. A. W. (1977). *Four Critical Years: Effects of College on Beliefs, Attitudes, and Knowledge*. San Francisco: Jossey-Bass.

Astin. A. W. (1982). *Minorities in American Higher Education*. San Francisco: Jossey-Bass.

Astin, A. W. (1984). Student involvement: a developmental theory for higher education. *Journal of College Student Personnel* 25: 297–308.

Astin, A. W., and Holland, J. L. (1961). The Environmental Assessment Technique: a new way to measure college environments. *Journal of Educational Psychology* 52: 308–316.

Astin, A. W., and Panos, R. J. (1969). *The Educational and Vocational Development of College Students*. Washington, DC: American Council on Education.

Atkins, N. D. (1982). College student performance, satisfaction, and retention. *Journal of Higher Education* 53: 32–50.

Bank, B. J., Slavings, R. L., and Biddle, B. J. (1986). Effects of peer, faculty, and parental influences on student retention. Paper presented at the meeting of the American Educational Research Association, San Francisco, April.

Bassis, M. S. (1977). The campus as a frogpond: a theoretical and empirical reassessment. *American Journal of Sociology* 82: 1318–1326.

Bean, J. P. (1985). Interaction effects based on class level in an explanatory model of college student dropout syndrome. *American Educational Research Journal* 22: 35–64.

Bean, J. P., and Metzner, B. S. (1985). A conceptual model of nontraditional undergraduate student attrition. *Review of Educational Research* 55: 485–540.

Beardsley, D. C., and Dowd, D. D. (1962). Students and the occupational world. In N. Sanford (ed.), *The American College: A Psychological and Social Interpretation of the Higher Learning* (pp. 597–626). New York: Wiley.

Becker, H. S., Geer, B., and Hughes, E. C. (1968). *Making the Grade: The Academic Side of College Life*. New York: Wiley.

Bengston, V. L. (1975). Generation and family effects in value socialization. *American Sociological Review* 40: 358–371.

Biddle, B. J., Bank, B. J., and Slavings, R. L. (1986). Norms, preferences, and retention decisions. Paper presented at the meeting of the American Educational Research Association, San Francisco, April.

Blau, P. M., and Duncan, O. D. (1967). *The American Occupational Structure*. New York: Wiley.

Blimling, G. S. (1988). The influences of college residence halls on students: A meta-analysis of empirical research, 1966–1985. Unpublished doctoral dissertation, Ohio State University.

Borow, H. (1966). The development of occupational motives and roles. In L. W. Hoffman and M. L. Hoffman (eds.), *Review of Child Development Research*, Vol 2 (pp. 373–422). New York: Russell Sage Foundation.

Bowen, H. R. (1977). *Investment in Learning: The Individual and Social Value of American Higher Education*. San Francisco: Jossey-Bass.

Braddock, J. H. (1981). The major field choices and occupational career orientations of black and white college students. In G. E. Thomas (ed.), *Black Students in Higher Education* (pp. 167–183). Westport, CT: Greenwood Press.

Bragg, A. K. (1976). *The Socialization Process in Higher Education*. (ERIC/ Higher Education Research Report No. 7). Washington, DC: American Association for Higher Education.

Bressler, M., and Wendell, P. (1980). The sex composition of selective colleges and gender differences in career aspirations. *Journal of Higher Education* 51: 650–663.

Brim, O. G., Jr. (1966). Socialization through the life cycle. In O. G. Brim, Jr., and S. Wheeler, *Socialization After Childhood: Two Essays* (pp. 1–49). New York: Wiley.

Chickering, A. W. (1969). *Education and Identity*. San Francisco: Jossey-Bass.

Chickering, A. W. (1974). *Commuting Versus Residential Students: Overcoming the Educational Inequities of Living Off-Campus*. San Francisco: Jossey-Bass.

Chickering, A. W., et al. (1981). *The Modern American College*. San Francisco: Jossey-Bass.

Clausen, J. A. (1968). Introduction. In J. A. Clausen (ed.), *Socialization and Society* (pp. 1–17). Boston: Little, Brown.

Conrad, C. F., and Blackburn, R. T. (1985). Program quality in higher education: a review and critique of literature and research. In J. C. Smart (ed.), *Higher Education: Handbook of Theory and Research*, Vol. 1 (pp. 283–308). New York: Agathon Press.

Curtis, R. L. (1974). The issue of schools as social systems: socialization effects as inferred from lengths of membership. *Sociological Quarterly*, 15: 277–293.

Davies, M., and Kandel, D. B. (1981). Parental and peer influences on adolescents' educational plans: some further evidence. *American Journal of Sociology* 87: 363–387.

Davis, J. A. (1964). *Great Aspirations*. Chicago: Aldine.

Davis, J. A. (1965). *Undergraduate Career Decisions*. Chicago: Aldine.

Davis, J.A. (1966). The campus as a frogpond: an application of the theory of relative deprivation to career decisions of college men. *American Journal of Sociology* 72: 17–31.

DeMartini, J. R. (1983). Social movement participation: political socialization, generational consciousness, and lasting effects. *Youth and Society* 15: 195–223.

Drew, D. E., and Astin, A. W. (1972). Undergraduate aspirations: a test of several theories. *American Journal of Sociology* 77: 1151–1164.

Duncan, O. D. (1961). A socioeconomic index for all occupations. In A. J. Reiss (ed.), *Occupations and Social Status* (Chap. 6 and Appendix B). New York: Free Press.

Eccles, J. S. (1986). Gender-roles and women's achievement. *Educational Researcher* 15(June/July): 15–19.

Eisenhart, M. A. (1985). Women choose their careers: a study of natural decision-making. *Review of Higher Education* 8: 247–270.

Endo, J., and Bittner, T. (1985). Developing and using a longitudinal student outcomes data file: the University of Colorado experience. In P. T. Ewell (ed.), *Assessing Educational Outcomes* (pp. 65–80). New Directions for Institutional Research, No. 47. San Francisco: Jossey-Bass.

Ethington, C. A., and Smart, J. C. (1986). A path analytic model of the decision to enter graduate school. *Research in Higher Education* 24: 287–303.

Feldman, K. A. (1969). Studying the impacts of college on students. *Sociology of Education* 42: 207–237.

Feldman, K. A. (1972). Some theoretical approaches to the study of change and stability of college students. *Review of Educational Research* 42: 1–26.

Feldman, K. A., and Newcomb, T. N. (1969). *The Impact of College on Students*. San Francisco: Jossey-Bass.

Feldman, K. A. and Weiler, J. (1976). Changes in initial differences among major-field groups: an exploration of the "accentuation effect." In W. H. Sewell, R. M. Hauser, and D. L. Featherman (eds.), *Schooling and Achievement in American Society* (pp. 373–407). New York: Academic Press.

Fendrich, J. M. (1976). Black and white activists ten years later: political socialization and left-wing politics. *Youth and Society* 8: 81–104.

Fox, R. N. (1986). Application of a conceptual model of college withdrawal to disadvantaged students. *American Education Research Journal* 23: 415–424.

Getzels, J. W. (1963). Conflict and role behavior in the educational setting. In W. W. Charters, Jr., and N. L. Gage (eds.), *Readings in the Social Psychology of Education* (pp. 309–318). Boston: Allyn & Bacon.

Goldsen, R. K., Rosenberg, M., Williams, R. M., Jr., and Suchman, E. A. (1960). *What College Students Think*. Princeton, NJ: D. Van Nostrand.

Greeley, A. M. (1967). *The Changing Catholic College*. Chicago: Aldine.

Hauser, R. M., Tsai, S., and Sewell, W. H. (1983). A model of stratification with response error in social and psychological variables. *Sociology of Education* 56: 20–46.

Hawkes, R. K. (1975). Norms, deviance, and social control: a mathematical elaboration of concepts. *American Journal of Sociology* 80: 886–908.

Hearn, J. C. (1980). Major choice and well-being of college men and women: an examination from developmental, organizational, and structural perspectives. *Sociology of Education* 53: 164–178.

Hearn, J. C., and Olzak, S. (1981). The role of college major departments in the reproduction of sexual inequality. *Sociology of Education* 54: 195–205.

Hoge, D. R. (1976). Changes in college students' value patterns in the 1950's, 1960's and 1970's. *Sociology of Education* 49: 155–163.

Holland, J. L. (1966). *The Psychology of Vocational Choice*. Waltham, MA: Blaisdell.

Holland, J. L. (1985). *Making Vocational Choices: A Theory of Vocational Personalities and Work Environments* (2nd ed.) Englewood Cliffs, NJ: Prentice-Hall.

Homans, G. C. (1950). *The Human Group*. New York: Harcourt, Brace & World.

Homans, G. C. (1961). *Social Behavior: Its Elementary Forms*. New York: Harcourt, Brace & World.

Huber, Ludwig (1980). Sozialisation in der Hochschule. In K. Hurrelmann and D. Ulich (eds.), *Handbuch der Sozialisationsforschung*. Weinheim-Basel: Beltz.

Hurrelmann, K. (1988). *Social Structure and Personality Development*. New York: Cambridge University Press.

Hyman, H. H., Wright, C. R., and Reed, J. S. (1975). *The Enduring Effects of Education*. Chicago: University of Chicago Press.

Jacob, R. (1957). *Changing Values in College: An Exploratory Study of the Impact of College Teaching*. New York: Harper & Row.

Jencks, C., Crouse, J., and Mueser, P. (1983). The Wisconsin model of status attainment: a national replication with improved measures of ability and aspiration. *Sociology of Education* 56: 3–19.

Kamens, D. (1974). Colleges and elite formation: the case of prestigious American colleges. *Sociology of Education* 47: 354–378.

Katchadourian, H. A., and Boli, J. (1985). *Careerism and Intellectualism Among College Students*. San Francisco: Jossey-Bass.

Kemper, T. D. (1968). Reference groups as perspectives. *American Sociological Review* 33: 31–45.

Kerckhoff, A. C. (1976). The status attainment process: socialization or allocation? *Social Forces* 55: 368–481.

Kett, J. (1977). *Rites of passage: Adolescence in America, 1790 to the Present*. New York: Basic Books.

Kohn, M. L. (1977). *Class and Conformity: A Study in Values* (2nd ed.). Chicago: University of Chicago Press.

Komarovsky, M. (1985). *Women in College*. New York: Basic Books.

Kuh, G. D., Bean, J. B., Bradley, R. K., Coomes, M. D., and Hunter, D. E. (1986). Changes in research on college students published in selected journals between 1969 and 1983. *Review of Higher Education* 9: 177–192.

Lacy, W. B. (1978). Interpersonal relationships as mediators of structural effects: college student socialization in a traditional and an experimental university environment. *Sociology of Education* 51: 201–211.

Lenning, O. T. (1982). Variable-selection and measurement concerns. In E. T. Pascarella (ed.), *Studying Student Attrition* (pp. 35–53). New Directions for Institutional Research, No. 36. San Francisco: Jossey-Bass.

Levine, A. (1980). *When Dreams and Heroes Died: A Portrait of Today's College Student*. San Francisco: Jossey-Bass.

Linton, R. (1936). *The Study of Man*. New York: Appleton-Century-Crofts.

Litten, L. H. (1982). Different strokes in the applicant pool: some refinements in a model of student college choice. *Journal of Higher Education* 53: 383–402.

Looker, E. D., and Pineo, P. D. (1983). Social psychological variables and their relevance to the status attainment of teenagers. *American Journal of Sociology* 88: 1195–1219.

Merton, R. K. (1968). *Social Theory and Social Structure*. New York: Free Press.

Metzner, B. S., and Bean, J. P. (1987). The estimation of a conceptual model of nontraditional undergraduate student attrition. *Research in Higher Education* 27: 15–38.

Meyer, J. W. (1970). The charter: conditions of diffuse socialization in schools. In W. R. Scott (ed.), *Social Processes and Social Structures* (pp. 564–578). New York: Holt, Rinehart & Winston.

Meyer, J. W. (1972). The effects of institutionalization of colleges in society. In K. A. Feldman (ed.), *College and Student: Selected Readings in the Social Psychology of Higher Education* (pp. 109–126). New York: Pergamon.

Moore, W. E. (1969). Occupational socialization. In D. A. Goslin (ed.), *Handbook of Socialization Theory and Research* (pp. 861–873). Chicago: Rand McNally.

Moos, R. H. (1979). *Evaluating Educational Environments*. San Francisco: Jossey-Bass.

Morgan, W. R., Alwin, D. F., and Griffin, L. J. (1979). Social origins, parental values, and the transmission of inequality. *American Journal of Sociology* 85: 156–166.

Mortimer, J. T. (1974). Patterns of intergenerational occupational movements: a smallest space analysis. *American Journal of Sociology* 79: 1278–1299.

Mortimer, J. T. (1976). Social class, work and the family: some implications of the father's occupation for familial relationships and sons' career decisions. *Journal of Marriage and the Family* 38: 241–256.

Mortimer, J. T., and Simmons, R. G. (1978). Adult socialization. In R. H. Turner, J. Coleman, and R. C. Fox (eds.), *Annual Review of Sociology*, Vol. 4 (pp. 421–454). Palo Alto, CA: Annual Reviews.

Nettles, M. T., Thoeny, A. R., and Gosman, E. J. (1986). Comparative and predictive analyses of black and white students' college achievement and experiences. *Journal of Higher Education* 57: 289–318.

Newcomb, T. M. (1943). *Personality and Social Change*. New York: Dryden Press.

Newcom, T. M., and Wilson, E. K., eds. (1966). *College Peer Groups*. Chicago: Aldine.

Newcomb, T. M., Koenig, K. E., Flack, R., and Warwick, D. P. (1967). *Persistence and Change: Bennington College and its Students After Twenty-Five Years*. New York: Wiley.

Nora, A. (1987). Determinants of retention among Chicano college students: a structural model. *Research in Higher Education* 26: 31–59.

Pace, C. R. (1979). *Measuring Outcomes of College: Fifty Years of Findings and Recommendations for the Future*. San Francisco: Jossey-Bass.

Pantages, T. J., and Creedon, C. F. (1978). Studies of college attrition: 1950–1975. *Review of Educational Research* 48: 49–101.

Parsons, T., and Platt, G. M. (1973). *The American University*. Cambridge: Harvard University Press.

Parsons, T., Shils, E. A., and Olds, L. (1951). Values, motives, and systems of action. In T. Parsons and E. A. Shills (eds.), *Toward a General Theory of Action* (pp. 45–276). New York: Harper Torchbooks (1962).

Pascarella, E. T. (1980). Student-faculty informal contact and college outcomes. *Review of Educational Research* 50: 545–595.

Pascarella, E. T. (1984). Reassessing the effects of living on-campus versus commuting to college: a causal modeling approach. *Review of Higher Education* 7: 247–260.

Pascarella, E. T. (1985a). College environment influences on learning and cognitive development. In J. C. Smart (ed.), *Higher Education: Handbook of Theory and Research, Vol. 1 (pp. 1–61).* New York: Agathon Press.

Pascarella, E. T. (1985b). Students' affective development within the college environment. *Journal of Higher Education* 56: 640–663.

Pascarella, E. T., and Chapman, D. W. (1983). A multi-institutional, path analytic validation of Tinto's model of college withdrawal. *American Educational Research Journal* 20: 87–102.

Pascarella, E. T., and Terenzini, P. T. (1980). Predicting freshman persistence and voluntary dropout decisions from a theoretical model. *Journal of Higher Education* 51: 60–75.

Pascarella, E. T., Terenzini, P. T., and Wolfle, L. M. (1986). Orientation to college and freshman year persistence/withdrawal decisions. *Journal of Higher Education* 57: 155–175.

Perun, Pamela J., ed. (1982). *The Undergraduate Woman: Issues in Educational Equity.* Lexington, MA: Lexington Books.

Peterson, M. W., Blackburn, R. T., Gamson, Z. F., Arce, C. H., Davenport, R. W., and Mingle, J. R. (1978). *Black Students on White Campuses: The Impacts of Increased Black Enrollments.* Ann Arbor: University of Michigan, Institute for Social Research.

Phelan, W. T. (1979). Undergraduate orientations toward scientific and scholarly careers. *American Educational Research Journal* 16: 411–422.

Regan, M. C., and Roland, H. E. (1982). University students: a change in expectations and aspirations over the decade. *Sociology of Education* 55: 223–228.

Reitz, J. G. (1975). Undergraduate aspirations and career choice. *Sociology of Education* 48: 308–323.

Richards, J. M., Jr. (1974). "Environments" of British Commonwealth universities. *Journal of Educational Psychology* 66: 572–579.

Rosenberg, M. (1957). *Occupations and Values.* Glencoe, IL: Free Press.

Sanford, N., ed. (1962). *The American College.* New York: Wiley.

Schrager, R. H. (1986). The impact of living group social climate on student academic performance. *Research in Higher Education* 25: 265–276.

Sewell, W. T., Haller, A. O., and Ohlendorf, G. O. (1970). The educational and early occupational status achievement process: replication and revision. *American Sociological Review* 35: 1014–1027.

Sewell, W. T., Haller, A. O., and Portes, A. (1969). The educational and early occupational attainment process. *American Sociological Review* 34: 82–92.

Shibutani, T. (1955). Reference groups as perspectives. *American Journal of Sociology* 60: 562–569.

Siegel, A. E., and Siegel, S. (1957). Reference groups, membership groups and attitude change. *Journal of Abnormal and Social Psychology* 55: 360–364.

Simpson, I. H. (1979). *From Student to Nurse: A Longitudinal Study of Socialization.* New York: Cambridge University Press.

Smart, J. C. (1985). Holland environments as reinforcement systems. *Research in Higher Education* 23: 279–292.

Smart, J. C. (1986). College effects on occupational status attainment. *Research in Higher Education* 24: 47–72.

Smart, J. C., and Pascarella, E. T. (1986). Socioeconomic achievements of former college students. *Journal of Higher Education* 57: 529–549.

Smith, E. J. (1981). The career development of young black females: the forgotten group. *Youth and Society* 12: 277–312.

Snyder, B. R. (1971). *The Hidden Curriculum*. New York: Knopf.

Solmon, L. C., and Taubman, P. J. (1973). *Does College Matter?* New York: Academic Press.

Solmon, L. C., and Wachtel, P. (1975). The effects on income of type of college attended. *Sociology of Education* 48: 75–90.

Spaeth, J. L., and Greeley, A. M. (1970). *Recent Alumni and Higher Education*. New York: McGraw-Hill.

Stern, G. G. (1970). *People in Context: Measuring Person-Environment Congruence in Education and Industry*. New York: Wiley.

Terenzini, P. T., Pascarella, E. T., Theophilides, C., and Lorang, W. (1985). A replication of a path analytic validation of Tinto's theory of college student attrition. *Review of Higher Education* 8: 319–340.

Terenzini, P. T., and Wright, T. M. (1986). Influences on students' academic growth during four years of college. *Research in Higher Education* 26: 161–179.

Thielens, W. W., Jr. (1966). *The Structure of Faculty Influence*. New York: Columbia University, Bureau of Applied Social Research.

Thomas, G. E., ed. (1981). *Black Students in Higher Education: Conditions and Experiences in the 1970's*. Westport, CT: Greenwood Press.

Thornton, R., and Nardi, P. M. (1975). The dynamics of role acquisition. *American Journal of Sociology* 80: 870–885.

Tinto, V. (1975). Dropout from higher education: a theoretical synthesis of recent research. *Review of Educational Research* 45: 89–125.

Tinto, V. (1982). Limits of theory and practice in student attrition. *Journal of Higher Education* 53: 687–700.

Tinto, V. (1987). *Leaving College: Rethinking the Causes and Cures of Student Attrition*. Chicago: University of Chicago Press.

Trow, M., ed. (1975). *Teachers and Students*. New York: McGraw-Hill.

Van Gennep, A. (1960). *The Rites of Passage*. (M. B. Vizedom and G. L. Caffee, trans.). Chicago: University of Chicago Press.

Vreeland, R., and Bidwell, C. E. (1965). Organizational effects on student attitudes: a study of the Harvard houses. *Sociology of Education* 38: 233–250.

Vreeland, R., and Bidwell, C. E. (1966). Classifying university departments: an approach to the analysis of their effects upon undergraduates' values and attitudes. *Sociology of Education* 39: 237–254.

Wallace, W. L. (1966). *Student Culture: Social Structure and Continuity in a Liberal Arts College*. Chicago: Aldine.

Walsh, W. B. (1973). *Theories of Person-Environment Interaction: Implications for the College Student*. (ACT Monograph 10). Iowa City: American College Testing Program.

Weidman, J. C. (1979). Nonintellective undergraduate socialization in academic departments. *Journal of Higher Education* 50: 48–62.

Weidman, J. C. (1984). Impacts of campus experiences and parental socialization on undergraduates' career choices. *Research in Higher Education* 20: 445–476.

Weidman, J. C. (1989). The world of higher educaton: a socialization-theoretical perspective. In K. Hurrelmann and U. Engel (eds.), *The Social World of Adolescents: International Perspectives* (pp. 87–105). Berlin-New York: de Gruyter/Aldine.

Weidman, J. C., and Friedmann, R. R. (1984). The school-to-work transition for high school dropouts. *Urban Review* 16: 25–42.

Weidman, J. C., and Krus, D. J. (1979). Undergraduates' expectations and images of college. *Psychological Reports* 45: 131–139.

Weidman, J. C., and White, R. N. (1985). Postsecondary "high-tech" training for women on welfare: correlates of program completion. *Journal of Higher Education* 56: 555–568.

Wheeler, S. (1966). The structure of formally organized socialization settings. In O. G. Brim, Jr., and S. Wheeler, *Socialization After Childhood: Two Essays* (pp. 53–116). New York: Wiley.

Wieder, D. L., and Zimmerman, D. H. (1976). Becoming a freak: pathways into the counter-culture. *Youth and Society* 7: 311–344.

Willie, C. V., and Cunnigen, D. (1981). Black students in higher education: a review of studies, 1965–1980. In R. H. Turner and J. F. Short, Jr. (eds.), *Annual Review of Sociology* Vol. 7 (pp. 177–198). Palo Alto, CA: Annual Reviews.

Wilson, R., Gaff, J. G., Dienst, E. R., Wood, L., and Bavry, J. L. (1975). *College Professors and their Impact on Students*. New York: Wiley.

Winch, R. F., and Gordon, M. T. (1974). *Familial Structure and Function as Influence*. Lexington, MA: D. C. Heath.

Winteler, A. (1981). The academic department as environment for teaching and learning. *Higher Education* 10: 25–35.

Winter, D. G., McClelland, D. C., and Stewart, A. J. (1981). *A New Case for the Liberal Arts*. San Francisco: Jossey-Bass.

Withey, S. B. (1971). *A Degree and What Else?* New York: McGraw-Hill.

Wrong, D. (1961). The oversocialized conception of man in modern sociology. *American Sociological Review* 26: 183–193.

Log-Linear Models: Applications in Higher Education Research

Dennis E. Hinkle
Virginia Polytechnic Institute and State University

James T. Austin
University of Illinois Urbana-Champaign

and

Gerald W. McLaughlin
Virginia Polytechnic Institute and State University

Often, data collected and analyzed in higher education research are qualitative or categorical rather than quantitative or continuous. Examples of qualitative variables are academic discipline, institution type, faculty rank, race, and gender to name but a few. Until recently, the statistical procedures available for analyzing data of this type were limited. While procedures have long been available for analyzing the association between two categorical variables in a two-dimensional table using chi-square statistics, procedures have not been available for analyzing the association among multiple variables in multidimensional cross-classification tables. For such tables, the usual approach was to analyze various combinations of variables in two-dimensional tables by sequentially combining the levels of the other variables or to analyze two-dimensional tables within the levels of other variables. Such an approach is subject to high Type I error rates but, more importantly, it does not allow the researcher to explore higher-order associations among the variables (Fienberg, 1980).

In the mid to late 1960s social scientists, along with statisticians, began to develop statistical techniques for simultaneous analysis of qualitative or categorical variables in multidimensional contingency tables. These techniques have been referred to as *log-linear contingency table analysis, logit analysis*, or more

An earlier and less extensive version of this chapter is found in B. Yancey, ed., *New Directions in Higher Education Research* (San Francisco: Jossey-Bass, 1988).

commonly, *log-linear models*. Those primarily responsible for these developments include Birch (1963), Bishop (1969), Bock (1970), Fienberg (1972), Grizzle, Starmer, and Koch (1969), Grizzle and Williams (1972), Goodman (1963, 1964, 1970, 1971a, b), Haberman (1972), Kastenbaum (1974), and Roy and Kastenbaum (1956). Even with these pioneering efforts, the use of log-linear models was limited until adequate textbooks were written (e.g., Bishop, Fienberg, and Holland, 1975; Fienberg, 1980; Goodman, 1978; Kennedy, 1983; Knoke and Burke, 1980), and until user-friendly computer programs were developed, such as BMDP-4F (BMDP Inc., 1985), SPSSX and SPSSPC (SPSS, Inc., 1986), SAS (SAS Institute, 1985), and SYSTAT (1986). In addition, a number of computer programs specifically designed for categorical data analysis have been written in the last 15 years, including MULTIQUAL (Bock and Yates, 1973), ECTA (Fay and Goodman, 1975), and FREQ (Haberman, 1979).

The historical roots of log-linear models date to Pearson's chi-square (χ^2) test of independence (1900) and Yule's cross-product ratio (1900). Pearson's χ^2 is defined as follows:

$$\chi^2 = \Sigma \frac{(O - E)^2}{E}$$

where O is the observed frequencies, and E equals the expected frequencies. While their work was restricted to 2×2 contingency tables, Bartlett (1935) used Yule's cross-product ratio to define and interpret second-order (three-variable) interaction in $2 \times 2 \times 2$ contingency tables. Concurrent with these developments was Fisher's (1924) work with maximum likelihood estimation and his development of a chi-square statistic, called the *likelihood ratio chi-square* (L^2.)

$$L^2 = 2\Sigma(O) \ln\left(\frac{O}{E}\right)$$

Both the Pearson χ^2 and the Fisher L^2 are distributed as chi-square when samples are sufficiently large and are asymptotically equivalent for very large samples. However, L^2 has more desirable properties (e.g., additivity) for analyzing log-linear models and is the goodness-of-fit statistic most often used. For a more thorough discussion of the development of statistical techniques for analyzing log-linear models, see Killion and Zahn (1976).

TABLE 1. Association Model

		Stay	Drop
Socioeconomic	High		
Status	Middle		
	Low		

ASSOCIATION MODELS VERSUS LOGIT MODELS

There are two types of log-linear models—association models and logit models. In association models, the purpose is to determine the independence or association between variables (Hinkle and McLaughlin, 1984). Kennedy (1983) refers to these models as "symmetrical" because the research question concerns only the presence or absence of an association between two variables, say **A** and **B**. For example, suppose a researcher wants to determine the relationship between the socioeconomic status and retention of community college students in transfer programs. The association between these two variables would be investigated for a sample of community college students; the contingency table for the data analysis might look like Table 1. For the data in this 3×2 contingency table, the appropriate analysis would be the test of independence using L^2 or χ^2.

In contrast, logit models seek to "determine whether subjects who fall in respective categories of one variable [**A**] differ appreciably in their response to another variable [**B**]" (Kennedy, 1983, p.7). Kennedy refers to these models as "asymmetrical" in that Variable **A** is considered the independent or explanatory variable and Variable **B** is the dependent or logit variable. For example, suppose a researcher selects samples of full professors, associate professors, and assistant professors and wants to determine if these three groups differ in their response to a questionnaire item relating to perceived faculty stress in higher education; the 2×3 contingency table for this investigation might look like that in Table 2. Note that the contingency tables in Table 1 and Table 2 are similar; however, the analysis of the data for Table 2 would be the chi-square test of homogeneity. Although the actual arithmetic of the chi-square tests for Table 1 and Table 2 are the same, the *post hoc* procedures and the interpretation of the results differ substantially (Marascuilo and McSweeney, 1977). For the association model of Table 1, one suggested *post hoc* procedure is to compute Cramer's V (Hinkle, Wiersma and Jurs, 1988), a measure of association that can be interpreted in much the same way as a product-moment correlation coefficient. For the logit model of Table 2, the *post hoc* procedures would be standardized residuals (ibid.)

TABLE 2. Logit Model

		Full Professor	Associate Professor	Assistant Professor
Response	Agree			
	Disagree			

TABLE 3. Freshman Retention Data

	Dropout	Stay	Total
White			
Male	262	863	1125
Female	351	1084	1435
Nonwhite			
Male	67	77	144
Female	70	85	155
Total	750	2109	2859

Source: DE Hinkle and GW McLaughlin (1984). Selection of models in contingency tables: a reexamination. *Research in Higher Education* 21:415–423.

or contrasts analogous to Tukey or Scheffe methods (Marascuilo and Mc-Sweeney, 1977).

HIERARCHICAL LOG-LINEAR MODELS FOR MULTIPLE VARIABLES

To illustrate the use of hierarchical log-linear models for multiple categorical variables, consider the data discussed by Hinkle and McLaughlin (1984) and found in Table 3.

In this example, the researcher was interested in the dropout rates for college students cross-classified on the basis of race and gender. While these data best illustrate an example for logit model analysis, we will use them to discuss the association model and then the logit model. For both, we begin by considering a hierarchy of "ANOVA-like" models, called the *Log-Linear Models* and then select the model that is most adequate in explaining the differences in the observed cell frequencies in the $2 \times 2 \times 2$ contingency table. For this three-variable example, one possible hierarchy of models is found in Table 4. The residual and component L^2 statistics computed in the analysis of the association model are also found in this table. We will explain these L^2 values as

**TABLE 4. Initial Hierarchical Analysis: Models and Likelihood
Ratio Chi-Square Values**

Model	Residual			Component		
	L^2	df	p	L^2	df	p
1 Null	2,818.96	7	.01			
2 R	771.28	6	.01	2,047.68	1	.01
3 R,S	735.16	5	.01	36.12	1	.01
4 R,S,T	62.33	4	.01	672.82	1	.01
5 T,RS	60.426	3	.01	1.91	1	.17
6 RS,RT	0.53	2	.76	59.89	1	.01
7 RS,RT,ST	0.23	1	.63	0.30	1	.58
8 RST	0.00	—	—	0.23	1	.63

we will illustrate the calculation of the L^2 statistic for the first three models; the calculation of the L^2 statistic for the remaining models is detailed in Fienberg (1980) or Kennedy (1983).

In association model analysis, Model 1 is referred to as the *null model* or the model that would indicate no association among the three variables. For this model, the frequencies would be expected to be uniformly distributed across the eight cells of the $2 \times 2 \times 2$ contingency table. That is, if there is no association among the variables, we would expect each cell to contain 2859/8 = 357.375 observations. To test the adequacy of the null model in explaining the distribution of the observed cell frequencies across the cells of the contingency table, the Fisher's L^2 statistic is computed. Obviously, the observed cell frequencies are not uniformly distributed across the cells and we would expect the L^2 statistic to exceed the critical value needed for statistical significance. For the above data, the residual L^2 (L_1^2) = 2,818.96, indicating that Model 1 does not adequately fit the the observed data. In other words the observed cell frequencies depart appreciably from the frequencies expected with this model.

The next three models sequentially fix the main marginal totals for the three variables. In Model 2, the marginal totals for the variable Race (**R**) are fixed in order to determine whether the distribution of cell frequencies in the $2 \times 2 \times 2$ contingency table can be explained by the fact that there are different numbers of whites and nonwhites in the sample. In this model, the 2,560 white students are uniformly distributed across the other 2×2 = 4 cells of the contingency table—640 in each cell. Similarly, the 299 nonwhite students are uniformly distributed across the corresponding 2×2 = 4 cells of the contingency table. The expected frequencies for Model 2 are found in Table 5. The residual L^2 statistic is computed to determine if Model 2 adequately fits the data. Since L_2^2

TABLE 5. Expected Cell Frequencies for Model 2

	Stay	Drop
White		
Male	640.0	640.0
Female	640.0	640.0
Nonwhite		
Male	74.75	74.75
Female	74.75	74.75

TABLE 6. Expected Cell Frequencies for Model 3

	Stay	Drop
White		
Male	562.5	562.5
Female	717.5	717.5
Nonwhite		
Male	72.0	72.0
Female	77.5	77.5

$= 771.28$, we would conclude that Model 2 does not adequately explain the distribution of cell frequencies for the $2 \times 2 \times 2$ contingency table. The component L^2 for this model is computed by subtracting the residual L^2 for Model 2 from the residual L^2 for Model 1, $L_1^2 - L_2^2 = (2,818.96 - 771.28) = 2,047.68$. Since the L^2 statistics are additive, this single degree-of-freedom component L^2 statistic indicates that there is an improvement of the fit to the data using Model 2 (that is, there is a difference in the number of whites and nonwhites in the sample). However, based upon the residual L_2^2 the fit is still not adequate. We will discuss the component L^2 in more detail in the section concerning model selection.

In the next model in the hierarchy, Model 3, the marginal totals for the variable Sex (**S**) are fixed. In this step, we investigate whether the distribution of cell frequencies in Table 3 can be explained by the fact that there are differences in the number of males (1,269) and females (1,590) in the sample having previously controlled for the marginal totals for the variable Race (**R**). For this model, the 1,125 white males are uniformly distributed across the two levels of the variable Retention (**T**). Similarly, the 1,435 white females, the 144 nonwhite males, and the 155 nonwhite females are uniformly distributed across variable **T**; these expected frequencies are found in Table 6. As for the first two models, the residual L^2 statistic is computed using the observed frequencies of Table 3 and the expected frequencies of Table 6. For this model, the residual $L^2 = 735.16$ indicating that Model 3 does not adequately fit the data and is not sufficient for explaining the distribution of observed cell frequencies of Table 3. The component L^2 for Model 3 is computed by subtracting L_3^2 from L_2^2 ($L_2^2 - L_3^2 = 771.28 - 735.16 = 36.12$). This component L^2 again indicates a significant improvement in the fit of the data (that is, there is a difference in the number of males and females in the sample) but, based upon the residual L^2 for Model 3, the fit is still inadequate.

The final one-variable model in the hierarchy is Model 4. For this model, the marginal totals for the variable Retention (**T**) are fixed. As indicated in the hierarchy, Model 4 is used to investigate whether the difference in the numbers of students who dropped out of school and those who stayed can explain the differences in the observed cell frequencies of Table 3 having previously controlled for the Race (**R**) and Sex (**S**) variables. The calculation of the expected cell frequencies for this model are slightly more complicated and thus are not given; the reader is referred to Fienberg (1980) and Kennedy (1983) for details. However, the residual L^2 for this model, $L_4^2 = 62.33$, is statistically significant indicating that Model 4 does not fit the data. The component L^2 is $735.16 - 62.34 = 672.82$. While this component L^2 indicates a difference in the number of subjects in the sample who dropped out of school and the number who stayed, this difference, combined with the differences in the number of whites and nonwhites and the number of males and females, is not sufficient for explaining the distribution of cell frequencies in the $2 \times 2 \times 2$ contingency table (see Table 3).

These first four models do not consider joint associations among the three variables in this study; they are concerned only with the differences in the marginal frequencies of the variables controlled sequentially. Since none of these models adequately fit the data, one or more of the higher order log-linear models in the hierarchy are necessary for explaining the distribution of cell frequencies in Table 3. These subsequent models deal sequentially with the three first-order (two-variable) associations (Models 5, 6, and 7) and the one second-order (three-variable) association (Model 8). The sequence of the models in the hierarchy is determined *a priori* by the researcher. For this example, we chose to examine the Race by Sex (**RS**) association—Model 5; the Race by Retention (**RT**) association—Model 6; and finally the Sex by Retention (**ST**) association—Model 7. However, the researcher may choose another sequence.

The residual L^2 for the Race by Sex association (**RS**) ($L_5^2 = 60.42$) is statistically significant indicating that Model 5 did not fit the data. In addition, the component L^2 ($62.33 - 60.42 = 1.91$) indicates that there is a nonsignificant Race by Sex association. Now consider Model 6 which considers the Race by Retention (**RT**) association; note that the residual L^2 ($L_6^2 = 0.53$) is not statistically significant. This result indicates that the expected cell frequencies, determined by controlling for the marginal totals for the three variables as well as the **RS** and the **RT** associations, do not differ from the observed cell frequencies. Note also that the component L^2 (60.42 − 0.53 = 59.89) is statistically significant indicating that the addition of the Race by Retention (**RT**) association to the hierarchy was significant in reducing the residual L^2, and thus the presence of an **RT** association.

Completing this example, consider Model 7. This model is used to determine whether a Sex by Retention (**ST**) association exists after controlling for the other models in the hierarchy. For this model, both the residual L^2 ($L_7^2 = 0.23$) and the component L^2 (0.53 − 0.23 = 0.30) are not significant. This was expected since the residual L^2 for Model 6 was already nonsignificant.

Finally, consider Model 8 which is called the *saturated model*. The residual L^2 for this model is always zero since the expected frequencies generated for this model equal the observed frequencies. For this example, the component L^2 is also nonsignificant indicating that less restrictive models in the hierarchy were able to fit the data. If previous models were not able to adequately fit the data, the residual L^2 would still be zero, but the component L^2 would be statistically significant. This result would indicate the presence of a three-variable association; that is, the simple association between two of the variables was not the same over the levels of the third variable.

Strategy for Model Selection

Kennedy (1983) presents a strategy for selecting the most appropriate log-linear model(s) when the models are considered in a hierarchy. The first step in this strategy is to begin at the bottom of the column of residual L^2 and go up the column looking for the first significant L^2. In our example, the first significant L^2 was for Model 5. This model and all less restricted models (1 through 4) are eliminated from further consideration. The second step is to begin at the bottom of the column of component L^2 and go up the column looking for the first significant component L^2. In the example, the first significant component L^2 was for Model 6. The more restricted models (7 and 8) would also be eliminated from further consideration. Using this strategy, we find that Model 6 would be the model of choice. However, when the associations among more than 4 or 5 variables are investigated, this strategy does not always identify a single model. For example, suppose that both the residual L^2 and the component L^2 for Model 6 were statistically significant. Further suppose that the residual L^2 for Model 7 was not significant but that the component L^2 was. This situation is illustrated in Table 7. Using the above strategy, the researcher would possibly eliminate Model 6 and interpret only Model 7. However, results such as those illustrated in Table 7 indicate the presence of both an **RT** and an **ST** association.

TABLE 7. Illustration for Model Selection

	Model	Residual	Component
Null	1	*	
R	2	*	NS
R,S	3	*	NS
R,ST	4	*	NS
T,RS	5	*	NS
RS,RT	6	*	*
RS,RT,ST	7	NS	*
RST	8	NS	NS

*Statistically significant.
NS Not Statistically significant.

TABLE 8. Screening Tables for Nonhierarchical Models

A. Tests that K-way and Higher Order Effects are zero

K	L^2	p
1	2818.96	<.0001
2	62.11	<.0001
3	0.23	.6319

B. Tests that K-way Effects are zero

K	L^2	p
1	2756.62	<.0001
2	62.33	<.0001
3	0.23	.6319

NONHIERARCHICAL LOG-LINEAR ANALYSIS

Researchers using log-linear models in the analysis of qualitative data quickly discover that the default options of the larger, mainframe computer software packages do not automatically provide the residual L^2 and the component L^2 that are discussed above; the researcher must sequentially enter the models and develop the tables containing both the residual L^2 and the component L^2. However, if the researcher cannot defend the use of a hierarchical approach and is only interested in whether there are one or more first-order (two-variable) associations or a second-order (three-variable) association, a different screening procedure is suggested. This procedure is illustrated in Table 8.

Note that there are two screening tables in Table 8. The first table involves testing that the k-way or higher order effects are zero; the second table involves the tests of which k-way effects are zero, where k is the number of variables. Consider the first screening table. The test that the "1"-way or higher order effects are zero is actually the test of Model 1, the null model; the residual $L^2 =$ 2,818.96. If this model is not statistically significant, we would conclude that the null model adequately fits the data and that there is no association among the variables. Since this model is statistically significant, the second step would be to look at the test of the "2"-way or higher order models which is actually the test of Model 4 ($L^2 = 62.33$). If this test is not significant, we would conclude that the differences in the marginal totals for one or more of the variables can explain the differences in the cell frequencies of the contingency table. Again, since this L^2 is still significant, we continue the screening procedure and look at the test of the "3"-way or higher order effect, which is actually the test of Model 7. Note that this L^2 is not statistically significant indicating that the 3-way effect (the three-variable association) is zero and that one or more of the two-variable associations are adequate for explaining the distribution of cell frequencies in the contingency table. If the test for $k = 3$ is significant, then the conclusion would be that Model 8, the saturated model, is necessary to fit the data and that a second-order (three-variable) association exists.

In the second screening table of Table 8, the L^2's values are component L^2 rather that residual L^2's. These L^2's are computed to test for the significance of "families" of models. In the first test, the family of single-variable models is considered and tested for statistical significance by subtracting the residual L^2 for Model 4 from the residual L^2 for Model 1 ($L_1^2 - L_4^2 = 2,818.96 - 62.33 = 2,756.63$). If this component L^2 is nonsignificant, then more than just the single-variable models are needed to fit the data and to explain the distribution of observed cell frequencies. Since this component L^2 is significant, one or more of the single-variable models are significant contributors and the data would be explored further to determine which of these single-variable models are significant.

The family of two-variable models is considered in the second test of this second screening table. The component L^2 for this second test is determined by subtracting the residual L^2 for Model 7 from the residual L^2 for Model 4 ($L_4^2 - L_7^2 = 62.33 - 0.23 = 62.10$). Since this component L^2 is statistically significant, one or more of the two-variable models are significant contributors to the explanation of the distribution of observed cell frequencies. In other words, one or more significant-order (two-variable) associations are present in the contingency table. Subsequent procedures, discussed below, are then used to determine which of these associations are significant.

The final step in the second screening table is the test of the component L^2 for Model 8. As indicated before, this component L^2 ($L_7^2 - L_8^2 = 0.23 - 0.00 = 0.23$) was nonsignificant and indicated that less restrictive models were sufficient for explaining the distributions of observed cell frequencies and that a second-

TABLE 9. Tests of Partial Associations

	L^2	p
Race by Sex (**RS**)	2.11	.1463
Race by Retain (**RT**)	0.30	.5819
Sex by Retain (**ST**)	60.08	<.0001
Race (**R**)	2047.68	<.0001
Sex (**S**)	36.12	<.0001
Retain (**T**)	672.82	<.0001

order (three-variable) association was not present in the data. As before, if this component L^2 had been significant, the conclusion would have been that Model 8 was necessary for fitting the observed data and that a second-order association existed.

Following these two screening procedures, the process becomes one of determining which of the families of models are required to fit the data. In our example, we determined from the screening procedures that one or more first-order (two-variable) associations are present in the data. In order to determine which ones are present, we recommend looking at the "partial L^2" for each of the two-variable models. This process is analogous to examining the partial regression coefficients in multiple regression analysis. Recall that in multiple regression analysis, each predictor variable is considered after controlling for all other variables in the regression equation. In log-linear analysis of association models, each first-order association is considered after controlling for all other first-order associations. The partial L^2's for our example are found in Table 9. Note that only the partial L^2 for the Race by Retention association (**RT**) (60.08) is significant. Note also that the Sex by Retention association (**ST**) (0.30) is the same as the component L^2 for Model 7 and is nonsignificant. We have also included the partial L^2's for the one-variable models. All three of these partial L^2 are statistically significant indicating that there are differences in the number of males and females, the number of whites and nonwhites, and the number of students who stay in school and the number who drop out. Obviously, these latter partial L^2's are of little importance to the researcher except for describing the sample. Thus, based upon the results in Table 9, we would conclude that there is a significant Race by Retention (**RT**) association present in the data.

In summary to this point, we have presented two approaches to log-linear analysis for association models. In the first approach, a hierarchical set of log-linear models is developed and tested sequentially. In determining which model or models should be interpreted, a screening strategy using both the residual and component L^2 was discussed. However, if the researcher is unwilling or unable to establish such a hierarchy *a priori*, a second screening

TABLE 10. Logit Model Analysis (Hierarchical)

	L^2	df	p
Enter race then sex			
Model			
5 **T,RS** (null model)	60.42	3	<.01
6a **RS,RT** (Race)	59.89	1	<.01
7a **RS,RT,ST** (Sex/Race)	0.30	1	.58
8 **RST** (Race × Sex)	0.23	1	.63
Enter Sex, then Race			
Model			
5 **T,RS** (null model)	60.42	3	<.01
6b **RS,ST** (Sex)	0.11	1	.74
7b **RS,ST,RT** (Race/Sex)	60.08	1	<.01
8 **RST** (Race × Sex)	0.23	1	.63

procedure was proposed. The second procedure identifies families of models that are needed to fit the data. Subsequently, partial L^2 statistics are considered to determine which members of the families are contributors to the fit.

The Logit Model

Now consider the analysis of the same data using the logit model approach. In this approach, the Retention (**T**) variable is considered as the dependent or logit variable with Race (**R**) and Sex (**S**) variables considered as the explanatory variables. For this approach, only Models 6, 7, and 8 from Table 4 are models of interest. That is, are there differences in the retention rates of whites and nonwhites (Model 6)? are there differences in the retention rates of males and females (Model 7)? and are there differences in the retention rates for the combination of the levels of the race and sex variables (Model 8)? Using ANOVA terminology, Model 6 is the Race main effect, Model 7 is the Sex main effect, and Model 8 is the Race by Sex interaction effect.

For the logit model, we can use either a hierarchical approach or a regression (partial L^2) approach; both approaches are illustrated in Table 10. Note that for both approaches, the "null model" is Model 5 as defined in the association model approach. This model contains all three one-variable models and the Race by Sex (**RS**) association. If this model adequately fits the data, then subsequent models, which are the models of interest, are unnecessary for explaining the distribution of observed cell frequencies.

In the hierarchical approach, the order of log-linear models tested is specified by the researcher. In the example, Model 6a is used to determine whether the

TABLE 11. Coefficient for $2 \times 2 \times 2$ Association Model

	Race		
	White	Nonwhite	
Retention			
Stay	1,947	162	2,109
Dropout	613	137	750
Total	2,560	299	2,859

ϕ = .152

retention rate is the same for both whites and nonwhites, i.e., the Race main effect (see Table 10). Model 7a is then used to determine whether the retention rate is the same for males and females, the Sex main effect, after controlling for the Race main effect. In the regression (partial L^2) approach, Model 7b would be used to examine the Race main effect after controlling for the Sex main effect; Model 7a would examine the Sex main effect after controlling for the Race main effect. For this example, the Race main effect is significant regardless of whether a hierarchical or partial L^2 approach is used and we would conclude that whites and nonwhites differ in retention rate. Note that the statement of this conclusion differs slightly from the statement for the association model approach.

Post Hoc Procedures

The *post hoc* procedures used in the analysis of simple log-linear models, like our example, are relatively easy to compute and interpret. In the association model approach, the researcher determines and reports the magnitude of the association between the Race (**R**) and Retention (**T**) variables combined over the Sex (**S**) variable. For this 2×2 contingency table, there are several measures of association that could be used including the phi (ϕ) coefficient (Hinkle et al., 1988). This 2×2 contingency table along with this measure is found in Table 11. For these data, ϕ = .152 and is interpreted as a correlation coefficient.

For the logit model, three *post hoc* procedures can be used: (1) standardized residuals (Hinkle et al., 1988); (2) Scheffe-type contrasts (Marascuilo and McSweeney, 1977); and (3) tests of the estimates of the parameters (Lee, 1977; Kennedy, 1983). We will illustrate the computation of the standardized residuals in interpreting the difference in retention for whites and nonwhites. Since the L^2 statistic is computed over all cells of the 2×2 table, a significant L^2 is an omnibus statistic and does not specify which of the cells are the major contributors to the statistical significance. To determine which cells are significant contributors, standardized residuals are computed for each cell using the following formula:

$$R = \frac{O - E}{\sqrt{E}}$$

where O is the observed frequency for the cell and E is the expected frequency. The observed frequencies (O), the expected frequencies (E), and the standardized residual R for each of the cells of this 2×2 contingency table are found in Table 12. Standardized residuals have been shown to be approximately standard normal (Haberman, 1973). Thus, when an R for a given cell exceeds 2.00 (in absolute value), we would conclude that the cell is a major contributor to the significant L^2 statistic. Further, if the sign of the R is positive, then that cell contains more observed frequencies than expected. Conversely, if the sign is negative, the cell contains fewer observed frequencies than expected. For the example, the standardized residuals in Table 12 indicate that there were fewer than expected whites $R = -2.260$) and more than expected nonwhites $R =$

TABLE 12. Standardized Residuals for $2 \times 2 \times 2$ Logit Model

	Race		
	White	Nonwhite	
Retention			
Stay			
O	1,947	162	2,109
E	1,888.37	220.63	
Dropout			
O	613	137	750
E	671.63	78.37	
Total	2,560	299	2,859

Standardized Residuals		
Race		
White	Nonwhite	
Retention		
Stay	1.347	−3.943
Dropout	−2.260	6.612

6.612) who dropped out of school and fewer than expected nonwhites ($\underline{R}$ = -3.943) who stayed in school.

A MORE COMPLEX EXAMPLE

The analysis and interpretation of log-linear models and the subsequent *post hoc* procedures for both association and logit models are relatively easy when each of the variables is dichotomous. However, the analysis and interpretation become more complex when the variables have more than two levels. Consider an example using the 1971–1980 Cooperative Institutional Research Project (CIRP) survey (Astin, 1982). In this example, we will consider the association among the following variables:

HS—Hard vs. Soft academic major
PA—Pure vs. Applied academic major
LN—Life vs. Nonlife academic major
RL—Extent to which current job was related to undergraduate major
CP—Extent to which college prepared them for their current job

The data for this example are found in Table 13. Note that the first three variables (**HS**, **PA**, and **LN**) are dichotomous with the **RL** variable having three levels and the **CP** variable having four levels. The resulting cross-classification has dimensions 2 × 2 × 2 × 3 × 4, or 96 cells.

For this example, we will consider both an association model approach and a logit model approach. In the association model approach, suppose the researcher does not specify a hierarchy and uses the second screening procedure discussed above; the two screening tables are found in Table 14. The L^2 statistics for the first screening table indicate that 1-way, 2-way, 3-way, 4-way, and higher order effects are statistically significant. However, in the second screening table, only the families of 1-way, 2-way, and 3-way effects are significant. Following the initial examination of the data, the researcher would use one of the recommended post hoc procedures for investigating the magnitude of the significant associations within the families of the two-variable and three-variable effects. The first step would be to consider the partial L^2 for each member of these families; these partial L^2 are found in Table 15. Since the purpose of this chapter is to illustrate the use of log-linear models rather than to provide a complete interpretation of all significant associations, we will only discuss the **PA** * **RL** and the **LN** * **PA** * **RL** associations (see Table 15). Since the **PA** variable has two levels and the **RL** variable has three levels, a 2 × 3 contingency table is needed to determine the magnitude of the association between these two variables. This table is developed by combining over the levels of the other three variables. The measures of association recommended for contingency tables larger than 2 × 2

TABLE 13. Data from CIRP Survey

Hard/soft (HS)	Pure/applied (PA)	Life/nonlife (LN)	Related (RL)	Job prep (CP)			
			Not related (1)	41	30	22	12
		Nonlife	Somewhat (2)	25	97	56	22
	Applied	(1)	Closely (3)	2	89	127	104
	(1)		Not related (1)	89	53	32	11
		Life	Somewhat (2)	13	39	43	13
Soft		(2)	Closely (3)	12	131	192	158
(1)			Not related (1)	114	115	82	16
		Nonlife	Somewhat (2)	9	60	58	27
	Pure	(2)	Closely (3)	7	47	94	81
	(2)		Not related (1)	125	137	85	33
		Life	Somewhat (2)	16	122	85	52
		(2)	Closely (3)	4	41	84	71
			Not related (1)	6	6	7	4
		Nonlife	Somewhat (2)	5	28	31	24
	Applied	(1)	Closely (3)	5	28	64	69
	(1)		Not related (1)	6	9	3	4
		Life	Somewhat (2)	2	16	6	3
Hard		(2)	Closely (3)	5	38	67	75
(2)			Not related (1)	22	24	14	12
		Nonlife	Somewhat (2)	5	36	36	17
	Pure	(2)	Closely (3)	2	19	41	33
	(2)		Not related (1)	24	17	19	6
		Life	Somewhat (2)	8	20	19	6
		(2)	Closely (3)	1	19	22	31

are Cramer's V and the symmetric λ (Hinkle et al., 1988). The 2×3 contingency table for the **PA** * **RL** association and the computed values for V and λ are found in Table 16. Again, these measures of association are interpreted in a manner similar to a correlation coefficient.

Now consider the **LN** * **PA** * **RL** association. For a significant three-variable association, we must investigate the two-variable associations within the levels of the third variable. For this example, we chose to investigate the **PA** * **RL** association within each of the two levels of **LN**. This strategy is analogous to "simple-effects" analyses in higher-order ANOVA. The two 2×3 contingency tables for the levels of **LN** are found in Table 17 along with the calculated values

TABLE 14. Screening Tables for Nonhierarchical Models

A. Tests that K-way and higher order effects are zero

K	L^2	p
1	3,506.232	<.0001
2	1,793.561	<.0001
3	188.255	<.0001
4	44.514	.0328
5	10.194	.1167

B. Tests that K-way effects are zero

K	L^2	p
1	1,712.671	<.0001
2	1,605.306	<.0001
3	143.741	<.0001
4	34.320	.0607
5	10.194	.1167

for V and λ for each. Note that the two measures of association are smaller for the nonlife academic majors ($V = .304$ and $\lambda = .142$) than for the life academic majors ($V = .404$ and $\lambda = 268$) indicating that the **PA** $*$ **RL** association is not the same in the two levels of the **LN** variable.

Now consider the logit model for this example using the **CP** variable as the logit variable. Without a specified hierarchy, the researcher would also use the two screening tables in Table 14 and the partial L^2 in Table 15 to identify which of the main effects and interactions are statistically significant. From Table 15, only the partial associations containing **CP** would be considered. Again, since the purpose of this chapter is to illustrate the use of log-linear models rather than provide a complete interpretation of all main and interaction effects, only the logit model main effect due to **HS** variable (i.e., the **HS** $*$ **CP** association) and the logit model **PA** $*$ **HS** interaction (i.e., the **PA** $*$ **HS** $*$ **CP** association) will be considered. For the **HS** main effect, the observed frequencies (O), the expected frequencies (E), and the standardized residuals (R) for each cell of the 2×4 contingency table are found in Table 18. These data indicate that, among graduates with a soft academic major, more than expected ($R = 2.076$) said college did not prepare them for their current job, and fewer than expected ($R = -2.668$) said that college prepared them very well. Conversely, among graduates with a hard academic major, fewer than expected ($R = -3.662$) said that college did not prepare them for their current job while more than expected ($R = 4.707$) said that college prepared them very well.

Now consider the **PA** $*$ **HS** logit model interaction; the standardized residuals are found in Table 19. The interpretation of these residuals is more complex.

TABLE 15. Tests of Partial Associations

	L^2	p
HS * PA * LN * RL	3.080	.2144
HS * PA * LN * CP	4.949	.1756
HS * PA * RL * CP	11.928	.0636
HS * PA * RL * CP	6.219	.3991
PA * LN * RL * CP	7.865	.2481
HS * PA * LN	.027	.8702
HS * PA * RL	.453	.7973
HS * LN * RL	14.763	.0006
PA * LN * RL	92.375	<.0001
HS *PA * CP	9.674	.0215
HS * LN * CP	6.335	.0964
PA * LN * CP	3.878	.2749
HS * RL * CP	7.502	.2769
PA * RL * CP	7.394	.2860
LN * RL * CP	.881	.9897
HS * PA	.454	.5003
HS * LN	35.497	<.0001
PA * LN	.479	.4887
HS * RL	44.063	<.0001
PA * RL	387.248	<.0001
LN * RL	16.901	.0002
HS * CP	16.705	.0008
PA * CP	11.743	.0083
LN * CP	2.546	.4869
RL * CP	928.598	<.0001
HS	1,089.241	<.0001
PA	1.923	.1655
LN	8.697	.0032
RL	236.521	<.0001
CP	376.267	<.0001

Note that the graduates with an applied and hard academic major have a pattern similar to that discussed above for the **HS** main effect, that is, fewer than expected ($R = -4.997$) said that college did not prepare them for their current job while more than expected ($R = 5.992$) said that college prepared them well. There were no significant standardized residuals for those graduates with an applied and soft academic major. Those graduates with a pure and soft academic major had a pattern similar to that discussed in the **HS** main effect; that is, more than expected ($R = 3.864$) said college did not prepare them for their current job

TABLE 16. V and λ for PA by RL Association

	Related		
	Not related	Somewhat	Closely
Applied	335	423	1,166
Pure	838	576	597

V = .327; λ = .198.

TABLE 17. V and λ for PA by RL Association Within the Levels of LN

Nonlife	Related		
	Not related	Somewhat	Closely
Applied	128	288	488
Pure	399	248	324

V = .304; λ = .142.

Life	Related		
	Not related	Somewhat	Closely
Applied	207	135	678
Pure	439	328	273

V = .404; λ = .268.

while fewer that expected ($R = -3.818$) said that college prepared them very well. An interesting anomaly in the data occurs for those graduates with a pure and hard academic major. The only standardized residual that was significant ($R = -3.343$) indicates that college prepared them well for their current job. This is in contrast to the results for the graduates with an applied and hard academic major mentioned above and might dictate further exploration.

SAMPLING AND STRUCTURAL ZEROS IN LOG-LINEAR ANALYSIS

In both previous examples, data sets with large sample sizes were analyzed. While large sample sizes are not a prerequisite for the analysis of log-linear models, such analyses are subject to the same restrictions as are all chi-square

TABLE 18. Standardized Residuals for the HS Main Effort

			CP			
			Not well	Fairly	Well	Very well
HS	Soft	O	457	961	960	600
		E	414.73	925.05	970.21	669.01
	Hard	O	91	260	322	284
		E	133.27	296.95	311.79	214.99

	Standardized Residuals			
	CP			
	Not well	Fairly	Well	Very well
HS Soft	2.076	1.182	-3.28	-2.668
HS Hard	-3.662	-2.144	0.578	4.707

TABLE 19. Standardized Residuals for the PA $*$ HS Intent

	CP			
	Not Well	Fairly	Well	Very Well
Applied				
Soft	-1.054	0.027	0.543	0.144
Hard	-4.997	-2.665	0.893	5.992
Pure				
Soft	3.864	1.651	-0.969	-3.818
Hard	-0.014	-0.288	-3.343	0.481

analyses; namely, no more than 20% of the cells should have expected frequencies (E) less than 5 and no cell can have zero entries (Hinkle et al., 1988). Consider the cross-classification table for the example using the CIRP data set; this table has $2 \times 2 \times 2 \times 3 \times 4 = 96$ cells (see Table 13). For such complex tables, large sample sizes are necessary in order to satisfy the requirement that fewer than 20% of the cell have expected frequencies less than 5. In this example, the sample size was 3,935 and there were no cells with expected frequency less than 5.

Zero cell frequencies can occur for one of two reasons; they can be either "sampling" zeros or "structural" zeros. Sampling zeros occur because the researcher uses a sample rather than the population. For cells in the population that have small frequencies, there is a possibility that a cell in the sample would contain no entries even though it is logically possible. For example, it is unlikely to find many grandparents under the age of 35 with bachelor's degrees, or males over 50 enrolled in nursing programs at community colleges, even in the largest national samples. In theory, the researcher could remove these zeros by increasing the sample size. Since this approach is often impractical, the researcher must resort to some other solution. One solution is to combine adjacent categories of the variable when it is practical and will not distort the data (Hinkle et al., 1988); however, this approach must be used with caution. A second approach is to add a small constant, such as .50, to each cell in the contingency table (Goodman, 1970). This is the method used most often, but it tends to be conservative and underestimate the parameters and their significance (Knoke and Burke, 1980). A third, but more complex, solution is to use maximum-likelihood estimates for the zero cell entries (Fienberg, 1980).

Structural zeros, on the other hand, arise from combinations that are logical impossibilities, such as male obstetrics patients. The major problem occurs when researchers fail to recognize that they have a structural zero rather than a sampling zero and try to remove it using the methods described above. This practice leads to uninformative analyses and must be avoided (Fienberg, 1980). The approaches for dealing with structural zeros are either the analysis of partial tables (Bishop, Fienberg, and Holland, 1975) or the use of "quasi-independence" models (Goodman, 1968).

USING LOG-LINEAR MODELS TO TEST FOR DISCRIMINATION

Log-linear analysis provides a rational procedure for testing the association between gender and these various personnel decisions, such as promotion and tenure, which are dichotomous, categorical variables. In these analyses, some writers advocate a search for the best-fitting model (Fienberg, 1980). However, the intent of hypothesis testing is not to let the data dictate the analysis, but to determine if a specified effect is statistically significant. Moreover, if a test procedure considers a large number of alternatives, some of which may be dropped from consideration if nonsignificant, then the nominal significance level is an underestimate of the actual significance level. For example, if 20 effects are tested using the .05 level of significance, then the probability is much greater than .05 that at least one effect will have an apparent significance of .05.

The solution to this dilemma is to develop rules for one specific test of an effect and to compute the probability for that test. In testing for *prima facie* evidence of discrimination, the first step is to identify the effect which can be uniquely interpreted as evidence of gender-based bias (if there are no other

TABLE 20. Data for Sex Descrimination Example

Year	Level	Gender	Decision	
			Yes	No
	To prof.	Male	25	13
1984		Female	3	4
	To assoc.	Male	44	13
		Female	6	4
	To prof.	Male	32	18
1983		Female	1	0‡
	To assoc.	Male	42	17
		Female	10	3
	To prof.	Male	23	27
1982		Female	0†	0†
	To assoc.	Male	41	11
		Female	7	0‡

†Structural zero.
‡Sampling zero.

explanations). It should be noted that such a procedure does not "prove" discrimination: no statistical procedure proves bias. The use of statistics only indicates whether the outcomes are related to gender, or some other factor, in a way not explained by the other elements in the model. If not, other evidence can then be considered as a basis for the bias.

Consider a logit model approach for the data in Table 20; the variables investigated are year of consideration (Y), level of promotion (L), and gender (S) with promotion outcome (D) as the logit variable. Note that the cells for females considered for promotion to full professor in 1982 are identified as structural zeros since no females were considered for this specific personnel action. In addition, there are two cells that are identified as sampling zeros: (1) females not promoted to full professor in 1983 and 2) females not promoted to associate professor in 1982.

In this example, the effect which must be considered as a cause for concern is the interaction of gender and the personnel decision, the logit model main effect due to gender, which indicates that the members of both sexes are not proportionally distributed within the categories of the decision (i.e., promotion). Where there are additional variables, their association with the gender-by-decision effect (the logit model interaction) must also be considered. The change in the fit of the model with the addition of these elements indicates the statistical significance of possible discrimination interactions. If there is an improvement in

TABLE 21. Expected Frequencies for Sex Discrimination Example

Year	Level	Gender	Decision	
			Yes	No
	To prof.	Male	24.1	14.9
1984		Female	4.9	3.1
	To assoc.	Male	42.9	15.1
		Female	8.1	2.9
	To prof.	Male	32.7	18.3
1983		Female	1.3	0.7
	To assoc.	Male	43.0	17.0
		Female	10.0	4.0
	To prof.	Male	23.5	27.5
1982		Female	0†	0†
	To assoc.	Male	42.6	10.4
		Female	6.4	1.6

†Structural zero.

fit associated with the inclusion of the model with these additional effects, then the *post hoc* procedures discussed earlier can be used to isolate the source of the significant effect(s).

The effects which can indicate possible cause for concern are based on the association of gender (**S**) and promotion outcome (**D**), that is, the logit model main effect due to gender (**SD**). In this specific example, there are also several higher-order association terms which contain the **SD** effect: its association with year, the logit model interaction (**SYD**); its association with level of promotion, the logit model interaction (**SLD**); and its association with both year and level of promotion, the second order logit model interaction (**SYLD**). If these terms are dropped from the model, the resulting analysis is based on **SLY, LYD**, and lower-order terms (e.g., **LY, SL, SY, YD, LD, A, S, L, Y**). Note that none of these terms contain the gender-decision interaction term.

The expected values for the **SD** model are shown in Table 21; they can be obtained by collapsing across gender, computing the proportion of members receiving the promotion, and multiplying the proportion by the number of each gender. For example, in 1982 there were 29 of 47 promoted so that the proportion (29/47) when multiplied by the number of males (39) gives 24.06 or the 24.1 shown in the table as the expected value for males. This reinforces the notion that this model produces expected values which are independent of a consideration of gender. The ability of this model to explain the observed frequencies is determined by computing the residual L^2 statistic, $L^2 = 4.18$.

TABLE 22. Tests of Partial Associations in Sex Discrimination Example

Effect	L^2	p
SLD	0.00	.9666
SYD	3.42	.1800
TYD	3.94	.1393
SLY	3.80	.0512
SD	0.18	.6699
LD	12.34	.0004
YD	0.43	.8074
SL	2.91	.0881
SY	1.32	.5174
LY	0.70	.7061
D	44.24	<.0001
S	185.67	<.0001
L	5.63	.0177
Y	0.53	.7689

With 5 degrees of freedom, the associated probability is .52. Thus, this model does fit the data and the models that include the **SD, SYD, SLD**, and the **SYLD** effects will not provide a significantly better fit. If, however, these latter models were necessary for fitting the data, then the researcher is advised to follow the exploratory strategy of testing models with the sequence dictated by the tests of partial associations (see Table 22). It must also be emphasized that the precision indicated by the printout should not be mistaken for accuracy, since each probability level represents the likelihood of a single outcome, not the probability of a large number of alternatives.

PATH ANALYSIS OF CONTINGENCY TABLES

Up to this point, the basic concepts and techniques of contingency table analysis have been discussed, including estimation, model screening, and *post hoc* procedures. Given the increasing use of causal modeling in educational, psychological, and sociological research (Bentler, 1980), we extend the discussion of logit analysis to the causal analysis of cross-classified data. Cook and Campbell (1979) note two goals for causal modeling: (1) estimating specific causal coefficients or (2) assessing the plausibility of different causal models for observed data. Given the current state of research in the behavioral sciences, the second goal is more appropriate for the purpose of this chapter, that is, to propose, test, and interpret alternative causal models for their fit to empirical data (Fienberg, 1980, p. 120).

Table 23. Data for Path Analysis Example

IQ	SES	Encouragement	College Plan	
			Yes	No
	Lower	Low	62	2276
Low		High	236	555
	Upper	Low	54	857
		High	540	644
	Lower	Low	99	976
High		High	481	442
	Upper	Low	97	544
		High	1,807	648

Source: WH Sewell and VP Shah (1968). Social class, parental encouragement, and cultural aspirations. *American Journal of Sociology* 73:559–572.

Where the data are at least intervally scaled, the appropriate procedure is path analysis (Wright, 1934). However, in this section, the focus is on path analysis with categorical data. Furthermore, only recursive causal models without feedback loops are considered. Since this presentation is not exhaustive, the reader is referred to several original sources. Fienberg (1980) devotes a chapter to the topic; Knoke and Burke (1980) and Kennedy (1983) also discuss causal modeling of contingency tables. Other sources include a series of articles by Goodman (1973a, b, 1979) and a chapter by Brier (1982). In addition, LISREL-type models for categorical data are discussed by Muthen (1984) and latent structure analysis by Lazarsfeld & Henry (1968).

To illustrate the application of logit analysis for a path analysis problem, consider the data previously analyzed by Sewell and Shah (1968). These investigators studied a random sample of 10,318 Wisconsin high school seniors, studying three exogenous and two endogenous variables. Their three exogenous variables were intelligence, gender, and socioeconomic status, which were believed to influence the two endogenous variables: reported parental encouragement toward attending college and subsequent reports of plans to attend college. Sewell and Shah (1968) based most of their analyses on interval level data, but they also presented a cross-tabulation of the data (p. 569). These data are the basis for our analyses and are presented in Table 23. For pedagogical purposes, two changes were made to simplify the analysis: (1) eliminating gender as an exogenous variable, and (2) collapsing intelligence (**I**) and socioeconomic status (**E**) into dichotomies. The latter change was made to enable a clearer interpretation of the parameter estimates generated by the log-linear analysis.

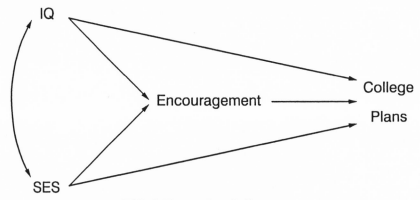

FIG. 1. Proposed path diagram.

An important first step in performing any path analysis is the construction of an explicit model relating the variables under investigation. This step is one of the major advantages of the causal modeling approach, since it forces researchers to specify *a priori* their assumptions about relations among the variables. The path diagram should be supported by previous research or theory, perhaps with competing models explicitly presented, because path analysis is a confirmatory technique. In path diagrams, arrows are used to represent causal and noncausal linkages. Curved, double-headed arrows represent noncausal associations which may be nonzero but are not interpreted as causal. These variables are given and are often referred to as exogenous or outside the causal system. Endogenous variables are the variables to be explained by the exogenous and other endogenous variables. Single-headed arrows represent directional and causal influences. As noted above, in recursive models the causal flow is presumed to be one-way. Notice that there are two types of causal effects: direct and indirect. *Direct* effects are unmediated and are transmitted directly from one variable to another. On the other hand, *indirect* effects are mediated by intervening variables in the causal model. A variable in a path diagram may have either or both types of effects on another variable. One possible model for this example is presented in Figure 1. In this model, intelligence (**I**) and socioeconomic status (**E**) are exogenous variables that precede parental encouragement (**C**), which in turn precedes reported college plans (**P**). The two exogenous variables also exert direct effects on college plans.

Following development of the path diagram, the next step is to determine estimates (lambdas) for the parameters in the path diagram using logit models. A sequential process is used in which one starts with the endogenous variable nearest to the exogenous variables and performs a series of logit analyses to estimate the "path coefficients," which are the parameter estimates (i.e., lambdas). The lambdas are analogous to betas in multiple regression analysis.

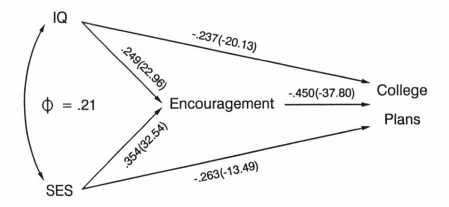

FIG. 2. Final path diagram.

Note carefully that the analogy between path analysis for interval data and path analysis for contingency table data breaks down if there are more than two levels of any variable. The complexity of the interpretation results from the fact that there is more than one parameter estimate when a polytomous variable is considered (Fienberg, 1980). The next step of the analysis consists of preparing a path diagram which includes the parameter estimates and perhaps a test of the fit of the overall model, indexed by the residual chi-square. Finally, some substantive interpretation should be applied to the final path diagram.

To test the model implied by the path diagram, one determines only the logit models implied by the path diagram(s) and tests only those models. That is, the screening procedure presented above for log-linear models is not appropriate when conducting a path analysis. Only the models specified by the path diagram are tested; parameter estimates generated from these analyses are then attached to the arrows. Therefore, for this example, we estimated three models to yield the final path diagram presented as Figure 2; these models are found in Table 24. The joint association among the two exogenous variables, SES and intelligence, was determined in the first model. The phi coefficient (ϕ) computed on the marginal table for these two variables equals .21, which indicates a significant, yet noncausal, association.

When estimating the path coefficients, it is important to control for all preceding variables to obtain the best estimates of effects. Note that second and third models in Table 24 include the main and interactive effects of all preceding variables before estimating the effects of interest.

To provide a substantive interpretation of the parameters attached to the causal arrows in Figure 2, it is important to remember that all variables are dichotomies.

TABLE 24. Models Tested in Path Analysis Example

Model 1	I,S,IS
Model 2	I,S,P,IS,IP,SP
Model 3	I,S,P,C,IS,IP,SP,ISP,IC,EC,PC

I = IQ.
S = SES.
P = Parental encouragement.
C = College plan.

Thus, the interpretation of the lambdas is that of the effect of the preceding variable on the logged odds of the response variable (Knoke & Burke, 1980; Kennedy, 1983). In addition to the path coefficients (lambdas) for the various paths, we have included, in parentheses, the z-value for the particular path coefficients. The z-values are standard normal deviates which are computed by dividing the lambdas by their standard errors. For example, the path from intelligence (I) to parental encouragement (C) is a positive .249 with a z-value equal to 22.96. Since the z-value is statistically significant, we conclude that those in the higher intelligence category are more likely to report high parental encouragement. Similarly, the path coefficient from socioeconomic status (E) to parental encouragement (C) is slightly larger and positive (.354) and also statistically significant ($z = 32.54$). Thus, we conclude that those in the higher socioeconomic category are more likely to report high parental encouragement.

Now consider the third model in Table 24 and the the effects of the measured variables on college plans (P). There are three effects of interest: (1) intelligence (I), (2) socioeconomic status (E) and (3) parental encouragement (C). Note in Figure 2 that all the lambda coefficients relating these variables to college plans are negative and statistically significant. Specifically, the path from intelligence to reported college plans is $-.237$, with an associated z-value of -20.13; the path from socioeconomic status to reported college plans is $-.263$, with an associated z-value of -13.49. Finally, the path from reported parental encouragement to reported college plans is $-.450$, with an associated z-value of -37.80. The negative signs are a function of how the data are coded, with the first category representing plans to attend college and the second category representing plans to not attend. The coefficients are interpreted as before, that is, as the effects of the independent variables on the logged odds of being in the two categories of the dependent variable.

Some significant problems still remain with the application of logit models to analyze qualitative path models. Goodman's analogy with continuous path analysis breaks down, according to Fienberg (1980) and Knoke and Burke (1980), where indirect effects and higher-order interactions are concerned.

Fienberg attributes part of the problem to the absence of a "calculus" for path coefficients. For example, Fienberg argues that only signs should be attached to paths, rather than parameter estimates as argued by Goodman. However, in defense of the use of log-linear analysis, it should be noted that there are no real procedures for handling interactions in quantitative path analysis.

The future of structural equation modeling with contingency table data would seem to lie in one of two directions. First, Muthen (1976, 1984) has recently developed a LISREL analogue, LISCOMP, to handle the problem of polytomous latent variables. This program is presently being tested for release. Second, latent structure techniques may represent another path of attack on this problem (Clogg, 1981).

SUMMARY

The purpose of this chapter was to present pertinent concepts and procedures for using log-linear and logit analysis in higher education research. We have made the distinction between symmetric and asymmetric designs in both the initial analysis and the *post hoc* procedures. The examples used illustrate the flexibility of the approach in both an analysis of variance and a regression framework. With these data, we hope that the reader will be able to evaluate the strengths and weaknesses of using log-linear models in higher education research.

REFERENCES

Astin, A. W. (1982). *Minorities in Higher Education*. San Francisco: Jossey-Bass.
Bartlett, M. S. (1935). Contingency table interactions. *Journal of the Royal Statistical Society Supplement* 2: 248–252.
Bentler, P. M. (1980). Multivariate analysis with latent variables: Causal modeling. *Annual Review of Psychology* 31: 419–456.
Birch, M. W. (1963). Maximum likelihood in three-way contingency tables. *Journal of the Royal Statistical Society* 25(Series B): 220–233.
Bishop, Y. M. M. (1969). Full contingency tables, logits, and split contingency tables. *Biometrics* 25: 119–128.
Bishop, Y. M. M., Fienberg, S. E., and Holland, P. W. (1975). *Discrete Multivariate Analysis: Theory and Practice*. Cambridge, MA: MIT Press.
BMDP, Inc. (1985). *Biomedical Data Programs Statistical Software Manual*. Berkeley: University of California Press.
Bock, R. D. (1970). Estimating multinomial response relations. In R. C. Bose et al. (eds.), *Contributions to Statistics and Probability*. Chapel Hill: University of North Carolina Press.
Bock, R. D., and Yates, G. (1973). *MULTIQUAL Loglinear Analysis of Nominal and Ordinal Qualitative Data by the Method of Maximum Likelihood*. Chicago: National Educational Resources.
Brier, S. S. (1982). Analysis of categorical data. In G. Keren (ed.), *Statistical and Methodological Issues in Psychology and Social Sciences Research*. Hillsdale, NJ: Erlbaum.
Clogg, C. C. (1981). New developments in latent structure analysis. In D. J. Jackson and

E. F. Borgatta (eds.), *Factor Analysis and Measurement in Sociological Research: A Multidimensional Perspective* Beverly Hills: Sage.

Cook, T. D., and Campbell, D. T. (1979). *Quasi-experimentation: Design and Analysis Issues for Field Settings* Chicago: Rand-McNally.

Fay, R. E., and Goodman, L. A. (1975). *ECTA Program: Description for Users.* Chicago: University of Chicago Press.

Fienberg, S. E. (1972). The analysis of incomplete multi-way contingency tables. *Biometrics* 28: 177–202.

Fienberg, S. E. (1980). *The Analysis of Cross-classified Categorical Data* (2nd ed). Cambridge, MA: MIT Press.

Fisher, R. A. (1924). The conditions under which χ^2 measures the discrepancy between observed observation and hypothesis. *Journal of the Royal Statistical Society* 87: 442–450.

Goodman, L. A. (1963). On methods for comparing contingency tables. *Journal of the Royal Statistical Society* 126(Series A): 94–108.

Goodman, L. A. (1964). Simultaneous confidence limits for cross-product ratios in contingency tables. *Journal of the Royal Statistical Society,* 26(Series B): 86–102.

Goodman, L. A. (1968). The analysis of cross-classified data: Independence, quasi-independence, and interaction in contingency tables with or without missing cells. *Journal of the American Statistical Association* 63: 1091–1131.

Goodman, L. A. (1970). The multivariate analysis of qualitative data: Interactions among multiple classifications. *Journal of the American Statistical Association* 65: 226–256.

Goodman, L. A. (1971a). The analysis of multidimensional contingency tables: Stepwise procedures and direct estimation methods for building models for multiple classifications. *Technometrics* 13: 33–61.

Goodman, L. A. (1971b). Partitioning of chi-square, analysis of marginal contingency tables, and estimation of expected frequencies in multidimensional contingency tables. *Journal of the American Statistical Association* 66: 339–344.

Goodman, L. A. (1973a). Causal analysis of data from panel studies and other kinds of surveys. *American Journal of Sociology* 78: 1135–1191.

Goodman, L. A. (1973b). The analysis of multidimensional contingency tables when some variables are posterior to others: a modified path analysis approach. *Biometrika* 60: 179–192.

Goodman, L. A. (1978). *Analyzing Qualitative/Categorical Data.* Cambridge, MA: Abt Books.

Goodman, L. A. (1979). A brief guide to the causal analysis of data from surveys. *American Journal of Sociology* 84: 1078–1095.

Goodman, L. A., and Kruskal, W. H. (1954). Measures of association for cross-classifications. *Journal of the American Statistical Association* 49: 732–764.

Grizzle, J. E., Starmer, C. F., and Koch, G. G. (1969). Analysis of categorical data by linear models. *Biometrics* 25: 489–504.

Grizzle, J. E., and Williams, O. D. (1972). Log-linear models and tests of independence for contingency tables. *Biometrics* 28: 137–156.

Haberman, S. J. (1972). Log-linear fit for contingency tables (Algorithm AS-51). *Applied Statistics* 21: 218–225.

Haberman, S. J. (1973). The analysis of residuals in cross-classified tables. *Biometrics* 29: 205–220.

Haberman, S. J. (1979). *Analysis of Qualitative Data* Vol. 1. New York: Academic Press.

Hinkle, D. E., and McLaughlin, G. W. (1984). Selection of models in contingency tables: A reexamination. *Research in Higher Education* 21: 415–423.

Hinkle, D. E., Wiersma, W., and Jurs, S. G. (1988). *Applied Statistics for the Behavioral Sciences*. (2nd ed.). Boston: Houghton Mifflin.

Kastenbaum, M. (1974). Analysis of categorized data: some well-known analogues and some new concepts. *Communications in Statistics* 3: 401–417.

Kennedy, J. J. (1983). *Introductory Log-linear Analysis for Behavioral Researchers*. New York: Praeger.

Killion, R. A., and Zahn, D. A. (1976). A bibliography of contingency table literature: 1900–1974. *International Statistical Review* 44: 71–112.

Knoke, D., and Burke, P. J. (1980). Log-linear models. Sage University Paper Series on Quantitative Applications in the Social Sciences, 07–020. Beverly Hills, Sage.

Lazarsfeld, P. F., and Henry, N. W. (1968). *Latent Structure Analysis*. Boston: Houghton Mifflin.

Lee, S. K. (1977). On the asymptotic variances of μ terms in loglinear models of multidimensional contingency tables. *Journal of the American Statistical Association* 72: 412–419.

Marascuilo, L. A., and McSweeney, M. (1977). *Nonparametric and Distribution-free Methods for the Social Sciences*. Monterey, CA: Brooks/Cole.

Muthen, B. (1976). Structural equation models with dichotomous dependent variables: a sociological analysis problem formulated by O. D. Duncan. Research Report 76–19, Department of Statistics, University of Uppsala, Sweden.

Muthen, B. (1984). A general structural equation model with dichotomous, ordered categorical, and continuous latent variable indicators. *Psychometrika* 49: 115–132.

Pearson, K. (1900). On a criterion that a given system of deviations from the probable in the case of a correlated system of variables is such that it can reasonably be supposed to have arisen from random sampling. *Philosophical Magazine* 50: 157–175.

Roy, S. N., and Kastenbaum, M. A. (1956). On the hypothesis of ''no interaction'' in a multi-way contingency table. *Annals of Mathematical Statistics* 27: 749–757.

SAS Institute Inc. (1985). *SAS User's Guide: Statistics, Version 5 Edition*. Cary, NC: SAS Institute.

Sewell, W. H., and Shah, V. P. (1968). Social class, parental encouragement, and educational aspirations. *American Journal of Sociology* 73: 559–572.

SPSS Inc. (1986). *SPSSX User's Guide* (2nd ed.). Chicago.

SYSTAT, Inc. (1986). *SYSTAT: The System for Statistics*. Evanston, IL.

Wright, S. (1934). The method of path coefficients. *Annals of Mathematical Statistics* 5: 161–215.

Yule, G. U. (1900). On the association of attributes in statistics: with illustration from the material of the childhood society. *Philosophical Transactions of the Royal Society* 194(Series A): 257–319.

Managing Uncertainty: Environmental Analysis/Forecasting in Academic Planning

James L. Morrison
*University of North Carolina at
Chapel Hill*

and

Thomas V. Mecca
*Piedmont Technical
College*

The external environment of institutions of higher education can be characterized by change and turbulence. Administrators of colleges and universities have witnessed major shifts in the demographics of their institutions' clientele. External agencies have tightened their control of policymaking and fiscal decisions made by the institutions' administrations. There has been a growing criticism of the value of the curriculum offered and the quality of instruction provided by many institutions of higher education, particularly in view of the importance of education in the increasingly competitive environment of the global economy. Less obvious, but no less significant, there has been a pervasive spread of electronic technologies through American society, challenging the dominant instructional and managerial paradigm found in the majority of American higher education institutions. In short, the accelerating rate, magnitude, and complexity of change occurring in all sectors of American society have created vulnerabilities and opportunities across the higher education "tableau" (Keller, 1983).

The rapidity and volume of changes have resulted in less lead time for administrators to analyze changes in their institutions' external environment and to formulate appropriate strategies. In addition, the risks and uncertainty involved in implementing a particular strategy or set of strategies have intensified. In summary, the turbulence in higher education's external environment challenges the capability of decisionmakers to effectively anticipate changing conditions.

This phenomenon of rapid environmental shifts led to a recognition among administrators and organizational theorists of the need for a comprehensive approach to institutional planning that emphasizes sensitivity to the effects of environmental shifts on the strategic position of the institution (Ellison, 1977; Cope, 1988). An administrator's analysis of the organization's environment is critical in accurately assessing the opportunities and threats that the environment poses for the institution and in developing the strategic policies necessary to adapt to both internal and external environments.

All organizations, including colleges and universities, are perceived by contemporary organizational theorists as social systems existing in and interacting with their environment (Aldrich, 1979; Scott, 1981). An organization's environment is essentially all those external factors that affect it or are perceived to affect it. Hall (1977) divides an organization's environmental factors into two categories: the limited number of factors that directly affect it (the task environment) and the almost unlimited number of factors that influence all organizations in the society (the general societal environment). In essence, the task environment is composed of the set of factors that are unique to each organization, while the general societal environment includes environmental factors that are the same for all organizations.

Factors in the task environment are readily apparent to college and university administrators (e.g., clients/students, revenue sources, and government educational policies and regulations). However, the distinction between the organization's task environment and the general societal environment is not always clear. Particularly under turbulent conditions, factors in the general societal environment "break through" into the organization's task environment (Kast and Rosenzweig, 1979). Consequently, changes in the general societal environment can, and often do, have significant effects on the organization, effects well documented in the literature of organizational analysis (Osborne and Hunt, 1974; Hall, 1977; Kast and Rosenzweig, 1979; Scott, 1981).

The uncertainty faced by a decision-maker in planning strategically is compounded by an increasingly dynamic and uncertain environment (Emery and Trist, 1965). Terreberry (1968) concluded that organizations must be prepared to adapt even more to the influence of external forces. Most environments are dynamic and, consequently, rich in possible opportunities as well as possible threats to the organization. Therefore, the strategic planner and policymaker cannot analyze the condition of the future environment by assuming that it will remain in a readily predictable state (i.e., in an orderly and incremental progression into the future).

Contingency approaches to organizational theory have focused upon the effect of environmental change in creating uncertainty for policymakers formulating organizational strategy (Anderson and Paine, 1975; Lindsay and Rue, 1980; Boulton et al., 1982; Miller and Friesen, 1980; Jauch and Kraft, 1986; Kast and

Rosenzweig, 1984). Duncan (1972) describes three factors that contribute to this sense of uncertainty: (a) a lack of information about environmental factors that would influence a given decision-making situation; (b) a lack of knowledge about the effects of an incorrect decision; and (c) the inability of the decision-maker to assess the probability that a given environmental factor will affect the success (or failure) of the organization or one of its subsystems in fulfilling its mission. In a later study, Leblebici and Salancik (1981) also found that the uncertainty experienced by a decision-maker arises from his or her inability to predict the outcomes of certain actions. This inability to predict decision outcomes is derived from two sources. The first is the nature of the world in which we live—multivariate, complex, and interrelated. The second is the probabilistic quality of our world—an event can occur tomorrow, next week, or next year that could affect the interrelationships of variables, trends, and issues. In essence, the more turbulent and complex the organization's environment appears, the less able an administrator is to anticipate the probability of success in implementing a particular strategy.

Traditional planning models are weak in identifying environmental changes and in assessing their organizational impact. In his analysis of the approaches to planning exhibited by American educational institutions, Ziegler (1972) identified two primary assumptions that characterize the weakness of these models: (a) the organization's environment will remain essentially static over time; and (b) the environment is composed of only a few variables that impact education. In essence, the underlying assumption of most current educational planning is that environmental change will be a continuation of the rate and direction of present (and past) trends. These trends are manifested in the "planning assumptions" typically placed in the first part of an institution's strategic or long-range plan. Therefore, many administrators implicitly expect a "surprise-free" future for their institutions. We know, however, that change, not continuation, will be the trend, and the further we go out into the future, the more true this will be. An approach is needed that enables administrators to detect signals of change in all sectors of the environment and to link environmental information to the organization's strategic management (Ansoff, 1975; Weber, 1984; Chaffee, 1985; Levy and Engledow, 1986; McConkey, 1987; Dutton and Duncan, 1987; Hearn, 1988).

The purpose of this chapter is to describe an approach to environmental analysis and forecasting that educational policymakers can employ in dealing with the level of uncertainty associated with strategic decision-making. Unlike traditional models of planning, such an approach does not lead decision-makers to conclude that the uncertainty they perceive in the external environment has been reduced. Rather, the focus of this approach is to enhance their capability to deal with a changing environment by making the perceived uncertainty in that environment explicit (Fahey, King, and Narayanan, 1981). This is accomplished through the analysis and evaluation of possible alternative future states of an organization's environment and the sources of change within it. In this chapter, we will explain one model of this approach and demonstrate its application in a case study. We conclude with an examination of the issues and questions posed by the application of this model to educational institutions, and we suggest directions for future research in this emerging methodological domain.

ENVIRONMENTAL ANALYSIS AND FORECASTING

Environmental analysis and forecasting are based upon a number of assumptions, among them the following (Boucher and Morrison, 1989):

- the future cannot be predicted, but it can be forecasted probabilistically, taking explicit account of uncertainty.
- Forecasts are virtually certain to be useless or misleading if they do not sweep widely across possible future developments in such areas as demography, values and lifestyles, technology, economics, law and regulation, and institutional change.
- Alternative futures including the "most likely" future are defined primarily by human judgment, creativity, and imagination.
- The aim of defining alternative futures is to try to determine how to create a better future than the one that would materialize if we merely kept doing essentially what is presently being done.

A model based upon assumptions like these is shown in Figure 1. Basically, the model states that from our experiences or through environmental scanning we identify *issues or concerns* that may require attention. These issues/concerns are then defined in terms of their component parts—*trends* and *events*. Univariate forecasts of trends and events are generated and subsequently interrelated through *cross-impact analysis*. The "most likely" future is written in a scenario format from the univariate trend and event forecasts; outlines of alternative scenarios to that future are generated by computer simulations from the cross-impact matrix. In turn, these *scenarios* stimulate the development of policies appropriate for each scenario. These policies are *analyzed* for their robustness across scenarios. The purpose of the entire exercise is to derive a final list of *policies* that effectively address the issues and concerns identified in the initial stage of the process. These policies are then implemented in *action plans*.

Issue Identification
A wide range of literature provides insights into how issues are recognized by decision-makers. Included is literature related to problem sensing and formulation (Kiesler and Sproull, 1982; Lyles and Mitroff, 1980; Pounds, 1969),

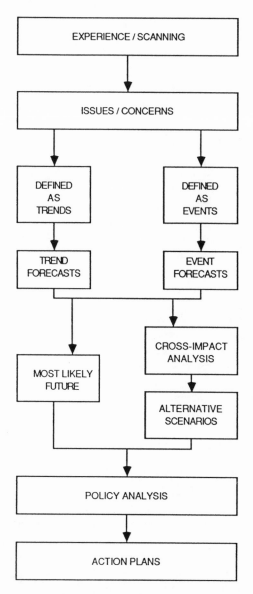

FIG. 1. Environmental Analysis/Forecasting Model (modified from Boucher and Morrison, 1989)

normative strategy development (Nutt, 1979), decision-making (Alexis and Wilson, 1967; Mintzberg, Raisinghani, and Theoret, 1976; Segev, 1976), and environmental scanning (Aguilar, 1967; Kefalas and Schoderbeck, 1973; King,

1982). Regardless of how issues are identified, there is agreement that inconsistencies perceived within the environment stimulate the decision-maker to further examine the issue (Dutton and Duncan, 1987).

The articulation of issues/concerns is particularly critical for effective strategic planning. A central tenet of strategic management pervading both the literature of organizational theory (Lawrence and Lorsch, 1967) and traditional business policy (Andrews, 1971) is that the proper match between an organization's external conditions and its internal capabilities is critical to its performance. Accordingly, the primary responsibility of the organizational strategist is to find and create an alignment between the threats and opportunities inherent in the environment and the strengths and weaknesses unique to the organization (Thompson, 1967).

A number of writers have recognized that the strategist's perceptions of the environment and the uncertainty it represents to the organization are key to the strategy-making process (Aguilar, 1967; Anderson and Paine, 1975; Bourgeois, 1980; Hambrick, 1982). Hatten and Schendel (1975) and Snow (1976) further suggest that the effectiveness of the strategy an organization pursues is dependent upon the strategist's ability to identify and evaluate major discontinuities in the environment. This ability is dependent upon the experience the strategist brings to this task as well as his or her ability to systematically scan the contemporary external environment.

Scanning

A major tool to identify discontinuities in the external environment is environmental scanning. Aguilar (1967) defined environmental scanning as the systematic collection of external information in order to lessen the randomness of information flowing into the organization. According to Jain (1984), most environmental scanning systems fall into one of four stages: primitive, *ad hoc*, reactive, and proactive. In the primitive stage, the environment is taken as unalterable. There is no attempt to distinguish between strategic and nonstrategic information; scanning is passive and informal. In the *ad hoc* stage, areas are identified for careful observation, and there are attempts to obtain information about these areas (e.g., through electronic data base searches), but no formal system to obtain this information is instituted. In the reactive stage, efforts are made to continuously monitor the environment for information about specific areas. Again, a formal scanning system is not utilized, but an attempt is made to store, analyze, and comprehend the material. In the proactive stage, a formal search replaces the informal searches characteristic of the earlier stages. Moreover, a significant effort is made to incorporate resulting information into the strategic planning process.

Aguilar suggests that environmental assessment is more effective where a formal search replaces the informal search of the environment. The formal search uses information sources covering all sectors of the external environment (social, technological, economic and political) from the task environment to the global environment. A comprehensive system includes specifying particular information resources (e.g., print, TV, radio, conferences) to be systematically reviewed for impending discontinuities. Examples of such systems are found mainly in the corporate world (e.g., United Airlines, General Motors); less comprehensive systems are now appearing in colleges and universities (Hearn and Heydinger, 1985; Morrison, 1987), although recent literature advocates establishing formal environmental scanning systems to alert administrators to emerging issues (Cope, 1988; Keller, 1983; Simpson, McGinty, and Morrison, 1987).

Structuring Issues

Issues may be *structured* by identifying their parts as trends or events. *Trends* are a series of social, technological, economic, or political characteristics that can be estimated and/or measured over time. They are statements of the general direction of change, usually gradual and long-term, and reflect the forces shaping the region, nation, or society in general. This information may be subjective or objective. For example, a subjective trend is the level of support for a public college by the voters in the state. An objective trend would be the amount of funding provided to all public institutions in the state. An *event* is a discrete, confirmable occurrence that makes the future different from the past. An example would be: "Congress mandates a period of national service for all 17–20-year-olds."

Structuring the issues involved in the planning problem includes developing a set of trends that measure change in individual categories, along with a set of possible future events that, if they were to occur, might have a significant effect on the trends, or on other events. The trend and event set is chosen to reflect the complexity and multidimensionality of the category. Ordinarily, this means that the trends and events will describe a wide variety of social, technological, economic, and political factors in the regional, national, and global environment.

Forecasting

Having defined the trend and event sets, the next step is to forecast subjectively the items in each of these sets over the period of strategic interest (e.g., the next 15 years). For trends, the likely level over this period is projected. This is an *exploratory forecast*. It defines our expectation, not our preference. (*Normative forecasts* define the future as we would like it to be with the focus on developing plans and policies to attain that future.) Similarly, the cumulative probability of each event over the period of interest is estimated, again on the same assumption.

It is important to distinguish between the terms *prediction* and *forecast*. Science depends upon theoretical explanation from which predictions can be made. With respect to the future, a prediction is an assertion about how some element of "the" future will, in fact, materialize. In contrast, a forecast is a probabilistic statement about some element of a possible future. The underlying form of a forecast statement is, "If A occurs, plus some allowance for unknown or unknowable factors, then maybe we can expect B or something very much like B to occur, or at least B will become more or less probable."

It is also important to distinguish the criteria for judging predictions and forecasts. Predictions are judged on the basis of their accuracy. Forecasts are judged, according to Boucher (1984, as reported in Boucher and Morrison, 1989), on the following criteria:

1. *Clarity*. Are the objects of the forecast and the forecast itself intelligible? Is it clear enough for practical purposes? Users may, for example, be incapable of rigorously defining "GNP" or "the strategic nuclear balance," but they may still have a very good ability to deal with forecasts of these subjects. On the other hand, they may not have the least familiarity with the difference between households and families, and thus be puzzled by forecasts in this area. Do users understand how to interpret the statistics used in forecasting (i.e., medians, interquartile ranges, etc.)?

2. *Intrinsic credibility*. To what extent do the results "make sense" to planners? Do the results have "face validity"?

3. *Plausibility*. To what extent are the results consistent with what the user knows about the world outside of the scenario and how this world *really* works or *may* work in the future?

4. *Policy relevance*. If the forecasts are believed to be plausible, to what extent will they affect the successful achievement of the user's mission or assignment?

5. *Urgency*. To what extent do the forecasts indicate that, if action is required, time must be spent fairly quickly to develop and implement the necessary changes?

6. *Comparative advantage*. To what extent do the results provide a better foundation now for investigating policy options than other sources available to the user *today*? To what extent do they provide a better foundation now for future efforts in forecasting and policy planning?

7. *Technical quality*. Was the process that produced the forecasts technically sound? To what extent are the basic forecasts mutually consistent?

These criteria should be viewed as filters. To reject a forecast requires making an argument that shows that the item(s) in question cannot pass through all or most of these filters. A "good" forecast is one that survives such an assault; a "bad" forecast is one that does not (Boucher and Neufeld, 1981).

Boucher and Neufeld stress that it is important to communicate to decision-makers that forecasts are transitory and need constant adjustment if they are to be helpful in guiding thought and action. It is not uncommon for forecasts to be criticized by decision-makers. Common criticisms are that the forecast is obvious; it states nothing new; it is too optimistic, pessimistic, or naive; it is not credible because obvious trends, events, causes, or consequences were over-looked. Such objections, far from undercutting the results, facilitate thinking strategically. The response to these objections is simple: If something important is missing, add it. If something unimportant is included, strike it. If something important is included but the forecast seems obvious, or the forecast seems highly counterintuitive, probe the underlying logic. If the results survive, use them. If not, reject or revise them (Boucher and Morrison, 1989).

A major objective of forecasting is to define *alternative* futures, not just the "most likely" future. The development of alternative futures is central to effective strategic decision-making (Coates, 1985). Since there is no single predictable future, organizational strategists need to formulate strategy within the context of alternative futures (Heydinger and Zenter, 1983; Linneman and Klein, 1979). To this end, it is necessary to develop a model that will make it possible to show systematically the interrelationships of the individually forecasted trends and events.

Cross-Impact Analysis

This model is a *cross-impact model*. The essential idea behind a cross-impact model is to define explicitly and completely the pairwise causal connections within a set of forecasted developments. In general, this process involves asking how the prior occurrence of a particular event might affect other events or trends in the set. When these relationships have been specified, it becomes possible to let events "happen"—either randomly, in accordance with their estimated probability, or in some prearranged way—and then trace out a new, distinct, plausible and internally consistent set of forecasts. This new set represents an alternative to the comparable forecasts in the "most likely" future (i.e., the "expected" future). Many such alternatives can be created. Indeed, if the model is computer-based, the number will be virtually unlimited, given even a small base of trends and events and a short time horizon (e.g., the next ten years).

The first published reference to cross-impact analysis occurred in the late 1960s (Gordon, 1968), but the original idea for the technique dates back to 1966, when the coinventors, T. J. Gordon and Olaf Helmer, were developing the game FUTURES for the Kaiser Aluminum Company. In the first serious exploration of this new analytic approach, the thought was to investigate systematically the "cross correlations" among possible future events (and only future events) to determine, among other things, if improved probability estimates of these events could be obtained by playing out the cross-impact relationships and, more important, if it was possible to model the event-to-event interactions in a way that was useful for purposes of policy analysis (Gordon and Haywood, 1968).

The first of these objectives was soon shown to be illusory, but the second was not, and the development of improved approaches of event-to-event cross-impact analysis proceeded (Gordon, Rochberg, and Enzer, 1970), with most of the major technical problems being solved by the early 1970s (Enzer, Boucher, and Lazar, 1971).

The next major step in the evolution of cross-impact analysis was to model the interaction of future events and trends. This refinement, first proposed by T. J. Gordon, was implemented in 1971–1972 by Gordon and colleagues at The Futures Group and was called *trend impact analysis*, or TIA (Gordon, 1977). Similar work was under way elsewhere (Helmer, 1972; Boucher, 1976), but TIA became well established, and it is still in use, despite certain obvious limitations, particularly its failure to include event-to-event interactions.

Two strands of further research then developed independently and more-or-less parallel with the later stages in the creation of TIA. Each was aimed primarily at enabling cross-impact analysis to handle both event-to-event and event-to-trend interactions and to link such a cross-impact modeling capability to more conventional system models, so that developments in the latter could be made responsive to various sequences and combinations of developments in the cross-impact model. One strand led to the joining of cross-impact analysis with a system dynamics model similar to the one pioneered by Jay Forrester and made famous in the first Club of Rome study (Meadows et al., 1972). This line of research—again directed by T. J. Gordon—produced a type of cross-impact model known as *probabilistic system dynamics*, or PSD.

The second strand led to a cross-impact model known as INTERAX (Enzer, 1979), in which the run of a particular path can be interrupted at fixed intervals to allow the user to examine the developments that have already occurred. The user can also examine the likely course of developments over the next interval and can intervene with particular policy actions before the run is resumed. Since the development of INTERAX, which requires the use of a mainframe computer, some work has been done to make cross-impact analysis available on a microcomputer. The Institute for Future Systems Research (Greenwood, SC) has developed a simple cross-impact model (Policy Analysis Simulation System—PASS) for the Apple II computer and an expanded version for the IBM AT. A comprehensive cross-impact model, *Bravo!*, will be released in mid-1989 by the Bravo! Corporation (West Hartford, CT) for an IBM AT (Morrison, 1988, July-August). These microcomputer based models greatly enhance the ability to conduct cross-impact analyses and, therefore, to write alternative scenarios much more systematically.

Alternative Scenarios

Scenarios are narrative descriptions of possible futures. A single scenario represents a history of the future. The "most likely" future, for example, contains all of the forecasts from the forecasting activity in a narrative weaving them together from some point in the future, describing the history of how they unfolded. Alternatives to this future are based upon the occurrence or nonoccurrence of particular events in the event set. Such alternatives define unique mixes of future environmental forces that may impact on a college or university. The range of uncertainty inherent in the different scenarios (which are, themselves, forecasts) changes the assumption that the future will be an extrapolation from the past (Zentner, 1975; Mandel, 1983). Within the context of an alternative future depicted by a scenario, the decision-maker can identify causal relationships between environmental forces, the probable impacts of these forces on the organization, the key decision points for possible intervention, and the foundations of appropriate strategies (Kahn and Wiener, 1967; Sage and Chobot, 1974; Martino, 1983; Wilson, 1978). By providing a realistic range of possibilities, the set of alternative scenarios facilitates the identification of common features likely to have an impact on the organization no matter which alternative occurs. It is conventional to create from three to five such histories to cover the range of uncertainty.

Numerous approaches can be taken in writing the scenarios, ranging from a single person writing a description of a future situation (Martino, 1983) to the use of an interactive computer model that uses cross-impact analysis to generate outlines of the alternatives (Enzer, 1980a,b; Mecca and Adams, 1985; Goldfarb and Huss, 1988). A broader range of scenario writing approaches is described by Mitchell, Tydeman, and Georgiades (1979), Becker (1983), and Boucher (1985).

Any of a number of scenario taxonomies, each with its own benefits and limitations, may be used to guide the development of a scenario logic (Bright, 1978; Ducot and Lubben, 1980; Hirschorn, 1980; Boucher, 1985). The most comprehensive of the taxonomies, however, is that of Boucher (1985) which has been updated in Boucher and Morrison (1989). In this taxonomy there are four distinct types of scenarios: the demonstration scenario, the driving-force scenario, the system change scenario, and the slice-of-time scenario. The first three types are characteristic of "path-through-the time" narratives; the fourth is a "slice of time" narrative. The following descriptions are derived from Boucher (1985) as updated in Boucher and Morrison (1989).

The *demonstration scenario* was pioneered by Herman Kahn, Harvey De Weerd, and others at RAND in the early days of systems analysis. In this type of scenario, the writer first imagines a particular end-state in the future and then describes a distinct and plausible path of events that could lead to that end-state. In the *branch-point* version of this type of scenario, attention is called to decisive events along the path (i.e., events that represent points at which crucial choices were made—or not—thus determining the outcome). Thus the branch points, rather than the final outcome, become the object of policy attention. As Kahn and Wiener (1967) point out, they answer two kinds of questions: (a) How might some hypothetical situation come about, step by step? and (b) What alternatives exist at each step for preventing, diverting, or facilitating the process?

The major weakness of the demonstration scenario, as Boucher (1985) points out, is that it is based upon "genius" forecasting and is, therefore, dependent upon the idiosyncrasies and experiences of individuals. However, this type of scenario (like all methods and techniques in this field) is useful in both stimulating and disciplining the imagination.

The *driving-force scenario*, perhaps the most popular type of scenario in governmental and business planning (Goldfarb and Huss, 1988; Ashley and Hall, 1985; Mandel, 1983), is exemplified by Hawken, Ogilvy, and Schwartz's *Seven Tomorrows* (1982). Here the writer first devises a "scenario space" by identifying a set of key trends, specifying at least two distinctly different levels of each trend, and developing a matrix that interrelates each trend at each level with each other. For example, two driving forces are GNP growth and population growth. If each is set to "high," "medium," and "low," there are nine possible combinations, each of which defines the scenario space defining the context of a possible future. The writer's task is to describe each of these futures, assuming that the driving-force trends remain constant.

The purpose of the driving-force scenario is to clarify the nature of the future by contrasting alternative futures with others in the same scenario space. It may well be that certain policies would fare equally well in most of the futures, or that certain futures may pose problems for the institution. In the latter case, decision-makers will know where to direct their monitoring and scanning efforts.

The major weakness of the driving-force scenario is the assumption that the trend levels, once specified, are fixed—an assumption that suffers the same criticism directed to planning assumptions in traditional long-range planning activities (i.e., they ignore potential events that, if they occurred, would affect trend levels). The advantage of this type of scenario, however, is that, when well executed, the analysis of strategic choice is simplified—a function of considerable value at the beginning of an environmental or policy analysis when the search for key variables is most perplexing.

The *system-change scenario* is designed to explore systematically, comprehensively, and consistently the interrelationships and implications of a set of trend and event forecasts. This set, which may be developed through scanning, genius forecasting, or a Delphi, embraces the full range of concerns in the social, technological, economic and political environments. Thus, this scenario type varies both from the demonstration scenario (which leads to a single outcome and ignores most or all of the other developments contemporaneous with it) and from the driving-force scenario (which takes account of a full range of future developments but assumes that the driving trends are unchanging), in that there is no single event that caps the scenario, and there are no *a priori* driving forces.

The system-change scenario depends upon cross-impact analysis to develop the outline of alternative futures. The writer must still use a good deal of creativity to make each alternative intriguing by highlighting key branch points and elaborating on critical causal relationships. However, this scenario suffers from the same criticisms that may be leveled at driving-force and demonstration scenarios: although everything that matters is explicitly stated, all of the input data and relationships are judgmental. Moreover, the scenario space of each trend projection is defined by upper and lower envelopes as a consequence of the cross-impacts of events from the various scenarios that are run. Although it is valuable to know these envelopes, this information by itself provides no guidance in deciding which of the many alternative futures that can be generated should serve as the basis for writing scenarios. This choice must be made using such criteria as "interest," "plausibility," or "relevance."

The *slice-of-time scenario* jumps to a future period in which a set of conditions comes to fruition, and then describes how stakeholders think, feel, and behave in that environment (e.g., 1984, *Brave New World*). The objective is to summarize a perception about the future or to show that the future may be more (or less) desirable, fearful, or attainable than is now generally thought. If the time period within the "slice of time" is wide, say from today to the year 2000, it is possible to identify the macro-trends over this period (e.g., Naisbitt's *Megatrends*, 1982). In this sense, a slice-of-time scenario is the same as the "environmental assumptions" found in many college and university plans. The weakness of this approach is that there is no explanation as to the influences on the direction of these trends, no plausible description of how (and why) they change over time.

Variations in these types of scenarios occur according to the perspective brought to the task by scenario writers. Boucher (1985) points out that writers using the *exploratory* perspective adopt a neutral stance toward the future, appearing to be objective, scientific, impartial. The approach is to have the scenario begin in the present and unfold from there to the end of the period of interest. The reader "discovers" the future as it materializes. The most common version of this mode, "surprise-free," describes the effects of new events and policies, although only likely events and policies are used. A second version, the "play-out" version, assumes that only current forces and policy choices are allowed to be felt in the future (i.e., no technological discoveries or revolutions are permitted).

Writers using the *normative* perspective focus on the question, "What kind of future might we have?" They respond to this question from a value-laden perspective, describing a "favored and attainable" end-state (a financially stable college and the sequence of events that show how this could be achieved) or a "feared but possible" end-state (merger with another institution).

In the *hypothetical* or *what-if?* mode, writers experiment with the probabilities of event forecasts to "see what might happen." In this mode, the writer explores the sensitivity of earlier results to changes in particular assumptions. Many "worst case" and "best case" scenarios are of this sort.

Boucher (1985) maintains that all scenarios may be placed in a particular type/mode combination. The current business-planning environment, for example, with its emphases on multiple-scenario analysis (Heydinger and Zenter, 1983), places a "most likely" future (exploratory, driving-force) surrounded by a "worst case" (normative—feared but possible, driving-force) and a "best case" (normative—desired and attainable, driving-force) scenario. Unfortunately, such a strategy ignores potentially important alternative futures from such type/mode combinations as the exploratory system change or exploratory driving-force scenarios. The choice of which scenario to write must be made carefully.

Policy Analysis
Policy analysis is initiated when the scenarios are completed. Since a scenario represents a type of forecast, it is evaluated by the same criteria described earlier (i.e., clarity, intrinsic credibility, plausibility, policy relevance, urgency, comparative advantage, and technical quality). Once these criteria are satisfied, each scenario is reviewed for explicit or implied threats and opportunities, the objective being to derive policy options that might be taken to avoid the one and capture the other. It is here that the value of this approach may be judged, for the exercise should result in policies that could not have been developed without having gone through the process.

Action Plans
Action plans are directly derived from the policy options developed through reformulating each option as a specific institutional objective. Responsibilities for developing detailed action plans and recommendations for implementation may be assigned members of the planning team. Typically, these staff members have knowledge, expertise, and functional responsibilities in the area related to and/or affected by the implementation of the strategic option. The resulting action plans are incorporated into the institution's annual operational plan as institutional objectives assigned to appropriate functional units with projected completion dates (Morrison and Mecca, 1988).

A CASE STUDY

The brief case study that follows illustrates the application of this approach to the strategic planning process of a two-year college. The institution, a public technical college located in the southeastern United States, is charged with offering a comprehensive program of technical and continuing education in concert with the economic and industrial development needs of its seven county service area. Like most two-year colleges, the institution's mission, role and program scope are greatly determined by the totality of its external relationships (Gollattscheck, 1983).

Several years ago, recognizing the institution's sensitivity to external change, the administration adopted a strategic planning process, ED QUEST, which incorporates the external analysis and forecasting approach described in this chapter. The participants in the process were drawn from across the college's administrative and instructional staff. The 15 members of the institution's planning team represented many of the functional areas of the college (e.g., instruction, continuing education, finance, and student services). The president and the three vice-presidents of the college were also members of the planning team. In addition to the 15 members of the planning team, 16 other staff members were selected based upon their expertise in a particular curriculum content area (e.g., business, engineering technology, industrial crafts) or for the "boundary-spanning" nature of their institutional role (e.g., admissions, job placement, financial aid, management development programs). Together, these individuals participated in environmental scanning and constituted a Delphi panel tasked to forecast relevant trends and events. The membership of this panel represented as broad a range of functional areas and organizational specialities as feasible.

Scanning the External Environment

The information and forecasts about environmental trends, issues, and developments that might have impact on the college's future were drawn from a variety of sources. Materials were obtained not only from education sources (e.g., *Chronicle of Higher Education, Change, Community College Journal*), but also from

- General sources (e.g., *US News and World Report, Newsweek, New York Times, Atlanta Journal*);
- "Fringe" publications (e.g., *Mother Jones, New Ages*);
- Periodicals covering four major areas—social, technical, economic and political (e.g., *Working Woman, American Demographics, High Technology, Business Week, Computer World*);
- Future-focused journals/newsletters (e.g., *The Futurist, What's Next, and the Issue Management Newsletter*);
- Additional information obtained from the institutional research office, including data on variables descriptive of the college's task environment (e.g., college-going rates of high school graduates, state revenues, demographic profile of state and region).

The intent of this information was to stimulate readers to identify possible future changes in the environment (i.e., trends, events, or issues) that would affect the college's future. The material was selected to provide an "information gestalt," within which members of the Delphi panel could begin to see patterns of change in the external environment. Using this material and personal experience, the members of the Delphi panel completed an open-ended questionnaire. This represents Round One (R1) of the Delphi survey. The questionnaire asked each respondent to identify several trends that would have major consequences for the college during the period of the next 11 years and to identify several events believed to have both a high likelihood of occurring at some time during the same period and, if occurring, a significant impact on the institution.

Forecasting External Changes
The R1 responses were used to develop the second-round (called R2) questionnaire. Typically, R1 responses reflected a general concern, "The demographics of our student body are changing rapidly." This concern needed to be restated into measurable trend statements, such as "the percentage of black students," "the percentage of Asian students," and "the percentage of those students older than 25 years of age." A related potential event statement was "The percentage of minority first graders in our area is greater than 50%."

The R2 questionnaire provided the Delphi panel members with the opportunity to forecast the set of trends (N = 78) and events (N = 60) over the period of the next 11 years (e.g., 1987 to 1997.) Representative trends on this questionnaire were as follows:

- Annual number of manufacturing jobs moving to the developing countries (e.g., Mexico, Korea) from the U.S.;
- Number of new jobs annually created by industrial development and expansion in the state;
- Number of industries in the southern U.S. using robots;
- Number of four-year colleges in the U.S. offering technical programs at the baccalaureate level.

Representative events on this questionnaire were as follows:

- A national opinion poll reveals that over 40% of the public believe that a general/liberal arts education is the best preparation for entering the job market.
- The federal government requires an 800 SAT or comparable ACT score for persons to be eligible to receive federal student aid.
- The state legislature mandates articulation policies and procedures among two-year colleges and four-year colleges.

- A major depression occurs in the U.S. (unemployment exceeds 15% for two consecutive years).

Panel members forecasted the level of each trend at two points in the future, 1992 and 1997, and estimated the probability that each event would occur at some time between 1987 and 1997. In order to relieve their anxiety about forecasting, they were instructed to provide their "best guess," and to indicate their first impressions. The purpose of requesting their forecasts as opposed to relying solely on forecasts of experts was to obtain the thinking of the chief decision-makers of the college as to their version of the "most likely" future. It is entirely possible that when faced with making these forecasts they may turn to the information initially provided, or they may seek other information. The assumption is that by having the decision-makers participate in the analysis, they "own" the analysis and, therefore, will find it creditable for developing policy options on the basis of the analysis.

In addition, panel members assessed the positive and negative consequences of each trend and event. This latter information was used to reduce the size of the trend and event set by eliminating those variables with lesser impact upon the institution.

Refining the Forecast

The forecasts of trends represented the panel's view of the "most likely" future of the college. In order to develop alternative scenarios to this future, it was necessary to conduct a third round (R3) Delphi, which focused on refining the probability estimates from the previous round (R2). This refinement was conducted using small groups from the Delphi panel. Initially, it was planned to use the Delphi panel to make these estimates as well as those estimates required to develop the cross-impact model (see below). This required each member of the Delphi panel to potentially make an enormous number of estimates. Although having the entire membership of the Delphi panel make all the estimates would have resulted in a single vision of the future of the group, it was decided that this task would be overwhelming to the individuals on the panel and would lead to panel "dropouts," a recurring problem in a large Delphi.

Therefore, to refine the forecast of events, the panel was divided into smaller groups, each being assigned a set of events and required to complete several estimates for each event: the earliest year the event's probability would first exceed zero and the event's probability of occurring by 1990 and by 1994. The procedure was for team members to (a) review R2 estimates for the median and interquartile range; (b) make a decision if, on the bases of earlier discussion, these estimates needed revision; (c) discuss the rationale for reestimation with other members of the group; and (d) make individual reestimations.

Developing the Cross-Impact Model

These groups were used to develop a cross-impact model that defined the interrelationships of events-on-trends and events-on-events. The events-on-trends model required the group to determine the impact of an event on the level of each trend. This was accomplished by the group providing both estimates of the magnitude of the event's maximum and "steady-state" impact on the trend's forecasted level (i.e., how long the maximum impact would remain to affect the trend level). In addition, group members estimated the number of years it would take from the initial occurrence of the event until it affected the trend, how long it would take for the effect of the event to reach its maximum effect, how long the maximum effect would last, and how long it would take for the impact of the event to decline until the trend reached a "steady state." For example, one event in the set was "voice-activated microcomputers available in the U.S." The impact of this event on the level of automation in U.S. offices was as follows: It would be five years before voice-activated microcomputers would begin to influence the level of office automation, and another two years before the maximum impact of a 40% increase in office automation would be reached. It was estimated that the maximum impact would continue for four years after which the impact would decrease over a three-year period to 30% steady-state impact.

The process of making these estimates was initially slow. After panel members grasped the concept of cross-impact analysis, however, the process proceeded at a smooth pace. The estimates from all teams were then reviewed by selected panel members. This step was necessary to ensure that there was consistency in the vision of the future represented by the cross-impact model's estimates.

Development of Alternative Scenarios

Once the cross-impact model was complete, a series of scenarios showing possible alternative future environments of the college were developed. The first scenario developed represented the college's "most likely" future. It described the content of the "expected futures" as defined by those trends identified as critical to the college's future. The specific character of this future was represented by the forecasted level of the trend based upon the implicit assumptions of each member of the panel. In this sense, the "most likely" future was a compilation of the planning assumptions used in most planning models, written in the form of a scenario.

Three other scenarios were created showing the alternative futures that could occur, should specific events happen in the future. Each of these scenarios described the changes in the level of the trends resulting from the impacts of a particular sequence of events over the period of the future which defined the strategic planning horizon for the college (10 years). In essence the alternative futures depicted in these scenarios represented a variation of the external environment described in the "most likely" scenario. The alternative scenarios were generated using PASS, an event-to-event and event-to-trend cross-impact model implemented on a personal computer. Within PASS, the "hits" for the event-to-event and event-to-trend sections of the model were determined from the cross-impact estimates made by the analysis teams. These estimates represented how the probability of a particular event would change, given the prior occurrence of an impacting event and how the level of a trend would change given the impact of a particular sequence of events. The result outlined a single path of development over time. Such paths were instructive to the planning teams, not only because they integrated the input estimates of the cross-impact model, but also because they described the alternative paths of developments that were, in fact, possible and redefined the context of the "most likely" future as represented by the changes in the levels of the impacted trends.

Conducting the Policy Analysis

The analysis of the implications of the four scenarios represented the policy analysis phase of the process. The planning team first evaluated the scenarios using the criteria previously mentioned in this chapter for judging forecasts. These criteria allowed the team to maintain the perspective that no scenario was to be viewed as a prediction of a future state of affairs of the college. Instead, there were an infinite number of possible alternative futures, each varying because of interactions among human choice, institutional forces, natural processes, and unknowable chance events. Each scenario, therefore, represented a probabilistic statement about some element of a possible future (i.e., forecast).

After the group had rigorously examined the scenarios, they assessed how the institution would be affected if the particular future described by the scenario materialized. This step was a critical part of the team's strategic planning process, because forecasts are of little or no value unless decision-makers estimate the degree and nature of the impact of change on the organization (Halal, 1984). Team members assessed the consequences of the scenario for the current and future mission of the organization. Also explored was the impact of the scenario on the institution's key indicators—factors that were perceived to make the difference between institutional success or failure (Rockart, 1979).

Once all scenarios had been reviewed, a list of implications was developed. These implications, common to all scenarios, represented those of critical importance to the establishment of institutional strategy (e.g., the demand for the college to develop more and varied outreach services, to provide both technical education and technology transfer activities, to adapt a core approach to its engineering curriculum, to demonstrate quality and excellence, and to operate in a context of more centralized governance at the state level). Those implications unique to a particular scenario represented possible conditions for which contingency strategies might have to be developed should the future described in the particular scenario emerge.

From these implications the planning team developed a list of institutional strategies. To ensure that strategies were appropriately focused, team members were directed to think of strategy as defining the relationship of the college to its external environment and as providing guidance to the institution's staff in carrying out their administrative and operational activities in six key decision areas: (a) basic mission; (b) array of programs and services; (c) types of students served; (d) geographic area served; (e) educational goals and objectives; and (f) competitive advantage(s) over competitors (e.g., low tuition, location). A strategy that affected one or more of these decision areas or the relationship between the college and the environment was considered a good candidate for adoption by the planning team. The potential of each strategy was assessed as to the degree it enhanced or inhibited institutional strengths and weaknesses previously identified by the planning team.

Those strategies estimated to enhance strengths or reduce weaknesses were examined as to their effectiveness across scenarios and then categorized with respect to the external implications they address. For example, a number of strategies focussed on the issue of educational excellence. Members of the team believed this issue would continue to grow as a public concern based upon the analysis of several of the scenarios; consequently, it was deemed important to make the college's community and staff perceive "quality" and "excellence" as important institutional values. Specific strategies identified by the planning team to accomplish this included:

- Publicizing institutional and faculty awards, honors, and innovative projects;
- Publicizing student achievements;
- Establishing a task force on institutional excellence to examine and make appropriate recommendations for improving any aspect of those educational programs and operations deemed "less than excellent";
- Expanding the number of major national conferences and meetings annually hosted by the college;
- Encouraging greater faculty participation in regional and national professional associations;
- Improving the quality of the college's adjunct faculty through increased salaries and involvement in the college's activities;
- Establishing an endowment fund to expand professional development opportunities available to the college's faculty and staff to ensure that all personnel remain current in their field of specialization;
- Establishing an instructional resource center in the college to provide support and training for all part-time and full-time faculty to maintain their instructional skills.

Another category of strategies was intended to reaffirm the institution's role as a catalyst for regional economic development. Strategies included:

- Expanding the capability of the college's continuing education program to provide start-up and ongoing job training and technical assistance for small business and service industries;
- Establishing a technology transfer consortium to assist businesses and industries in the region to improve their productivity through the application of new technologies for existing production processes;
- Establishing an ongoing program of conferences and workshops for local and community groups to foster regional economic and community activities;
- Establishing an advanced technology education center for the "factory of the future" to provide technical training and technology transfer services to industries in the region.

Incorporating the Strategies into the College's Ongoing Activities
The planning team was asked to discuss these strategies with members of their staffs. The vice president for planning circulated this list of strategies and their corresponding objectives to all members of the planning team. At a half-day meeting, the team reviewed suggested objectives for each strategy and selected those objectives they believed the college should emphasize in its annual operational plan, allocating appropriate resources. Periodically during the year the president and the vice presidents reviewed the progress made in accomplishing the objectives.

Benefits and Limitations
An evaluation of the process by the members of the planning team indicated that the planning process was successful in producing information describing changes in the external environment relevant to the future of the college and in stimulating strategies that would not have been developed without going through the process. More specifically, team members felt that the process provided a systematic approach to the identification and analysis of external information. This viewpoint was best summarized by several members of the team who said that the process caused the team "to look at the future in an organized manner," and it "gave order to all the data that are out there" by helping the college's planning team to "structure the data so they can be matched with what we are about [and] what we are trying to do."

Overall, the team members thought that this planning approach increased their awareness and ability to assess the implications of external changes for the institution's future. Several members of the team said that it, "forces members [i.e., the planning team] to look at issues which would be overlooked and . . . aids in broadening the participant's perspective." Members of the planning team also indicated that the alternative scenarios were useful in developing a number of strategies and that the process provided a systematic approach for identifying those strategies that were to be given priority for implementation.

The incorporation of the strategies selected for implementation into the college's ongoing management activities, however, did not go smoothly. This was not surprising in that Gray (1986) found that the difficulties encountered in the implementation of strategic plans were the source of the greatest discontent among corporate executives (p. 90). In this case, planning-team members felt that there was a gap between the college's strategic planning process and its operational planning. The perception of a number of members was that the results of the process were not used in their entirety. Members also noted that the strategies were added to previously determined priority assignments of staff, thus increasing work loads and resulting in incompatible demands. In other words, the new strategies were implemented without work assignments being "uncoupled" from strategies previously developed by the administration (Hobbs and Heany, 1977).

The problem of implementation was also related to what team members viewed as another problem—the lack of wider participation in the process among other members of the faculty and staff. While team members believed that the process facilitated the development of a consensus regarding the strategic directions of the institution among members of the planning team, they generally did not perceive this consensus reaching other members of the faculty and staff. Consequently, the results of the strategic planning process were perceived to be mandated by some staff. The importance of this problem is supported by the conclusion that Cleland and King (1974) draw that an organization's success in strategic planning is more sensitive to the overall organizational culture within which the planning is accomplished than the planning techniques and processes used (p. 70).

Some planning-team members were critical about the techniques and procedures used during the process. Several individuals believed that the scope of the environmental scan was too narrow and concentrated too heavily on technological and economic changes in the environment. There was far from unanimity on this point. One team member's sole criticism of the process was that the information from the scan was of little value and should rather have concentrated on the economic and employment data reflective of the local economy of the college's service area. Most team members thought, however, that the environmental scan and the trend and event statements contained on the Delphi's R2 questionnaire reflected changes in all sectors of the environment affecting the college.

Lastly, team members thought the procedures followed for evaluating the robustness and probable effectiveness of the strategies needed to be strengthened. More specifically, it was pointed out that short of a subjective assessment of the impact on college expenditures, the complete financial implications of implementing a particular strategy would not be known until after it was selected. Also, several individuals believed that in addition to assessing the strategies' impact on the institution's strengths and weaknesses, it would have been useful if the strategies had also been assessed as to their impact on the college's key indicators. With the availability of the PASS model, such an assessment was technically feasible, as it allows the user to incorporate policies (i.e., strategies) and trend data for each indicator into the cross-impact model of the institution's future environment.

PROBLEMS, ISSUES, AND NEEDED RESEARCH

This approach to planning and associated research methods and techniques is derived from the development of technological forecasting by military planners in the years that followed World War II in an attempt to avoid being unprepared for future wars. Technological forecasting differed from traditional planning methods in that findings were based upon judgments about the future and were used to develop complex scenarios (as opposed to identifying only the next generation of military-related breakthroughs). However, according to Enzer (1983), it was not until the mid-1960s that technological forecasting was placed into an analytical framework with such supporting methods as the Delphi, scenario writing, cross-impact analysis, and system dynamics, through the work of Gabor (1964), Jantsch (1967), Kahn and Wiener (1967), and de Jouvenel (1967).

As one might expect with such a newly developing field, there are a variety of problems and issues associated with external analysis and forecasting. Indeed, Boucher (1977) identified some 300 unique problems and issues in this emerging area in a survey of the literature and of leading researchers in the futures field; Coates (1985) identified almost as many in a survey of issues managers. Space permits only a limited description of the most pressing issues for further research in this area.

Methodological Issues

Forecasting the "most likely" and alternative futures using the approach described here is based on soft, judgmental data, data based upon intuitive, often theoretically unstructured insights into real-world phenomena. Indeed, one of the major problems in this area of inquiry is the inadequacy of current theories of social change. Boucher (1977) found that none of the competing theories existing then or now (personal communication, August 1988) had predictive value. If our understanding of social change were more highly developed, forecasting the future would be much less problematic.

Improving methods of forecasting involves the question of how the validity of results obtained by the construction of a simulation model about the future can be measured. Of course, the concept of validity is difficult to apply to the study of the future. For this reason, many forecasters emphasize that accuracy is not a criterion for evaluating forecasts, for it is impossible to identify and assess the impact of all future events. Therefore, the best criteria we can develop at present are that forecasts be credible, plausible, and internally consistent given the information we have as a result of our scan and given our state of knowledge vis-á-vis social change.

Reliability and validity are also problems in judgmental forecasting. There has been some research on the extent to the same methods produce the same results. Martino (1983) reviewed a number of studies that reported a similarity of results across different Delphi studies. However, Sackman (1974) found that the similarity of forecasted median dates for events from some of these Delphi studies were statistically low. The effect of expert and nonexpert panels on the potential validity of judgmental forecasting has also been difficult to assess. Proponents argue that there is evidence that the more expertise panel members have, the better the forecast. Sackman (1974) reviewed a variety of Delphi studies comparing forecasts of experts with those of nonexperts and found that there was no difference. Studies by Campbell (1966) and Salancik, Weger, and Helfer (1971) came to essentially the same conclusion. Unfortunately, there has been little recent research on reliability and validity in judgmental forecasting.

Moreover, there has been little research on the relative advantages of different methods of eliciting forecasts from a group (e.g., questionnaires, interviews, computer terminals, face-to-face discussion), and on the extent to which forecasts derived through the use of these different techniques differ (Boucher, personal communication, August 1988). Perhaps one reason for the lack of research on these questions is the paucity of university-based programs that incorporate a responsibility for developing the concepts and methodology of forecasting. Another reason may be due to the pragmatic use of this approach to planning. That is, a major function of this approach to planning is to involve decision-makers in thinking about the future in ways that they have not thought previously. Ideally, they should be involved in all forecasting activities so that they "own" the products of the analysis and, therefore, are comfortable in using this analysis to stimulate the development of policy options that can be implemented in action plans. They use forecasts by experts (as reported in the literature or through personal communications) to assist them in making their own forecasts. In so doing, they become "smart" about current and forecasted changes and use this increasing alertness to conduct their managerial and planning responsibilities. The process of scanning, forecasting, and planning, therefore, may be more important to the future of the organization than the product of any particular round of forecasting or planning. Consequently, the validity of the analysis is not as crucial as it would be in other research activity.[1]

There are a number of questions related to one of the major tools used by forecasters—the Delphi. Olaf Helmer (1983), one of the developers of the Delphi technique, has posed the following research questions (fp 118): What degree of anonymity is most helpful to the performance of a panel? How should the questioning process be structured? How can information from a variety of individuals from a variety of disciplines be best used? How stable is a panel's judgment over time? What is the optimal panel size? How can the performance of forecasters be calibrated? Be enhanced? What data, data-processing facilities, simulations, communication devices or models would be most helpful to forecasters? How can control for the systematic bias of forecasters be obtained?

There are also a number of issues related to a tool essential to forecasting alternative scenarios—cross-impact analysis. For example, the cross-impact matrix is constructed in a bivariate, first-order impact fashion (if Event A occurs, does it affect the probability of Event B occurring and, if so, to what extent?). It is too unwieldy and complex for this technique to handle the possibility of two or more events jointly affecting the probability of another event. Too, Helmer (1983) notes the problem of "double-accounting"; i.e., "if event A has a direct impact on event C but also has an indirect impact on it via another event, B, how can we make sure that this indirect impact is not also reflected in the direct impact of A on C and thus counted twice?" (p. 120).

Implementation Issues

Most educational leaders can readily identify pressing concerns and issues facing colleges and universities on the basis of their reading, experience in managing issues, and discussions with colleagues, both at home and around the world. Frequently, however, this identification is limited without the benefit of a comprehensive environmental scan of critical trends and potential events in the social, technological, economic, or political environments from the local to the global levels. Moreover, a systematic and continuous scanning process is crucial to the successful implementation of an external analysis/forecasting approach to planning in order to reevaluate the forecasts to determine if they need to be reestimated on the basis of new information generated in the scan.

Developing and institutionalizing a systematic, comprehensive environmental scanning function requires a commitment of time and resources that at present only major corporations (e.g., General Motors), trade associations (e.g., American Council of Life Insurance), think tanks (e.g., Standford Research Institute) and some philanthropic organizations (e.g., United Way of America) have been willing to do. A number of colleges (e.g., St. Catherine) and universities (e.g., Arizona State, Colorado, and Minnesota) have conducted periodic scans, but the only comprehensive, ongoing system reported in the literature is at the Georgia Center for Continuing Education (Simpson, McGinty, and Morrison, 1987). There may be several reasons for this state of affairs. One is the resource commitment required in (a) obtaining sufficient readers to regularly scan a variety of information sources, (b) maintaining the files manually and electronically, and (c) obtaining time of busy administrators and faculty members to review, discuss, and use the pertinent information developed in the process. Pflaum (1985) argues, for example, that many scanning processes do not survive because of the time and energy required to sustain them by volunteers. Ptaszynski, in applying the ED QUEST model in the School of Management at Wake Forest University, reported that their planning team thought that they were wasting valuable professional time scanning irrelevant material, time that detracted from the more important analysis phase (personal communication, May 28, 1988).

There are attempts under way to develop environmental scanning consortia. United Way of America, for example, encourages colleges and universities to participate in its electronic environmental scanning network, although it has not yet established a separate subnet for higher education (Morrison, 1987). Even with such assistance in maintaining a shared data base, however, the question of how to best use the scarce time available for the major decision-makers remains an issue.

Studies Needed
In addition to the research implications of the discussion above in the advancement of this important area of inquiry, there are a number of specific studies needed. For example, the general approach to external analysis and forecasting advanced here has been applied only in a small two-year technical college. How applicable is this model to other types of educational organizations and units (e.g., academic departments, four-year colleges, research universities, state systems of higher education)? A number of case studies are under way that apply this approach to a learning resources center in a dental school (Raney, personal communication, August 1988), to the admissions program of a school of management (Ptaszynski, 1988), to a department of training and development in a university hospital (Clay, personal communication, August 1988), to a consortium of church-related colleges (May, 1987), and to a doctoral-degree-granting university (Porter, personal communication, May, 1988). More are needed. Such studies could include a focus on actual decision-making behaviors of educational leaders engaged in formal analysis, forecasting, and planning activities. Others could focus on comparisons of effectiveness (as measured by outcomes) of those institutions using this approach to those not using the approach, controlling on relevant third variables (e.g., selectivity, type of control, institutional size, financial support).

Winkler (1982) identified several promising research directions when considering modeling decisionmaking problems under uncertainty that are relevant to the approach described in this chapter. First, the link between the creative process and the model-formulation stage of decision-making under uncertainty has not been explored, although Mendell (1985a) has developed a set of rules for improving an individual's ability to create mental scenarios of the future and a framework of questions designed to stimulate consciousness of the future implications of current phenomena (1985b).

Winkler (1982) also suggested the development of decision-aids involving user-friendly computer software for modeling decision-making problems under uncertainty, preferably in an interactive mode. The cross-impact models noted in this chapter such as PASS and *Bravo!* are designed to enable users to generate outlines of scenarios of future environments and of organizational performance simultaneously. It is possible to examine each alternative scenario for developments that give the future its special character and, thereby, to identify those events that are particularly "bad" or "good." Policy options may then be designed to increase the probability of "good" events and decrease the probability of "bad" events. By including these policies in the cross-impact model, it is possible to treat them analytically in the same manner as events (i.e., estimate their effects on the events and trends in the model), and to rerun the computer simulation to create alternative scenarios that contain policies as well as events and trends. This is known as *policy-impact analysis* (Renfro, 1980). Although such decision-aids are available, there is no evidence in the literature that they are being used in external analysis and forecasting in colleges and universities. As Norris and Poulton (1987) note, there is a dire need for case studies to illuminate the applicability of this approach to educational planning.

The applicability of catastrophe theory to sociopolitical forecasting is another direction for possible research. Catastrophe theory defines sudden changes and discontinuities in the behavior of natural and social systems (Woodcock and Davis, 1978). Zeeman (cited in Smith, 1980) points out that catastrophe theory "can be applied with particular effectiveness in those situations where gradually changing forces or motivations lead to abrupt changes in behavior" (p. 26). Although a relatively young science, catastrophe theory is beginning to be applied in planning. For example, analysts at a major corporation adapted the approach for modeling alternative "catastrophes" of discontinuous and divergent change in the motivational forces of growth and profit that control business behavior (Smith, 1980). One can only speculate as to the value in the decision-making process of alternative scenarios generated by computerized cross-impact models incorporating the mathematical modeling approach of catastrophe theory.

There are dozens of other research possibilities to improve this approach to academic planning, of which only two additional ones will be mentioned here. First, there is a need for a current handbook on external analysis and forecasting that can guide college and university institutional researchers and planners in this promising methodology. The only published guides (Fowles, 1978; Henckley and Yates, 1974), although good, are dated. Second, there is a need for a national research effort on the future of higher education, with corresponding implications for academic planning in America's diversified system of colleges and universities. This effort should include an environmental scanning/ forecasting data base, housed either with the U.S. Department of Education or at one of the major professional associations (American Association for Higher Education, American Council on Education, Association for Institutional Research, or the Society for College and University Planning). This data base should be electronically accessible to the higher education research and planning community. Moreover, portions of the annual meetings of professional associations could focus on the implications of this evolving data base for academic planning and provide professional development opportunities in current techniques of external analysis and forecasting.

CONCLUSIONS

The purpose of environmental analysis/forecasting in academic planning is to provide college and university administrators information that can facilitate better decision-making, particularly in making decisions affecting the long-range future of their institutions. Given that we live in an age of "future shock," when changes in the external environment occur with ever-increasing rapidity, educational leaders are faced with a future that most assuredly will be different from the present. This chapter has reviewed the salient literature describing a basic approach used to manage this uncertainty—identifying issues/concerns based upon experience and upon environmental scanning, structuring issues in the form of trends and events, forecasting the "most likely" future of these trends and events, assessing the interrelationships of these trends and events through cross-impact analysis, and producing alternative scenarios of plausible futures that stimulate the development of viable and robust strategic options that can be incorporated in specific institutional plans. This approach varies from a traditional long-range planning approach based upon a single set of environmental assumptions about the future in recognizing that, although the future is a continuation of existing trends, it is subject to modification by events that have some probability of occurrence. Indeed, environmental uncertainty is caused by potential events. We cannot predict the future, because uncertainty is a product of our incomplete understanding of trends, potential events and their interrelationships. However, by using the best available information we have, we can anticipate plausible alternative futures and, thereby, limit the number of unanticipated possibilities to the smallest possible set.

Acknowledgments. Many of the ideas expressed in this chapter were developed in earlier field work by the first author with Wayne I. Boucher, who continued to provide advice, and encouragement while this manuscript was being prepared. In particular, the sections on cross-impact analysis and scenarios draw heavily on his work as reported in Boucher and Morrison, 1989. In addition, the authors would like to express appreciation to Blanche Arons, Carol Binzer, Maria Clay, Joseph Coates, Robert Cope, Gay Davis, David Dill, Christopher Dede, William Held, Lee May, Elizabeth Markham, Sherry Morrison, and James Ptaszynski for their helpful comments on earlier versions of the manuscript. Of course, the views expressed here, and any errors, are solely the responsibility of the authors.

Notes

1. This view is not shared by everyone, however. James Ptaszynski (personal communication, May 28, 1988) and David Snyder (personal communication, January 29, 1989) argue that college and university planning teams should not engage in forecasting, but rely solely on forecasts produced by experts.

REFERENCES

Aguilar, F. J. (1967). *Scanning the Business Environment*. New York: Macmillan.
Aldrich, H. (1979). *Organizations and Environments*. Englewood Cliffs, NJ: Prentice-Hall.
Alexis, M., and Wilson, C. Z. (1967). *Organizational Decision Making*. Englewood Cliffs, NJ: Prentice-Hall.
Alter, S., Drobnick, R., and Enzer, S. (1978). A modeling structure for studying the future. (Report No. M-33). Los Angeles, CA: University of Southern California, Center for Futures Research.
Anderson, C. R., and Paine, F. T. (1975). Managerial perceptions and strategic behavior. *Academy of Management Journal* 18: 811–823.
Andrews, K. R. (1971). *The Concept of Corporate Strategy*. Howewood, IL: Dow Jones-Irwin.
Ansoff, H. I. (1975). Managing strategic surprises by response to weak signals. *California Management Review* 18(2): 21–33.
Armstrong, J. S. (1978). *Long-Range Forecasting*. New York: Wiley.
Asher, W. (1978). Forecasting: an appraisal for policy makers and planners. Baltimore, MD: John Hopkins University Press.
Ashley, W. C., and Hall, L. (1985). Nonextrapolative strategy. In J. S. Mendell (ed.), *Nonextrapolative Methods in Business Forecasting* (pp. 61–76). Westport, CT: Quorum Books.
Ayres, R. V. (1969). *Technological Forecasting and Long-Range Planning*. New York: McGraw-Hill.
Barton, R. F. (1966). Realight and business policy decisions. *Academy of Management* (June), pp. 117–122.
Becker, H. S. (1983). Scenarios: importance to policy analysts. *Technological Forecasting and Social Change* 18: 95–120.
Berquist, W. H., and Shumaker, W. A. (1976). Facilitating comprehensive institutional development. In W. H. Berquist and W. A. Shumaker (eds.), *A Comprehensive Approach to Instructional Development* (pp. 1–48). New Directions for Higher Education No. 15. San Francisco, CA: Jossey-Bass.
Blaylock, B. K., and Reese, L. T. (1984). Cognitive style and the usefulness of information. *Decision Science* 15: 74–91.

Boucher, W. I. (1976). *An Annotated Bibiography on Cross-Impact Analysis*. Glaston-bury, CT: Futures Group.

Boucher, W. I., ed. (1977). *The Study of the Future: An Agenda for Research*. Washington, DC: U.S. Government Printing Office.

Boucher, W. I. (1982). Forecasting. In J. S. Nagelschmidt ed., *Public Affairs Handbook: Perspectives for the 80's* (pp. 65–74). New York: AMACOM.

Boucher, W. I. (1984). *PDOS Technical Advisors' Final Report: Chapters Prepared by Benton International, Inc.* Prepared for the Futures Team of the Professional Development of Officers Study (PDOS), Office of the U.S. Army Chief of Staff. Torrance, CA: Benton International.

Boucher, W. I. (1985). Scenario and scenario writing. In J. S. Mendell (ed.), *Nonextrapolative Methods in Business Forecasting* (pp. 47–60). Westport, CT: Quorum Books.

Boucher, W. I., and Morrison, J. L. (1989). *Alternative Recruiting Environments for the U.S. Army*. Alexandria, VA: Army Research Institute.

Boucher, W. I., and Neufeld, W. (1981). Projections for the U.S. consumer finance industry to the year 2000: Delphi forecasts and supporting data, Report R-7. Los Angeles: Center for Futures Research, University of Southern California.

Boucher, W. I., and Ralston, A. (1983). Futures for the U.S. property/casualty insurance industry: final report, Report R-11. Los Angeles: Center of Futures Research, University of Southern California.

Boulton, W. R., Lindsay, W. M., Franklin, S. G., and Rue, L. W. (1982). Strategic planning: determining the impact of environmental characteristics and uncertainty. *Academy of Management Journal* 25: 500–509.

Bourgeois, L. J. (1980). Strategy and environment: a conceptual integration. *Academy of Management Review* 5: 25–39.

Bright, J. R. (1978). *Practical Technology Forecasting Concepts and Exercise*. Austin, TX: Sweet Publishing Company.

Cameron, K. (1983). Strategic reponses to conditions of decline. *Journal of Higher Education* 54: 359–380.

Campbell, G. S. (1971). Relevance of signal monitoring to Delphi/cross-impact studies. *Futures* 3: 401–404.

Campbell, R. M. (1966). A methodological study of the utilization of experts in business forecasting. Unpublished doctoral dissertation, University of California at Los Angeles.

Chaffee, E. E. (1985). The concept of strategy: from business to higher education. In J. C. Smart (ed.), *Handbook of Theory and Research in Higher Education* (pp. 133–172). New York: Agathon Press.

Cleland, D. I., and King, W. R. (1974). Developing a planning culture for more effective strategic planning. *Long-Range Panning* 7(3): 70–74.

Coates, J. F. (1985). Scenarios part two: alternative futures. In J. S. Mendell (ed.), *Nonextrapolative Methods in Business Forecasting* (pp. 21–46). Westport, CT: Quorum Books.

Coates, J. F. (1986). *Issues Management: How You Plan, Organize, and Manage Issues for the Future*. Mt. Airy, MD: Lomand.

Cope, R. G. (1978). *Strategic Policy Planning: A Guide for College and University Administration*. Littleton, CO: Ireland Educational Corporation.

Cope, R. G. (1981). *Strategic Planning, Management, and Decision Making*. Washington, DC: American Association for Higher Education.

Cope, R. G. (1988). *Opportunity from Strength: Strategic Planning Clarified with Case Examples*. Washington, DC: Association for the Study of Higher Education.

Dalkey, N., and Helmer, O. (1963). An experimental application of the Delphi method to the use of experts. *Management Science* 9(3): 458–467.

Dede, C. (1989). Strategic planning and future studies in teacher education. In W. Robert Houston (ed.), *Handbook of Research on Teacher Education*. New York: Macmillan.

de Jouvenel, B. (1967). *The Art of Conjecture*. New York: Basic Books.

Dill, W. R. (1958). Environment as an influence on managerial autonomy. *Administrative Science Quarterly* 2: 409–443.

Dube, C. S., and Brown, A. W. (1983). Strategy assessment: a rational response to university cutbacks. *Long-Range Planning* 17: 527–533.

Ducot, C., and Lubben, G. J. (1980). A topology for scenarios. *Futures* 12(1): 51–59.

Duncan, O. D. (1973). Social forecasting: the state of the art. *The Public Interest* 17: 88–118.

Duncan, R. B. (1972). Characteristics of organizational environments and perceived environmental uncertainty. *Administrative Science Review* 17: 313–327.

Duperrin, J. C., and Godet, M. (1975). SMIC 74—A method for constructing and ranking scenarios. *Futures* 7: 302–341.

Durand, J. (1972). A new method for constructing scenarios. *Futures* 4: 323–330.

Dutton, J. E., and Duncan, R. B. (1987). The creation of momentum of change through the process of strategic issue diagnosis. *Strategic Management Journal* 8: 279–295.

Ellison, N. (1977). Strategic planning. *Community and Junior College Journal* 48(9): 32–35.

Emery, F. E., and Trist, E. L. (1965). The causal texture of organizational environments. *Human Relations* 18: 21–32.

Enzer, S. (1970). A case study using forecasting as a decision-making aid. *Futures* 2: 341–362.

Enzer, S. (1977). Beyond bounded solutions. *Educational Research Quarterly* 1(4): 21–33.

Enzer, S. (1979). *An Interactive Cross-Impact Scenario Generator for Long-Range Forecasting, Report R-1*. Los Angeles: Center for Futures Research, University of Southern California.

Enzer, S. (1980a). INTERAX—An interactive model for studying future business environments: Part I. *Technological Forecasting and Social Change* 17(2): 141–159.

Enzer, S. (1980b). INTERAX—An interactive model for studying future business environments: Part II. *Technological Forecasting and Social Change* 17(3): 211–242.

Enzer, S. (1983). New directions in futures methodology. In James L. Morrison and Wayne I. Boucher (eds.), *Applying Methods and Techniques of Futures Research* (pp. 69–83). San Francisco: Jossey-Bass.

Enzer, S., Boucher, W. I., and Lazar, F. D. (1971). *Futures Research as an Aid of Government Planning in Canada, Report R-22*. Menlo Park, CA: Institute for the Future, August.

Etzioni, A. (1968). *The Active Society: A Theory of Societal and Political Processes*. New York: Free Press.

Fahey, L., King, W. R., and Narayanan, V. K. (1981). Environmental scanning and forecasting in strategic planning: the state of the art. *Long-Range Planning* 14: 32–39.

Fisher, G. (1987). When oracles fail: A comparison of four procedures for aggregating probability forecasts. *Organizational Behavior and Human Performance* 28: 96–110.

Fowles, J., ed. (1978). *Handbook of Futures Research*. Westport, CT: Greenwood Press.

Gabor, D. (1964). *Inventing the Future*. New York: Knopf.

Gibson, R. (1968). A general systems approach to decision-making in schools. *The Journal of Educational Administration* 6: 13–32.

Goldfarb, D. L., and Huss, W. W. (1988). Building scenarios for an electric utility. *Long-Range Planning* 21: 79–85.

Gollattscheck, J. F. (1983). Strategic elements of external relationships. In G. A. Myran (ed.), *Strategic Management in the Community College* (pp. 21–36). New Directions for Community Colleges, No. 44. San Francisco: Jossey-Bass.

Gordon, T. J. (1968). New approaches to Delphi. In J. R. Wright (ed.), *Technological Forecasting for Industry and Government* (pp. 135–139). Englewood Cliffs, NJ: Prentice-Hall.

Gordon, T. J. (1977). The nature of unforeseen developments. In W. I. Boucher (ed.), *The Study of the Future*. (pp. 42–43). Washington, DC: U.S. Government Printing Office.

Gordon, T. J., and Haywood, A. (1968). Intitial experiments with the cross-impacts matrix method of forecasting. *Futures* 1(2, December): 100–116.

Gordon, T. J., Rochberg, R., and Enzer, S. (1970). *Research on Cross-Impact Techniques with Applications to Selected Problems in Economics, Political Science, and Technology Assessment, Report R-12*. Menlo Park, CA: Institute for the Future, August.

Gray, D. H. (1986). Uses and misuses of strategic planning. *Harvard Business Review* 64(1): 89–97.

Guerjoy, H. (1977). A new taxonomy of forecasting methodologies. In W. I. Boucher (ed.), *The Study of the Future: An Agenda for Research*. Washington, DC: U.S. Government Printing Office.

Guild, P. B. (1987). How leaders' minds work. In L. T. Sheive and M. B. Schoenheit (eds.), *Leadership: Examining the Elusive* (pp. 81–92). Washington, DC: 1987 Yearbook of the Association for Supervision and Curriculum Development.

Gustafson, D. H., Shulka, R. K., Delbecq, A. L., and Walster, G. W. (1973). A comparative study of difference in subjective likelihood estimates made by individuals, interactive groups, Delphi groups, and nominal groups. *Organizational Behavior and Human Performance* 9: 280–291.

Halal, W. E. (1984). Strategic management: the state-of-the-art and beyond. *Technological Forecasting and Social Change* 25: 239–261.

Hall, R. H. (1977). *Organizations: Structure and Process*. Englewood Cliffs, NJ: Prentice-Hall.

Hambrick, D. C. (1982). Environmental scanning and organizational strategy. *Strategic Management Journal* 2: 159–174.

Hatten, K. J., and Schendel, D. E. (1975). Strategy's role in policy research. *Journal of Economics and Business* 8: 195–202.

Hawken, P., Ogilvy, J., and Schwartz, P. (1982). *Seven Tomorrows*. New York: Bantam.

Hearn, J. C. (1988). Strategy and resources: Economic issue in strategic planning and management in higher education. In J. C. Smart (ed.), *Handbook of Theory and Research in Higher Education* (pp. 212–281). New York: Agathon Press.

Hearn, J. C., and Heydinger, R. B. (1985). Scanning the university's external environment. *Journal of Higher Education*: 56(4) 419–445.

Helmer, O. (1972). Cross impact gaming. *Futures* 4: 149–167.

Helmer, O. (1983). *Looking Forward: A Guide to Futures Research*. Beverly Hills, CA: Sage.

Helmer, O., and Rescher, N. (1959). On the epistemology of the inexact sciences. *Management Science* 1: 25–52.

Henckley, S. P., and Yates, J. R., eds. (1974). *Futurism in Education: Methodologies*. Berkeley, CA: McCutchan.

Heydinger, R. B., and Zenter, R. D. (1983). Multiple scenario analysis as a tool for introducing uncertainty into the planning process. In J. L. Morrison, W. L. Renfro, and W. I. Boucher (eds.), *Applying Methods and Techniques of Futures Research* (pp. 51–68). New Directions for Institutional Research No. 39. San Francisco: Jossey-Bass.

Hirschorn, L. (1980). Scenario writing: a developmental approach. *Journal of the American Institute of Planners* 46: 172–183.

Hobbs, J. M., and Heany, D. F. (1977). Coupling strategy to operating plans. *Harvard Business Review*: 55(3): 119–126.

Hogarth, R. M. (1978). A note on aggregating opinions. *Organizational Behavior and Human Performance* 21: 40–46.

Hogarth. R. M., and Makridakis, S. (1981). Forecasting and planning: an evaluation. *Management Science* 27(2): 115–138.

Ireland, R. D., Hitts, M. A., Bettsm, R. A., and DePorras, D. A. (1987). Strategy formulation processes: differences in perceptions of strengths and weaknesses indicates and environmental uncertainty by managerial level. *Strategic Management Journal* 8: 469–485.

Jain, S. C. (1984). Environmental scanning in U.S. corporations. *Long-Range Planning* 17: 117–128.

Jantsch, E. (1967). *Technological Forecasting in Perspective*. Paris: Organization for Economic Cooperation and Development.

Jauch, L. R., and Kraft, K. L. (1986). Strategic management of uncertainty. *Academy of Management Review* 11(4): 77–790.

Jones, J., and Twiss, B. (1978). *Forecasting Technology for Planning Decisions*. New York: Petrocelli.

Joseph, E. (1974). An introduction to studying the future. In S. P. Henchley and J. R. Yates (eds.), *Futurism in Education: Methodologies* (pp. 1–26). Berkeley, CA: McCutchen.

Kahn, H., and Wiener, A. (1967). *The Year 2000*. New York: Macmillan.

Kahneman, D., Slovic, P., and Tversky, A. (1982). *Judgment Under Uncertainty: Heuristics and Biases*. New York: Cambridge University Press.

Kane, J., and Vertinsky, I. B. (1975). The arithmetic and geometry of the future. *Technological Forecasting and Social Change* 8: 115–130.

Kast, F. L., and Rosenzweig, J. (1979). *Organization and Management: A Systems Approach*. New York: McGraw-Hill.

Kefalas, A., and Schoderbeck, P. P. (1973). Scanning the business environment: some empirical results. *Decision Science* 4: 63–74.

Keller, G. (1983). *Academic Strategy: The Management Revolution in American Higher Education*. Baltimore: Johns Hopkins University Press.

Kiesler, S., and Sproull, L. (1982). Managerial response to changing environments: perspectives on problem sensing from social cognition. *Administrative Science Quarterly* 27: 548–570.

King, W. (1982). Using strategic issue analysis in long-range planning. *Long-Range Planning* 15: 45–49.

Klein, H. E., and Newman, W. H. (1980). How to integrate new environmental forces into strategic planning. *Management Review* 19: 40–48.

Kotler, P., and Murphy, P. (1981). Strategic planning for higher education. *Journal of Higher Education* 52: 470–489.

Lawrence, P., and Lorsch, J. (1967). *Organization and Environment*. Boston: Harvard Business School.

Leblebici, H., and Salancik, G. R. (1981). Effects of environmental uncertainty on information and decision processes in banks. *Administration Science Quarterly* 26: 578–598.

Lee, S. M., and Van Horn, J. C. (1983). *Academic Administration: Planning, Budgeting and Decision Making with Multiple Objectives*. Lincoln: University of Nebraska Press.

Lenz, R. T. (1987). Managing the evolution of the strategic planning process. *Business Horizons* 30: 74–80.

Lenz, R. T., and Engledow, J. L. (1986). Environment analysis: the applicability of current theory. *Strategic Management Journal* 7: 329–346.

Lindsay, W. M., and Rue, L. W. (1980). Impact of the organization environment on the long-range planning process: a contingency view. *Academy of Management Journal* 23: 385–404.

Linneman, R. E., and Klein, H. E. (1979). The use of multiple scenarios by U.S. industrial companies. *Long-Range Planning* 12: 83–90.

Linstone, H. A., and Simmonds, W. H., eds. (1977). *Futures Research: New Directions*. Reading, MA: Addison-Wesley.

Linstone, H. A., and Turoff, M., eds. (1975). The Delphi method: techniques and application. Reading, MA: Addison-Wesley.

Lozier, G. G., and Chittipedi, K. (1986). Issues management in strategic planning. *Research in Higher Educaiton* 24(1): 3–13.

Lyles, M., and Mitroff, I. (1980). Organizational problem formulation: an empirical study. *Administrative Science Quarterly* 25: 102–119.

Mandel, T. F. (1983). Futures scenarios and their use in corporate strategy. In K. J. Albert (ed.), *The Strategic Management Handbook* (pp. 10–21). New York: McGraw-Hill.

Martino, J. P. (1983). *Technological Forecasting for Decision-Making* (2nd ed.). New York: North-Holland.

May, L. Y. (1987). Planning for the future of United Methodist education. Draft Ph.D. dissertation proposal, School of Education, University of North Carolina at Chapel Hill.

McConkey, D. D. (1987). Planning for uncertainty. *Business Horizons* 00: 40–45.

McKenney, J. L. and Keen, P. (1974). How managers' minds work. *Harvard Business Review* 52: 79–90.

Meadows, D. H., Meadows, D. L., Randers, J., and Behrens, W. W., III (1972). *The Limits to Growth*. New York: Universe Books.

Mecca, T. V., and Adams, C. F. (1981). *The Educational Quest Guide: Incorporation of Environmental Scanning into Educational Planning*. Greenwood, SC: Institute for Future Systems Research.

Mecca, T. V., and Adams, C. F. (1982). ED QUEST: an environmental scanning process of educational agencies. *World Future Society Bulletin* 16: 7–12.

Mecca, T. V., and Adams, C. F. (April, 1985). Policy analysis and simulation system for educational institutions. Paper presented at the Annual Meeting of the American Educational Research Association, Chicago, April. (ERIC Document Report Reproduction Service No. ED 265–632)

Mendell, J. S. (1985a). Putting yourself in the scenarios: a calculus of mental manipulations. In Jay S. Mendell (ed.), *Nonextrapolative Methods in Business Forecasting* (pp. 77–80). Westport, CT: Quorum Books.

Mendell, J. S. (1985b). Improving your ability to think about the future: training your consciousness. In Jay S. Mendell (ed.), *Nonextrapolative Methods in Business Forecasting* (pp.81–90). Westport, CT: Quorum Books.

Merriam, J. E., and Makover, J. (1988). *Trend Watching*. New York: AMACOM.

Michael, D. H. (1973). *On Planning to Learn and Learning to Plan*. San Francisco: Jossey-Bass.

Miller, D., and Friesen, P. H. (1980). Archetypes of organizational transitions. *Administrative Science Quarterly* 25: 268–299.

Miller, D., and Friesen, P. H. (1983). Strategy-making and environment: the third link. *Strategic Management Journal* 4: 221–235.

Milliken, F. J. (1987). Three types of perceived uncertainty about the environment: state, effect, and response uncertainty. *Academy of Management Review* 12(1): 133–143.

Miner, F. C. (1979). A comparative analysis of free diverse group decision-making approaches. *Academy of Management Journal* 22(1): 81–93.

Mintzberg, H. (1978). Patterns in strategy formation. *Management Science* 24(9): 934–948.

Mintzberg, H., Raisinghani, D., and Theoret, A. (1976). The structured of unstructured decision processes. *Academy of Management Review* 21: 246–275.

Mitchell, R. B., and Tydeman, J. (1978). Subjective conditional probability modeling. *Technological Forecasting and Social Change* 11: 133–152.

Mitchell, R. B., Tydeman, J., and Georgiades, J. (1979). Structuring the future application of a scenario generating procedure. *Technological Forecasting and Social Change* 14: 409–428.

Morrison, J. L. (1987). Establishing an environmental scanning/forecasting system to augment college and university planning. *Planning for Higher Education* 15(1): 7–22.

Morrison, J. L. (1988). Developing an environmental scanning/forecasting capability: implications from a seminar. Paper presented at the meeting of the Society for College and University Planning, Toronto, Canada, July–August.

Morrison, J. L., and Mecca, T. U. (1988). *ED QUEST—Linking Environmental Scanning for Strategic Management*. Chapel Hill, NC: Copytron.

Morrison, J. L., Renfro, W. L., and Boucher, W. I. (1983). *Applying Methods and Techniques of Futures Research*. New directions in institutional research, No. 39. San Francisco: Jossey-Bass.

Morrison, J. L., Renfro, W. L., and Boucher W. I. (1984). *Futures Research and the Strategic Planning Process: Implications for Higher Education*. ASHE-ERIC Higher Education Research Report No. 9, 1984. Washington, DC: Association for the Study of Higher Education.

Morrison, J. L., Simpson, E., and McGinty, D. (1986). Establishing an environmental scanning program at the Georgia center for continuing education. Paper presented at the 1986 annual meeting of the American Association for Higher Education, Washington, DC, March.

Nanus, B. (1979). *QUEST—Quick Environmental Scanning Technique* (Report No. M34). Los Angeles: University of Southern California, Center for Futures Research.

Naisbitt, John (1982). *Megatrends*. New York: Warner Books.

Nelms, K. R., and Porter, A. L. (1985). EFTE: An interactive delphi method. *Technological Forecasting and Social Change* 28: 43–61.

Norris, D. M., and Poulton, N. L. (1987). *A Guide for New Planners*. Ann Arbor, MI: The Society for College and University Planning.

Nutt, P. (1979). Calling out and calling off the dogs: managerial diagnosis in public service organizations. *Academy of Management Review* 4: 203–214.

Nutt, P. (1986a). Decision style and its impact on managers and management. *Technological Forecasting and Social Change* 29: 341–366.

Nutt, P. (1986b). Decision style and strategic decisions of top executives. *Technological Forecasting and Social Change* 30: 39–62.

Osborne, R. N., and Hunt, J. L. (1974). Environment and organization effectiveness. *Administrative Science Quarterly* 18: 231–246.

Pflaum, A. (1985). External scanning: an introduction and overview. Unpublished manuscript, University of Minnesota, March.

Porter, A. L. (1980). *A Guidebook for Technology Assessment and Impact Analysis.* New York: Elsevier Science.

Pounds, W. F. (1969). The process of problem finding. *Industrial Management Review* 2: 1–19.

Ptaszynski, J. G. (1988). ED QUEST as an organizational development activity. Ph.D. dissertation proposal, School of Education, University of North Carolina at Chapel Hill.

Pyke, D. L. (1970). A practical approach to delphi. *Futures* 2(2): 143–152.

Quade, E. S. (1975). *Analysis for Public Decisions.* New York: American Elsevier.

Renfro, W. L. (1980). Policy impact analysis: a step beyond forecasting. *World Future Society Bulletin* 14: 19–26.

Renfro, W. L. (1983). *The Legislative Role of Corporations.* New York: American Management Association.

Rockart, J. F. (1979). Chief executives define their own data needs. *Harvard Business Review* 57: 81–93.

Sackman, H. (1974). *Delphi Assessment: Expert Opinion, Forecasting, and Group Process. Report R-1283-PR.* Santa Monica, CA: Rand Corporation.

Sage, D. E., and Chobot, R. B. (1974). The scenario as an approach to studying the future. In S. P. Henckley and J. R. Yates (eds.), *Futurism in Education: Methodologies* (pp. 161–178). Berkeley, CA: McCutchen.

Salancik, J. R., Wenger, W., and Helfer, E. (1971). The construction of Delphi event statements. *Technological Forecasting and Social Change* 3: 65–73.

Scott, W. R. (1981). *Organizations: Rational, Natural and Open Systems.* Englewood Cliffs, NJ: Prentice-Hall.

Segev, E. (1976). Triggering the strategic decision-making process. *Management Decision* 14: 229–238.

Shane, H. G. (1971). Future-planning as a means of shaping educational change. In *The Curriculum: Retrospect and Prospect.* Chicago: National Society for the Study of Education.

Shirley, R. C. (1982). Limiting the scope of strategy: a decision based approach. *Academy of Management Review* 7: 262–268.

Simpson, E., McGinty, D., and Morrison, J. L. (1987). The University of Georgia continuing education environmental scanning project. *Continuing Higher Education Review* (Autumn), pp. 1–19.

Slocum, J. W., and Hellriegel, D. (1983). A look at how managers' minds work. *Business Horizons* 26: 56–68.

Smith, W. C. (1980). Catastrophe theory analysis of business activity. *Management Review* 6: 27–40.

Snow, C. C. (1976). The role of managerial perceptions in organizational adaption: an exploratory study. *Academy of Management Proceeding* 249–255.

Steiner, G. A. (1979). *Strategic Planning.* New York: Free Press.

Taggart, W., Robey, D., and Kroeck, K. G. (1985). Managerial decision styles and cerebral dominance: an empirial study. *Journal of Management Studies* 22: 175–192.

Tanner, G. K., and Williams, E. J. (1981). *Educational Planning and Decision-Making.* Lexington, MA: D. C. Heath and Co.

Terreberry, S. (1968). The evolution of organizational environments. *Administrative Science Quarterly* 12: 590–613.

Terry, P. T. (1977). Mechanisms for environmental scanning. *Long-Range Planning* 10: 2–9.

Thomas, P. S. (1980). Environmental scanning: the state of the art. *Long-Range Planning* 13: 20–25.

Thompson, J. D. (1967). *Organizations in Action.* New York: McGraw-Hill.

Uhl, N. P. (1983). Using the Delphi technique in institutional planning. In N. P. Uhl (ed.), *Using Research for Strategic Planning: New Directions for Institutional Research No. 37.* San Francisco: Jossey-Bass.

Utterbach, J. M. (1979). Environmental analysis and forecasting. In Dan E. Schendal and Charles W. Hoffer (eds.). *Strategic Management: A New View of Business Policy and Planning.* Boston: Little, Brown.

Van de Ver, A. H., and Delbecq, A. L. (1974). The effectiveness of nominal, Delphi and interacting group decision making processes. *Academy of Management Journal,* 17(4): 605–621.

Vanston, J. H., Frisbie, W. P., Lopreato, S. C., and Poston, D. L. (1977). Alternate scenario planning. *Technological Forecasting and Social Change* 10: 159–88.

van Vught, F. A. (1987). Pitfalls of forecasting: Fundamental problems for the methodology of forecasting from the philosophy of science. *Futures* (April), pp. 184–196.

Wagschall, P. H. (1983). Judgmental forecasting techniques and institutional planning. In J. L. Morrison, W. L. Renfro, and W. I. Boucher (eds.), *Applying Methods and Techniques of Futures Research: New Directions for Institutional Research No. 39.* San Francisco: Jossey-Bass.

Weber, C. E. (1984). Strategic thinking—dealing with uncertainty. *Long-range Planning* 17: 61–70.

Wheelwright, S., and Makridakis, S. (1980). *Foreasting Methods for Management* (3rd ed.), New York: Wiley.

Wilson, I. A. (1978). Scenarios. In J. Fowles (ed.), *Handbook of Futures Research* (pp. 225–247). Westport, CT: Greenwood Press.

Winkler, R. L. (1982). State of the art: research directions in decision-making under uncertainty. *Decision Science* 13: 517–533.

Woodcock, A., and Davis, M. (1978). *Catastrophe Theory.* New York: Avon Books.

Woodman, R. W., and Muse, W. V. (1982). Organization development in the profit sector: lessons learned. In J. Hammons (ed.), *Organization Development: Change Strategies* (pp. 22–44). New Directions for Community Colleges No. 31. San Francisco: Jossey-Bass.

Zentner, R. D. (1975). Scenarios in forecasting. *Chemical and Engineering News* 53: 22–34.

Ziegler, W. L. (1972). *An Approach to the Futures-Perspectives.* Syracuse, NY: Syracuse University Research Corporation, Educational Policy Research Center.

Author Index

Subject Index

A

AAUP Project to Improve College Teaching, 168

Academic careers and labor markets, 134-149
  academic hierarchies, 146
  demographic trend analysis, 135-138
  entry job effects on career, 147-148
  human capital theory, 134-135, 138-140
  institutional ascription model, 135, 142-144, 146
  labor market outcomes, 147
  screening or "job competition" model, 135, 140-142, 146
  structural perspectives, 135, 144-145
  temporal changes, 148-149

Academic planning, *see* Administrative strategies

Academic tracking, 281

Action plans, 367, 374

Adaptive strategy, 13-15, 17, 19-20, 22

Administrative strategies, 44-54. *See also* Strategy in systems of higher education
  cognitive and symbolic, 50-51
  environmental analysis, *see* Environmental analysis and forecasting in academic planning
  forecasting, 360-362, 369-370. *See also* Environmental analysis and forecasting in academic planning
  latent functions of impossibility, 51-54
  successful, 46-47
  unsuccessful, 48-50

Adult education and the paradigm revolution, 98

Alternative scenarios, 363-367, 371-372

Archives, campus. *See* Campus archives and office of institutional research

Art education
  evaluation of instruction, 166
  paradigm revolution, 98-99

Assessment, *see* Faculty evaluation

Association models, 325-326

Athletic scholarships, 206-207

B

Basic Educational Opportunity Grant (BEOG), 214, 216, 221

Behavioral and cognitive strategies, administrative, *see* Administrative strategies

BEOG (Basic Educational Opportunity Grant), 214, 216, 221

Boards, educational system, 1, 3, 9, 24-25, 27, 31, 36-37. *See also* Systems of higher education

Branch-point scenario, 364-365

Budgets, 180, 200, 202
  pricing strategies
  student financial aid, 213-221. *See also* Financial aid, student

Business administration and the paradigm revolution, 77-80

Business communications and the paradigm revolution, 82-83

C

Cafeteria System, 158

Campus archives and office of institutional research, 180-195
  cliometrics, 187-192
  example, 182-185
  historical HEGIS, 185-187
  numerical planning, 180-182
  policy issues, 192-193

Canada, 169

Capital, human, 134-135, 138-140

Careers, academic
  faculty career stages, 173
  labor markets, *see* Academic careers and labor markets

T